European Integration Theory

European Integration Theory

SECOND EDITION

Antje Wiener
Professor of Political Science, University of Hamburg, Germany

Thomas Diez
Professor of International Relations, University of Birmingham, UK

OXFORD
UNIVERSITY PRESS

OXFORD

UNIVERSITY PRESS

Great Clarendon Street, Oxford OX2 6DP
United Kingdom
Oxford University Press is a department of the University of Oxford.
It furthers the University's objective of excellence in research, scholarship,
and education by publishing worldwide. Oxford is a registered trade mark of
Oxford University Press in the UK and in certain other countries

First published 2004
Second edition 2009
Reprinted 2012

British Library Cataloguing in Publication Data
Data available

Library of Congress Cataloging in Publication Data
Data available

ISBN 978-0-19-922609-2

Printed and bound by CPI Group (UK) Ltd, Croydon, CR0 4YY

In memory of Ernst Haas who so greatly inspired generations of integration scholars.

■ PREFACE

European integration theory is a vibrant but dispersed field. With this book, we hope to further the debate among and between the multitude of approaches that have been put forward since the early 1960s. In a time when the political significance of the European Union is increasing while its legitimacy is ever more contested, engagement with different explanations of integration, conceptualizations of European governance, and critiques of the status quo as well as normative debates about its future seem to us of the utmost importance not only for students of integration but for public debate in general. We are hoping to make a contribution to this debate, as well as to furthering the theorizing of European integration itself.

The idea for this book was first sketched out during a sunny coffee break at an ISA convention in Los Angeles; its taking shape owes much to follow-up conversations during a weekend in Belfast and a hike in the hills of Northern Ireland in October 2000. Since its first publication in 2004, the book has become a standard reference for those interested in the field, and thus Oxford University Press has asked us to do a second edition. While change in theory does not develop as quickly as new historical developments in the actual integration process occur, such a second edition seemed nonetheless appropriate. In revising the volume, we have drawn on feedback from students (both our own and elsewhere), reviews, and ten anonymous referee reports. As a consequence, we have added new chapters (on political economy and political theory) as well as new authors, and have asked our 'old' authors not only to update their chapters but also to respond to comments we had received. Each chapter now also includes a number of core questions with which students can check their learning outcomes.

Since the first edition was published, the massive enlargement towards the east has been accomplished, and the European constitutional treaty has been signed and then rejected in the ratification process; its successor, the Treaty of Lisbon, is presently also awaiting its uncertain fate after voters in Ireland gave it the thumbs down. Both developments are crucial for the set-up of this volume. Enlargement is the test case that we have asked all authors to address in order to compare approaches. Constitutional questions we identify as a core challenge for integration theory to address; a field that originated from the field of international relations and set out to explain the anomaly of states pooling their sovereignty rather than the normative consequences this may have for governance.

We therefore hope that this new edition will not only provide an even better and more comprehensive teaching tool than its predecessor, but that it also addresses some of the core issues European integration faces in the present and near future. In compiling this edition, Ruth Anderson at Oxford University Press proved to be a friendly but persistent force, without whom this project would not have taken off. We are also grateful to Eleni Christodoulou who helped us in the final stages of compiling the manuscript. Above all, however, we would like to thank our students in Bath, Belfast, Birmingham, and Trento, who encouraged us in our undertaking and whose discussions of the chapters have been more insightful than they probably thought at the time.

This book is dedicated to the late Ernie Haas, without whom it probably would never have been written in the first place, and whose innovative and committed contribution to European integration theory is greatly missed.

Antje Wiener and Thomas Diez

■ CONTENTS

■ NOTES ON CONTRIBUTORS

Claudia Attucci is currently a Marie Curie postdoctoral fellow at University College London. Her research and publications include 'An Institutional Dialogue on Common Principles. Reflections on the EU Charter of Fundamental Rights', in Dobson and Føllesdal (eds) *Political Theory and the European Constitution* (Routledge, 2004) and 'European Values and Constitutional Traditions in the EU Charter of Fundamental Rights', in Heit (ed.) *Die Werte Europas* (Munster, 2006).

Richard Bellamy is Professor of Political Science and Director of the School of Public Policy, University College London (UCL), University of London. Recent publications include *Liberalism and Pluralism: Towards a Politics of Compromise* (Routledge, 1999), *Rethinking Liberalism* (Continuum, 2000, 2005), and (as co-editor) *The Cambridge History of Twentieth Century Political Thought* (Cambridge University Press, 2003), *Lineages of European Citizenship* (Palgrave, 2004) and *Making European Citizens* (Palgrave, 2006). His *Political Constitutionalism: A Republican Defence of the Constitutionality of Democracy* was published by Cambridge University Press in 2007 and his *Citizenship: A Very Short Introduction* by Oxford University Press in 2008.

Michael Burgess is Professor of Federal Studies and the Director of the Centre for Federal Studies at the University of Kent. Among his publications are *Comparative Federalism: Theory and Practice* (Routledge, 2006) and *Multinational Federations* (Routledge, 2007), co-edited with John Pinder, and *Federalism and the European Union: The Building of Europe 1950–2000* (UCL Press, 2000) and *Comparative Federalism and Federation* (Harvester Wheatsheaf, 1993; edited with Alain C. Gagnon).

Alan W. Cafruny is Henry Bristol Professor of International Affairs at Hamilton College. His publications include *Europe at Bay: In the Shadow of US Hegemony* (Lynne Rienner, 2007; with Magnus Ryner) and *A Ruined Fortress: Neoliberal Hegemony and Transformation in Europe* (Rowman and Littlefield, 2003; co-edited with Magnus Ryner).

Thomas Diez is Professor of International Relations in the Department of Political Science and International Studies, University of Birmingham (UK). His publications include *The European Union and Conflict Resolution* (Cambridge University Press, 2008; co-edited with Mathias Albert and Stephan Stetter) and *Cyprus: A Conflict at the Crossroads* (Manchester University Press, 2009; co-edited with Nathalie Tocci).

Birgit Locher is a Political Consultant and Research Fellow at the University of Tübingen, Germany. Her publications include *Norms, Advocacy-Networks and Policy Change: Trafficking in Women in the European Union* (VS-Verlag, 2007) and *Transnational Activism in the UN and the EU: A Comparative Study* (Routledge, 2008; co-edited with Jutta Joachim).

Andrew Moravcsik is Professor of Politics and International Affairs, and Director of the European Union Program, at Princeton University's Woodrow Wilson School. He has written widely on European integration, transatlantic relations, international organization, international relations theory, defence-industrial globalization, and global human rights. He is Senior Fellow at the Brookings Institution, Contributing Editor at *Newsweek* magazine, and has served in policy positions in the US, Europe, and Asia.

Arne Niemann is Lecturer in European Integration Studies and International Relations at the Department of Political Science, University of Amsterdam. His publications include *Explaining Decisions in the European Union* (Cambridge University Press, 2006).

B. Guy Peters is Maurice Falk Professor of Government at the University of Pittsburgh, and Distinguished Professor of Comparative Politics at Zeppelin University (Germany). He is also co-editor of the European Political Science Review. His most recent publications include *Debating Institutionalism* (co-edited with Jon Pierre and Gerry Stoker), *Implementing New Public Management in Eastern Europe and Central Asia* (Central European Press) and *The Politics of Bureaucracy* (6th edn, Routledge).

John Peterson is Professor of international Politics at the University of Edinburgh. Recent publications include *The European Union: How Does It Work?*, 2nd edn (Oxford University Press, 2008; co-edited with Elizabeth Bomberg and Alexander Stubb), and *The Institutions of the European Union* 2nd edn (Oxford University Press, 2006; co-edited with Michael Shackleton).

Jon Pierre is a research professor in the Department of Political Science, University of Gothenburg. His recent publications include *The Handbook of Public Administration* (Sage, 2003), *Handbook of Public Policy* (2006) (both co-edited with Guy Peters), and *Debating Institutionalism* (Manchester University Press, 2008; co-edited with Guy Peters and Gerry Stoker).

Mark A. Pollack is Associate Professor of Political Science at Temple University, Philadelphia. He is the author of *The Engines of European Integration: Delegation, Agency, and Agenda Setting in the European Union* (Oxford University Press, 2003), and co-author, with Gregory C. Shaffer, of *When Cooperation Fails: The Global Law and Politics of Genetically Modified Foods* (Oxford University Press, 2009).

Elisabeth Prügl is Associate Professor of International Relations at Florida International University. Among her publications are *The Global Construction of Gender: Home-based Work in the Political Economy of the 20th Century* (Columbia University Press, 1999) and 'Feminism and Constructivism: Worlds Apart or Sharing the Middle Ground?' with Birgit Locher in *International Studies Quarterly* (March 2001).

Thomas Risse holds the Chair in International Politics at the Free University of Berlin's Otto Suhr Institute of Political Science. He is co-editor of the *Handbook of International Relations* (Sage, 2002) and of *Transforming Europe. Europeanization and Domestic Change* (Cornell University Press, 2001).

J. Magnus Ryner is Professor of International Relations at Oxford Brookes University. His publications include *Capitalist Restructuring, Globalisation and the Third Way: Lessons from the Swedish Model* (Routledge, 2002) and *Europe at Bay: In the Shadow of US Hegemony* (Lynne Rienner, 2007; co-authored with Alan Cafruny).

Frank Schimmelfennig is Professor of European Politics at the Center for Comparative and International Studies, ETH Zurich, Switzerland. His publications include *The EU, NATO, and the Integration of Europe* (Cambridge University Press, 2003) and *International Socialization in Europe* (Palgrave, 2006; with Stefan Engert and Heiko Knobel).

Philippe C. Schmitter is a Professor of Political Science at the European University Institute (EUI). Among his publications on the EU are *Governance in the European Union* (Sage, 1996; with Gary Marks, Fritz Scharpf, and Wolfgang Streeck) and *How to Democratize the European Union . . . and Why Bother?* (Rowman and Littlefield, 2000).

Ole Wæver is Professor of International Relations at the University of Copenhagen. He is co-author of *Security: A New Framework for Analysis* (Lynne Rienner, 1998; with Barry Buzan and Jaap de Wilde) and *Regions and Powers: The Structure of International Security* (Cambridge University Press, 2003).

Antje Wiener is a Professor of Political Science at the University of Hamburg, Germany. Her publications include *The Invisible Constitution of Politics: Contested Norms and International Encounters* (Cambridge University Press, 2008), *Contested Meanings of Norms: The Challenge of Democratic Governance beyond the State* (a special issue for *Comparative European Politics*, 5(1), Palgrave, 2007), *The Social Construction of Europe* (Sage, 2001; co-edited with Thomas Christiansen and Knud Erik Jørgensen), and *'European' Citizenship Practice—Building Institutions of a None- State* (Westview, 1998).

1 Introducing the Mosaic of Integration Theory

Thomas Diez and Antje Wiener

The Relevance of Integration Theory

The Dual Purpose of this Book

There is surely no shortage of books on European integration. This is a booming field, and readers will know better than anyone else the difficulties in choosing the appropriate literature. It is all the more surprising then that very few of these books are dedicated to the theory of European integration, especially when it comes to introductions and overviews. Most of them deal with the history of the integration process and its main actors, with the European Union's formal institutions and particular policies, or with present and future member states' policies, and barely spare a chapter on theoretical perspectives. This is not to say that there is no work done on integration theory. Indeed, this is in many respects a vibrant field that has overcome the impasses of the past. Yet, except for a few notable exceptions that we will return to in the course of this introduction (above all, Rosamond 2000 and Jørgensen, Pollack, and Rosamond 2007, and in German, Bieling and Lerch 2005), concise overviews of the field of integration theory remain rare.

This is therefore what we set out to do in this book: first, to provide an introduction to integration theory, its various approaches and how they have developed, to those who have started to study European integration, and are interested (as, we argue below, anyone studying European integration should be) in the theories of their field; second, to provide an overview of the field and take stock of its achievements to date, but also its problems, for those who are involved in the development of European integration theory, and who want to make sense of the sometimes confusing array of approaches that have been proliferating since the 1960s.[1] In doing so, we suggest that as the European integration process has progressed, its analyses have moved away from being predominantly concerned with either providing a normative template for a future European polity or with explaining the integration process within a social scientific framework grounded in International Relations (IR) theory. Increasingly, scholars have turned to or incorporated a more critical or 'problematizing' approach, therefore reflecting both concerns with the integration process and developments in IR theory since the 1980s, while others have treated the European Union (EU) as a political system that faces general problems of governance and therefore should not solely be treated as the exception to international politics that needs explaining. Neither of these developments means that

IR as a discipline has become irrelevant to the analysis of European integration, and it in many ways continues to structure the major debates, but the field as a whole has certainly become a lot more varied.

To this end, we have invited eminent scholars who have contributed significantly to the development of a particular theoretical approach, to take part in this 'stocktaking'. We have asked them to reflect upon the development, achievements, and problems of 'their' approach according to a set pattern, which we will introduce below and which will allow for comparing and relating individual approaches to each other. In this introduction, we want first to make the case for the relevance of theory when studying European integration. We then proceed to give a broad overview of the phases of theorizing European integration, thereby surveying the theoretical approaches that we have included in this volume and providing our rationale for this particular selection. The following section introduces the comparative framework that provided the guide for the chapters. This will include a discussion of the nature of the relationships between theories, a theme that we return to in the conclusion of this book. Finally, building on this discussion, we introduce the pattern of each chapter and provide an overview of the book.

We should add that the process of stocktaking would make no sense if it did not lead to the further development of theory. To that extent, we would not want to see this book read purely to understand and replicate existing theories, but rather as the starting point for criticizing and reformulating existing approaches, bringing them together in novel ways, and to move beyond them. We would like to see both colleagues and students involved in this project—it is probably fair to say that without the critical engagement of their students, none of the authors of this book could have made the contribution they did to European integration theory.

What is Integration Theory?

In order to talk meaningfully about integration theory, its two constitutive terms 'integration' and 'theory' need to be defined. This is less straightforward than it may at first seem, since both terms are heavily contested.

Let us turn to *integration* first. Ernst Haas, one of the most influential neofunctionalist integration theorists (see also Niemann with Schmitter in Chapter 3), once defined integration as the process 'whereby political actors in several, distinct national settings are persuaded to shift their loyalties, expectations and political activities toward a new centre, whose institutions possess or demand jurisdiction over the pre-existing national states' (Haas 1958: 16). This is a broad definition, which includes both a social process (the shifting of loyalties) and a political process (the construction of new political institutions with a direct say in at least a part of their member states' affairs). Not all theorists would include both aspects in their definition, and there are reasons why Haas, from his perspective, emphasized the social element of integration. As will become clear in Chapter 3, functionally defined actors are core promoters of integration in neofunctionalism.

A less demanding definition preferred by intergovernmentalists, coming from a different angle within the spectrum of integration theory, focuses instead more narrowly on the creation of political institutions to which member states subscribe. For an overview of integration theories as the present volume attempts to provide, insisting on coverage of both social and political integration would have been far too demanding and would have led to the exclusion of theoretical approaches otherwise seen as central to the debate. Therefore, while we have sympathies for Haas's definition, we have in the following included approaches that tackle at least the political integration process, while some of them go beyond this and deal with social integration as well.

While this may seem broad enough as a common denominator for most of traditional integration theory, it is nonetheless too restrictive to account for some of the later developments in what may broadly be seen as the field of integration theory. In both of the definitions above, integration is first and foremost a *process*: both neofunctionalists and intergovernmentalists are more concerned with the process of integration than with the political system to which that integration leads. However, since the 1980s various authors have focused specifically on the shape of what they call a new system of governance emerging in the EU. While they are more concerned with the *outcome* than the process of integration (see Marks, Hooghe, and Blank 1996; Marks, Scharpf, Schmitter, and Streeck 1996), their work is included in our understanding of integration theory, because it now undeniably forms an important part of that field, as the field has moved towards accepting the EU as a polity that needs to be understood better.

Secondly, what is *theory*? Again, understandings differ, and as above, we endorse a definition that allows us to include a broader range of approaches. Narrowly defined, theory is understood as a causal argument of universal, transhistorical validity and nomothetic quality, which can be tested through the falsification of a series of hypotheses (King, Keohane, and Verba 1994; Przeworski and Teune 1982). Some of the chapters discussed in this book will stick to this narrow definition, many however will not. Instead, they use theory in a rather loose sense of abstract reflection, which despite its abstract nature can nonetheless be context-specific, for instance by taking its point of departure in the consideration of a particular policy field of the EU. To make this point clearer, it helps to consider that theory serves different purposes. Some theoretical approaches explain policy outcomes or decision-making behaviour, others criticize or 'problematize' general trends on the basis of abstract considerations; some fit particular developments into a larger classificatory scheme, others seek to provide normative guidance (see for example Woods 1996). In each case, theory means something else: Different theoretical approaches to European integration are informed by different understandings of the meaning and purpose of theorizing.

To distinguish these different understandings from the narrow definition of theory outlined above, we will use the term 'integration theory' when we mean the *field* of theorizing the process and outcome of (European) integration, while we use the term 'theoretical approaches' when we refer to the *individual* ways of dealing with integration, some, but not all of which may be classified as theories in the narrow sense. What they all share, however, is that they are not solely concerned with the development of particular policies, but that they want to make a contribution to the reflection on European integration and governance.

European integration theory is thus the field of systematic reflection on the process of intensifying political cooperation in Europe and the development of common political institutions, as well as on its outcome. It also includes the theorization of changing constructions of identities and interests of social actors in the context of this process.

Why Study Integration Theory?

For many students, the main purpose of studying integration theory will be to gain a better understanding of how the EU works. To do so, students require first and foremost knowledge about how these institutions are set up and how they work so as to identify organizational competences, the role and function of a particular institution according to the Treaties, or access points for lobbying activities. From this perspective, the value added by theory is not immediately obvious—instead, empirical facts appear to provide sufficient information. Why then study integration theory? There are, at least, three reasons.

First, theories in the narrow sense of the term help us to explain processes and outcomes of integration, which not only leads to a better understanding of the current set of institutions, but may also help to formulate expectations about future developments and institutional behaviour.

Second, apart from the set-up, role, and function of formal institutions, many readers will, for example, be concerned with questions of democratic reform and legitimacy. On the one hand, these *do* require detailed knowledge about the EU's institutions. Yet, on the other hand, they also require a deeper understanding of the normative issues at stake, such as: what should legitimacy be based on? Or: what form of democracy is appropriate for a polity beyond the nation state? Many approaches that do not fit the narrow scientific definition of theory address such issues and assist and encourage further reflections upon them.

Third, and arguably more importantly, 'pure' empirical knowledge of how institutions work is impossible and would in any case not be very meaningful. It is *impossible* since the representation of empirical facts is always based on particular concerns, and assumptions about the nature of the EU and the finality of the integration process, which often remain unreflected. Integration theory helps to highlight and problematize these concerns and assumptions. 'Pure' empirical knowledge is *not very meaningful* in the sense that since any empirical representation is imbued with such assumptions, to concentrate only on the 'facts' provides a superficial understanding that disregards at least some of the political disputes 'underneath' the surface. To sum this point up, analysing integration is not only a technical matter, but involves particular understandings and conceptualizations of integration and the EU, for which we need integration theory.

Two examples illustrate this point. The first one concerns the nature of foreign policy decision-making within the EU. To observers who base their assessment on organizational design, the EU's Common Foreign and Security Policy (CFSP) is by and large identified as a matter of the Council and therefore intergovernmentally organized. Not quite so, argue others (see e.g. Jørgensen 1997; Glarbo 2001; Øhrgaard 1997). While it is true that formally, CFSP is primarily a matter between governments and does not fall within the scope of the Commission, this characterization misses some of the informal, 'societal' developments that have created a dense web of consultation with integrative effects that are not captured by the intergovernmentalist picture. These take place on the social level through the creation of a diplomatic community within the EU (Glarbo 2001), or the projection of normative power in international politics on the basis of common values and norms (Manners 2002; Sjursen 2006a; Diez and Manners 2008), and they have political consequences, such as the so-called 'coordination reflex', the widespread tendency to coordinate foreign policy with other member states rather than going it alone. The extent to which this is true is a matter of empirical analysis, but the important point is that these studies employ a particular theoretical approach that allows them to bring to the fore the social dimension of the integration process, even in areas formally characterized by intergovernmentalism (see also Risse on social constructivism in Chapter 8).

The second example concerns the development of citizenship in the EU. Here, formal institutional approaches would find that Union citizenship was 'invented' at the intergovernmental conference that prepared the treaty revisions at Maastricht. As such, it is often seen as a 'thin' institution with little substantive importance. Yet some authors have pointed out that elements of (market-) citizenship, i.e. fundamental rights of working citizens, had been included in the treaties before, and that the way European citizenship emerged at Maastricht was in fact conditioned by previous legal cases, rulings, and provisions (O'Leary 1996; Kostakopoulou 2001; Kadelbach 2003). Others have pointed out that previous 'citizenship practice', i.e. the policies and political processes that forge the institutionalized terms of citizenship within a particular context, had constructed elements of citizenship rights, access, and belonging that shaped the formulation of Union citizenship later on (Wiener 1998; see also Meehan 1993; Shaw 2007). The citizenship case demonstrates that the assessment of an institution's meaning depends on the type of theoretical approach chosen to study the problem. Whether one regards the institutionalization of EU citizenship with the Maastricht Treaty as an important development will, for instance, depend on the theoretical assumptions about context, institutional role, and function, i.e. whether citizenship is approached from a normative, liberal or, indeed, dogmatic legal perspective. Furthermore, the process of integration raises questions about theoretical assumptions and contested concepts, for example, the question of whether such citizenship undermines the familiar concept of modern (national) citizenship. All of these are questions that are ultimately of a theoretical nature in the sense of this book, and the theoretical vantage point one takes is crucial to how one answers them.

Reviewing the history of European integration demonstrates that there have been a number of occasions that are hotly debated in the integration literature, mostly due to analysts approaching them from different theoretical angles. The following is just a brief selection of controversies, some of which we will get back to in more detail later on:

The role of state interests in the founding years: From a realist perspective[2] in the IR sense of the term, integration and especially the developments in the founding years are largely down to the interests and power of big member states, during that phase particularly France and Germany, with France wanting to control Germany and Germany having an interest in getting back onto the international stage (see for example Pedersen 1998).

Against this, neofunctionalists have emphasized the role of private and sector interests (see Chapter 3), whereas political economy approaches put the spotlight onto the setting of integration within a broader context of capitalist hegemony (see Chapter 12).

The lack of major institutional developments in the 1970s: The 1970s are often labelled the 'doldrum years' of integration (and, as it were, integration theory), because political integration seemed to stagnate, whereas others have argued that below the surface a lot of changes took place that would prepare for the reinvigoration of integration and integration theory in the latter half of the 1980s (Caporaso and Keeler 1995). Furthermore, outside political science, legal scholars have advanced the argument of 'integration through law', focusing on increasing legal interdependencies and corresponding shifts in the meaning of sovereignty (Capeletti *et al.* 1985).

The agreement on the Single European Act (SEA) (1986): The agreement on institutional change introduced with the SEA raised a number of new questions for integration theory. Having been forged at an intergovernmental conference, it led to a re-launch of the theoretical debate discussing the role and formation of state preferences in the negotiations towards the SEA (Moravcsik 1991, 1993; see also Chapter 4), on the one hand, and emphasizing the role of the Commission, informal processes within the Committee of Permanent Representatives (COREPER), and the influence of private actors such as the European Round Table of Industrialists, on the other (Wincott 1995; Hayes-Renshaw, Lequesne, and Mayor Lopez 1992; Ross 1995; Bornschier 2000; see also Chapter 12).

All of these controversies need to be investigated empirically, but they cannot be reduced to a simple testing of alternative hypothesis, nor can they be addressed purely by 'thick description' (W. Wallace 1996). Instead, seemingly competing theories often shed a different light on the issue that is enabled by a particular theoretical perspective.

Integration Theory: A Broad Overview

Phases of European Integration Theory

Having established the relevance of integration theory, we will in the following provide a broad overview of its development. This places the theoretical approaches in their historical disciplinary context.

We suggest that the development of integration theory can be divided into three broad phases (see also Wiener 2006). These are preceded by a normative proto-integration theory period. We identify the three phases as explanatory, analytical, and constructive, respectively. A note of caution is in order, however. Since most approaches combine various dimensions of theory, the distinction among the respective phases is not as clear-cut as analytically suggested. The phases are therefore meant to identify the emergence, development, and, at times, dominance of particular theoretical tendencies, but we do not mean to suggest that these were the only (and sometimes not even the dominant) ones. In Table 1.1, we have left the endpoints of these phases open, since work in one tradition tends to continue after the emergence of new tendencies in theorizing. However, when

Table 1.1 Three phases in integration theory

Phase	When?	Main themes	Main theoretical reference points
Explaining integration	1960s onwards	How can integration outcomes be explained?	Liberalism, realism, neoliberalism
		Why does European integration take place?	
Analysing governance	1980s onwards	What kind of political system is the EU?	Governance, comparative politics, policy analysis
		How can the political processes within the EU be described?	
		How does the EU's regulatory policy work?	
Constructing the EU	1990s onwards	How and with which social and political consequences does integration develop?	Social constructivism, poststructuralism, international political economy
		How are integration and governance conceptualized? How should they be?	Normative political theory
			Gender approaches

we mention end dates in the following text, these are to signify a shift within European integration theory towards new approaches.

Similarly, although perhaps to a lesser extent, the dates provided for the beginnings of our three phases are also problematic. In 1970, Haas (E. B. 1970: 635), for instance, had already conceptualized the then European Community as an 'anarchoid image of a myriad of unity' with significant 'asymmetrical overlapping' and 'infinitely tiered multiple loyalties', and Lindberg and Scheingold (1970) analysed the EC as a 'would-be polity'. Both of these works address issues characteristic of the phase of 'analysing governance' in European integration theory, which we will further develop below, yet they had been published at least a decade before. We would nonetheless argue that our three phases identify the major tendencies in the development of European integration theory. They are also significant as the general self-image of the discipline, although not everyone would agree with our identification of a third phase in particular.

The normative proto-integration period predates the actual development of political integration in Europe. It is an important precursor of the three phases of integration theory building. Functionalism is typical of this normative period. As part of a broader set of early 'liberal' approaches to IR, it saw states and their sovereignty as the core problem of a war-prone world. Popular in the interwar years and in the immediate aftermath of the Second World War, with David Mitrany's *A Working Peace System* (1943) as the core publication, it had a strong normative agenda, namely how, through a network of transnational organizations on a functional basis, one could constrain states and prevent future war. This was a global concern and had no direct relation to European integration—as a matter of fact, Mitrany was an opponent of regional integration that he saw as undermining his global concerns and replicating rather than transcending a state-model (Mitrany 1966; see Rosamond 2000: 36–8). Early federalism, too, can be located in this period. As a political movement it was more directly related to particular developments in Europe, for example in the form of calls for a European federation made during the interwar years by actors as different as the German Social Democrats (see Schneider 1977; Hrbek 1972) and the conservative Hungarian Count Coudenhove-Kalergi (1971). Again, state sovereignty was a core problem for federalists only to be overcome by political organization at a higher level, although in contrast to Mitrany's functionalist model, this new political organization would bear many features of the state.

With the *first phase* roughly lasting from the signing of the Treaty of Rome until the early 1980s, we enter European integration theory proper. Despite the realist attempts to integrate them into their worldview, and conceptualize integration as an effect of the power play between states, the early successes of integration challenged the existence of the territorial state system, which is at the core of realist assumptions. It therefore also challenged the overwhelming predominance of realism in IR after the disillusionment with liberal theories after the Second World War and its aftermath. Accordingly, integration theory initially sought to explain the processes of institution-building above the state, which was not supposed to happen within a realist picture of the world. Two theoretical approaches came to dominate the debate. Both were based on rational actor assumptions, while locating the push and pull for the integration process on different levels and in different societal realms.

Neofunctionalists, in line with their broad definition of integration, took up functionalist ideas and explained the move away from the anarchic state system and towards supranational institution-building by focusing on societal and market patterns and how they pushed elites towards advocating supranational institutions within their policy areas. Because of the functional interconnectedness of policy areas, these shared policy initiatives in so-called 'low politics' areas were seen as having the potential for 'spilling over' into other policy areas, at first to those closely related to market policy, but ultimately beyond (*functional spillover*). This assumption the neofunctionalists shared with their predecessors. Yet they recognized that such spillovers were far from automatic, and so in addition to this, they expected actors, who had shifted their loyalties and redefined their identities, to actively demand further integration (*political spillover*). In particular, actors responsible for governance on the supranational level (in the EU case, above all the European Commission) were considered to push (or 'cultivate') integration because they had an interest in integration as such (*cultivated spillover*). While sticking to the normative agenda of funcionalism, neofuctionalists therefore paid greater tribute to the necessity of central political institutions. Chiming with the development of IR at the time, and the social sciences generally speaking, they also had an explicit *social scientific* (in contrast to a predominantly normative) interest in creating a *general* theory of regional integration that was applicable beyond the singular case of Europe (see in particular Ernst Haas's as well as Philippe Schmitter's work; Haas 1961, 1967, 1970; Haas and Schmitter 1964; and Niemann with Schmitter in Chapter 3 of this book). In a different but not dissimilar way, Karl W. Deutsch (1957) saw integration coming about through the increased communication and interaction across borders, which gave his theoretical approach the name 'transactionalism'.

These arguments were opposed by intergovernmentalists who explained supranational institution-building as the result of bargains struck between nation states with specific geopolitical interests that militated towards a 'pooling' of sovereignty in specific historical circumstances. In doing so, intergovernmentalists stuck to the core arguments of realism while still explaining aberrations from the realist worldview (Hoffmann 1966). The debate between supporters of integration as 'the rescue of the nation state' (Milward 1992), on the one hand, and as the overcoming of the nation state, on the other, which began in this first phase of integration theory, has remained a consistent factor in social science analysis to this day. While liberal intergovernmentalism, one of the core theoretical approaches since the late 1980s, does not deny the societal impact on supranational institution-building, as the theorization of societal preference formation in Moravcsik's work demonstrates (see Schimmelfennig and Moravcsik in Chapter 4), their focus has been on governmental actors whose capacity for decisions was enhanced by supranational institutions, but not constrained by them. Institutions, according to this view, are designed for particular purposes and under control of the actors who created them. However, in line with the emerging consensus between neorealists and neoliberals in IR in the 1980s, Moravcsik combines 'realist' state-centrism on the international level with a 'liberal' focus on state preference formation, rather than referring to given geopolitical interests, and sees institutions beyond the nation state as a standard feature of international politics, even though they are largely dependent on the continued support of their member states. To that extent, Moravcsik relates much more to the neoliberal than the realist camp in IR; after all, neoliberals, too, concede that the state is central to international politics and have therefore given up one of the core normative aims of classical liberalism as outlined above.

For a new generation of integration theorists, however, institutions were not mere tools in the hands of their creators, but had themselves an important impact on both the integration process and the development of European governance. As neoinstitutionalists have demonstrated, institutions can cause 'unintended consequences' (North 1990), making the process of institution-building less easily reversible than the intergovernmentalists would have it (Pierson 1996). A particularly dramatic example of unintended consequences was the largely underestimated push to further integration by the Single European Act (Weiler 1999). In terms of European integration theory, this led to the revival and revision of classic integration theories in the form of liberal intergovernmentalism (Moravcsik 1991) and neofunctionalism (Stone Sweet 2002; Sandholtz and Zysman 1989; Tranholm-Mikkelsen 1991). It also marks the starting point for a shift of focus in theoretical approaches to European integration away from IR Theory towards comparative politics, not least out of a recognition that the EU's complex institutional set-up seemed to be here to stay. Meanwhile, even within IR, there emerged a greater recognition of different forms of institutionalized cooperation in international politics, first in the form of 'regime theory', then in the theorization of what Czempiel and Rosenau (1992) aptly called 'governance without government'.

This *second phase* considerably broadened the scope of empirical research and theoretical reflection on European integration, and introduced a greater degree of interdisciplinarity. It brought comparative and institutionalist approaches to the foreground of integration theory, following questions of what kind of polity the EU really is and how it operates—as Thomas Risse-Kappen (1996) famously put it, to 'explore the nature of the beast'. Among the concepts developed during this phase to answer these questions are the EU as a system of 'multilevel' (Marks, Hooghe, and Blank 1996) or 'network governance' (Jachtenfuchs and Kohler-Koch 1996), or as a 'multiperspectival polity' (Ruggie 1993). Others focused on the way in which policies are made through the analysis of policy networks (Peterson 1995a; Peterson and Bomberg 1999). A key process analysed was the 'Europeanization' of governance rules, institutions, and practices across the EU (Cowles et al. 2001). Questions of institutional adaptation and misfit and of good governance including legitimacy, democracy, and transparency are other issues addressed by works in this second phase of integration theories. They clearly reflected the shifting agendas of both IR and comparative politics in an era in which governance structures, it seemed, could no longer be contained within the nation state and therefore called for an analysis that integrated both fields.

To some extent, the *third phase* of integration theory is marked by the return of IR theory, although of a different kind. During the 1980s and 1990s, IR theory was characterized by the rise of a variety of critical and constructivist approaches, which drew their inspiration from developments in other fields of social theory. Scholars questioned both the ontological and epistemological assumptions on which traditional approaches had been built. Social constructivists, for instance, demonstrated the relevance of ideas, norms, institutions, and identities for international politics and pointed to the interdependence of the structure of the state system, on the one hand, and the agency of those involved in international politics, on the other. Post-structuralists problematized core concepts of IR theory and drew attention to the discursive construction of our understanding of international politics. Critical theorists and feminists not only developed important critiques of the contemporary international system, but also often offered alternatives paths towards what they saw as a more just world. In the field of political economy, too, scholars took on a more critical outlook and increasingly referred to the problems brought about by the hegemony of capitalism as a particular political-economic system.

These developments coincided with the move towards political union in the 1991 Maastricht and the 1996 Amsterdam Treaties. Under the pressure of massive enlargement and constitutional revision, integration theory faced the challenge of analysing and problematizing the interrelated processes of widening and deepening. Different from the first two phases, which sought to explain or analyse either institution-building on the supranational level, or institutional change on the meso- and substate levels, this third phase of integration theory thus faced the more encompassing task of theorizing the goal or finality of European integration, the competing ideas and discourses about European governance, and the normative implications of particular EU policies. Accordingly, apart from problem-oriented theorizing, works during this phase have been concerned with questions about our understanding of integration, how particular policy areas have been defined and developed in the way they did, and what political effects these definitions and historical processes have had.

This third phase therefore focuses on substantial questions about 'constructing' (and limiting) European integration. It is in answering these questions that the critical and constructivist approaches in IR theory were taken up,[3] alongside or combined with in-sights from the 'constitutional turn' later in the second phase, which, sparked by the Maastricht and Amsterdam Treaties and the increased public debate about the legitimacy of European governance, brought normative questions about the EU's constitution from political theory to the heart of the analysis of governance (see Chapter 11). Social con-structivism, especially, has in some respects drawn on, and in turn contributed to insights of governance approaches. In particular, it has addressed issues of the development of the EU's formal and informal institutions, as well as processes of Europeanization, although as far as the latter are concerned, its focus has been on the Europeanization of identities rather than institutions and policies (see Risse in Chapter 8).

Approaches Covered in this Book

The theoretical approaches discussed in this book cover the three phases of integration theory, including their normative precursor. We have therefore divided the book into three corresponding parts: explaining European integration, analysing European govern-ance, and constructing the European Union.

Part One, *Explaining European Integration*, contains first a chapter on federalism. While federalism is first and foremost a normative theory, it has been used more recently in a comparative fashion to explain, analyse, or devise particular features of the Euro-polity (Koslowski 2001; Nicolaidis and Howse 2001). Furthermore, scholars such as Morav-csik (1998) have derived hypotheses about the particular institutional choices made in intergovernmental conferences for European governance from federalism. Together with neofunctionalism and intergovernmentalism, federalism can be seen as a triad of theories that are often, although problematically so, as we will argue below, presented as compet-ing with each other. Accordingly, Chapter 3 is devoted to neofunctionalism and Chapter 4 to intergovernmentalism, both of which take IR theories as a starting point to attempt an explanation of why integration takes place, and why policy-makers choose particular policies and institutional arrangements.

In Part Two, *Analysing European Governance*, we turn our focus to those approaches that first and foremost try to understand and analyse the EU as a type of political system. Chap-ter 5 reflects on the development of governance approaches. It explicitly links the study of European integration to broader debates and analytical frameworks in political science. Focusing more on the analysis of policy-making processes and drawing on a different set of political science literature, Chapter 6 discusses the policy network approach to the analy-sis of European governance, at the core of which is the explanation of particular policy decisions with the configuration of the respective policy field. While such an approach often produces very detailed empirical studies, it is nonetheless a *theoretical* approach in that it advances general arguments about the nature of the policy-making process and its outputs within a complex governance setting. Chapter 7 looks at the contribution that various 'new institutionalisms' have made to the study of European governance, analysing in particular the impact of institutions on policy-making and the overall development of governance, as well as the shaping of those institutions by political actors. The focus in this chapter is on rationalist and historical institutionalism, whereas sociological institutionalism is discussed as part of social constructivism in Chapter 8. This chapter acts as a kind of bridge to Part One and Part Three. Social constructivists are interested in what kind of 'beast' the EU is (Risse-Kappen 1996) and how political processes and identities change within the integration process. They link to the approaches in Part Three in that they stress the constructed characteristic of European integration and governance and the interplay of structure and agency in this construction. Yet they also link to the approaches covered in Part One in that they try to explain this construction, highlighting the role of ideas and norms together with interests, rather than focusing predominantly on the latter, as neofunctionalists and intergovernmentalists tend to do. Social constructivists also share with most approaches in both Parts One and Three a strong affiliation with IR: while social constructivism by no means originated there, it found its way into the study of European integration via the work that developed in IR since the late 1980s.

Finally, Part Three, *Constructing the European Union*, deals with those more recent approaches that add a critical dimension to studying the European Union. This part includes, in Chapter 9, a discussion of discursive approaches to the analysis of European integration, some of which have used post-structuralist concepts taken mostly from IR theory to problematize conceptions of European integration and governance, while others have tried to use those concepts to develop an explanatory framework for the analysis of the European policies of member states, drawing on the constraints that predominant discourses set for the formulation of EU policy. Gender approaches, which are covered in Chapter 10, share the critical and problematizing line with discursive approaches, building in part on the advances of feminist approaches in other disciplines and focusing on how European integration and EU policies build on and (re)produce a particular image of 'women' and 'men', implicitly or even explicitly favouring one over the other. In their critical and problematizing mode, both Chapters 9 and 10 tackle some of the core normative problems of European integration and EU governance as it has developed over the decades, including above all the notion of a crisis of legitimacy of supranational governance. These issues relate to the broader questions posed by political theory as a subfield of political science, and so it is little surprise that political theorists have increasingly found interest in the EU. Chapter 11 covers the input from this field to European integration theory. As a final contribution before our conclusion, Chapter 12 provides an overview of political economy approaches to the study of European integration and governance. Again, these have increasingly focused on critical interrogations of the integration process and its consequences, but instead of tackling predominantly conceptual issues as discursive approaches do, their main arguments relate to the capitalist system as it is embedded in the current configuration of the Single Market and Economic and Monetary Union.

The list of approaches covered in this book is obviously not exhaustive of all the approaches available to the student of European integration. We have included what we believe are currently the most salient and influential approaches in European integration theory, and by including some of the more recent developments, we will have already expanded the scope of what is conventionally taught as the core of the discipline. Nonetheless some of the omissions may prove more controversial than others. Two require particular justification.

First, we have not included a chapter on transactionalism. While we agree with those who would like to see this approach given much more attention than it currently receives, because it would refocus our attention to the social, rather than the political integration process, we cannot ignore that, a few exceptions aside, hardly anyone has followed the lead of Karl Deutsch in this respect. In addition to this, Deutsch's focus was on NATO and the transatlantic 'security community', rather than on European integration per se (but see Deutsch *et al.* 1967). It is telling that one of the few recent pieces that comes close to transactionalism subsumes Deutsch's work under neofunctionalism, and focuses on transnational exchange as one of the independent variables influencing the form of supranational organization, rather than on different forms of community as a result of communication across borders (Stone Sweet and Sandholtz 1997).

A second omission in this book is that of 'pure' economic theories of integration. In this respect, we do not believe that there can be a purely economic theory of European integration as defined above, which is above all a political and social process. To the extent that economic theories exist in this field, they are looking at particular aspects and especially the effects of economic integration, and are thus not theories of European integration as such (see Balassa 1962; El-Agraa 1982). Economic theories have, however, found their way into some of the approaches covered, such as liberal intergovernmentalism, where predictions about the outcome of domestic bargains over national interests are made on the basis of economic theorems, or political economy, which however criticizes the division of economics from the other social sciences, and they are therefore discussed within these contexts. However, we do not think that an economic theory as such is currently playing a major part in the integration theory debates, nor are we convinced that it should be.

Last but not least, the approaches included in this book have in their majority (but by no means all) been formulated by scholars working in English, and within the Anglo-Saxon scholarly community. This is a problem to the extent that we are thereby imposing a narrative of the development of European integration theory on scientific communities that may have had a very different experience, and we may have overlooked important and exciting theoretical developments in that process—European integration theory outside the Anglo-Saxon boundaries may indeed be 'the best kept secret' (Jørgensen 2000 for international relations theory; see also Friedrichs 2004). Having said that, the success of approaches beyond national boundaries requires its formulation in what is increasingly becoming the lingua franca of academia. This is not to say that there are no interesting developments outside what is accessible in English. It is also true that there are particular academic styles that differ between national academic communities, and that translating from another language into English does not always properly convey the meaning of the original. As an overview and a stocktaking exercise, we had to base our selection on what we regarded as success across borders, and English-speaking publications remain in many ways the yardstick for such an exercise, even if this is problematic.

Studying Integration Theory

Contexts of Theoretical Development

The story of integration theory can be told from a chronological angle or with a focus on theoretical debates and the specific issues covered. Our account combines a chronological perspective with a perspective on debates because there are distinct themes and controversies to particular *phases* of European integration theory. Telling the story of integration theory in these terms is not uncommon (cf. the overviews by Caporaso and Keeler 1995; Bache and George 2001; Rosamond 2000; Eilstrup-Sangiovanni 2006). More contested is the question of how the theoretical approaches relate to each other. There are two aspects to this issue. The first relates to the emergence of theories and the movement from one dominant approach to another, and can therefore be seen as a contribution to the history and sociology of European integration studies. The second is concerned with the 'fit' of theories (above all whether they are compatible or competing with each other), and is therefore a contribution to theory-building in itself.

Starting with the historical–sociological approach, there are two factors that are often seen as influencing the development of theories, the academic and the sociopolitical context (Rosamond 2000: 9). The academic context consists of debates and problems that are pursued in the wider scientific context of a particular field as well as the legacies of previous debates in the field itself. Of particular importance in this context are 'paradigms' that provide researchers with guideposts about how to conduct and present their studies (see Kuhn 1964). The sociopolitical context, in contrast, consists of factors outside of academia, such as the development of the object under analysis, the influence of sponsors on research agendas, or the discursive restrictions set by a particular political climate. In addition, both of these contexts can be coloured by national differences.

Our account of the three phases of European integration theory above provides plenty of examples for how the study of European integration has followed the ups and downs of its subject. The rise, fall, and comeback of neofunctionalism in the 1950s, following the Empty Chair crisis and the Single European Act respectively, provide the most obvious case. The relation between the sociopolitical context and the development of theory is, however, not a one-way street. Thus, not only was neofunctionalism developed on the basis of what happened in Western Europe in the 1950s, neofunctionalism itself also became the quasi-official ideology in the Commission and other parts of the EC institutions. Ironically, as George and Bache (2006) point out, it is today often used by so-called Eurosceptics to increase fears of a technocratic, centralized, and undemocratic super-state, whereas governments supportive of further integration tend to resort to the intergovernmentalist rhetoric of sovereignty being only 'pooled' in order to alleviate these fears.

While the influence of the EU's development on integration theory may be obvious, the academic context has been no less forceful in shaping the way in which integration has been conceptualized and analysed. As Rosamond (1995: 394) argues, theoretical approaches to the analysis of European integration 'have arisen in the context of dominant perspectives in the broad arena of social scientific inquiry' and are 'bound up with intellectual fashion and debates between and within different theoretical paradigms'. Thus, if we had included a list of major works in other social sciences and neighbouring fields in this introduction, we would have seen that theoretical movements in European integration studies are often preceded by or run in parallel with developments in disciplines such as political science, legal studies, and IR in particular, as our overview has demonstrated. Neofunctionalism provides yet again a good example with its social-scientific turn against earlier versions of functionalism (see Caporaso and Keeler 1995: 32–4; Kelstrup 1998: 24).

European integration also became an instrument for the pursuit of academic controversies in that it served as ammunition for the critique of the dominant, state-centred realist paradigm (George and Bache 2006); and again this mirrors debates in IR and political science more widely. Thereby, the neofunctionalism versus intergovernmentalism debate became embedded in a discourse in which the model of the state remained at the core, either on the national or on the European level (see Rosamond 1995), which in turn hindered the development of a debate about legitimacy 'beyond the state' (Kelstrup and Williams 2000: 8). That such a debate eventually became possible is not only due to the acceptance of the EU as a polity discussed above (see Hix 1994: 10), but also to the development of normative, critical, and constructivist approaches in other social sciences that could be imported into the third phase of European integration theory (Kelstrup and Williams 2000: 1, 9). Similarly, the comparativist project of the second phase benefited greatly from the previous development of neo-institutionalist research in sociology, which provided comparativists with new concepts to analyse political institutions as an important influence on politics in their own right.

Interestingly, it is the academic context where national differences seem to matter most, rather than the sociopolitical context, and the problem of language discussed earlier plays a crucial part in this. It is perhaps ironic that most of the classic integration theories have been developed in the United States, rather than within Europe. This, however, can be explained by the dominance of theory-driven American social science in international relations (see Wæver 1998a), from which the approaches in the crucial first phase of integration theory developed. 'European' approaches have traditionally tended to be much more historically or normatively oriented, or have been engaged in detailed empirical studies of particular policies (Smith and Ray 1993). Only with the advent of the second and the third phase of integration theory are there more clearly audible European voices—most of them advocating a form of social inquiry that is different from the American social science model. Among these voices, there is also a certain degree of differentiation along national or regional lines, although whether this is more than coincidental would require further analysis. To give but two examples, discursive studies of the EU have by and large emerged from a Scandinavian context (e.g. Hansen and Wæver 2002; Larsen 1997a, b; Neumann 1999; Wæver 1998b), whereas two major studies on ideas and European governance have originated in Germany (Jachtenfuchs *et al.* 1998; Marcussen *et al.* 2001). Further research would have to be done to substantiate these initial findings, but they are striking enough to suggest that particular approaches often have a regional centre.

Competing or Complementary Approaches?

The importance of sociopolitical and academic contexts for the development of integration theory raises fundamental questions about the relationship of individual approaches to each other. Does the discussion in the last section imply that instead of moving to one unified theory, these approaches offer different perspectives that are largely determined by the contexts in which they are developed? Are these perspectives mutually exclusive, and can the arguments they put forward be tested against each other? How, in short, is one to compare the different theoretical approaches?

At the extremes of this debate are, on the one hand, the notion of scientific progress, where through falsification our knowledge of integration advances, and, on the other hand, the notion of incommensurable paradigms, which, in effect, construct and talk about different realities, and between which a dialogue is hardly possible. If we take the different understandings of theory advanced above, the more scientifically minded will generally tend towards the former, those with a broader understanding of theory towards the latter pole. Consequently, Moravcsik (1998) for instance, in his major contribution to the development of European integration theory, tests different theories against each other in order to establish a (liberal-intergovernmentalist) ground on which future theory can build. His exchange with Diez as well as with Risse and Wiener on the value of this contribution, however, can serve as an example for talking past each other because of very different agendas, concepts, and definitions that emerge from very different contexts (see Diez 1999c; Moravcsik 1999c, 2001c; Risse and Wiener 2001).

While we agree that scientific progress is ultimately influenced by its academic and sociopolitical context, we nonetheless find the argument of incommensurability problematic. Most integration theories have been developed within the context of Western academia, and although their pedigree differs, and consequently their ontological and epistemological foundations, they share quite a lot of common ground, as will become more obvious when reading through the chapters of this book. To the extent that they are incompatible, this is a consequence not of their inherent incommensurability, but of the claims they make about their scope. In other words, many theorists make broader claims such as 'explaining integration', when what they really do is a much more limited enterprise, for instance explaining results of intergovernmental conferences, criticizing a particular conceptualization of integration, or seeking to understand the historical development of a particular aspect of integration. This problem, as well as the criticism of it, is not new. Puchala already remarked in 1972 that

different schools of researchers have exalted different parts of the integration 'elephant'. They have claimed either that their parts were in fact whole beasts, or that their parts were the most important ones, the others being of marginal interest.

Puchala (1972: 268)

Inappropriate scope claims take an ontological and an epistemological form. Ontologically, approaches often explicitly or implicitly claim to provide a theoretical approach to (European) integration as such, while they in fact focus on a particular process or outcome. If this claim is relaxed, it should be possible to combine different approaches depending on the subject of analysis. Epistemologically, approaches would only be incommensurable if they claimed to have the same purpose and if they were directly related to reality. If, however, we assume that approaches can have different purposes, and if, perhaps more controversially, we further assume that our understanding of reality is always mediated by particular discursive contexts, which seems particularly opportune in the face of the multiperspectival character of the European Union (Ruggie 1993), then it is possible to see different approaches adding to a larger picture without being combined into a single, grand theory.

Even if two approaches agree on the aim of explaining integration, for instance, they might still be difficult to compare if what they mean by integration (ontological scope claim) are two different things. Moravcsik, for instance, focuses on political integration and the role of intergovernmental bargains, whereas neofunctionalists such as Stone Sweet and Sandholtz (1997) see integration as a much more social process happening in part through what they call 'transnational exchange' between member states societies (see also Branch and Øhrgaard 1999; on liberal intergovernmentalism see also Rosamond 1995: 398). All of these are respectable accomplishments in their own rights, and hardly testable against each other (see also Hix 1994: 3). Yet, at the same time, this does not necessarily make them incommensurable once there is a certain modesty introduced regarding the scope of the argument made.

The approaches in this book therefore can be seen as providing different perspectives on the subject of integration, each contributing to our overall understanding of the subject. They cannot easily be lumped together to form a grand theory of integration because one needs to adopt one's own viewpoint in order to 'make them work', and we therefore differ in this respect from the project of developing an overarching framework as it was eventually pursued even by Puchala (1972). However, they are not always direct competitors either, although some of them will indeed formulate hypotheses that can be tested against each other. Instead, one might see them as stones in an always-incomplete *mosaic*. The picture of integration that emerges from them is a multifaceted one—a point we will have to revisit in the conclusion to this volume, together with some of the questions this raises about the advancement and value of theory.

For now, it is important to develop an understanding of the main dimensions along which these approaches differ. We consider two such dimensions as particularly important. One is about the functions of theory briefly referred to above; the other is about the areas that the approaches analyse.

The Functions of Theory

There are three main functions of theory (broadly understood), and these run roughly parallel to the three main phases of integration theory identified above.

1. *Theory as explanation or understanding.* Although explaining and understanding approaches differ widely in the epistemological claims they make, and consequently in the methodologies they apply (see Hollis and Smith 1990), they share a common purpose in the sense that they ask why (explaining) or how (understanding) an event has come about. To that extent, they ask for reasons and/or causes for something to happen (on reasons and causes, see the discussion in Wendt (1999) and S. Smith (2000)). They differ predominantly in relation to the degree to which they consider their arguments generalizable or dependent on specific contexts, warranting different methodologies. The approaches in the first phase of integration theory have asked these sorts of questions, and most of them have leaned towards the 'explanation' variant. More recent approaches such as social constructivism have sometimes asked

similar questions, and while most social constructivists would see themselves in the 'understanding business', at least some of them have leaned towards 'explaining'.

2. *Theory as description and analysis.* This might at first seem like a waste-bin category, but it is not. Approaches in this category focus on the development of definitions and concepts with which to grasp particular developments, practices, and institutions. They provide labels and classifications. In that sense, explaining and understanding approaches have to presuppose descriptive and analytical approaches because the latter provide the former with the concepts on the basis of which events can be explained or understood. Likewise, an 'underlying theory' is an important part of any classificatory exercise (Grigorevich Mirkin 1996: 23). In the second phase of integration theory, we would expect a focus on description and analysis because one of the aims of these approaches was to provide a vocabulary with which to capture 'the nature of the beast' (Risse-Kappen 1996), to 'classify' the EU as a polity and to understand its main features and processes.

3. *Theory as critique and normative intervention.* While approaches in the first two categories take the development of integration more or less as a given, other approaches question the route that the integration process, or a particular policy, has taken, or develop norms and principles for the future of integration. Approaches in this category therefore either problematize a given development, or they develop normative alternatives. Theory in this understanding is often much closer to what one might call philosophy, or perhaps only 'abstract reflection', but in the form of normative theory, it has always had its rightful place in the canon of political theory, and many critical theories have recently been added to this (Tully 2002, 2008). At least some of the approaches included in our third phase of integration theory fall into this category.

If theory has such different purposes, it would be unfair and not even valid to hold one approach accountable on the basis of criteria set by another one. Evaluating and weighing theoretical approaches against each other therefore always has to take account of the principal function or purpose that the approach assigns to itself, unless we want to impose one common purpose on all theoretical approaches.

The Areas of Theory

It is, however, not only the purpose of theory that varies, but also the area, or the 'object' of particular approaches. Analysing member states' integration policy is different from, although related to, reflecting on the best institutional set-up for the EU, and consequently may require a different methodology. These areas of theory are a second, independent dimension on which theoretical approaches can differ from each other. Again, we propose three different areas, which we have delineated along the triad of polity, policy, and politics.

1. *Theory dealing with polity.* 'Polity' refers to the political community and its institutions. Approaches falling into this category would be those analysing the 'nature of the beast', those explaining how the EU's institutional structure came

about, or those trying to find constitutional alternatives on the basis of normative considerations, to give examples taken from all three functions of theory.

2. *Theory dealing with policy*. 'Policy' includes the actual measures taken to tackle concrete problems, and theoretical approaches in this area analyse and compare their content, or critically reflect upon them. This includes aspects such as 'policy style, the general problem-solving approach, the policy instruments used, and the policy standards set' (Börzel and Risse 2000: 3). However, to qualify as theory according to our definition above, such analyses need to be brought onto an abstract level, for instance by drawing out general patterns of policy content, or reflecting on the normative underpinnings within a policy field.

3. *Theory dealing with politics*. 'Politics' comprises the process of policy-making and the daily struggles and strategies of political actors dealing with each other. It is about the bargaining between governments, the influence of particular interest groups, or the dominance of a specific style of how decisions are reached. Approaches concerned with politics look at such issues as why technocratic governance prevails over participatory governance, how interest groups try to influence the policy-making process, or how particular groups are systematically disadvantaged by the dominant political style.

As these definitions have illustrated, it would be rather difficult empirically to stick strictly to one of these areas. Any discussion of polity is likely to involve constitutional frames in which policy-making takes place, or which restrict the content of policy, as well as the implication of constitutional arrangements for politics. Nonetheless, approaches are likely to emphasize one or the other, and not deal with all three poles of the triad in equal measure. Moreover, to the extent that they want to explain, they will use polity, policy, and politics either as the *explanandum* (what is to be explained) or the *explanans* (the explaining factor). However, a theoretical approach such as neofunctionalism might aim at explaining integration outcomes (here polity), while focusing on their explanation (here politics). Therefore, one has to specify how the areas of theory figure within each approach.

The Mosaic of Integration Theory

Combining these two dimensions, we arrive at what we call the mosaic of integration theory. Keeping the caveats raised above in mind, theoretical approaches can be located in the nine cells of Table 1.2. Its character as a 'mosaic' comes from the fact that each approach can be seen as a stone that adds to the picture that we gain of the EU. This picture is likely to remain unfinished, as new approaches will add new stones to change the picture. To reiterate, our point is that rather than directly competing with each other, each approach contributes to the emerging picture in its own limited way. The contributions can be ambiguous—as is the EU itself in many ways—but they are not necessarily mutually exclusive and incommensurable, as is often assumed. Placing an approach in

Table 1.2 The functions and areas of (integration) theory

	Polity	Policy	Politics
Explanatory/understanding			
Analytical/descriptive			
Critical/normative			

a particular part of the mosaic therefore clarifies with which approaches it actually competes in a rather narrow field.

Even if this is the case, however, any two approaches may still not be directly testable against each other. The example of liberal intergovernmentalism versus neofunctionalism illustrates this. In this case, while both approaches want to explain the political process of reaching a decision, and to some extent the outcome of that process in terms of its effects on the polity, they analyse different aspects of the decision-making process because they start from a different definition of integration. The distinction of various analytical areas is therefore a rather general one that always needs to be supplemented by a closer look at the basic concepts and definitions that approaches use within their area. This is not only true for the area- but also for the function-dimension. Because we have lumped together explaining and understanding, analytical and descriptive, critical and normative, approaches even within one cell are not necessarily directly comparable, as the epistemological claims they make differ widely, and thus the scope of their argument.

As we have pointed out above, approaches will usually find themselves in more than one category. The mosaic should not be seen as an exercise in compartmentalization. Quite the opposite: it is a heuristic device that allows us to move beyond fruitless debates in which approaches operating in different areas and pursuing different purposes talk past each other. Besides, even though approaches will cross the imaginary boundaries of the identified fields, they will tend to focus on one or the other—life is too short, and book space too restricted to deal with everything.

Reviewing Integration Theory

The Structure of the Chapters

Although the structure of individual chapters varies, they all address a set of questions that will help in the comparison between theoretical approaches and the assessment of their compatibility or incommensurability. Each author was asked to summarize the origins of the approach covered, its main arguments, and development over time. As the majority of the authors were substantially involved in the development of 'their' approach, these sections are to be seen not only as an introduction, but also as a reflection on the current state of the art of each approach in relation to earlier work. Chapters also include an overview of the main debates surrounding approaches, including the criticism raised from the perspective of other approaches, the main current questions facing authors, and potential ways forwards.

However, in order to come to a consistent and reflected comparison of the approaches, we have asked authors to include a section in which they provide an example of a specific puzzle that they think 'their' approach is particularly apt to address, and which in the past has been a focus of many works written in this tradition. If our argument about European integration theory as a mosaic holds, we expect approaches to differ in their 'best case', or in the area that they focus upon. We have furthermore asked authors to include a section in which they summarize, or speculate on, how works written from their approach have addressed, or would address the issue of enlargement as a test case. Again, we expect the contributions to focus on different areas of, but also to ask different types of questions about enlargement, illustrating the different functions of theory.

On the basis of these two sections where authors provide examples of how their approaches deal with concrete issues, we will return in the conclusion to the questions raised in this introduction, but we also invite readers to make their own comparisons when reading this book, and to use these sections as a starting point for critical reflections on the past or ongoing debates summarized in each chapter, and thereby pushing European integration theory forward.

Past, Present, and Future

'Past, present, and future' provides an organizing theme for this book in a double sense. First, each chapter, by reflecting on the origins and development of each approach, on the main puzzles addressed and the state of the art, and on the current challenges and ways forward, addresses the past, present, and future of each approach. Secondly, the three parts of this volume reflecting the three phases of European integration theory can be seen as an expression of past, present, and future: past in the sense of a set of approaches that have been with us since the early days of integration theory, have been developed to a considerable degree, and have influenced subsequent generations of integration scholars; present in the sense that a lot of theoretical work today has shifted towards questions of governance that combine international relations and comparative politics; and future in the sense that a set of novel approaches raises a number of issues which, although unlikely to dominate theoretical development in the future, will have to be taken into account, as they are now taken into account in other social sciences.

We have already made clear that we do not wish to reinforce some of the fault(y) lines along which the field of European integration theory was divided in the past. Instead, we see in the present a healthy trend towards a proliferation of approaches that contribute to an ever more faceted and nuanced picture of the European Union, its history and its development. What we would like to see in the future is neither the development of one single grand theory, nor the isolation and non-communication between approaches. The following chapters should help to clarify from where each approach comes, and the scope of its argument, so that a critical but constructive and open debate can thrive.

■ NOTES

1. This is a revised and amended version of the introduction chapter to the first edition to this volume. We are grateful to a number of reviewers for their comments. Previous versions of the original chapter were presented at the First Pan-European Conference on European Union Politics in Bordeux, September 2002, the Biennial Convention of the European Union Studies Association in Nashville, March 2003 and at seminars at Koç, Sabançi, and Boğaziçi Universities Istanbul. We are grateful to Knud Erik Jørgensen, Daniel Wincott, the co-panellists and audiences, and our students in Belfast and Birmingham.

2. When we use the term 'realism' in this chapter, we refer to realism as a particular tradition in international relations theory, rather than as an epistemological position.

3. There have of course been critical approaches to European integration all along. See for example, international political economy approaches, informed by Marxism and post-Marxism (e.g. Deppe 1976; Holland 1980), which posed themselves as alternatives to the mainstream in the 1970s and 1980s (see Chapter 12), but they were always confined to a few niches, and did not gain as much popularity as the more recent approaches covered here, although there has over the past decade or so been a resurgence of related approaches in the form of what one could call the 'Amsterdam School', covered in Chapter 12 of this volume.

■ STUDY QUESTIONS

1. What is the importance of theory in the study of European integration?

2. What can be seen as the three broad phases of theorizing European integration and governance and why?

3. What are the main influences on the development of European integration theory? Elaborate, distinguishing between real world events and conceptual debates.

4. How do different theoretical approaches relate to each other? Does this apply to all approaches in an equal way?

5. What are the three functions of theory?

PART ONE

Explaining European Integration

<table>
<tr><td>

2

</td><td>

Federalism

Michael Burgess

</td></tr>
</table>

Introduction

In this chapter I want to explore the relationship between federalism and European integration. In doing so, my main aim is to demonstrate the relevance of the federal idea to the building of Europe. However, it is imperative at the outset to begin with a preliminary caution. This is that federalism is a word that has been used to describe different phenomena. In practice it can excite and arouse passionate political controversy as well as exerting a calm moderating influence simply because it means different things to different people in different contexts at different times. Small wonder, then, that it has been used and abused in equal measure. Any meaningful analysis of federalism must take account of what I shall call 'empirical context'. 'Federalism' suggests disunity and fragmentation in India and in the United Kingdom (UK) while it implies the exact opposite in Germany and the United States of America (USA). Even in established federations there are widely varying perspectives about the word federal or federalism.

When we focus upon European integration, the empirical context looms particularly large because it has transcended the familiar level of the nation state to the level of an unknown 'ever closer union among the peoples of Europe', as the Preamble to the Treaty of Rome states; a union that currently includes intergovernmental, supranational, federal, confederal, and functional elements. This hybrid Europe, with its complex institutions, structures and procedures that defy precise definition and categorization in conventional political science terms, is widely deemed today to be moving toward what looks increasingly like a federal destination. Step by step, in piecemeal, incremental fashion, the European Community (EC) has evolved into the European Union (EU) which is now on the threshold of a constitutional and political Europe that is a federal Europe, but not necessarily a federal state as we know it.

For those who advocate a federal Europe, the gradual evolution of a 'Community' into a 'Union' during the last half-century is a firm vindication of the continuing strength and vitality of the federal idea. The relations between states and peoples in the voluntary union that was first created in 1951 by the Treaty of Paris with the European Coal and Steel Community (ECSC), and then extended in 1957 to include both the European Economic Community (EEC) and the European Atomic Energy Community (EAEC) in the Treaties of Rome, continue to widen and deepen. One consequence of this unending process of economic and political integration is that in many important respects the 'peoples' of the European member states have now become citizens, if not quite a single people, of the EU.

Given the empirical reality that is the contemporary EU, it comes as little surprise to learn that federalism, sometimes referred to as the 'f' word, has acquired much more credibility today than at any time since its heyday in the early post-war years. Indeed, the sheer pace of European integration since the ratification of the Single European Act (SEA) in 1987 has unquestionably revived the fortunes of the federal idea. Consequently, a political idea that historically and philosophically has always been about different forms of human association and organization, and that antedates the modern state in Europe, is also now representative of a particular theoretical approach to the analysis of European integration.

Historically, federalism has been associated with the conventional processes of state-building and national integration. It has been construed as a particular way of bringing together previously separate, autonomous, or independent territorial units to constitute a new form of union based upon principles that, broadly speaking, can be summarized in the dictum 'unity in diversity'. This dictum refers to a union of states and peoples, but it is a particular kind of union. It is a voluntary union whose principal purpose is to recognize, preserve, and formally accommodate distinct interests, identities, and cultures according to the Latin term *foedus*—from which the term federal derives—meaning covenant, compact, bargain, or contract. This formal agreement is rooted in the idea of an equal partnership between the respective partners to the bargain based upon the notion of mutual reciprocity: the idea that participants will not only make decisions for the general welfare of the whole, but that they will also refrain from taking decisions that knowingly do harm either to other members or to the union as a whole. There is a sense, then, of a moral commitment to the comity of the membership that constitutes the union.

Past federations have been founded upon distinct territorial identities and interests as well as upon minority cultures, substate nationalisms, religious differences, and a range of socio-economic factors that served to underline societal cleavages having political salience. The unity of federations therefore has traditionally been based upon the preservation and promotion of certain federal values that together allow these differences and diversities to breathe and flourish. Federal values are enshrined in written constitutions that entrench these diversities in order to sustain the original purpose of the union. Later on, during the course of the federation's constitutional and political evolution, new bargains or agreements might be struck between new interests and identities that emerge and these enable the union to adapt and adjust to contemporary change in order to maintain political legitimacy, order, and stability. Established federations in Europe that have been highly successful in this process of conflict management include Switzerland, Germany, and Austria, while the USA, Canada, Australia, India, and Malaysia have also achieved different forms and levels of unity and integration that are admired outside Europe. Indeed, Switzerland and India stand out as remarkable examples of how multinational, multilingual and multicultural federal unions can survive and sustain impressive levels of unity built upon federal principles. It is no accident therefore that Switzerland, in particular, is frequently singled out as a model for the future evolution of the EU (McKay 2001).

Federal models, of course, have their limitations. The EU is not intended to become either the USA or a Switzerland writ large. There is no historical precedent for the kind of union that Europe is busy constructing. The road to federal union along which the EU seems to be travelling has no signposts or footprints to follow. Previous federations have emerged as a result of conscious political actions that first created a written constitution as the foundation of the new state whereas the EU has evolved uniquely as the result of concrete economic steps based upon international treaties whose goals have been rooted, at best, in ambiguity. There can be no doubt, however, that while the means to building Europe have been principally economic, the underlying imperative of post-war European integration has been political. There has, in short, been a complex interaction between economics and politics in the pursuit of national self-interest by the member states of the EU that has resulted in a new kind of federal union the like of which has never before been seen.

Federalism and European Integration

I will begin with a short survey of the origins of the federal idea together with a sketch outline of its relationship to the modern state in Europe. This historical and philosophical background context is crucial to a basic understanding of the relevant contemporary concepts and their interrelationships. Consequently there is a need to define our fundamental concepts first, such as federalism, federation, confederation, the modern state, and European integration, before our exploration can proceed.

The Federal Idea

The origin of the federal idea, in the words of Davis (1978: 2), is 'wreathed in mist' and it has evolved over several centuries long before the emergence of the modern state in Europe, but for our purposes in this chapter it is worth noting that the meaning of *foedus* constituted the first serious challenge to Jean Bodin's classic conception of the state almost as soon as his *Les Six Livres de la Republique* was first published in 1576 and quickly became the standard rationalization of the unitary monarchical state (Tooley 1955). The rise of the modern state in Renaissance Europe during the sixteenth and early seventeenth centuries went hand in hand with the emergence of sovereignty as a conceptual instrument for the organization of power in the state. The seventeenth and eighteenth centuries witnessed the gradual development and consolidation of the modern territorial state as the sole legitimate source of public order and political authority. The state was 'sovereign' in the sense that it admitted no rival or competing authority within its own territorially demarcated boundaries. The modern territorial sovereign nation state—the *Westphalian* state—was predicated upon the assumption that there was a final and absolute political authority in the political community.

The significance of Bodin for the emergence of the federal idea about the organization of the state resided in the imperative to refute his rigid, unyielding conception of the state and sovereignty. As Davis observed (1978: 46–7), it might initially seem paradoxical to include Bodin in a survey of the federal idea and Europe but to omit him completely would actually be 'a grave error' for:

whether by the force of repulsion or resistance, his catalytic influence on federal theory cannot be ignored . . . other jurists could no more evade Bodin than successive generations of political jurists could free themselves from the questions—who commands, and how many masters can there be in a stable state, one, two, three or more?'

Bodin's legacy was enduring. For two centuries up until the American colonists challenged the constitutional, political and ultimately the military might of the British empire in the War of Independence in 1776, and substituted the federal idea for its imperial counterpart as a form of political organization, the notion of the independent sovereign state as centralized, absolute, and indivisible with the supreme power resident in a monarch answerable only to God and natural law dominated political and diplomatic discourse in continental Europe. Indeed, even as the reformist idea of a contractual limit placed upon the supreme power—a constitutional monarchy—gradually gained currency in England in the seventeenth century, traces of the Bodinian conception of the state survived in the European mindset until well into the twentieth century. This Bodinian conception of the state was directly opposed to that propounded by Johannes Althusius in his *Politica Methodice Digesta,* (known as the 'Politics') first published in 1603, which articulated a set of federal principles as the basis for the modern state. As a German Calvinist intellectual and political magistrate who emerged from the late sixteenth-century Reformist tradition, Althusius is rightly seen as the father of modern federalism in the continental European tradition out of which the personalist strand of federalism developed over 350 years later (M. Burgess 2000: 7–11; Hueglin 1999: 222–4).

What, then, do we mean by the federal idea and how is it related to European integration? We have already noted that the term 'federal' derives from the old Latin word *foedus* meaning some kind of covenant, contract or bargain. It is also important to remember that the act of forming such a covenant is rooted in the core principles of equality, partnership, reciprocity, mutuality, toleration, recognition, and respect. Davis (1978: 3) refers to the cognate term *fides* meaning faith and trust, so that covenantal federalism has evolved over the centuries to refer to a voluntary union of entities, be they persons, a people, communities, or states. In short, it is a 'vital bonding device of civilisation'. However, while this description tells us something about the nature of this kind of union, it does not explain how it must be structured, nor does it identify the principles that shape such unions.

When we refer to terms such as reciprocity, mutuality, equality, recognition and respect, we already have a sense of what is at stake here. In the memorable language of Albert Venn Dicey (1915: 75), the fundamental prerequisite that always underpins this form of association is the sentiment of *union,* but not *unity.* In other words, the purpose of the union is to integrate different entities but not to assimilate them. The presumption of a federal union, then, is that it is a union but a particular kind of union. It is a union based upon the formal constitutional recognition of difference and diversity. Previously discrete, distinct or independent entities come together to form a new whole, in which they merge part of their autonomous selves while retaining certain powers, functions, and competences fundamental to the preservation and promotion of their particular cultures, interests, identities, and sense of self-definition. The usual shorthand expression of this peculiar trait is Daniel Elazar's (1987: 12) reference to 'self-rule and shared rule'. Typically a federal union can be said to have two faces: it is both a unifying force and a means to maintain difference and diversity, and it is precisely this inherent ambiguity in the federal concept that periodically has been the root cause of genuine confusion and misunderstanding. Conventionally people have used the term to describe both the process of political unification—the building of a state by aggregation—and the diffusion of power within an established state, or the process of disaggregation. However, federalism is directly related to both unity and diversity and expresses both of these simultaneously.

Federalism, Federation, and Confederation

In this very brief sketch outline, the basic appeal of the federal state lies precisely in its institutional and structural capacity both to accommodate and reconcile different kinds of union with different kinds of diversity. Federations exist because they formally acknowledge, via constitutional entrenchment, the sorts of identities and diversities that constitute that sense of difference so essential to a living, breathing, pluralist social and political order. It is important to understand that the federal principles identified above can be structured and institutionalized collectively in a variety of different ways. No federation is identical to another. The way that salient differences and diversities are incorporated in each federal state and how they adjust and adapt to changing circumstances will be shaped and determined by unique historical factors. The formal constitutional expression of federal principles might require only that a union be a confederation—a union of states—rather than a single state: a federation. As we shall see, the EU represents a new kind of federal order.

   Let us consider some definitions in order to clarify what has been surveyed so far. There is a firm conceptual distinction between *federalism* and *federation*, originally introduced into the mainstream literature by Preston King in 1982, where the former is identified as the original and persistent driving force of the latter. Accordingly federalism can be construed as political ideology and/or political philosophy and it comprises the assorted identities and interests that are grouped around historical, cultural, social, economic, ideological, intellectual, and philosophical factors, making it effectively the sustaining dynamic that was the federation's original *raison d'être*. Federation is therefore defined by King (1982: 77) as 'an institutional arrangement, taking the form of a sovereign state, and distinguished from other such states solely by the fact that its central government incorporates regional units in its decision procedure on some constitutionally entrenched basis'. The relationship between these two concepts is clearly complex. Federalism informs federation and vice versa. Moreover, while it is perfectly possible to have federalism without federation, 'there can be no federation without some matching variety of federalism' (1982: 76). Diversity notwithstanding, all federations are composite states that constitute a single people.

Confederation, however, is something that is conceptually distinct from both federalism and federation but is often either ignored or overlooked in the mainstream literature on the federal idea and European integration. This is a mistake because confederation is significant for a deeper understanding of what is meant by a federal Europe. Murray Forsyth (1981) has defined confederation as a union of *states* in a body politic in contrast to a federation that is a union of *individuals* in a body politic, suggesting the unity of one people or nation. Conceptually, of course, the matter is neither as simple nor as straightforward as these definitions would imply because the distinctions between federation and confederation are in practice sometimes rather blurred and imprecise, but they do nonetheless convey the basic historical differences between these phenomena (see also Riley 1973).

Federalism in the context of the EU is the application of federal principles to the process of European integration where the term 'integration' refers to the sense of a coming together of previously separate or independent parts to form a new whole. Charles Pentland (1973: 21) defined integration as 'a process whereby a group of people, organized initially in two or more independent nation-states, come to constitute a political whole which can in some sense be described as a community'. The point is that a new totality of relations between states and peoples is created and the utility of the term depends upon which particular approach to integration is adopted. Before we leave this section, let us summarize briefly what we mean by the federal idea and European integration.

We have seen that at the core of the federal idea is the principle of association. In the context of our subject, it is based upon the notion of a voluntary union of states and peoples—the result of a bargain, treaty, contract or covenant freely entered into—that is binding upon its members and rooted in mutual respect, recognition, reciprocity, tolerance, consent, and equality. The shape and structure of this federal union are determined by the declared goals of the covenant and the historical circumstances that brought it into being. Since it is integration and not assimilation that is the main goal of the EU, the federal principles identified above suggest that it will be founded upon self-rule and shared rule. The federal idea is also an organizing concept that is essentially anti-absolutist and anti-centralist, its watchwords being autonomy, solidarity, pluralism, citizenship as well as the principle of subsidiarity, which provides that political decisions should be taken at the lowest possible level and which has implications for the building of a union from the bottom upwards rather than a hierarchical top-down approach (European Commission 1992; M. Burgess 2000).

Unions, however, are not confined by their origins. They evolve in both size and scope, and new bargains are formulated and agreed based upon changing circumstances. New policy agendas constantly emerge that allow for adjustment and adaptation so that federal unions are subject to an endless debate about the principles of governance and interminable disputes about rival teleologies. This is as it should be, but as we shall see, there is a price to be paid for the relentless pursuit of the perfect union. One of the main problems for students of European integration is how to explain and understand the nature of this curious union that has evolved principally from a series of economic steps and is wholly unprecedented. We can begin to appreciate its significance by looking more closely at federalist theory and practice.

Federalist Theory and Practice

Three Strands of Federalism after the Second World War

It is often claimed that in terms of political practice the federalist movement had its hey-day in the early post-war years that were remembered chiefly for the Hague Congress of May 1948 in which the federalists were particularly active and influential. Known as the Congress of Europe, this was an assembly of representatives of political organizations, comprising 750 delegates from 16 countries, committed to both European integration and cooperation. It met in May 1948 in the Hague and adopted several resolutions calling for a European union or federation with its own institutions, a common market, monetary union and a charter of human rights linked to a European court. This congress gave birth to the European Movement, a broad-based national federation of groups dedicated to the cause of European integration.

It is certainly true that the federalist movement was conspicuous during these years and that its political influence was seriously underestimated by British political elites, but it is not the case, as some observers have claimed, that it petered out in 1954 when the pioneering projects for a European Defence Community (EDC) and a European Political Community (EPC) abruptly collapsed. To accept this interpretation would be to distort the history of the post-war federalist movement. It suggests that their influence was merely transitory when in reality it displayed a strong continuity of thought and practice throughout the subsequent half-century.

The appeal of the federal idea to many Europeans can be located in both the threat of war and the practical experience of the Second World War (Burgess 1989). It was largely among the members of the anti-fascist European Resistance that the federal idea was originally nurtured as the answer to Europe's post-war destiny. For them the defeat of Hitler was only the first step. It offered a golden opportunity for Europeans to return to fundamental questions and the ferment of political ideas and discussions about the role of federalism in post-war European integration was clearly established in the various plans for European union that were drawn up in the years between 1939 and 1945 (Wilkinson 1981; Lipgens 1985). Of course it is very important to note that while the crystallization of the federal idea was essentially part of the *intellectual* Resistance to Hitler and was tantamount to a *spiritual* revolution of ideas, federalism also comprised many radically different conceptions of Europe and divergent political strategies about how to achieve what was broadly conceived of as a 'federal' Europe.

Probably the most famous federalist document to emerge during the war years was the Ventotene Manifesto of 1941. Drawn up by a small nucleus of Italian federalists led by Altiero Spinelli and Ernesto Rossi, federal ideas, attitudes, and assumptions were lucidly expressed in what was one of the first Resistance declarations devoted to European integration (Lipgens 1982; Pinder 1998). It remained, however, a monument to an idea that was never implemented. Immediately after the war, the European nation states regrouped and re-established themselves, thus effectively rejecting federation as the solution to European unity. Nonetheless, if it is true that the Resistance programme—and the spiritual revolution that it symbolized—was effectively defeated and abandoned by the conservative restoration of the immediate post-war years, the federal idea did not disappear with it. On the contrary, it survived in the plethora of influential interest groups that sprouted across Western Europe after 1945 and it was vigorously sustained in the European Union of Federalists (EUF) founded in Basle in December 1946. Indeed, one scholar has noted that in 1948 in France alone there were 17 European federalist groups, each with between 50 and 4,000 members (Greilsammer 1979), and it was during the late 1940s that renowned federalists like Alexander Marc, Henri Brugmans, and Denis De Rougemont began to formulate highly elaborate federalist doctrines which were eventually to play a part in the ideological split in the EUF during 1955–56.

From a practical policy-making standpoint, the impact of the federalists upon the EDC and EPC projects of the early 1950s was incontestable. Indeed, the attempt to launch them was made 'largely as a result of federalist pressure' and 'federalist ideas also contributed a great deal to the content of the proposals' (Cardozo 1987). Spinelli's role in this episode was particularly noteworthy (M. Burgess 2000). As Secretary-General of the Italian Movimento Federalista Europeo (MFE), it was he who was instrumental in channelling the Italian government's support toward a federal solution for the EPC which was to have a directly elected European assembly, powers of taxation and a joint decision-making structure. Spinelli's federalist strategy was what he called 'democratic radicalism', being built upon the idea of a major role for a parliamentary assembly in drafting a new treaty for Europe. This came to be known as 'the constitutional method' whereby an elected European assembly would act as the embryonic constituent voice of the European peoples and serve to mobilize a dynamic European public opinion in the quest to establish a popular European federation. As we shall see, it departed sharply from the competing political strategy of Jean Monnet who became Spinelli's great rival in the concerted post-war drive to champion a federal Europe. Monnet was the first President of the supranational High Authority of the ECSC during 1951–55 and he led the Europe-wide Action Committee for a United States of Europe until 1975, always believing that the political strategy of small, concrete, economic steps would *culminate* in a federal Europe. In complete contrast, Spinelli's own radical strategy meant *starting* with the political institutions and a popularly endorsed treaty that would be quickly translated into the familiar statist language of a constitution. It was a fundamental strategic difference founded upon competing conceptions of a federal Europe that has served indelibly to characterize both the theory and the practice of European integration up until the present day (M. Burgess 2000).

In addition to Monnet's 'federalism by instalments' and Spinelli's self-styled 'democratic radicalism' (for a more detailed discussion, see below), there existed another important strand of federalist thought that merits inclusion in our survey. This is what is variously labelled 'integral', 'personalist', or Proudhonian federalism (see also Roemheld 1990) and encapsulates a fairly broad range of political and sociological ideas based upon the notion of a European society and the spread of federalist values across the established boundaries of European states. Derived mainly from the philosophical writings of Marc, Brugmans, and de Rougemont, mentioned above, the pantheon of personalist writers would also include Robert Aron, Emmanuel Mounier, and Daniel Rops. Put simply, the basic intellectual position of the personalists revolves around the dignity of the human person and it involves a highly searching critique of advanced capitalism. Its normative, prescriptive predisposition is to restore man as a whole person by rescuing him from the modern capitalist state whose mass society has effectively cut him off from his family, neighbours, and local associations, reducing him to the isolation of anonymity in a monist world where he finds himself confronted by global society. As an isolated individual, man is ultimately cut off from himself. Personalism, in bringing man back in touch with society, seeks also to bring political authority back to human beings as complex, responsible members of society. It does this by active citizen participation in decision-making processes, decentralization to the grass roots, local autonomy, and respect for personal differences. The upshot of this personalist federalism is a quite elaborate, sophisticated way of looking at European integration, but while it has retained its ideological distinctiveness it has suffered from the problem of how precisely to translate these ideas into practical action. It is no easy task to try to change attitudes and mentalities among mass publics (Kinsky 1979). In this respect, federal theory and practice seem to have been decidedly decoupled and it is therefore easy to understand why many federalists describe the personalists as Utopian federalists (M. Burgess 2000).

The three strands of federalism identified above underline the rich tradition of philosophical, ideological, and empirical ideas, influences, and strategies that have been developed in response to the drive for European integration. Rival federalists with competing perspectives in the post-war years have been constantly engaged in the contest for practical relevance and if it is true that Monnet's approach to the building of Europe has been the most successful of these political strategies, this does not to imply that the others have become redundant. Indeed, many of Spinelli's assumptions and beliefs about the need for a constitutional and political Europe to build upon Monnet's economic foundations have been vindicated since the ratification of the Single European Act (SEA) in 1987. The implications of this ideological and strategic contest for federalism and European integration strongly suggest that the role of EU member states as propulsive forces in helping to build a federal Europe has actually been underestimated by federalists themselves and should be much more effectively integrated into federalist theory. While certainly not wishing to construct a federal Europe that follows traditional processes of state-building and national integration which have produced the nation states of today, the relevance of existing federal models as 'comparators' is nonetheless well worth more than a moment's reflection (Sbragia 1992; McKay 2001). What, then, can be learned from comparative federalism as a distinct approach to understanding the EU as a new federal order? As a new federal model, what light can comparative federalism shed on the future shape of the EU?

Comparative Federalism and the EU

The internal coherence of the comparative federalism approach acts as a filter to ensure that we are comparing like with like. This means that in practice it is perfectly possible to construe the EU—in Elazar's terms—as yet another species or variety of the overarching genus 'federalism'. It also means, on this reckoning, that federation itself—the federal state—becomes merely one species of the larger genus, federalism. This in turn enables those scholars who adopt Elazar's conceptual framework to argue in a consistent vein that there are many different 'federal forms' and that 'the federal principle does not necessarily mean establishing a federal system in the conventional sense of a modern federal state' (Elazar 1987: 10–12). Elazar always believed that scholars had a duty to be vigilant with their concepts in order to ensure that they remained both useful and relevant to the contemporary world and he also urged them to keep re-conceptualizing in order to understand and explain the changing world. This desire to keep pace with a changing world chimed conveniently with his conception of federalism and the evolution of the EU. Consequently, the curious admixture of federalism, confederalism, supranationalism, and intergovernmentalism that characterized the EU provided scholars with fresh insights and new perspectives about federalism and European integration theory.

This is the approach that has recently been adopted by scholars who at the start of the twenty-first century have looked either normatively to a new 'federal vision of governance' (Nicolaidis and Howse 2001) in order to respond to a perceived legitimacy crisis in multilayered democracies or empirically to a renewed quest for comparative insights into the functioning and evolution of multilevel political systems (Menon and Schain 2006). Predictably the utilization of both normative and empirical orientations to engage largely systemic properties in the USA and the EU has been the most obvious result. The USA invented modern federation in 1789 and its widely acknowledged success as the first 'national federation' guaranteed its intellectual and practical status as the yardstick of federal progress for well over a century and a half up until the end of the Second World War. Indeed, its influence on the European federalists as the classic federal model persisted into the 1950s and early 1960s.

There is much in the EU–USA comparison, then, that remains attractive to scholars of European integration and its current manifestation in the EU. The USA has been the dominant federal model for a very long time. Today, however, the undoubted success of the EU—especially the Single European Market (SEM), EMU, enlargement, and its recent constitutional and political evolution—has made it in many important respects a rival model of federal practice and evolution. The EU constitutes 27 constituent member states that, together with a single currency and a central bank, form an integrated SEM with a combined population of over 370 million people, making it not only a serious economic competitor for the USA but also offering itself as an alternative federal model for the future. Indeed, Elazar regarded the EU as already having replaced the USA as the new federal paradigm in world politics (Elazar 1995, 2001).

There is no doubt that the EU–USA comparison continues to appeal to many social scientists, particularly from the contemporary standpoints of institutional analysis, developmental processes, and public policy dynamics. However, while the choice of the USA remains a popular comparison for such scholars, this has not deterred them from extending the range of comparative analyses to include federations much closer to home. Recent perspectives on comparative federalism in the EU and Germany and in the EU and Switzerland (Borzel and Hosli 2003; Church and Dardanelli 2005) have underlined the continuing desire to search for fresh insights and persistent patterns of development.

The conceptual framework that is adopted, as mentioned above, determines both the possibilities and the limitations of comparative federalism and the EU. However, one area that constitutes both a limitation and a possibility lies in the underdeveloped field of multinational federalism. None of the comparisons already identified—the USA, Germany, and Switzerland—are multinational federations and this is significant because the idea of a federal Europe, however it is defined, embraces the fixed conception of a *multinational* EU. This fundamental attribute is widely acknowledged to be a feature that is simply inescapable and cannot be erased. Since we have already seen that the USA constitutes a model of the archetypal *national* federation and the trajectory of EU evolution is certainly not directed toward a new national state, it makes sense for future research efforts to be directed towards empirical case studies, such as Belgium, Spain, and India, that exhibit the basic cultural–ideological characteristics of a multinational union of states and peoples. Whatever else the EU is and might become, it will remain a multicultural, multilingual, multi-ethnic and ultimately multinational union of constituent states and peoples.

Liberal Intergovernmentalism and Federalism

Clearly, different aspects of *both* comparative politics and IR can be comfortably accommodated in the quest to explain and understand European integration. However, students of European integration theory should be cautious about recent theoretical trends and developments that have spawned a new model, dubbed Liberal Intergovernmentalism (LI) by its author, Andrew Moravcsik, who, in a series of seminal articles published in the 1990s, has produced probably the most elaborate of the current explanations for the building of Europe (Moravcsik 1991, 1993, 1997, 1998).

The implications of LI for federalism are both serious and damaging because federalism is relegated to the margins of serious analytical discussion. For those who seek to reinstate federalism as a perfectly rational approach to European integration, LI is a model that is fundamentally flawed. Moravcsik's important contribution to the intellectual debate about European integration is obviously to be welcomed, but it has never effectively come to terms with why and how the contemporary EU has evolved in such a strong federal direction. The biggest stumbling-block to a meeting of minds on this question seems to hinge upon the way he construes federalism itself. His early articles simply failed to incorporate federalism in his analysis at all, while he was successively able to dismiss it as irrelevant merely by subsuming it within neofunctionalism so that it was rendered virtually invisible (see the treatment of federalism in Moravcsik 1998: 16–7, 27–33, 52–9). His more recent contributions (1998, 2001a) have witnessed a significant willingness to confront what many observers see self-evidently as a federal Europe, but even here there is some evidence of serious intellectual discomfort.

Moravcsik has begun to remove federalism from the shadow of neofunctionalism but its recognition has still not extended much beyond that of a subordinate category labelled 'the geographical explanation of national preferences' (1998: 70). Moreover, the claim made for different kind of 'institutional choice', based upon the 'pooling and delegation of sovereignty', being reduced to 'federalist versus nationalist ideology' appears superficially plausible but is actually over-simplified and assumes what needs to be proved. For example, the assumption that federalism predicts 'systematic variation across countries rather than across issues' is highly questionable. So-called 'federalist' countries do not consistently favour 'delegation and pooling' independently of 'substantive consequences of cooperation' nor is it convincing to claim that 'pro-European' groups will always favour 'pooling and delegation' independently of 'substantive concerns' (1998: 70).

In a recent essay that finally confronts the question about whether or not European integration has evolved to such an extent in social, economic, political, legal, and constitutional terms that we can now make claims to have a federal Europe, Moravcsik has described the EU as 'an exceptionally weak federation' (2001a: 186). He is, however, clearly uncomfortable with this description, adding that it might well be thought of 'as something qualitatively different from existing federal systems' and much preferring to refer to it as 'a particular sort of limited, multilevel constitutional polity designed within a specific social and historical context' (2001: 186–7).

Considering his established concern for analytical rigour and methodological prowess, these are surprisingly equivocal conclusions derived from his own assessment of the EU's current policy and institutional capacity, which he construes as weak. Clearly it is one thing to seek to derive 'standardized hypotheses' leading to the 'generalizability of conclusions' about European integration (2001: 2), but it is quite another to explain why the evolution from a *community* to a *union* has been a federal evolution.

Moravcsik's construction of federalism is conceptually shallow and incomplete. His failure to give it the detailed attention it deserves means that instead of explaining federalism he *explains it away*. Yet there is clearly some scope for applying his methods to federal evolution in the same way that he uses them to explain and understand supranational developments. Without wishing to labour the point about Moravcsik's most recent detailed work (see the discussion in Chapter 4), it might assist towards a deeper understanding and appreciation of the nature of the debate between federalism and LI if we take a closer look at one particular area where both schools of thought entertain strong but divergent viewpoints and interpretations. This pertains to the constitutional evolution of the EU, and it has been chosen for inclusion in this chapter precisely because it serves as a convenient example or case study to demonstrate how federalism can be used effectively to explain the building of political Europe. By its very nature, this case study propels us into the area of history and theory or, more accurately, historical revisionism and its theoretical implications for European integration. Let us return, then, to the conceptual world of federalism and the shift from Monnet's 'functionalism' to Spinelli's 'constitutionalism'.

Federalism and the Constitutional Evolution of the EU

In practice, the question of a constitution for Europe has never been at the forefront of the public debate about European integration. It has only recently emerged on the official policy agenda of the EU member states. As we shall see, Monnet's peculiar approach to the building of Europe rendered such a requirement redundant. Consequently it has been deliberately eschewed as irrelevant to the nebulous goal stated in the preamble to the Treaty on European Union of an 'ever closer union among the peoples of Europe'. Indeed, in hindsight, such a strategy at any time in the post-war evolution of the European project would have been tantamount to suicide. Member state governments were neither willing nor able even to contemplate, let alone introduce, such a proposal that would have been peremptorily rejected as chimerical.

In these circumstances, then, it might seem strange to refer to the constitutional evolution of the EU. However, this is not the case. Monnet's own political strategy for the construction of a federal Europe lay in what we might call issue avoidance. He sought to build Europe by avoiding a damaging confrontation with issues that might conceivably call national sovereignty directly into question. The constitutional evolution of the European project would occur, as it were, almost imperceptibly by adding institutional pieces to the larger jigsaw in incremental fashion. The process was made crystal clear in the famous public speech of 9 May 1950 in which the French Foreign Minister, Robert Schuman, declared the goal of a united Europe:

Europe will not be made all at once, or according to a single plan. It will be built through concrete achievements which first create a de facto concrete solidarity. The coming together of the nations of Europe requires the elimination of the age-old opposition of France and Germany. Any action taken must in the first place concern these two countries . . . The pooling of coal and steel production should immediately provide for the setting up of common foundations for economic development as a first step in the federation of Europe . . . this proposal will lead to the realization of the first concrete foundation of a European federation indispensable to the preservation of peace.

Nelsen and Stubb (1994: 11–12)

The Schuman Declaration was silent about a European constitution. This was something that, if it occurred at all, would arrive in its own time as the logical result of a highly successful pioneering experiment in economic integration. Let us explore this apparent conundrum a little further.

It is the argument of this chapter that history and theory are the key to understanding the relationship between federalism and European integration, and that integral to this relationship are the ubiquitous role of Jean Monnet and the nature of Monnet's Europe. This refers to Monnet's own unique approach to the building of post-war Europe that relied, as we have seen, upon piecemeal, cumulative concrete steps leading to a federal Europe. By forging specific functional links between states in a way that did not directly challenge national sovereignty, Monnet believed that the door to federation would gradually be opened. These so-called 'functional' links were primarily economic activities and they were perfectly expressed in the ECSC initiative of the early 1950s. This novel form of sectoral supranational organization would be the foundation of the European federation that would evolve only slowly to engage national elites in a process of mutual economic interest. These concrete benefits would gradually form that crucial solidarity—the common interest—which Monnet believed indispensable for the removal of physical and mental barriers.

If we glance at a preliminary sketch outline of what became the Schuman Plan, this continuity in Monnet's thinking is quite striking. Since Franco-German union could not be achieved at once, a start would have to be made by 'the establishment of common bases for economic development' (Monnet 1978: 295). The goal of a federal Europe would be attained via Franco-German union that would itself be realised 'through the interplay of economics and institutions' necessitating 'new structures on a European scale' (Monnet 1978: 295). The approach to federation, which Monnet called 'the ECSC method' of establishing 'the greatest solidarity among peoples', implied that gradually other tasks and other people would become subject to the same common rules and institutions—or perhaps to new institutions—and this experience would 'gradually spread by osmosis' (Monnet 1978: 392–3). No time limits were imposed on what was clearly deemed to be a long, slow, almost organic, process of economic and political integration. The following extract from Monnet's *Memoirs* is worth quoting at length:

We believed in starting with limited achievements, establishing de facto solidarity, from which a federation would gradually emerge. I have never believed that one fine day Europe would be created by some great political mutation, and I thought it wrong to consult the peoples of Europe about the structure of a Community of which they had no practical experience. It was another matter, however, to ensure that in their limited field the new institutions were thoroughly democratic; and in this direction there was still progress to be made . . . the pragmatic method we had adopted would . . . lead to a federation validated by the people's vote; but that federation would be the culmination of an existing economic and political reality, already put to the test . . . it was bringing together men and practical matters.

Monnet (1978: 367)

This exceptionally lucid explanation of how Monnet viewed the path to federation not only underlines the authenticity of his federalist credentials, it also confirms the European project as quintessentially a federal project that would need to engage the constitutional question only at some distant, undefined date in the future. Monnet's 'method' was based upon the bold assumption that 'political' Europe would be the 'culminating point of a gradual process' so that Europe would experience a qualitative change in the constitutional and political relations between states and citizens. However, this metamorphosis would happen only when 'the force of necessity' made it 'seem natural in the eyes of Europeans' (Monnet 1978: 394–5). Consequently Monnet's approach to a federal Europe rendered constitutionalism—the building of political Europe—contingent upon cumulative functional achievements.

It was precisely at this juncture—in the interaction between politics and economics—that Altiero Spinelli entered the theoretical debate. The mistake that Spinelli attributed to Monnet was inherent in the functional approach which neglected to deal with 'the organization of political power at the European level' (author's interviews with Spinelli, September 1983 and February 1985). This meant that the political centre remained weak and largely impotent, lacking the capacity to go much beyond what already existed and unable to adapt to new forces and problems encountered at the European level. Here the focus shifted to the role of the European institutions. For Monnet, institutions were crucial but his conception differed significantly from Spinelli's in the extent to which he viewed their development as akin to organic growth arising directly out of functional performance. Spinelli, in contrast, had a much more positive conception of institutions. As the bedrock of political integration, they had to be solid. He believed that Europe could not afford the 'wait and see' policy of Monnet: what was urgently required if Europe was not to suffer political immobilism and stagnation was institutional reform.

In summary, then, Spinelli believed that Monnet's Europe was vulnerable to paralysis at some point in the future because it failed to confront the realities of organized political power. The central institutions would remain weak and the predicted shift from *quantity* to *quality* would not occur precisely because of Monnet's excessive reliance upon functionalist logic. Consequently the constitutional and political evolution of Europe would simply be stunted. This fervent conviction prompted Spinelli to confront the political implications of Monnet's Europe by engaging the difficult and controversial task of attempting to forge ahead in the 1980s with building 'political' Europe (M. Burgess 2000). Since the SEA in 1987, therefore, the public debate about the future of Europe—its institutional architecture, policy scope, and membership size— has become so controversial precisely because it is at heart a constitutional debate, that is, a debate about constitutionalizing the European construction.

The conceptual and strategic differences between the two major protagonists in the federal cause had enormous theoretical implications for the building of Europe. Today there appears to be an emerging consensus among informed commentators on the EU that we have now reached the limits of Monnet's conception of European integration. It is now time for statesmen and politicians to address Spinelli's concerns. Europeans have to recognize and deal with the emerging federal reality that is staring them in the face. Together the Maastricht, Amsterdam, Nice, and Lisbon Treaties have combined to build upon Monnet's Europe by accelerating and accentuating its federal direction. The failure (finally conceded in 2006) of the Constitutional Treaty to achieve unanimous popular endorsement in the EU of 27 member states did not mean the abandonment of a constitutional and political Europe. It was merely a temporary setback on the long road towards a federal Europe. As Spinelli once remarked, it is necessary to experience failures in the struggle to build political Europe so that we are the better prepared to know when there can be successes. After all, this has been the practical historical experience of federalism and European integration. It is in this light that we should construe the current interlude between the official negotiations that produced the recent European Reform Treaty (also known as the Lisbon Treaty) in 2007 that awaits formal ratification in 2008 in the member states. Considerable institutional and policy evidence has, nonetheless, accumulated to substantiate the claim that the EU already constitutes a federal Europe. It is a new federal model (Burgess 2006).

The historical and theoretical background context sketched out above, then, suggests a number of things. First, we have reached a new crossroads in the EU's economic and political evolution that has enormous empirical and theoretical implications for federalism and European integration. Secondly, the generation of increasing public concern and controversy about the future of Europe indicates the heightened engagement of mass publics in the integration process largely, but not solely, because this crossroads represents the shift from Monnet's functionalism to Spinelli's constitutionalism that is implicit in the building of political Europe. Thirdly, the EU is about to move from the formal language of treaty to what will in effect be the discourse of constitution that is indicative of the member states' collective perception of the union as more than just an intergovernmental reality.

Federalism and the Enlargement of the EU

The enlargement of the EU was always a part of the 'Community psyche'. Article 237 of the Treaty of Rome makes it clear that 'any European state may apply to become a member of the Community' (Treaty of Rome 1957). According to Article 240, the Treaty was also concluded 'for an unlimited period' so that here was the institutional and policy framework for a voluntary union of states and citizens that was pledged to infinite membership expansion in Europe for an indefinite period. Moreover, the basis for a *federal* union, though never explicitly established, was always at least a distinct *possibility* given the institutional implications of Article 138 concerning direct elections to the European Parliament (EP) together with those of Articles 171–7 relating to the powers of the European Court of Justice; the principle of Qualified Majority Voting (QMV); and, finally, the establishment of an executive body (the European Commission) in Article 155 that, once appointed, was independent of the member state governments and accountable to the EP.

The current EU of 27 constituent units has grown in size from the original 6 founding members via a series of piecemeal, incremental steps that has no discernible pattern and no inherent logic beyond the fact of expansion. Each enlargement in 1973 (the UK, Denmark, and Ireland), 1981 (Greece), 1986 (Spain and Portugal), and 1995 (Sweden, Finland, and Austria) has been the result of ad hoc individual negotiations and a series of compromises carefully designed to accommodate the specific needs and requirements of both the evolving EU and its applicant states. The end of the Cold War and the sudden and dramatic collapse of communism throughout eastern Europe, however, ushered in a completely new era with a distinctly different dynamic in terms of European integration. This time, 12 countries were knocking at the EU's door in what sometimes seemed to be an undignified scramble for membership that posed unprecedented problems for the European project. The countries that were accepted for membership in 2004 included Poland, Hungary, the Czech Republic, Slovakia, Slovenia, Latvia, Lithuania, Estonia, Malta, and Cyprus, thus increasing its size from 15 to 25 constituent units. Bulgaria and Romania were refused formal membership until 2007 when their inclusion brought the total number of member states to its current 27.

The so-called 'Copenhagen criteria', confirmed in June 1993, specified three main economic and political preconditions which can be conveniently summarized as:

1. the acceptance of liberal democratic institutions based on the rule of law, respect for human rights, and the protection of minorities;

2. the existence of a functioning market economy; and

3. the ability to take on the obligations of membership, including political, economic, and monetary union.

Even with these formidable admission criteria, the socio-economic, political, legal, and financial implications for the EU remain colossal. The dramatic increase in membership size has not seriously impeded the evolution of integration in other areas, such as the Lisbon Treaty on European reform. However, the admission of so many countries with so many different national goals and policy priorities has undeniably altered the very nature of the European project and introduced different dynamics that cannot be gainsaid.

From a federalist perspective, the overriding imperative is clearly to seek to accommodate all of the applicants without seriously damaging the *acquis communautaire*, the agreed set of norms and rules within the Union, and to continue to pursue an agenda for wide-ranging reform that already existed but which has become much more urgent since 1989–90: and the range of reforms is extensive. Its general focus would be to enhance the federal and confederal elements that the EU already exhibits at both the institutional and policy levels. The battery of reforms includes inter alia the following proposals: further extensions of Qualified Majority Voting (QMV) in the Council of Ministers (CM); more accountability and transparency of decision-making in the CM; the election of the President of the European Commission from the EP; the power of the EP to force the resignation of individual commissioners; the extension of the co-decision procedure to the remaining legislative areas that it does not cover; a larger EU budget, with extended EP scrutiny; and enhanced Commission participation in the emerging European Security and Defence Policy (ESDP). Federalists would also like to see the series of opt-outs originally negotiated by the UK, Sweden, and Denmark that included EMU, the CFSP, defence, and citizenship, become opt-ins in order to allow the EU to function more efficiently and democratically, and to buttress its external role as a unitary actor that can speak with a single voice in world affairs. A federal Europe that works would be one that utilized to the full the dictum 'common solutions to common problems' and the fulfilment of all the conditions identified above would certainly be sufficient to justify calling the EU federal (Pinder 1998).

The questions that the challenge of enlargement poses for federalism and the federalists are really related to the maintenance of unity and diversity in both institutions and policies. Some of these have already been identified above, but institutional reform concerns the strengthening of the central supranational institutions—the Commission, EP, and the ECJ—in the wake of the relatively recent emergence of the intergovernmental conference method (1985–2007) of union-building, while policy matters are essentially about enhancing the EU's policy capacity and implementation, such as in the fields of ESDP, labour markets in the SEM and energy policy. It is important to note that the promotion of federalist values and principles—reciprocity, mutual respect, recognition, tolerance, and consent—can still be pursued if they are conducted through the existing institutional channels of the EU that represent the member state governments, such as the Council of Ministers and the European Council that constitute the confederal dimension of the European project. The EU, we are reminded, is a political, economic, social, and legal hybrid that is characterized by a combination of federal, confederal, supranational, and intergovernmental features.

Enlargement of the EU, then, does not necessarily mean that the federal and confederal elements in its future evolution will be attenuated. On the contrary, the accentuation of difference and diversity will be counterbalanced by protection of the *acquis* and the commitment of applicant states to EMU and the SEM. The main threat to the EU—the impracticability of existing decision-making processes and problems of policy implementation—would be removed with the successful ratification of the Lisbon Treaty. This is imperative if the EU is not be permanently shackled by undue reliance upon an intergovernmental institution based upon consensus-building that is inherently fragile and ephemeral. The Lisbon Treaty has the possibility to ensure that decision-making processes will ultimately connect with the federal reality of how to divide and share power and competences equitably in the union. After all, the EU has evolved in a series of incremental steps that have gradually enhanced the federal and confederal characteristics in European integration so that 'self-rule and shared rule' is its shorthand definition.

Enlargement must not be construed solely as a negative challenge or threat to the union because it is also an opportunity to strengthen it, and this is how we should view the prospects of the Lisbon Treaty, 2007. It, too, symbolizes yet another crossroads in the overall process of building Europe and it furnishes one of those periodic moments to pause for reflection, reappraisal and revision in order to adapt and adjust to changing circumstances. New bargains are struck, fresh impetus is given to integration and the EU's institutional mechanisms, its decision-making procedures and its policy capacity are all buttressed to meet the challenges of an expanding union. The next few years will therefore constitute a period of consolidation, but the larger the union becomes, the more that federal and confederal principles and values will act as the operative means to achieve the goal of 'an ever closer union' among European states and peoples.

Conclusion

This chapter has explored the conceptual relationship between federalism, federation, confederation, and European integration. It has defined the basic terms and looked at some of the problems and pitfalls involved in theory and practice, taking the opportunity to make some brief comparisons and contrasts with functionalism, neofunctionalism, and liberal intergovernmentalism. The relevance of the federal idea to European integration has been examined by a series of brief excursions into history and theory, a short case study of the EU's constitutional evolution and a concise assessment of the enlargement issue from the standpoint of federalist perspectives. Each of these areas has confirmed the significance of federalism and the federalists to the post-war historical evolution of the European project.

One outstanding contemporary change that already has colossal implications not only for federalism, but also for theories of European integration in general, is the engagement of mass publics in the future direction of the EU. The increasing use of referenda to obtain political legitimacy for new treaty arrangements suggests a veritable sea change in the integration process. The building of Europe can no longer progress according to a permissive consensus. Member state governments can no longer rely upon their electorates for automatic confirmation of elite decisions and there is clear evidence that a chasm has opened up in elite–mass relationships concerning the future of Europe. The implication of this increasing reliance upon intergovernmental conferences for new treaties that must be ratified by parliaments and peoples harbours many problems for federal political strategies in national arenas where the 'f' word remains extremely sensitive in mainstream political discourse, but these strategic problems are likely to be overtaken by events if the current reform treaty is successfully ratified. The new treaty that has been substituted for the earlier Constitutional Treaty should not be underestimated in its capacity to bring about a much more effective federal Europe, with a stronger political leadership, as a result of institutional reform and new streamlined decision-making procedures. At the very least it is likely to bring to a close the phase that we might come to describe as 'intergovernmental treaty making' in the history of European integration.

If we turn to the question of theoretical convergence, there would appear to be some evidence of an intellectual rapprochement in many important respects between federalism, neofunctionalism, and liberal intergovernmentalism. There is, for example, an increasing tendency to be more realistic and less fanciful about theories of European integration than in the past and this has resulted in a much lower level of intellectual expectations. However, all three approaches acknowledge, admittedly to differing degrees, the reality of supranational actors and institutions, the significance of selective contributions to European integration made by individual statesmen, the impact of changing national policy preferences, the interaction of intra- and extra-EU events and circumstances, the complex interrelationship between economics and politics, the relevance of path dependency, and the intellectual sensitivities to both international relations and comparative politics methodologies. Of course federalism and a revised neofunctionalism both have normative as well as empirical properties absent from liberal intergovernmentalism and, as already mentioned above, there is some evidence of a willingness to be more open-minded about recommending comparative federalism as a useful benchmark for identifying various pathways to the building of Europe. Alberta Sbragia (1992: 262–3), for example, implicitly accepted the conceptual distinction between federalism and federation when she noted that 'one can have what might be called segmented federalism, that is, treaty-based federal arrangements in certain policy arenas, without having a formal, constitutionally based federation'. Or again, 'a federal-type organization could evolve without becoming a constitutionally based federation in the traditional sense'. This would make 'the study of federations useful in thinking about the Community's future'.

■ GUIDE TO FURTHER READING

Key Primary Works

Elazar, D.J. (1995) 'From statism to federalism: a paradigm shift', *Publius: The Journal of Federalism*, 25(2), 5–18. This is an important federalist perspective on the shift from the Westphalian state to new forms of federal union that have drawn their inspiration from the post-war evolution of the EU.

Lister, F.K. (1996) *The European Union, the United Nations and the Revival of Confederal Governance* (London: Greenwood Press). This is a very interesting and thought-provoking thesis about the revival of confederal principles in the world of states.

Pinder, J. (1986) 'European community and nation-state: a case for a neo-federalism?', *International Affairs*, 62(1), 41–54. This is now a classic article on the arguments for a new kind of federal Europe.

Rossiter, C. (ed.) (1961) *The Federalist Papers* (New York: New York American Library). This is the classic collection of papers written by Hamilton, Jay, and Madison in defence of the proposed new American constitution that has subsequently become a philosophical treatise on government and is frequently alluded to in contemporary analyses of European integration.

Other Important Primary Works

Burgess, M. (ed.) (1996) 'Federalism and the European Union', Special Issue of *Publius: The Journal of Federalism*, 26(4), 1–162. This is an important collection of contemporary essays on various dimensions of the subject.

Carney, F.S. (ed.) (1995) *Politica: Johannes Althusius* (Indianapolis, IN: Liberty Fund). This is the best translation and survey of the political ideas of Althusius.

Hueglin, T.O. (1999) *Early Modern Concepts for a Late Modern World: Althusius on Community and Federalism* (Waterloo, ON: Wilfrid Laurier University Press). This survey has become important for the contemporary debate about the revival of the federalist ideas of Althusius in the context of European integration.

King, P. and Bosco, A. (eds) (1991) *A Constitution for Europe: A Comparative Study of Federal Constitutions and Plans for the United States of Europe* (London: Lothian Foundation Press). This is important for the range of material germane to the emergence of ideas about a federal constitution for Europe.

Pinder, J. (1993) 'The new European federalism: the idea and the achievements', in Burgess, M. and Gagnon, A.G. (eds) *Comparative Federalism and Federation: Competing Traditions and Future Directions* (Hemel Hempstead: Harvester Wheatsheaf), 45–66. This is now a classic chapter on the emergence of 'incremental federalism' in European integration.

Ross, G. (1995) *Jacques Delors and European Integration* (Oxford: Polity Press). This is indispensable for an understanding of the federal ideas, influences, and strategies of the former President of the European Commission during the period 1985–95.

Vernon, R. (ed.) (1979) *The Principle of Federation by P.-J. Proudhon* (Toronto: University of Toronto Press). The best survey of Proudhonian ideas of federalism and their continuing practical significance.

■ **STUDY QUESTIONS**

1. What are the core principles of federalism? What is their significance for the EU?
2. Is it correct to claim that Monnet made the first steps in the building of a federal Europe easy but the later steps more difficult?
3. What are the lessons that can be learned from a comparative analysis of the EU and the USA?
4. Do you think that an EU of 27 member states will strengthen or weaken the idea of a federal Europe?
5. How far do you think that the current EU constitutes a new federal model in the world of states?

3 Neofunctionalism

Arne Niemann with Philippe C. Schmitter

Introduction

Amongst the earlier theories of regional integration, neofunctionalism is distinguished both in its sophistication and ambition, and in the amount of criticism that it has attracted. The theory was first formulated in the late 1950s and early 1960s, mainly through the work of Ernst Haas and Leon Lindberg in response to the establishment of the European Coal and Steel Community (ECSC) and the European Economic Community (EEC). The theory was at its prime until the mid-1960s, during which time the evolution of European integration seemed to vindicate its assumptions. Shortly before the publication of E.B. Haas's seminal book, *The Uniting of Europe,* in 1958, cooperation on coal and steel under the ECSC had 'spilled over' into the EEC and the European Atomic Energy Community (Euratom). In addition, the formation of the customs union ahead of schedule and the progress made on the Common Agricultural Policy supported the neofunctionalist claims. From the mid-1960s, the theory was criticized increasingly, particularly because of several adverse empirical developments, the culmination of which was the Empty Chair crisis of 1965–66 when French President Charles de Gaulle effectively paralysed the Community. In the late 1960s and early 1970s neofunctionalists made attempts to revise some of their hypotheses and claims, but in the mid-1970s Haas declared the theory to be obsolete. With the resurgence of the European integration process in the mid-1980s, however, neofunctionalism made a substantial comeback. Since the 1990s, some endeavours have been made to newly revise the original approach.

We proceed as follows: after identifying neofunctionlism's intellectual roots, we specify early neofunctionalism's core assumptions and hypotheses, including its central notion of 'spillover'. We then review the criticisms that have been levelled against it before turning to later revisions of the theory. The next section looks at some most-likely cases; and the final section analyses the case of enlargement.

Intellectual Roots

Neofunctionalism finds its intellectual antecedents at the juncture between functionalist, federalist and communications theories, while also drawing indirectly on the 'group theorists' of American politics. Haas and Lindberg, the two most influential and prolific neofunctionalist writers, combined functionalist mechanisms with federalist goals.

Like functionalism, neofunctionalism emphasizes the mechanisms of technocratic decision-making, incremental change, and learning processes. However, although the theory has been dubbed neofunctionalism, this is in some respects a case of 'mistaken identity' (cf. Groom 1978), since it departed significantly from Mitrany's functionalism (Mitrany 1966, 1975). Whereas functionalists held that form, scope, and purpose of an organization was determined by the task that it was designed to fulfil, neofunctionalists attached considerable importance to the autonomous influence of supranational institutions and the emerging role of organized interests. While the former did not limit integration to any territorial area, the latter gave it a specifically regional focus. Moreover, where Mitrany attached importance to changes in popular support, neofunctionalists privilege changes in elite attitudes.

Another important figure in neofunctionalism's intellectual inheritance was Jean Monnet. The importance of functional spillover, which will be elaborated below, was already recognized by Monnet before it was given an explicit academic label, and neofunctionalism was not only an analytical framework: it was also a normative guide for action. Both Haas and Lindberg reveal considerable sympathy for the project of European unification in their writings. Although Haas argued that the purpose of his theory was merely to describe, explain, and predict (Haas 1970: 627–8), it was also meant to prescribe (cf. Tranholm-Mikkelsen 1991: 4).

Early Neofunctionalism

To determine exactly what neofunctionalism stands for is no straightforward undertaking, as the theory has come to mean different things to different people. There are a number of reasons for this. First, it became increasingly difficult to distinguish what exactly qualified as neofunctionalist thought because the theory underwent a series of reformulations in the late 1960s and early 1970s. The original versions of Ernst Haas and Leon Lindberg were revised and modified by a number of writers, such as Philippe Schmitter, Stuart Scheingold, and Joseph Nye, but also by Haas and Lindberg themselves. Secondly, there have been internal disagreements within the neofunctionalist school of thought. Neofunctionalist scholars differed on the dependent variable problem (the question of the end state of integration), whether, and to what extent, loyalties shifted to the new centre,[1] and whether depoliticization or politicization constituted a precondition for the spillover process.[2] Thirdly, the uncertainty about the substance and boundaries of neofunctionalist thought also gave rise to much semantic confusion. Terms such as 'spillover' and '*engrenage*', for example, have been taken to mean different phenomena. Conversely, similar or identical ideas have been disguised by different terminologies. A fourth problem arises from very selective and narrow interpretations of the approach by some of its critics.[3]

To alleviate the existing confusion, we seek to define key neofunctionalist terms, assumptions, and hypotheses during the course of this chapter. As a starting (and reference) point we go back to early neofunctionalist theorizing from Haas's seminal work, *The Uniting of Europe*, published in 1958, to roughly the late 1960s.

Definition of Integration

Neofunctionalism offers no single authoritative definition of integration. Its practition-ers have revised their definition over time. Both Haas and Lindberg held integration to be a process as opposed to an outcome or (end-)state. They also agreed that integration involved the creation and role expansion of regional institutions. Moreover, they both stressed change in expectations and activities on the part of participating actors. Whilst Lindberg restricted his study to the European Economic Community (EEC), Haas based his analysis on the ECSC, but extended his conclusions to both the EEC and the European Atomic Energy Community (Euratom). Haas defined integration as:

the process whereby political actors in several distinct national settings are persuaded to shift their loyalties, expectations and political activities toward a new centre, whose institutions possess or demand jurisdiction over the pre-existing national states. The end result of a process of political integration is a new political community, superimposed over the pre-existing ones.

Haas (1958: 16)

Lindberg offers a somewhat different definition:

(1) The process whereby nations forego the desire and ability to conduct foreign and domestic policies independently of each other, seeking instead to make joint decisions or to delegate the decision-making process to new central organs: and (2) the process whereby political actors in several distinct settings are persuaded to shift their expectations and political activities to a new centre.

Lindberg (1963: 6)

It should be noted that, unlike Haas, Lindberg, in not suggesting any endpoint for the integration process, implicitly acknowledged that the breadth and depth of integration could be in constant flux. Lindberg also suggested that political actors merely shift their expectations and not their loyalties to a new centre. Thus, Lindberg's conception and definition of integration can be seen as more cautious.[4]

Underlying Assumptions

The essence of the theory can be derived from a set of fundamental precepts, some of which have been hinted at in the neofunctionalist understanding and definition of integration. First, in line with the mainstream of US political science of the time, the early neofunctionalists aimed at general theory-building. In its initial conception, neo-functionalism understood itself as a 'grand' or general theory of integration—claiming applicability regardless of when and where it occurred (cf. Haas 1961: 366ff; Haas and Schmitter 1964: 706–7, 720). Secondly, integration is understood as a process. Here neo-functionalists fundamentally differ from intergovernmentalists who tend to look at iso-lated events (mainly treaty negotiations) and assume them to be repetitions of the same power game. Implicit in the notion of process is the contrary assumption that integration processes evolve over time and take on their own dynamic. Third, neofunctionalism is 'pluralist' in nature. In contrast to traditional realist theories, it contests both that states are unified actors and that they are the only relevant actors. Instead, neofunctional-ists assume that regional integration is characterized by multiple, diverse, and changing actors who are not restricted to the domestic political realm but also interact and build coalitions across national frontiers and bureaucracies (Haas 1964a: 68ff). Fourth, neofunctionalists see the Community primarily as 'a creature of elites'. While Haas (1958: chs 5 and 6) devoted much of his attention to the role of non-governmental elites, Lindberg (1963: ch. 4) largely focused on governmental elites. Neither ascribed much importance to the role of public opinion. The conclusion was that there was a 'permissive consensus' in favour of European integration (Lindberg and Scheingold 1970: 41) and that this would suffice to sustain it. Fifth, although Haas did not mention it, he seems to have assumed uninterrupted economic growth in Europe (cf. Holland 1980). Linked to this was a more explicit 'end of ideology' assumption, i.e. that these increasingly prosperous societies would focus primarily on the pursuit of wealth rather than nationalist, socialist, or religious ideals.

Neofunctionalism is mainly a theory about the dynamics of European integration. Five assumptions encapsulate the driving forces behind its progress.

1. Its practitioners assume rational and self-interested actors (Haas 1970: 627), who (nevertheless) have the capacity to learn and change their preferences. Interest-driven national and supranational elites, recognizing the limitations of national solutions, provide the key impetus. The shift of expectations, activities, and (perhaps eventually) loyalties towards the new centre is also seen as one which is primarily motivated by actors' interests. However, these self-regarding motives are not perceived as constant. They are likely to change during the integration process, as actors learn from the benefits of regional policies and from their experiences in cooperative decision-making (Haas 1958: 291). Neofunctionalists contest the intergovernmentalist assumption of interest aggregation exclusively at the national level through some hermetic process. Instead, Haas (1958: 9–10) argued that membership in the ECSC altered the way that interest groups and, later, member governments, perceived their interests.

2. Once established, institutions can take on a life of their own and progressively escape the control of their creators. Concerned with increasing their own powers, employees of regional institutions become agents of further integration by influencing the perceptions of participating elites (both private and public), and therefore governments' (national) interest.

3. Early reformulations of the theory stressed the primacy of incremental decision-making over grand designs. Moreover, seemingly marginal adjustments are often driven by the unintended consequences of previous decisions. This effect arises from the incapacity of most political actors to engage in long-term purposive behaviour as they 'stumble' from one decision into the next, especially when engaging in such an innovative task as regional integration. Decisions in this arena are normally taken with highly imperfect knowledge of their consequences and frequently under the pressure of deadlines (Haas 1970: 627).

4. Neofunctionalists reject the conventional realist axiom that all games played between actors are necessarily zero-sum in nature. In the Community setting exchanges are often better characterized as positive-sum games and a 'supranational' style of decision-making, which Haas defined as 'a cumulative pattern of accommodation in which the participants refrain from unconditionally vetoing

proposals and instead seek to attain agreement by means of compromises upgrading common interests' (Haas 1964a: 66).

5. Haas agreed with the assumption made by some economists, such as Pierre Uri who was the chief economist of the ECSC in the 1950s, that emerging functional interdependencies between whole economies and their productive sectors tends inexorably to foster further integration (Haas 1958: 372f). Probably on the basis of this assumption, Haas initially believed that the spillover process would be automatic, which led him to predict the emergence of a political community in Europe before the end of the transitional period established by the Rome Treaty (Haas 1958: 311).

The Concept of Spillover

This set of assumptions forms the basis for the initial neofunctionalist explanation of the integration process in Europe. Its conception of change is succinctly encapsulated in the notion of spillover. The term was first applied in two distinctive manners: (1) it was used as a sort of shorthand for describing the occurrence of (further) integration; and, (2) it was used to identify the driving force and inherent logic of integration via increased functional/economic interdependence.[5] Haas (1958: 383) described an 'expansive logic of sector integration' whereby the integration of one sector leads to 'technical' pressures pushing states to integrate other sectors. The idea is that some sectors are so interdependent that it is impossible to isolate them from the rest. Thus, the integration of one sector at the regional level is only practicable in combination with the integration of other sectors, as problems arising from the functional integration of one task can only be solved by integrating yet more tasks. Haas (1958: 297) held that sector integration 'begets its own impetus toward extension of the entire economy'. For example, the viability of integration in the coal and steel sectors would be undermined unless other related sectors such as transport policy followed suit, in order to ensure a smooth movement of necessary raw materials. In the literature the term *functional spillover* later came to denote the functional–economic rationale for further integration (cf. Lindberg and Scheingold 1970).[6]

Haas and Lindberg also considered support for the integration process amongst economic and political elites to be of great significance. National elites had to come to perceive that problems of substantial interest could not be effectively addressed at the domestic level, not least because of the above-mentioned functional-economic logic. This should lead to a gradual learning process whereby elites shift their expectations, political activities and—according to Haas—even loyalties to a new European centre. Consequently, national elites would come to promote further integration, thus adding a political stimulus to the process. Haas (1958: 312–13) in particular focused on the pressures exerted by non-governmental elites. Those pressures include the altered perceptions of political parties, business and professional associations, trade unions or other interest groups. This implies that integration in a particular sector leads the relevant interest groups to move part of their activity to a higher level of aggregation and therefore gradually shift their focus and expectations to European institutions. Presuming that they would perceive positive benefits from their regional experiences, these private organizations should support further integration (cf. Haas 1958: chs 8 and 9).

Lindberg, for his part, attributed greater significance to the role of governmental elites and socialization processes. He drew attention to the proliferation of EU working groups and subcommittees which, by bringing thousands of national officials into frequent contact with each other and Commission officials, had given rise to a complex system of bureaucratic interpenetration. These interaction patterns, Lindberg argued (1963: ch. 4), increase the likelihood of socialization processes occurring amongst national civil servants within the Council framework. Given the effect of these mechanisms, neofunctionalists challenged the classic intergovernmental vision of Community decision-making as based only on national strategic bargaining and postulated the existence of a supranational problem-solving process, 'a cumulative pattern of accommodation in which the participants refrain from unconditionally vetoing proposals and instead seek to attain agreement by means of compromises upgrading common interests' (Haas 1958: 66). It was further implied that these socialization processes, by fostering consensus formation amongst agents of member governments, would eventually lead to more integrative outcomes (Lindberg 1963: chs 1 and 4; Lindberg and Scheingold 1970: 119). This process was later termed *engrenage*.[7] Neofunctionalists also argued that socialization processes and particularly the increased habit of national elites to look for European solutions in solving their problems would help to generate a shift of expectations and perhaps loyalties towards the new centre on the part of national elites. The integrative pressures exerted by national (governmental and non-governmental) elites were later termed *political spillover* in the literature (Tranholm-Mikkelsen 1991: 5).

A further impetus for regional integration would be provided by the role of those employed by supranational institutions. Haas emphasized how the High Authority of the ECSC and, later, the European Commission facilitated agreement on integrative outcomes. As opposed to lowest common denominator bargaining, which he saw as inherent in strictly intergovernmental decision-making, supranational systems were characterized by 'splitting the difference' and more significantly a bargaining process of 'upgrading common interests'. Parties agree that they should have a common stand in order not to jeopardize those areas in which consensus prevails. The participants in such negotiations tend to swap concessions in related fields under the auspices of an institutionalized mediator such as the Commission. Governments do not feel as if they have been bullied. Common interests are upgraded to the extent that each participant feels that, by conceding something, it has gained something else. In addition, Haas saw the Commission as the main actor cultivating the underlying logic of functional–economic interdependence. In line with his assumption of rational actors, Haas foresaw the gradual expansion of its mandate as commensurate with the increasing breadth and depth of integration, thus providing the process with yet more impetus (Haas 1961: 369ff, 1964a: 75ff). Lindberg emphasized the Commission's cultivation of ties with national elites. He pointed out that it occupies a privileged position of centrality and authority, enabling it not only to direct the dynamics of relations among states but also the relations of interest groups within each state. According to Lindberg (1963: 71), the Commission's cultivation of contacts with national civil servants and interest groups would in time lead to the Commission's progressive 'informal co-optation' of member states' national elites to help realise its European objectives. The integrative role attributed to the Commission (or supranational institutions more generally) was later termed *cultivated spillover* (Tranholm-Mikkelsen 1991: 6).

Criticisms

Neofunctionalism is probably the most heavily criticized integration theory. After the passing of its heyday in the mid-1960s, critiques of neofunctionalism emerged from inter-governmentalist scholarship (e.g. Hoffmann 1995: 84ff), and also increasingly from within the neofunctionalist camp itself—not least that of its self-critical founding father (Haas 1976: 175ff). Even after he pronounced the theory obsolescent, and after Lindberg 'retired' from studying the EEC/EC, critiques of their works flourished in the 1980s (Holland 1980; Webb 1983; Taylor 1983), and have not been out of fashion ever since (e.g. Moravcsik 1991, 1993; Milward 1992: 11–12; Risse-Kappen 1996: 56ff). It is important to note, how-ever, that a number of criticisms levelled against neofunctionalism misrepresent its claims, distort its arguments or interpret the theory selectively.[8]

For this reason, not all of the critiques are justified. For example, scholars have errone-ously accused the theory of failing to account for unintended consequences (McNamara 1993: 309) or for its supposed deficiency to recognize that loyalties and identities tend to be multiple.[9] Its critics have also exaggerated neofunctionalism's predictive pretensions and, especially, Haas's pronouncement of a political community as a likely outcome of the integration process before the end of the 12-year transitional period referred to in the Treaty of Rome (1958: 311), although neofunctionalists had avoided making such assumptions about an end-state as early as the beginning of the 1960s (Haas 1960: 1964b; Lindberg 1963: 6). In addition, the theory was, somewhat unfairly, disparaged for ex-planatory shortcomings on issues beyond its research focus and analytical spectrum, such as questions related to the nature of interest representation and intermediation in the EU (cf. Hix 1994: 6) or the initiation of the integration process in Europe (cf. Milward 1992: especially ch. 1). However, this latter line of criticism does have a certain validity given the early neofunctionalist aspirations to grand theorizing, an issue that will be taken up below. A more extensive account of contestable critiques vis-à-vis neofunctionalist theory has been provided elsewhere (Niemann 2000: 13–23).

Nevertheless, some criticisms provide more pertinent and fundamental challenges. First, neofunctionalism has been criticized for its grand theoretical pretensions. It has been rightly argued that neofunctionalism does not and cannot provide a general theory of regional integration in all settings, especially not of their origins; it presumes that member countries are relatively developed and diversified in their productive systems and that they have democratic polities. In addition, the theory provides certain analyti-cal tools to deal with only a particular type of questions, i.e. those related to *explaining* integration.

Both 'liberal intergovernmentalist' (e.g. Moravcsik 1993: 475ff) and 'liberal interdepend-ence' theorists (Keohane and Nye 1975, 1977) have questioned its assertion that spillover is inevitable and its seemingly exclusive reliance on economic determinism. In *The Uniting of Europe* Haas did consider the spillover process to be more or less automatic (Haas 1958: ch. 8). Later reformulations introduced qualifications to the likelihood of its occurrence. Some of these constituted sensible delimitations, such as the requirement that the task assigned to institutions had to be inherently expansive, i.e. functionally interdependent upon other issue areas (Lindberg 1963: 10). Other specifications pointed into the right direction, but were rather ad hoc, not sufficiently elaborated and not adequately linked with the main body of theory, like Haas's notion of the 'dramatic political actor' (Haas 1968: preface) or Lindberg's claim that spillover cannot be expected to take place in the absence of a will to proceed on the part of the member states (Lindberg 1963: 11). It is no exaggeration to state that early versions of neofunctionalism lack a sufficient coherent and comprehensive specification of the conditions under which spillover will occur.

Other critics have taken issue with neofunctionalism's alleged actor-centredness (Jørgensen and Christiansen 1999: 4). Neofunctionalist thought was not devoid of structural elements. For example, the functional–economic rationale based on the interdependence of sectors, which has also been referred to as functional spillover, is essentially a structural pressure. However, one may argue that neofunctionalism gives undue prominence to actors—especially, in the role assigned to supranational civil servants and representatives of sectoral interests—and that agents and structural explanations need to be linked with one another more adequately.

More orthodox theorists of international relations have long protested that neofunctionalists systematically (and naively) underestimated the continued impact of sovereignty consciousness and nationalism as barriers to the integration process (Hoffmann 1995: especially 75–84). Examples such as the French 'empty chair' politics under Charles de Gaulle or British policies under Margaret Thatcher illustrate the significance of these conceptions—although later neofunctionalists would point out that these incidents did not prevent further expansion of the tasks and authority of the EU in the longer run.

More economically minded critics (Holland 1980; Webb 1983) observed that the concept of spillover was connected to the implicit assumption that economic growth would continue unabated in the capitalist world, and that all member states would benefit more or less equally from that growth (cf. Haas 1964a: 68). In the 1950s and 1960s, many economists shared this optimistic outlook, not least because Western free-market economies were enjoying a period of unprecedented growth and duration. By the 1970s however, falling growth rates and rising unemployment produced a reappraisal. It has been suggested that the stagnation of the integration process and the shift of the institutional balance in the EC in favour of intergovernmental decision-making can be attributed in part to this worsening economic climate. Spillover, whether functional, political, or cultivated, was an allegedly fair weather process. Under less favourable circumstances, member states 'have appeared both uncertain and defensive and frequently unwilling to take the Community option' (Webb 1983: 21).

A number of authors (Hoffmann 1995; Webb 1983; George 1991) have observed that neofunctionalists failed to take the broader international context into account adequately. They argued that the European Community is only a part of the world economy, and that the international system prevents any possibility of insulating Europe from its effects. Hoffmann (1995: 84) saw external factors as a disintegrative force and contended that diverse responses to its pressures by member states would create unbridgeable divisions and even ruptures. His criticism overlaps with Webb's and Holland's on the changing (international) economic climate. Conversely, other writers have emphasized the integrative impact of external pressures. Schmitter (1996: 13), for example draws attention to European monetary policy cooperation, which began to evolve after US President Nixon's decision to take the dollar off the gold standard in 1971. Haas himself saw neofunctionalism's neglect of the wider world context as a serious shortcoming (Haas 1968:

preface). He eventually came to the drastic conclusion that the entire research focus on regional integration needed to be switched to the wider issues of interdependence (Haas 1976: 208).

Finally, neofunctionalists have come under warranted criticism for their lack of attention to domestic political processes and structures. It has been argued that they underestimated the role of national leadership by wrongly assuming that decision-makers were only 'economic incrementalists' and 'welfare seekers'. They may also have overestimated the role of interest groups in influencing policy, and assumed too much homogeneity in the pressures that would be brought to bear on different governments (cf. Hansen 1973; George 1991). Moreover, as pointed out by Moravcsik (1993: 477), neofunctionalism fails to explain government choices on the basis of models of pressure from predictable distributive coalitions. Lindberg himself conceded this deficiency. Together with Scheingold, he pointed out that neofunctionalism describes domestic processes, but says little about underlying causes of disparate national demands for integration. However, no means of rectifying this shortcoming was proposed (cf. Lindberg and Scheingold 1970: 284).

Modified Neofunctionalist Accounts

In response to the numerous criticisms, as well as to events occurring in the integration process itself, a few neofunctionalists undertook to reformulate their theory in the 1960s and early 1970s. Some of their modifications provide useful insights, while others have proved of limited utility. Critics would say that the theory became increasingly reactive to ad hoc occurrences and, therefore, so indeterminant in its conclusions as to provide no clear direction for research (e.g. Moravcsik 1993: 476). In any case, by the 1970s, most academic observers had dismissed neofunctionalism as either out of date or out of touch. Many turned to purely descriptive accounts that eschewed any attempt at theorizing. Others attempted to subsume the experience of European integration within the confines of orthodox theories of international relations—whether realist, neorealist, or liberal.

However, a few scholars have implicitly—or sometimes even explicitly—recognized the continuing value of neofunctionalism, suggesting that the approach still contains some useful building blocks for contemporary theorizing (e.g. Keohane and Hoffmann 1991; Marks *et al.* 1996; Pierson 1996). Others even argued that it may be worth resurrecting the theory in light of the Community's resurgence in the mid-1980s (Taylor 1989; Tranholm-Mikkelsen 1991).

In addition, it is noticeable from studying the wider literature on European integration theory that some of the more recent approaches bear considerable resemblance to neofunctionalism and that neofunctionalist insights have also informed other theoretical approaches (such as multilevel governance) in a number of ways,[10] although few authors have given explicit credit to neofunctionalism. Most plainly drawing on neofunctionalist thought and also most openly acknowledging their neofunctionalist roots (without however seeming to intend to revise the theory), Alec Stone Sweet and Wayne Sandholtz put forward their 'supranational governance' approach, which emphasizes the role and importance of transnational exchange, EU rules, and supranational institutions. They argue that cross-border transactions generate a demand for Community rules that EC institutions seek to supply. Once Community legislation develops, supranational society emerges as (business) actors realize that one set of rules is preferable to 15 or more sets of (national) rules. Actors working within the new Community framework would then test the limits of EC rules. This would in turn lead to more precise rules (due to the clarifications from EC adjudicators) that develop ever further away from the original intentions of member governments. Stone Sweet and Sandholtz argue that the transfer of competence to the Community is uneven and depends on the intensity of demands for EC regulation in a given issue area. Most significantly they depart from (early) neofunctionalism by leaving open whether actors' loyalties and identities eventually shift to the European level and by laying greater emphasis on the relevance of intergovernmental bargaining in EC politics (cf. Stone Sweet and Sandholtz 1997; Sandholtz and Stone Sweet 1998).

Their supranational governance account has been criticized in several respects. For example, it has been noted that they largely ignore the potential impact of the external/international realm, which is peculiar because Sandholtz had earlier co-authored a well-known article in which the influence of international competitive pressures constituted an important aspect for explaining the 1992 project (cf. Sandholtz and Zysman 1989). In addition, the supranational governance account has been criticized for remaining trapped in the old 'neofunctionalist–intergovernmentalist' dichotomy, for example, by privileging certain types of actors (supranational institutions) and by concentrating on limited parts of empirical reality (day-to-day developments) (cf. Branch and Øhrgaard 1999). While this may indeed be seen as a substantial shortcoming, it also needs to be pointed out that the intergovernmentalist–neofunctionalist debate remains an important one, albeit not as important as it used to (cf. Rosamond 2000: 2; Jachtenfuchs 2001: 255; Niemann 2006: 305–8).

Very few scholars have overtly identified themselves as neoneofunctionalists and deliberately sought to revise the original theory. Philippe Schmitter is one of them. As a former student of Ernst Haas who refused to accept his mentor's declaration of obsolescence, he first turned to the task of revision in the early 1970s and then again 30 years later. In terms of the basic driving forces of integration Schmitter not only points to endogenous tensions and contradictions related to the regional integration project, but also to the importance of external/exogenous factors—not just as an impediment but as a potentially facilitating factor in the integration process. As for the role of supranational institutions in fostering integration, he belatedly emphasized the role of the European Court of Justice in making major contributions to the assertion of EU supranationality. Schmitter illustrates the dynamic of his revised approach through a model of decision cycles. 'Initiating cycles', which the present European Union has passed through long ago, are followed by 'priming cycles' that account for the changing dynamics of member states in between decision cycles.

> The major difference between 'initiating' and 'priming' cycles . . . comes from the rising importance of distinctive regional processes. With each successive crisis resolved as the common institutions emerge from the initiation cycles, regional-level rules . . . gain in significance to the point that they begin to overshadow the opinions and actions of national governments, associations and individuals.
>
> Schmitter (2004: 61)

As regional processes begin to have greater effect, national actors may become more receptive to changing the competencies and authority of regional institutions.

However, in his revised theory Schmitter rejects the 'automaticity of spillover' assumption. Strategic responses other than spillover are conceptualized, such as (1) 'spill-around', the proliferation of functionally specialized independent, but strictly intergovernmental, institutions; (2) 'build-up', the concession by member states of greater authority to the supranational organization without expanding the scope of its mandate; (3) 'muddle-about', when national actors try to maintain regional cooperation without changing/adjusting institutions; and (4) 'spillback', which denotes withdrawal from previous commitments by member states. He points out that, as far as European integration is concerned, so far each of the (priming) decision cycles has generated further imbalances and contradictions thus avoiding encapsulation, a state of stable self-maintenance. He also implies that the EU has not yet reached the 'transforming cycle', where the potentialities for functionally integrating their economies (would) have been exhausted and the emphasis would be placed on the integration of polities.

Another revised neofunctionalist framework was developed by Arne Niemann (cf. Niemann 1998, 2000, 2004, 2006). Taking early neofunctionalism as a starting point, he departs from the original approach in several ways. First, the ontological scope is slightly broadened—somewhat beyond what Haas (2001) post hoc described as 'soft rational choice' for the original neofunctionalist account—towards a wider and more inclusive ontology by encroaching 'soft' constructivism to a larger extent than Haas (2001) attributed to early neofunctionalism. This extension was undertaken for two reasons.

1. While some elements of (early) neofunctionalism can be solidly located in the rational choice tradition, with rational, intentional, and self-interested actors (cf. Burley and Mattli 1993: 54–5), other elements were more reminiscent of constructivist thought with actors capable of learning processes,[11] and his account places more explicit emphasis on socialization, deliberation, and learning than did Haas's early neofunctionalism for explaining EU decision outcomes.

2. Whereas early neofunctionalism viewed agents as predominant and paid relatively little attention to structure,[12] Niemann's revised neofunctionalist framework attributes to structure and agency a more equal status. Embracing the concept of structuration (Giddens 1984), he emphasizes the interdependence of structures (e.g. functional interdependencies, the EU/international system of states/institutional order) and agents (ranging from governmental elites to private and supranational actors). Hence, structure and agency mutually constitute each other.

Niemann's revised approach should be understood as a wide-ranging, but partial, theory that is only intended to account for part of the process of regional integration in Europe, namely that of explaining EU decisions and their impact upon integration. The latter is no longer viewed as an automatic and exclusively dynamic process, but rather occurs under certain conditions and is better characterized as a dialectic[13] process, i.e. the product of both dynamics and countervailing forces. The latter are explicitly conceptualized in his framework. Countervailing forces may either be stagnating (directed towards standstill) or opposing (directed towards spillback) in nature. In particular, two concrete countervailing forces are accommodated in the revised neofunctionalist framework: first there is 'sovereignty-consciousness', which encapsulates actors who oppose delegating sovereignty/competences to the supranational level and is linked to national traditions, identities and ideologies. Second, 'domestic constraints and diversities' signify national governments' restricted autonomy to act due to constraints by actors (e.g. lobby groups or coalition partners) or structural limitations (such as a country's economy, demography, or legal tradition) in the domestic political system. This is exacerbated by the economic, cultural, legal, demographic or other diversities between member states, which may entail considerable adjustment costs for some and thus obstruct integrative endeavours.

While the conceptualization of countervailing forces contains a key element in Niemann's revised framework, he also further develops and specifies the dynamics of integration. Functional spillover is broadened in scope to go beyond merely economic linkages and is freed from its deterministic ontology—implying that functional structure has to be found plausible and compelling by actors in order to be acted upon—thus reflecting a 'soft' functionalism. Functional 'pressures from within'—which capture pressures for increased cooperation within the same, rather than another, sector—are made more explicit and upgraded as an explanatory tool. So is cultivated spillover—the concept that originally denoted the role of the Commission/High Authority—which is also widened to include the integrative roles played by the Council Presidency, the European Parliament, and the European Court of Justice. Building on Schmitter (1969, 1970), 'exogenous' spillover is incorporated into his framework to account for the tensions and contradictions originating outside the integration process itself. In addition, political spillover, which broadly speaking conceptualizes the role of non-governmental elites, is also stretched. Interest groups are taken to be influenced not only by endogenous-functional, but also by exogenous and domestic structures. 'Social' spillover is separated from political spillover for a more clear-cut explaination of reflexive learning and socialization processes. The concepts of communicative and norm-regulated action are incorporated into social spillover to describe and explain these processes more adequately. Learning and socialization are no longer regarded as constant (as implied by early neofunctionalists) but as being subject to conditions. These conditions, as well as the conditions for the other sorts of spillover, are set out in his revised framework (cf. especially Niemann 2006).

Schmitter's and Niemann's revised neofunctionalist accounts may also provide scope for some criticism: for example, the parsimony of early neofunctionalism is lost to some extent, since their (spillover) formulations and (bivariate/multivariate) hypotheses are rather more complex than the original theory.

In the introduction to the 2004 edition of the *Uniting of Europe*, Haas made a final contribution to European integration theory. While this piece does not constitute an outright attempt to revise his neofunctionalist theory, he makes some important reflections on how new developments in IR and political science theory relate to, challenge, and (potentially) stimulate neofunctionalism. In particular, Haas makes it his task to see how neofunctionalism 'can become part of a respectable constructivism' (Haas 2004: xvii). He suggests that neofunctionalism may be considered a forerunner, and part of, constructivism. Haas also considers the utility of (old and new) institutionalist approaches. He concludes that revised neofunctionalist approaches benefited from institutionalist thinking, as a result of which the neofunctionalist tradition, in his view, 'has a new lease on life' and should be considered 'no longer obsolescent' (Haas 2004: liii).

Most-likely Cases and the Conditions for Spillover

Generally speaking, the neofunctionalist research agenda predominantly focuses on explaining EU decision processes and outcomes. However, no one case easily qualifies as a best case application of the theory. This is due to the fact that—based on the insight that the concept of spillover needs to be carefully delimited—the conditions for the occurrence of the neofunctionalist dynamics are quite numerous, and that these conditions also vary across spillover pressures. Hence, rather than trying to identify one best case, we will discuss the conditions of spillover for the different pressures, while at the same time pointing to issue areas where these conditions have been broadly met. While the automaticity of spillover assumption was gradually phased out of neofunctionalism, few scholars have sought systematically to delimit the concept of spillover and the neofunctionalist dynamics. We will thus consider the various neofunctionalist pressures mainly along the conditions that we derived from our own work (e.g. Niemann 2006; Schmitter 2004).

As for functional spillover—the situation/process in which the original integrative goal can be assured only by taking further integrative action, which in turn creates circumstances that require further action—perhaps the most important condition is that functional pressures have to be *perceived* as compelling. Functional spillover is a structural pressure and structures need agents to translate those pressures. Functional pressures do not 'determine' behaviour in any mechanical or predictable fashion. They contain an important element of human agreement. However, we can approximate when actors are more likely to perceive such pressures are persuasive, namely when the original issue area and the objectives therein are (considered) salient, and when the interdependence with areas where further action is (regarded as) strong (cf. Niemann 2004, 2006).[14]

A case illustrating strong functional pressure is the spillover from the internal market to the area justice and home affairs. If the single market—including the free movement of persons—was to be completed, certain compensatory measures were (considered) necessary in areas such as visa, asylum, immigration, and police cooperation. The original issue area and the objectives therein, i.e. completing the internal market, were indeed very salient. Considerable significance was attached to it partly because, amongst the four freedoms, the free movement of persons has the most direct bearing on the lives of individual citizens (Fortescue 1995: 28). From an economic perspective, the proper functioning of the single market would be jeopardized, unless this principle was put into practice (European Commission 1985: 6). Also, the functional interdependence between the free movement of persons and certain policy areas is strong. The most obvious functional link may be the one with external border control and visa policy. States are unlikely to waive the power of internal controls, unless they can be provided with an equivalent protection with regard to persons arriving at external frontiers. This implies shifting controls to the external borders and also a common visa policy, regulating short-term admission to the EC. There is also a strong rationale for a common asylum policy, as otherwise the restrictive efforts of one member state would be undermined by liberal policies of another state. The fear was that the abolition of internal borders would lead to an increased internal migration of asylum seekers denied asylum in the first country, and to multiple applications for asylum (Achermann 1995; Niemann 2008).

Thus, the functional rational itself was strong indeed. In addition, national and supranational elites also very much bought into it. One can argue that actors' *perception* of the pressure as a necessity was even greater than the *logic* of the argument as deduced from a 'factual' analysis of cause-and-effect mechanisms. For example, it can be argued that the intra-EU borders (or borders in general) have always been permeable and that the abolition of border control makes less difference than widely held (cf. Huysmans 2000: 759). Despite this gap/flaw in the functional rationale, the Commission and member governments overwhelmingly accepted the functional link, and also reproduced it so that eventually it acquired the status of knowledge, outside the realm of the contestable (cf. den Boer 1994).

A second set of conditions attached to the concept of functional spillover is that decision-makers (1) do not anticipate that further integration in one area may create problems in other areas, which in turn would lead to further (possibly undesired) integration (so that they refuse to take the first integrative step); or (2)—when further spillovers are anticipated—that the benefit of the first integrational step is sufficiently salient that it outweighs the concerns about later spillover effects into other areas. Usually the latter condition applies. Given restricted time horizons, decision-makers tend to be less concerned with the safeguarding sovereignty, than with creating the conditions of continued domestic success (Pierson 1996). However, these conditions are certainly not always met. For example, in the negotiations concerning the scope of the Common Commercial Policy at the Amsterdam Inter-governmental Conference (IGC), a number of member governments did see the benefits of bringing trade in services under the scope of Article 113. However, it was feared by some member states (and in fact seemed likely from the perspective of the Council legal service) that this would foster the process of internal Community liberalization in the area of services and that the Commission could use the backdoor of Article 113 to regulate in areas which fell under member states' competence. Hence, from the first integrational step (expanding the scope of Article 113) undesired spillover into another area (internal Community services liberalization) was feared. Although there were other areas of scepticism among these delegations, the anticipation of spillover, which was regarded as more costly than the benefits of extending Community competence, contributed to member governments' refusal to bring services under the scope of the Common Commercial Policy at Amsterdam (Niemann 2006: ch. 3).

As pointed out by Schmitter (1969: 163) and by Pierson and Leibfried (1995) functional interdependencies are most likely to occur in the presence of 'high issue density'. Pierson (1996: 137) has demonstrated that with an increase of issue areas at the European level there is an exponential expansion of connections between issue areas. For example, with four issue areas there are six possible connections, while with eight areas the number of potential connections rises to 28. Hence, this would suggest that there is growing potential for functional linkages and functional spillover processes as the integration process proceeds. This may also help to explain the resurgence of integration since the 1992 project (cf. McNamara 1993: 320–1). A number of studies have highlighted the potential integrative force of functional pressures, especially in terms of spillovers from the 1992 project to EMU (Mutimer 1989), to the domain of social policy (Pierson and Leibfried 1995) and to energy policy (Matlary 1997).

In terms of political spillover—the integrative pressures exerted by (national governmental and especially non-governmental) elites realizing that problems of substantial interest cannot be satisfactorily solved at the domestic level—certain conditions are conducive to this dynamic. First, we will focus on the role of non-governmental elites. Interest groups are (more) likely to seek supranational solutions when

1. the potential gains from European integration are high;

2. interest groups can easily ascertain the benefits of EU activity;

3. the relevant issue area has for some time been governed by the EU/EC, so that organized interests had a chance to familiarize themselves with the Community policy process, to coordinate on the European level, and for learning processes to occur;

4. functional spillover pressures or—as some of the revised neofunctionalist approaches would allow for—internationally induced incentives drive or reinforce the rationale for seeking supranational solutions (cf. Niemann 2006: ch. 5).

A number of empirical studies have confirmed the impact of interest groups and political spillover pressures on (integrative) policy outcomes. Sandholtz and Zysman (1989) and Green Cowles (1995) have pointed to the influence of European business, and especially the European Round Table of Industrialists, on the 1992 programme during the negotiations leading to the SEA. Here, the above conditions were (very) largely met. The potential gains from the internal market were high. Apart from the Commission's favourable estimations concerning economic growth and improved business conditions, firms and interest groups could themselves easily ascertain the benefits of the 1992 project, as one set of rules and regulations clearly constituted a significantly more beneficial economic environment than 12 (or more) different ones. In addition, a globalizing world economy and growing international competition provided an important spur for the internal market project (Green Cowles 1995). There are other areas were the political spillover pressures seem to have been at work. David Cameron (1995) has argued that a transnational community of European (central) bankers helped to frame the debate on EMU at Maastricht. O'Reilly and Stone Sweet (1998) have found that business and consumer groups played an important role in the transfer of competence to the Community in the field of air transport.

In other areas political spillover dynamics proved less substantial. Niemann (1998, 2006) has argued that the development of the PHARE programme and the 1996–97 negotiations on the extension of EU external trade competence to the area of services have been accompanied by rather insubstantial support from organized interests. These cases have shown that a lack of transparency and complexity (of General Agreement on Tariffs and Trade [GATT]/World Trade Organization [WTO] rules and decision-making of the PHARE programme) can hinder interest group involvement, as it obscured the benefits of supranational governance (especially in the trade case) or confused actors concerning where to start lobbying (as in the case of the PHARE programme). Moreover, in both cases—even that concerning the extension of the Common Commercial Policy—the economic stakes were (perceived as) not that high, certainly when compared with, say, the SEM (cf. Niemann 2006: ch. 5).

Neofunctionalists also stressed the role of governmental elites as well as *socialization, learning,* and (in Niemann's revised version) *deliberation,* especially with regard to the increasing number of (Council and other) working groups and committees. A number of conditions can be specified for these processes. Socialization, deliberation, and learning processes

1. need time to develop;
2. tend to be significantly constrained if important members of a working group/ committee are distrusted;
3. are impaired when issues become politicized;
4. can be offset in the case of adverse bureaucratic pressures in national ministries and administrations;
5. tend to be obstructed when negotiations are rather technical in nature and negotiators do not possess enough expertise;
6. may be impeded when officials are a priori against changing their norms and habits and feel that they have been dragged into EU/EC cooperation (cf. Niemann 2006).

Where these conditions take on favourable values socialization and learning process can unfold and have an integrative bearing on outcomes, for instance in the case of the PHARE programme. When these conditions are partly/largely not met—as for example in the case of the discussions on the 1996–97 reform EU trade policy (cf. Niemann 1998, 2006: chs 3 and 4)—this dynamic is significantly obstructed and has no impact.

More generally, studies suggest for instance that an *esprit de corps* tends to develop in Council committees over time and that membership matters in terms of civil servants' construction of role conceptions and attitudes (Trondal 2002). Beyers and Dierickx (1998) have found that intense informal cooperation between national delegates has developed, that common attitudes to different negotiation partners have been adopted and that the importance of non-state institutional actors has been recognized even by officials from traditionally more Eurosceptic member states. Egeberg (1999: 471) has held that national officials involved in EU decision-making are generally characterized by a substantial degree of collective responsibility which is reflected in the overall willingness to shift and reformulate their positions. The recent scholarship also suggests that the EU and its institutions are, of course, not the only socializing mechanisms, but that national institutions and the domestic realm, more generally, also provide important, and often prevailing, socializing sources and mechanisms (e.g. Beyers 2002: 23; Egeberg 1999: 470–1).

As for cultivated spillover, the integrative pressure exerted by supranational institutions, we will here focus on the role of the Commission. The following factors condition its policy entrepreneurship:

1. its ability to forge internal cohesion (Nugent 1995);
2. the Commission's capacity to shape the agenda—not only where it has an exclusive right of initiative, but also in the second and third pillars and at IGCs—for example by proactively tabling proposals, skilful timing of proposals, and maintaining close ties with the Presidency;

3. the cultivation of relations with member governments, interest groups, or other actors, i.e. securing support for its policies by making use of its strategic position of being centrally located within a web of policy networks and relationships (Mazey and Richardson 1997);

4. its ability to build consensus and broker compromises, often while upgrading common interests (Nugent 1995);

5. the instrumentalization of functional (and exogenous) spillover pressures, i.e. promoting further integration by drawing on such rationales in the debate (Sandholtz 1993; Héritier 1998);

6. the Commission's capacity to know the limits of its entrepreneurial leadership so as not to overplay its hand vis-à-vis the member states (cf. Pollack 2001).

In addition, there are a number of (background) factors affecting its role which are largely beyond the control of the Commission. First, in the absence of (effective) interest groups the Commission is deprived of potential allies and may not succeed in the pursuit of its objectives (Nye 1971). Secondly, Commission leadership is most effective when supported by a significant political actor, such as a powerful member state (George 1996: 44). Thirdly, it has been pointed out that institutions may register the greatest impact on policy outcomes in periods of swiftly changing events, uncertainty and incomplete information and during periods of policy adaptation (cf. Peterson 1992; Sandholtz 1993).

A number of studies have revealed the Commission's ability to play a proactive and integrative leadership role. This has been indicated by research in the fields of telecommunications (Sandholtz 1993), energy (Matlary 1997), air transport policy (O'Reilly and Stone Sweet 1998), information technology (Sandholtz 1992), structural policy (Marks 1992), environmental policy (Sbragia 1993), in the launch of the 1992 project (Sandholtz and Zysman 1989), and in paving the way for monetary union (Jabko 1999). These cases are accompanied by many of the above-mentioned favourable conditions for Commission assertion. In cases largely characterized by an absence of these conditions, such as the Amsterdam IGC negotiations on reforming the Common Commercial Policy—in which the Commission lacked internal coherence, overplayed its hand and was largely unsupported by interest groups or key member states—the Commission's impact tends to remain very marginal (cf. Niemann 2006: ch. 3).

Test Case: Enlargement

Early neofunctionalism paid little attention to the geographical expansion of the ECSC and EEC. This is not surprising since neofunctionalism had passed its prime before the first EC enlargement in 1973 (cf. Schimmelfennig and Sedelmeier 2002: 501). However, Haas (1958: 313–17) did talk about a 'geographical spillover'. For him such a process was beginning to take place with Britain. The latter's rapprochement to the ECSC was spurred by the fear of isolation and successful integration of economies on the continent, which threatened Britain's future access. Apart from Haas's explicit, if limited, mention, how suitable are neofunctionalism's conceptual tools for shedding light on the case of enlargement? Arguably, its toolkit should go some way to explaining the Community's geographical growth. Our subsequent analysis will particularly focus on the recent case of Eastern enlargement.

First, the neofunctionalist definition of integration as a *process* is much in keeping with standard definitions and descriptions of enlargement, which is commonly also characterized as a 'gradual process' (Schimmelfennig and Sedelmeier 2002: 503).

Secondly, neofunctionalism provides some scope for explaining why a substantial number of countries began to queue for EU membership. The EU's magnetism was to a considerable extent due to the high level of integration it had reached, which made accession attractive and exclusion costly (Vachudova 2007: 107). In addition, the EC was in many ways an economic and political success story. It had cemented the peace on the continent, spurred economic prosperity, and displayed significant dynamism since the mid 1980s with the 1992 project, the decision on EMU and first steps towards political union. Moreover, the Community had begun to play a proactive and constructive role in the relations with the Central and Eastern European Countries (CEEC), first in terms of bilateral trade agreements in the (late) 1980s, later through its coordination of aid for the G-24, the PHARE programme, and—more controversially—the negotiation and conclusion of the Europe Agreements. The demand for EU enlargement can partly be derived from neofunctionalism's basic tenet: integration leads to tensions, contradictions, and demands, which can only be resolved by taking further integrative action. Here, however, this does not take the form of bringing more sectors under the governance of the Community, but of expanding the territorial scope of the integration project. While the above process is much in the spirit of spillover, the conceptual link to the outside world/international realm was weak within early neofunctionalism. This was later resolved, to some extent, by conceptualizing for what was coined 'externalization' (Schmitter 1969) or 'exogenous spillover' (Niemann 2004, 2006).

Thirdly, neofunctionalism also adds to our understanding when considering the role of supranational institutions, especially the Commission. The latter has impacted on the enlargement process, primarily in an integrative and autonomous way. It has played a considerable role in channelling the process (and thus sometimes managed to augment its own position), starting with its proactive and successful attempt to attain the mandate to coordinate the Community's aid policy (Niemann 1998). Later, the Commission acted as a broker by fostering cooperation between the EU member states and applicant countries, thereby 'generating and selling new conceptions of the future of European integration', and thus influencing the agenda and exercising some control over the pre-accession process (Vachudova 2007: 114). It has also been argued that the Commission played an autonomous role in (often successfully) advocating the accommodation of candidates' preferences, for example by making skilful use of the policy process (Sedelmeier 2002). Moreover, it has been held that the Commission (successfully) encouraged a larger enlargement in order to reinforce its own position and role by keeping itself in the enlargement business (Vachudova 2007).

Fourth, the role of interest groups in the enlargement process also partly corroborates neofunctionalist theorizing. The most influential interest group, the European Round

Table of Industrialists (ERT), lobbied in a coordinated, transnational fashion.[15] The ERT promoted the accession of the CEEC, as this promised to facilitate access to the Central Eastern European markets (cf. Holman 2001; Bieler 2002). Neofunctionalists had suggested that interest groups would suggest further integration (here enlargement), once they become aware of the benefits of existing integration (Haas 1958). This seems to be the case with the ERT, even if a long-term shift of expectations and, especially, loyalties to the European level, anticipated by Haas (1958: chs 8 and 9) is more doubtful. Also the actual influence of the ERT on policy outcomes is unclear. Interesting to note is the close collaboration between the Commission and the ERT, for example, in terms of devising the pre-accession strategy (Holman 2001: 173; Bieler 2002: 590), something that is easily squared with neofunctionalist writings on the cultivation of interests. Other aspects of the role of organized interests in the enlargement process have been more problematic. For instance, some associations representing sectors in uncompetitive positions were against the enlargement process (Jachtenfuchs 2002: 654). This would seem to contradict early neofunctionalism, which assumed a more homogenous and favourable evolution of organized interests towards supporting further integration.

Overall, neofunctionalism enhances our understanding mostly in terms of accounting for some of the driving forces behind the process of enlargement. Yet it goes somewhat beyond that, as it also indicates certain rationales for further integration flowing from enlargement. Most obviously, there is the well-known functional link between widening and deepening. For instance, once enlargement had become an internal goal, problems were anticipated in terms of decision-making for policy areas ruled by unanimity. Unanimity was already regarded as problematic by some with 15 member states. With 25 (or 27) and the corresponding diversification of interests and increased heterogeneity, it was feared that those areas still governed by unanimity would become even more susceptible to deadlock. This functional pressure stemming from enlargement has been one factor accounting for the successive extension of QMV, for example in EU migration policy (Niemann 2008).

However, as stated earlier, (revised) neofunctionalism is best viewed as a partial theory which provides insights only for certain research questions, largely situated toward explaining EU decision outcomes. Important issues on which neofunctionalism leaves us in the dark include the relevance and role of (varying) domestic actor constellations and structures in the applicant countries for the enlargement process, the implications of enlargement for the nature of the EU political system, the social and political consequences of geographical expansion, and the normative dimension of EU enlargement.

Conclusion

Although neofunctionalism has been widely criticized and some of these criticisms have revealed major deficiencies, it remains an important approach for conceptualizing and explaining the dynamics of European integration. There are several reasons for this: firstly, as the case illustrations have indicated, neofunctionalism (still) has a very useful toolkit for analysing salient issues, mainly revolving around explaining EU decision processes and outcomes. Even though this has been an old and long-standing research question, it will continue to be a prominent one. Secondly, neofunctionalism has inspired subsequent theorizing and later approaches have drawn extensively (if not always, explicitly) on its assumptions and hypotheses which in turn provided useful building blocks for a number of frameworks. Thirdly, neofunctionalism has proven to be capable of reformulation, partly owing to the nature of its theoretical assumptions/formulations, and partly due to the propensity for self-reflection and self-criticism of its authors.

Hence, rather than confining its relevance to specific conditions prevailing at the time of its formulation five decade ago, the student of regional integration should recognize that neofunctionalism has been and still is an evolving theory. Its location between the disciplines of international relations and comparative politics enhances its potential for explaining a highly unorthodox and unprecedented process of transformation that virtually by definition cannot be captured by either of these. As such the neofunctionalist research agenda is by no means exhausted. There is continued potential for developing the theory, not least in further specifying the conditions under which the different types of spillover pressure are likely to unfold. Thus, it still needs work, but that should be taken as a challenge rather than as an excuse for dismissing the neofunctionalist approach.

■ NOTES

1. On the latter two issues, compare, for example, Haas (1958: 16, 311) with Lindberg (1963: 6). See also the subsequent discussion on the definition of integration.

2. Compare for instance Haas (1961), who believed that issue areas need to be depoliticized and characterized by pragmatic interest politics in order to spill over, with Schmitter (1969: 166). The latter pointed out that politicization was a necessary driving force for the progression of the integration process.

3. Perhaps the most striking example of such a kind of selective and misleading reading of the neofunctionalist approach is the work of Alan Milward (1992: 11–12).

4. Contrary to the conventional reading and misinterpretation of neofunctionalism, Haas actually held that such a shift in loyalties need not be absolute or permanent, allowing for multiple loyalties (Haas 1958: 14). In addition, soon after devising his original definition of integration, Haas downplayed the previously amalgamated endpoint (Haas 1960), and also abandoned shifting *loyalties* as a defining characteristic of integration. Instead, he emphasized the transfer of *authority* and *legitimacy* (Haas 1970: 627–8, 633).

5. As described below, later on the term spillover was used to explain all the different neofunctionalist dynamics.

6. The terminologies of functional, political, and cultivated spillover were not part of the first generation neofunctionalist vocabulary.

7. See Taylor (1983: 9–10). It should be noted that the term '*engrenage*' has been given different meanings by different authors which has led to considerable semantic confusion: Pinder (1991: 26, 32) calls '*engrenage*' what Lindberg meant by 'informal co-optation' (see later in this subsection). Wallace (1990: 17) stretches the term to include the reorientation of economic interests among mass publics. Finally, Nye (1971: 51–2) and Russell (1975: 61–2) attached a wholly different meaning to the term. Their notion of *engrenage* can be seen as a variation of functional spillover.

8. Also cf. Rosamond (2005) who suggests that Haas has been misread on several points.

9. For a misinterpretation of neofunctionalism on this point, see Marcussen and Risse (1997). Contrary, to Marcussen and Risse, Haas has already acknowledged the existence of multiple identities in Haas (1958: 5, 9, 14).

10. On the similarities and overlaps of neofunctionalism with other approaches see Niemann (2006: 302–5).

11. See for example Haas (1958: 291–2); Lindberg and Scheingold (1970: 119). I agree with Rosamond (2005: 242, 250) who suggests that Haas's neofunctionalism was shot through with an interest in cognitions, perception, and the sociological dimension of institutionalized interaction', and that the deployment of constructivist vocabulary benefits (revised) neofunctionalist theory. See also Haas (2001, 2004) who made the relationship between neofunctionalism and constructivism a prominent theme in his final contributions to European integration.

12. However, structure was arguably more important in (early) neofunctionalism than acknowledged by Haas (2001: 29), given the emphasis on functional–economic interdependencies.

13. Tranholm-Mikkelsen (1991: 18–19) has suggested viewing integration as a dialectical process. Although this is where he saw the limitations of neofunctionalism, he does not seem to make this suggestion with a view to reforming the theory.

14. As the brackets in the previous sentence suggest, even these criteria are not entirely materially/ objectively determinable, but leave scope for varying perception, as will be further illustrated below.

15. Haas (1958: chs 8 and 9) had suggested that interest groups would increasingly organize a Brussels-based umbrella organization and conduct their lobbying efforts in a coordinated manner transnationally.

■ GUIDE TO FURTHER READING

Haas, E.B. (1958) *The Uniting of Europe: Political, Social and Economic Forces, 1950–7* (London: Stevens). This seminal work has provided the foundation of (early) neofunctionalist theory. Now in its third edition, the book is one of the most frequently referenced titles in the entire literature on European integration.

—— (1970) 'The study of regional integration: reflections on the joy and anguish of pretheorizing', *International Organization,* 24(4), 607–44. This self-critical piece provides a useful specification of Haas's earlier work.

—— (2001) 'Does constructivism subsume neo-functionalism?', in Christiansen, T., Jørgensen, K.E., and Wiener, A. (eds) *The Social Construction of Europe* (London: Sage), 22–31. An important post-hoc reflection of his earlier work in the context of constructivist theory.

Journal of European Public Policy (2005), 12(2), Special Issue in Honour of Ernst Haas. An edited collection of papers that reviews different aspects of Haas's neofunctionalism.

Lindberg, L. (1963) *The Political Dynamics of European Economic Integration* (Stanford, CA: Princeton University Press). This is also a neofunctionalist classic. While Haas (1958) focused on the ECSC, Lindberg here concentrated his analysis on the EEC.

Niemann, A. (2006) *Explaining decisions in the European Union* (Cambridge: Cambridge University Press). This book analyses, restates, and develops (earlier) neofunctionalist theory and assesses the usefulness of the revised neofunctionalist framework on three cases studies.

Schmitter, P. (1969) 'Three neo-functional hypotheses about international integration', *International Organization,* 23(2), 161–6. A concise formulation of the concept of spillover.

—— (1970) 'A Revised Theory of Regional Integration', *International Organization,* 24, 836–68. A useful though complex modified neofunctionalist account that the author later used as a basis for further revision (cf. Schmitter 2004).

Tranholm-Mikkelsen, J. (1991) 'Neo-functionalism: obstinate or obsolete? A reappraisal in the light of the new dynamism of the EC', *Millennium: Journal of International Studies,* 20(1), 1–22. A useful commentary and a fine systematization of neofunctionalist thought.

■ **STUDY QUESTIONS**

1. Explain the concept of spillover. What is its value-added for theorizing European integration?

2. Discuss the criticisms that have been levelled against neofunctionalism. To what extent and in which regard has neofunctionalism been fairly/justifiably criticized?

3. What contribution has neofunctionalism made to theorizing European integration?

4. (How) can neofunctionalist theory be modified/reformulated so as to account for the European integration process of the late twentieth century and early twenty-first century?

5. To what extent and how has neofunctionalism influenced and informed more recent theoretical approaches? Which approaches to theorizing European integration/governance seem to have been particularly inspired by neofunctionalist thought?

4 Liberal Intergovernmentalism

Andrew Moravcsik and Frank Schimmelfennig

Introduction

Liberal Intergovernmentalism (LI) has acquired the status of a 'baseline theory' in the study of regional integration: an essential first cut explanation against which other theories are often compared.[1] In this chapter we argue that it has achieved this dominant status due to its theoretical soundness, empirical power, and utility as a foundation for synthesis with other explanations. We begin by outlining the main assumptions and propositions of LI in the section 'Liberal intergovernmentalism as theory'. We then discuss common criticisms levelled against it and examine the scope conditions under which LI is most likely to explain state behaviour(s). We subsequently explore two cases: one, agricultural policy, where LI is expected to perform well, and another, enlargement, where it might be expected to face difficulties and go on to examine briefly the current state of the European Union. We conclude by pointing out LI's openness to dialogue and synthesis with other theories and reiterating its status as a baseline theory of European and regional integration.

Liberal Intergovernmentalism as Theory

There are several characteristics of LI that have contributed to its standing as a baseline theory.

First, LI is grounded in broader social science theory. It seeks to modernize integration theory by drawing on general political science theory. It is an application of 'rationalist institutionalism', a general approach used to study interstate cooperation in world politics (see also Pollack, Chapter 7 this volume). Although LI draws on insights from traditional schools in European integration studies that treat the EU (or regional integration) as a unique or sui generis activity—particularly neofunctionalism (see Chapter 3 in this volume), but also, to a lesser extent, traditional 'intergovernmentalism', as developed by Hoffmann (1966, 1982, 1995)—LI seeks to ground these insights in a more consistent and rigorous core of microfoundational assumptions. This allows LI, in contrast to traditional schools of European integration, to specify the motivations of social actors, states, and leaders, and to derive predictions of aggregate behaviour or dynamic effects from their interaction that can be subjected to empirical tests (Moravcsik 1998: 13–14; 2005).

Second, LI is a 'grand theory' that seeks to explain the broad evolution of regional integration. LI is a theoretical synthesis or framework, not a narrow theory of a single political activity. It argues that one cannot explain integration with just one factor, but instead seeks to link together multiple theories and factors into a single coherent approach appropriate to explaining the trajectory of integration over time.

Third, LI is parsimonious. Though multi-causal, LI remains simple. Its basic premises can be summarized in a few general interrelated propositions, which deliberately seek to simplify EU politics, stressing the essential and excluding certain secondary activities. At the same time, it should be noted, LI rejects monocausal explanation, arguing that a minimum of three theories, arrayed in a multistage model—one each of preferences, bargaining, and institutions—are required to explain integration. The precise specification of each theory, moreover, varies by issue area and circumstance. This is hardly an overly simplistic account. Still, the aspiration to parsimony differentiates LI from atheoretical concepts like 'multilevel governance'—a descriptive metaphor rather than a theory that subsumes nearly all possible political interrelationships found in the EU, including those predicted by LI (Jachtenfuchs 1997: 17; cf. Hooghe and Marks 2001).

Yet the primary source of LI's success lies not in its generality, ambition, parsimony or other formal attributes, but in the apparent accuracy of the substantive assumptions and empirical predictions it advances about European politics. What are these?

At the most fundamental level, LI rests on two basic assumptions about politics. The first is that states are actors. The EU, like other international institutions, can be profitably studied by treating states as the critical actors in a context of anarchy. That is, states achieve their goals through intergovernmental negotiation and bargaining, rather than through a centralized authority making and enforcing political decisions. The European Community (EC) 'is best seen as an international regime for policy co-ordination' (Moravcsik 1993: 480). This assumption is not 'realist': national security is not the dominant motivation, states power is not based on coercive capabilities, state preferences and identities are not uniform, and interstate institutions are not insignificant (Keohane and Nye 1977). LI simply acknowledges a blunt empirical fact about contemporary institutions like the EU: member states are 'masters of the treaty' and continue to enjoy pre-eminent decision-making power and political legitimacy.

The second basic LI assumption is that states are rational. Rationalism is an individualist or agency assumption. Actors calculate the utility of alternative courses of action and choose the one that maximizes (or satisfies) their utility under the circumstances. Collective outcomes are explained as the result of aggregated individual actions based on efficient pursuit of these preferences—albeit subject to the information at hand and uncertainty about the future. Agreement to cooperate, or to establish international institutions, is explained as a collective outcome of interdependent (strategic) rational state choices and intergovernmental negotiations.

One way to restate the states-as-actors and rationality assumptions is as follows. Decisions to cooperate internationally can be explained in a three-stage framework: states first define preferences, then bargain to substantive agreements, and finally create (or adjust) institutions to secure those outcomes in the face of future uncertainty.[2] Each stage is separate, and each stage is explained by a separate theory. Cooperation outcomes are explained only at the end of the multicausal sequence (Moravcsik 1989, 1998). To be useful in analysing European integration in particular, the framework is further specified using precise theories of preferences, bargaining, and institutionalization. It asks: what type of domestic preferences should be expected to matter most in Europe? Which bargaining dynamics should shape European agreements? What factors explain institutional design? LI adopts one specific theory for each step, a 'liberal' or societal theory of national preference formation, a bargaining theory of international negotiations, and a functional theory of institutional choice. Each of these LI explanations puts forward concrete propositions, derived from theory, to be evaluated against alternative explanations.

In *The Choice for Europe* (1998), Moravcsik addressed these questions by investigating the evolution of the EU from 1955 to 1992, from 'Messina to Maastricht'.[3] He asked whether:

1. national preferences were driven by general geopolitical ideas and interests or by issue-specific (generally economic) interests;

2. substantive bargaining outcomes were shaped by the manipulation of information by supranational entrepreneurs and information asymmetries or by intergovernmental bargaining on the basis of asymmetrical interdependence;

3. the choice of EU institutions reflected federalist ideology, the need for technocratic management, or an interest in securing credible member state commitments.

The basic argument of choice, in its most condensed form, is that

EU integration can best be understood as a series of rational choices made by national leaders. These choices responded to constraints and opportunities stemming from the economic interests of powerful domestic constituents, the *relative power* of states stemming from asymmetrical interdependence, and the role of institutions in bolstering the *credibility of interstate commitments*.

Moravcsik (1998: 18, italics added)

Let us consider each of these three stages in turn, and the precise reasons why Moravcsik and other liberal intergovernmentalists have reached these theoretical conclusions.

National Preferences

Despite the wide range of domestic actors involved in preference formation—and often the wide range of actors involved in foreign policy-making itself—LI continues to treat the state as a unitary actor because it assumes that domestic political bargaining, representation, and diplomacy generate a consistent preference function.[4] According to liberal theories of international relations, 'the foreign policy goals of national governments vary in response to shifting pressure from domestic social groups, whose preferences are aggregated through political institutions' (Moravcsik 1993: 481). The fundamental goals of states—or 'state preferences'—are neither fixed nor uniform: they vary among states and within the same state across time and issues according to issue-specific societal interdependence and domestic institutions (Moravcsik 2008).

The key here is the term 'issue-specific'. Note that LI's basic theoretical claim is not—contrary to common misunderstanding—that 'producer interests prevail' or 'economics dominates policy'. It is that state preferences are driven by issue-specific preference functions about how to manage globalization, not linkage to general policy concerns. The appropriate issue-specific model differs by substantive issue. In economic issue areas, the proper model of the national interest generally derives from a balance or equilibrium between producer interests (insider business and workers), on the one hand, and taxpayers and those interested in regulation, on the other (Grossman and Helpman 1994). The latter will loom larger in areas where the regulatory component is more salient, such as environmental policy, immigration, and development aid. In non-economic issue areas (e.g. foreign policy), the economic element may be far less important in the issue-specific calculation and the issue dominated by non-economic concerns (Wincott 1995; Moravcsik 1995, 1998: 26, 50).

In the specific case of the European Union, where most of the initial policy issues were indeed economic and the prospect of internal warfare among democratic capitalist states was remote, Moravcsik's empirical analysis confirms that the preferences of national governments regarding European integration have mainly reflected concrete economic interests rather than other general concerns like security or European ideals. Moravcsik finds that, initially, the central impetus for post-war European integration arose from the great post-Second World War shift from north–south inter-industry trade and investment (i.e. exchanges of manufactures for primary goods) to north–north intra-industry trade and investment (i.e. exchanges of similar manufactures or commodities) (Milward 2000). Concrete preferences emerged 'from a process of domestic conflict in which specific sectoral interests, adjustment costs and, sometimes, geopolitical concerns played an important role' (Moravcsik 1998: 3). Governments pursued integration as 'a means to secure commercial advantages for producer groups, subject to regulatory and budgetary constraints' and 'the macro-economic preferences of ruling governmental coalitions' (Moravcsik 1998: 3, 38). This was true even in certain cases almost universally believed to be dictated by geopolitical and ideological concerns, such as General de Gaulle's opposition to British membership and supranational institutions.

Yet economic interests do not tell the whole story: Moravcsik points out that geopolitical interests (even more than ideology) also had an important impact on European integration. Of the 15 cases (five decisions across three countries) studied in *The Choice for Europe*, forces of economic globalization played an important role in all, yet in fully half geopolitics and ideology had an important secondary impact. In at least three cases, significant outcomes might have been reversed without them (Moravcsik 1998: 474). Overall, Moravcsik concludes, 'naked economic preferences would probably have led to a highly institutionalized pan-European free trade area with flanking policies of regulatory harmonization and monetary stabilization' (Moravcsik 1998: 6).

Substantive Bargains

The national preferences of different states rarely converge precisely. To explain the nature of substantive outcomes of international negotiations among states with different national preferences, LI deploys (following rationalist institutionalism) a bargaining theory of international cooperation. States must overcome collectively suboptimal outcomes and achieve coordination or cooperation for mutual benefit, yet at the same time they must decide how the mutual gains of cooperation are distributed among the states. Collective and individual interest often conflict, with hard bargaining over distributional gains sapping the willingness and ability of states to cooperate. In this context, bargaining theory argues that the outcome of international negotiations, that is, whether and on which terms cooperation comes about, depends on the relative bargaining power of the actors.

Bargaining power in international politics, as in social life, may result from many factors. LI posits that in the EU context, asymmetrical interdependence, that is, the uneven distribution of the benefits of a specific agreement (compared to those of unilateral or alternative possibilities known as 'outside options') and information about preferences and agreements play a crucial role. Generally, those actors that are least in need of a specific agreement, relative to the status quo, are best able to threaten the others with non-cooperation and thereby force them to make concessions; and those actors that have more and better information about other actors' preferences and the workings of institutions are able to manipulate the outcome to their advantage.

LI seeks to explain the efficiency of bargaining and the distribution of gains from substantive cooperation among states whose preferences have been explained. The historical data in *The Choice for Europe* portrays processes of hard bargaining, in which credible threats to veto proposals, to withhold financial side-payments, and to form alternative alliances excluding recalcitrant governments carried the day. The distributive outcomes reflected the relative power of states based on patterns of asymmetrical interdependence: those who gained the most economically from integration, relative to unilateral and collective alternatives, compromised the most on the margin to realize gains, whereas those who gained the least (or for whom the costs of adaptation or alternatives were highest) tended to enjoy more clout to impose conditions (Moravcsik 1998: 3).

This account downplays the role of informational asymmetries in bargaining, thereby challenging traditional accounts of integration emphasizing potential inefficiencies in bargaining. Both federalists and neofunctionalist accounts have stressed the role of 'ideational entrepreneurs' such as the Commission president and federal idealists like Jean Monnet and Jacques Delors. Such theories are based on the assumption, sometimes implicit, that the costs of negotiating (transaction costs) are high and that entrepreneurs armed with better information, ideas, prestige, or contacts are therefore able to influence national governments (Sandholtz and Zysman 1989; Ross 1995; cf. Moravcsik 1999a, b). LI argues, in contrast, that such third parties are usually not required to reach efficient interstate agreements, precisely because they rarely possess information or expertise unavailable to states. Moravcsik's empirical research transaction costs in Europe are generally low relative to the substantive benefits states receive from cooperation and their capacity to provide entrepreneurship on their own behalf. Information and ideas are plentiful and relatively symmetrically distributed among states: there is little evidence that states are less informed or equipped to act than other actors. Given a positive array of state preferences, decentralized interstate negotiations in the EU reliably produce efficient outcomes, with few potential gains 'left on the table'. To be sure, in exceptional cases, supranational entrepreneurs have appeared to have been required for efficient bargaining outcomes to emerge; the Single Act of 1986 appears to have been one such case (Moravcsik 1999a).

Institutional Choice

To explain the establishment and design of international institutions, once a substantive agreement is struck, IR rationalist institutionalism relies mainly on a 'regime-theoretical' account. This perspective conceives of international institutions as instruments to cope with unintended, unforeseen, and often unwanted consequences. LI follows 'neoliberal institutionalism' (Keohane and Nye 1977) in stipulating that international institutions are often necessary conditions for durable international cooperation. In this respect, LI concurs with some claims traditionally attributed to neofunctionalist (or historical institutionalist) theory: states deliberately delegate authority to supranational organizations capable of acting against the subsequent preferences of governments (cf. Fligstein and Stone Sweet 2001: 1208); and institutions incorporate unintended, and unwanted consequences under conditions of uncertainty—an essential component of regime theory (Keohane 1984; cf. Pierson 1996).[5]

Above all, however, institutions help states reach a collectively superior outcome by reducing the transaction costs of further international negotiations on specific issues and by providing the necessary information to reduce the states' uncertainty about each other's future preferences and behaviour. States establish rules for the distribution of gains according to the pre-existing bargain and reduce the costs of coordinating their activities, monitoring the behaviour of others, and mutually sanctioning non-compliance. Accordingly, issue-specific problems of cooperation caused by, above all, the severity of distributional conflict and enforcement problems and by uncertainty about the preferences of other actors and the future states of the world, require and yield different institutional designs (Koremenos *et al.* 2001).

LI argues that issue-specific variation in the delegation and pooling sovereignty reflect the issue-specific concerns of national governments about each other's future ability to comply with the substantive deals reached (either in the sense of strict enforcement or further elaboration of a bargain). Most EU procedures, however, simply set norms and procedures for more efficient bargaining and reduction of uncertainty (Majone 1994). In such cases of pure 'coordination', governments may delegate decisions to common decision-making, or delegate them to the EU—as in the case of some 'standard-setting' decisions—in order to reduce the transaction costs of determining a common solution (Scharpf 1999: 165–6). Cases of outright delegation for this purpose are rare, because governments are generally able to manage such situations.

Cases of more extensive delegation—for example, the use of qualified majority voting, Commission right of proposal, the powers of the European Central Bank, the negotiating mandates of the European Commission, the adjudicatory power of the European Court of Justice, Europe's modest fiscal centralization—are more often aimed at resolving problems of control, sanctioning, and incomplete contracting through credible pre-commitment (Pollack 2003; Franchino 2007). By transferring sovereignty to international institutions, governments effectively remove issues from the varying influence of domestic politics and decentralized intergovernmental control, which might build up pressure for non-compliance if costs for powerful domestic actors are high (Moravcsik 1998: 9, 73).

It is important to remember, however, that the EU differs from national governments in that it has little fiscal capacity (2 per cent of European public spending), no coercive capacity, and an extremely small administration (barely the size of a small European city). Outside of areas like competition, monetary, and trade policy, most EU rules are implemented, administered, and enforced by national officials (Franchino 2007; Moravcsik 2007). The key is credible domestic commitment by strengthening the national executive (Moravcsik 1994) or the national judicial branch (Burley and Mattli 1993; Alter 1998), or the very domestic groups that support the policy in the first place (Bailey *et al.* 1997) vis-à-vis other domestic forces favouring non-compliance. These mechanisms are quite consistent with the liberal view of international relations on which LI is based, in which we expect the most fundamental guarantee of the irreversibility of integration to lie in the evolution and adaptation of national preferences and institutions themselves, not with international regimes (Moravcsik 1998: 493). The process of Europeanization, sometimes seen as a challenge to LI theory, is in fact an essential part of it. European integration is not about replacing the nation state, but about 'rescuing' and adapting it—to use historian Alan Milward's (2000) term—to cope with globalization.

Theoretical Criticism and Scope Conditions

Some object that LI's claim to explain the broad trends in regional integration is exaggerated.[6] First, 'rational-choice institutionalists' charge that LI—after all initially designed as a theory of grand bargains—cannot explain everyday decision-making, and thus is limited to only a small sliver of EU policy-making in which institutions play a disproportionately small role. Second, 'historical institutionalists' (HI) argue that LI focuses only on conscious intergovernmental decision-making at treaty-amending moments, thereby overlooking many 'unintended' or 'undesired' consequences that occur as a result of treaty amendments. Thus, they charge, LI gives a misleading impression of integration as a whole. Third, others point to empirical examples where LI propositions do not seem to hold. To what extent can LI accurately account for European integration as a whole? And where does it reach its limits?

LI is, by assumption, a theory of intergovernmental decision-making under anarchy. It does not explicitly theorize pre-existing institutional rules. Generally this is interpreted to mean, concretely, that LI is narrowly limited to treaty-amending decisions, while other theories such as rational-choice institutionalism are more appropriate to everyday decision-making or interstitial decisions in between formal treaty amendments (Peterson 1995; Pollack 2005). The latter models incorporate richer institutional detail needed to calculate the effects of the specific rules under which nations vote, set agendas, or interact with the European Commission or Parliament (see Chapter 7 this volume; Garrett and Tsebelis 1996). A large literature has emerged based on formal analysis of institutions and of legal procedures and cases, purporting to show the formal reasons why such institutional details may matter, and providing anecdotal evidence that they do.

While these criticisms contain small kernels of theoretical truth, they are overstated. True, LI works best when decision-making is taking place in decentralized settings under a unanimity requirement rather than in settings of delegated or pooled sovereignty under more complex and nuanced decision rules. Yet, recent empirical research suggests that LI theory applies far more broadly than is commonly supposed, including much everyday EU decision-making. The reason is that many decisions within the EU are taken by *de facto* consensus or unanimity, even when the formal rules seem to dictate otherwise.

- The European Council, where member states act by consensus, increasingly initiates EU policy. The Council has increased its relative influence in recent decades, taking over from the Commission as de facto agenda-setter for the EU (Ludlow 1991).

- In the EU legislative process, the Council of Ministers rarely votes, but instead acts by informal consensus, even in considering basic economic legislation. The presidency seeks an informal consensus, often negotiating with recalcitrant states until agreement is reached—a process decisively shaped by LI factors such as ideal points, national preference intensities, and the resulting credibility of veto threats.

- When the Council of Ministers does vote, it formally decides under supermajoritarian (70 per cent) rules—a threshold higher than that required to amend most national constitutions. Hence, recent empirical studies suggest, the basic factors highlighted by LI theory such as ideal points, asymmetrical interdependence, and alternatives to agreement, generally remain dominant structural elements in any understanding of institutional process, whereas factors like precise institutional design, the composition of the Parliament, or the views of the Commission appear to have almost no impact on outcomes (cf. Garrett and Tsebelis 1996; Achen 2006). Nor do these tests suggest that the relative size of governments—a variable stressed by realist integration theorists like Joseph Grieco but not by LI—is of much importance (Grieco 1996).

- There are many other areas of EU decision-making where informal, consensual decision-making appears to prevail, including: the 'second and third pillars' of the EU (Common Foreign and Security Policy and Justice and Home Affairs), where governments can opt out, and incremental changes in the scope of legislation that take place by unanimous decision under general clauses of the Treaty of Rome, and intergovernmental 'comitology' procedures that oversee implementation, though the latter are less well-understood (Zeitlin and Pochet 2005).

This is not to say, of course, that LI explains everything or that institutional design never matters in EU policy. Indeed, the stress placed by LI theory itself on the deliberate delegation and pooling of sovereignty implies that institutions matter. Obviously many detailed EU legal procedures of delegate authority, for example central banking, supranational adjudication, and competition policy, all presume semi-autonomous legal power. Still, the analysis above implies that LI theory applies far beyond 'treaty-amending decisions', well into the realm of everyday EU decision-making.

Some critics offer an even sharper criticism. Proponents of historical (or supranational) institutionalism object that an analysis of the EU's constitutional evolution that only examines intergovernmental decisions that advance integration is incomplete.

HI theorists concede to LI that governments enter rationally into grand bargains. Yet once they do so, such agreements may have unanticipated or undesired consequences. These consequences will be difficult to redress, moreover, because domestic societal and institutional actors will have made costly adaptations to new circumstances (Pierson 1996: 30–4).

Underlying such claims are two dynamics. One is a drift in national preferences. Prior bargains may seem inconvenient if national preferences suddenly shift, perhaps after a change in government, a major economic shock, or policy learning. The other is a drift in the function of institutions. Supranational organizations may also 'work to enhance their own autonomy and influence within the European polity', thereby uncomfortably constraining governments in unexpected ways (Sandholtz and Stone Sweet 1998: 26). If such feedback or spillover dominates integration, the EU's long-term trajectory will only *appear* to be shaped by intergovernmental decisions and LI's structural factors. The real long-term dynamics will be a combination of random external shocks and constrained adaptation that generate a path-dependent process of integration.

The most frequently cited example of the HI dynamic is the assertion of the legal supremacy and autonomy by the European Court of Justice (ECJ). During the 1960s and 1970s, the ECJ interpreted its competences in an integrationist manner unanticipated and initially undesired by governments. This process helped strengthen national courts, private litigants, and occasionally the Commission, thereby influencing the distribution of gains from market liberalization, and encouraging states to accept institutions and enforcement schemes that the ECJ helped design (Burley and Mattli 1993; Alter 1998). Another example is 'interstitial' institutional change beyond and between formal treaty changes (Hix 2002; Stacey and Rittberger 2003; Farell and Héritier 2007). Because treaties are incomplete contracts, they give rise to bargaining between the Council, the Commission, and the Parliament that redistribute competences and prefigure later formal treaty revisions.

In showing that EU institutional arrangements can drift away from initial expectations, HI studies surely have a valid empirical point. Yet we should resist overinterpreting these examples. LI (and 'rational institutionalist' IR theory more generally) not only can explain many such cases and accommodate undesired consequences. In fact, LI assumes their existence! If unanticipated consequences did not exist, there would be no need for international institutions to elaborate 'incomplete contacts' to begin with. The reason for institutions is precisely to elaborate agreements and credibly lock in compliance against defection by future unsatisfied governments.

Anecdotes of unhappy governments and interest groups therefore do not by themselves constitute compelling evidence against LI. Unforeseen or initially undesired policies may change over time simply and as expected by LI due to changes in state preferences, power, and information. Insofar as such interstitial change results from interstate decisions—or tacit intergovernmental consent—it may well be explicable by LI. This is the case even if other actors, such as the European Parliament, are involved in their elaboration, and regardless of whether or not the change is ratified by treaty amendment. It quite often simply reflects the working out of the uncertainty and indeterminacy inherent in the initial bargain—or any political process. The question, therefore, is whether this uncertainty is so great as to divert integration fundamentally from its course, as HI theory suggests.

This is an empirical question—and one in which the evidence tends to support the LI position (Kleine 2008). Fundamental shifts in the integration process without the consensual support of the member states or threats of exclusion—the critical factors predicted by LI—remain modest. State preference functions regarding integration have tended to be rather stable over time. Governments foresaw many policy consequences often said to be unforeseen: the Common Agricultural Poilcy, for example—the case that led Fritz Scharpf to apply the HI ('joint decision trap') model to the EU, on which Pierson draws—cannot plausibly be viewed as an unintended consequence, since European governments were quite aware of the consequences of their actions (Scharpf 1988: 251; Pierson 1996: 144; Moravcsik 1998). The past 15 years of EU politics have disconfirmed, for example, the central prediction of Paul Pierson's otherwise admirably rigorous article on HI, namely that the EU Social Protocol has 'tremendous' potential to generate 'unanticipated consequences' (Pierson 1996: 155; also Pierson and Leibfried 1995).

Still, it is important to note that LI is not a universal theory. LI explains integration under most conditions, but not under those that violate its assumptions about preferences, bargaining, and credible commitments. One of the advantages of employing more explicit theory is that we can be more precise about its scope: the scope of a theory is defined by its assumptions; where they do not obtain, the theory does not apply. Two such limitations are important to keep in mind.

First, LI best explains policy-making in issue areas where social preferences are relatively certain and well defined. The LI explanation of state preferences, which focuses on issue-specific societal interests concerning interdependence, should work better, the 'more intense, certain, and institutionally represented and organized' those societal pressures are (Moravcsik 1998: 36) and the less 'uncertainty there is about cause–effect relations' (Moravcsik 1999a: 171). Conversely, 'the weaker and more diffuse the domestic constituency behind a policy' (ibid.) and the more uncertain or modest are 'the substantive implications of a choice', the less predictable are national preferences and the more likely ideological preferences and beliefs, or other factors, may be influential (Moravcsik 1998: 486–9; Moravcsik and Nicolaïdis 1999: 61). Thus LI advances a second-order prediction: the variance of outcomes should be correlated with the underlying uncertainty in the circumstances being analysed.

This is precisely what we observe. Across EU policies, the most reliably predictable national preference functions are those in agriculture and trade, where economic preferences are stable. Countries have held consistent preference functions for decades, shifting incrementally in response to changing market conditions and more suddenly in response to overt policy failures (Moravcsik 1998: 493). Similarly, the logic of credible commitment obtains where institutional delegation and pooling has modest and diffuse consequences with generally positive-sum consequences. Where national preferences involve large and predictable downside risks, we observe the construction of international institutions that maintain national prerogatives (Kleine 2008). Thus in agriculture, the member states privilege the status of national ministers, restrict the role of the European Parliament, and employ voting rules that maintain tighter national control (Moravcsik 1998: 488). Less predictable are national preferences in economic areas such as monetary policy, where economic knowledge is more uncertain and the distribution of costs and benefits more diffuse. Beliefs about the efficacy of monetary policy strategies may have mattered as much as underlying political economy (McNamara 2002). Even less predictable are the politics of constitutional reform in circumstances, such as the recent European Constitutional deliberations, where substantive concerns are not invariably salient. Recent EU constitutional deliberations since 2001 have been overwhelmed by such shifting and weak ideological beliefs (Moravcsik 2006).

Second, intergovernmental bargaining based on asymmetrical interdependence dominates interstate bargaining except in rare conditions of high transaction costs and asymmetrical information, when supranational entrepreneurs may wield influence. Basic theories of bargaining, negotiation, and international regimes predict that decentralized non-coercive negotiations will be more efficient where information is plentiful and distributed widely (Coase 1960). Only when governments lack critical information, expertise, bargaining skills, and legitimacy that third parties can provide are the latter likely to be influential. Moravcsik argues that entrepreneurship—or formal institutionalization—is required not so much in situations where international bargaining is complex, difficult or new, per se, but when domestic coordination problems are severe (1999a: 282–5). In Moravcsik's analysis, the Single European Act (SEA) is the only major case in which these conditions have applied, and even then only partially. The failure of European multinational firms to discover their common interests and to organize for effective collective action, and the failure of interest groups and domestic ministers to aggregate the numerous bureaucratically disparate proposals into an integrated internal market package, gave supranational entrepreneurs in the Commission and the Parliament a comparative advantage in initiating the SEA, mobilizing a latent transnational constituency, and generating a more efficient outcome (Moravcsik 1999a: 292–8).

To illustrate these basic points about LI's scope and empirical power, we now consider an 'easy' and a harder case for the theory.

An Easy Case: Agriculture

The easy case is the initial creation of the Common Market during the 1960s: the removal of internal tariffs and quotas, and the harmonization of external barriers into a common external trade policy, as well as the creation of the Common Agricultural Policy (CAP). Agriculture is an 'easy' case because it creates ideal conditions for the application of LI, which works well when there are certain and intense preferences, clear positive-sum benefits, and clear credible commitment problems. To this day, the CAP remains a core element of the 'European bargain' and continues to consume the better part of the EU's budget. It remains among the most important single foreign economic policies pursued by any industrialized government today—fundamentally shaping the domestic and global political economy of developing nations, as well as transatlantic relations. Farmers' associations have intense preferences, are highly organized, and exercise a strong influence on governments. In no country does public policy stray far from their demands—an ideal condition for the application of LI.

The initial task in any LI analysis is to explain state preferences by understanding the structure of issue-specific domestic societal interests—in this case economic ones. In agriculture, more than any other sector, national preferences were skewed toward producer interests, due to the large size and highly organized nature of the farm sector, and the diffuse and unorganized groups of taxpayers and consumers who were forced to foot the bill. In the 1960s, state preferences concerning a common agricultural policy varied strongly among the major governments and were closely related to producer preferences on agricultural trade inside and beyond the EC. Internal documents, overt domestic unrest and pressure, and the willingness of the government to take diplomatic risks suggest that the French preferences were particularly intense. This reflected importance of the agricultural sector in the three countries: 'Farming employed 25 percent of Frenchmen, 15 percent of Germans, and only 5 percent of Britons. Germany and Britain were large net importers but only marginal exporters of agricultural goods' (Moravcsik 1998: 89–90), while France was a large surplus producer and exporter. Whereas Germany and Britain were uncompetitive in agriculture, French exports were expected to benefit greatly from intra-EC liberalization as long as high prices relative to the world market were guaranteed. Britain as a net importer was interested in maintaining its preferential agreement with the Commonwealth in order to buy agricultural products at relatively low prices. By contrast, Germany with its still sizeable and politically influential agricultural sector 'sought to maintain high support prices behind protective barriers' (Moravcsik 1998: 98). National preferences mirrored the size and competitiveness of commodity sectors: France 'most intensely favored liberalization of commodities trade within a preferential European zone with modest support prices', yet 'strongly opposed agricultural trade liberalization in the GATT'. Germany opposed internal liberalization 'unless very high common support prices were paid' but 'was prepared to make GATT concessions . . . that preserved domestic arrangements': Britain was 'sceptical of any agricultural policy' and favoured a liberalization of global agricultural trade instead (Moravcsik 1998: 161).

Turning from preferences formation to interstate bargaining, LI would predict that France's comparatively strong interest in creating the CAP would place it in an inferior bargaining position on this issue. It needed to give up more, or press its neighbours more, in order to secure agreement. How exactly did this work? The conventional story is that it occurred through issue-linkage, that is, by France offering concessions on entirely unrelated issues it was less interested in. The French government linked the acceleration of internal tariff removal to a schedule for the adoption of the CAP, threatening to block industrial liberalization if Germany did not give up its favoured bilateral agricultural trade agreements, and 'held up the EC's mandate for the Kennedy round of GATT negotiations to force German concessions on the CAP' (Moravcsik 1998: 206–8). Yet the extent to which any country can impose losses on other interest groups in the name of cross-issue linkage is limited by this group's ability to organize and exert pressure. French industrialists did not really oppose the EEC or GATT agreement, nor did German farmers oppose the CAP: there was thus no real quid pro quo at the level of sectoral interests.

The more fundamental story of the CAP, according to Moravcsik, was instead one of convergence of interest—collusion—between German and French farming interests at the expense of French and German consumers, taxpayers, and technocrats, as well as third-country (e.g. US) producers and the European Commission. French farmers gained preferential access to German markets and higher support prices. In exchange, the CAP was structured on terms that suited German farmers: long transition periods for bilateral quotas, high subsidies, and price supports. Even the modest disadvantage to a few German farmers from slightly lower wheat prices was more than offset by extremely high EU support prices for animal products, the mainstay of German agriculture, resulting in a massive increase in overall German production and exports (Moravcsik 1998: 212–13). The real opponents to this deal were not German farmers but neoliberal finance officials like Ludwig Erhard. To persuade them, de Gaulle worked hard to create the appearance of a credible threat that he would withdraw from the EU entirely if the CAP were not created. Yet he was careful never to put himself in a position of having to make good on the threat—when he threatened to, French farmers rebelled and he backed down (Moravcsik 2001b: 37, 2001c: 53). Here—and only here, that is, within the context of an acceptable political economy bargain—did geopolitical ideology play a role, in the form of de Gaulle's efforts to embarrass German politicians into accepting a deal by threatening to undermine the EEC.

This bargaining outcome demonstrates, furthermore, the near total lack of influence by the European Commission influence as a 'supranational entrepreneur'. To be sure, the Commission was involved in the negotiations throughout, and generations of analysts have mistaken involvement for real influence (cf. Lindberg 1963). Hence the 'closed', high-priced comprehensive, and administratively decentralized agricultural policy was 'the precise opposite of what the Commission had sought'. The Commission always favoured, as it does to this day, a liberal, self-financing, more centralized policy to further the structural adjustment (Moravcsik 1998: 205–6, 161). One reason why the Commission had little power is that member states were in fact better informed about each others' preferences and about the intricacies of agricultural policy than was the Commission; they easily defeated the proposals of Commissioner Mansholt (Moravcsik 1998: 230–2). Convergence of interest and relative bargaining power, not entrepreneurship by insiders, dictated the final outcome.

Turning finally to institutional choice, preferences and behaviour in the creation of the common market reflected concerns about credible commitment, as LI predicts. Again, the establishment of the CAP provides a clear example. Despite its allegedly federalist attitudes, the German government resisted qualified majority voting on the CAP because it feared being forced into lower levels of protection for its agricultural producers. In spite of its purportedly ideological aversion to supranational institutions, France under de Gaulle insisted on a centralized CAP and external trade policy in order to assure German compliance and to lock in permanent financing at high price levels before Britain was admitted. EU agricultural policy was from the start to be decided by unanimity vote without a right of proposal for the Commission—a textbook setting for hard intergovernmental bargaining. Since then agriculture has been subject to a particular form of representation in which national agriculture ministers have direct influence unequalled in other specific issue-areas. From an LI perspective, this institutional 'capture' is endogenous. It is precisely because agricultural interests are so strong, and because nearly all industrialized governments are committed to their subsidization where necessary, that they are privileged in EU-level negotiations.

A More Difficult Case: Liberal Intergovernmentalism and Enlargement

Decisions to 'widen' the EU, just like treaty amendments to 'deepen' the EU, involve intergovernmental negotiations under unanimity. Yet they are more complex for LI to explain. While enlargement triggers some intense and concrete distributional issues, particularly for new members, whose entire economic orientation may depend on membership, and for existing members—EU budgetary flows and trade and investment issues being matters of some importance—the interests involved for existing members are in other ways more diffuse. Existing policies as well as the acquis communautaire generally remain unchanged, the overall size of the new members is generally small compared to the existing EU and, in any case, any net EU budgetary impact is small compared to national budgets or positive trade effects. The result is to render this a somewhat more ambiguous case for LI theory—in which costs and benefits, and thus state calculations, are more imprecise.

Still, LI predicts that members will calculate the advantages of enlargement in terms of the costs and benefits of socioeconomic interdependence of various types. New members will strongly seek membership in an existing trade bloc, while existing members will move more slowly to promote enlargement, led by those whose interdependence relationship with potential new members is the most positive. They would also exploit their superior bargaining power with applicants to impose conditions, create exceptions and transition periods, and provide side payments, thereby mitigating disadvantages to those existing members who directly compete with new members for subsidies or markets.

In *The Choice for Europe*, only the issue of British membership in the 1960s is analysed in some detail (Moravcsik 1998: 164–220). According to Moravcsik, both British desire for membership and French opposition to it were economically motivated. Whereas Britain's commercial interests were harmed by exclusion from the customs union, France feared low-price commercial competition and, most of all, British opposition to the CAP. This interpretation challenges the conventional view that de Gaulle was opposed to British entry for ideological or geopolitical reasons having to do with anti-Americanism, NATO, or resentments left over from the Second World War. (Only the explanation of German support for the French opposition to British membership has to resort to geopolitical interests: its economic interests were closer to the British than to the French.) France dropped its opposition only after the CAP was established. Even then the French government demanded a permanent financing arrangement for the CAP as a condition of UK entry. In the negotiations on British membership, the British bargaining position was weak because Britain 'was more commercially dependent on the Six than vice versa' (Moravcsik 1998: 220). Britain preferred membership to exclusion and was therefore willing to make major concessions to France, which had little economic interest in British membership and could thus extract those concessions (mainly on the CAP) in exchange for giving up its veto (Mattli 1999; Gstöhl 2002).

What about the Eastern enlargement of the EU in recent years? We begin with national preference formation. Member states took a range of positions, which can be largely—but not entirely—explained by their patterns of interdependence, geographical position, and economic structure (Schimmelfennig 2001). These positions diverged on both the speed and extent of preferred enlargement: along the dimension of speed, 'drivers' advocated an early and firm commitment to Eastern enlargement, whereas 'brakemen' were reticent and tried to put off the decision; along the second dimension of extent, one group of member states pushed for a limited (first) round of enlargement focusing on the central European states, whereas others favoured an inclusive approach for all 10 candidates (see Table 4.1).

The distribution of enlargement preferences largely mirrors the geographical position of the member states. Except for Greece and Italy, the countries bordering on central and eastern Europe were the drivers of enlargement; except for Britain, the more remote countries were the brakemen. This is as LI would predict, since the member states' geographical position can be understood as a proxy variable for 'the imperatives induced by interdependence and, in particular, the . . . exogenous increase in opportunities for cross-border trade and capital movements' that should determine national preferences according to Moravcsik (1998: 26). Member states on the eastern border of the EU are both more likely to benefit from trade with central and eastern Europe, and have a greater interest in managing negative externalities—unwanted immigration, social problems, crime, pollution—that might cross borders in the absence of integration. The negative position of countries like Italy and Greece, despite their border position, reflects the potential losses enlargement imposed via trade and budgetary competition on the poorer, less highly developed, and more agricultural among existing members—as LI predicts. Less-developed member states were likely to be more adversely affected by competition over the EU agricultural and structural fund budget, as well as by trade integration with the East, since they specialize in the same traditional and resource-intensive industries (like agriculture, textile, and leather as well as metalworking) as the CEE economies (Hagen 1996: 6–7).

Geopolitical or ideological interests seem to have been decisive in some cases, particularly, as LI predicts, where governments lack no intense economic interest. Some member states acted on the fear that future Central and Eastern European (CEE) members would side with Germany in EU decision-making, a standard interpretation of French reticence towards enlargement (see e.g. Grabbe and Hughes 1998: 5), but emphasis on the Mediterranean region may have affected the Greek and Italian positions, too. Central and eastern Europe is neither geographically close nor economically important to Britain, yet Britain pushed for expansion. Some attribute British commitment to enlargement to the Europhobia of the Conservative governments, which calculated that widening the EU would prevent its further deepening and even dilute the achieved level of integration

Table 4.1 Member state enlargement preferences

	'Small bang' (Limited enlargement)	'Big bang' (Inclusive enlargement)
Drivers (quickly)	Austria, Finland, Germany	Britain, Denmark, Sweden
Brakemen (slowly)	Belgium, Luxembourg, Netherlands	France, Greece, Ireland, Italy, Portugal, Spain

(see e.g. Grabbe and Hughes 1998: 5), though insiders report that Britain favoured the need to stabilize Europe to tragedies such as Yugoslavia (Wall 2008). Still, LI goes far toward predicting the nature of state preferences for and against Eastern enlargement.

Turning from national preference formation to interstate bargaining, Moravcsik and Milada Vachudova successfully apply LI theory to recent Eastern enlargement and argue that it resembles the British case. Whereas market expansion is usually profitable to members and non-members alike, non-members generally benefit more, due to their enormous one-sided dependence on EU markets. The collective GNP of all 10 Eastern candidates is below 5 per cent of that of the current members, and whereas the share of EU exports and imports of the total foreign trade of the candidates rose to between 50 and 70 per cent in the 1990s, their share of EU foreign trade remained below 5 per cent. The inflow of Western capital is critical for the CEE economies whereas the impact of Eastern economies in the Western economies is far smaller—easing their adaptation and increasing their bargaining power.

Moravcsik and Vachudova argue that asymmetrical interdependence had decisive implications for bargaining over enlargement. 'Applicant countries . . . consistently found themselves in a weak negotiating position vis-a-via their EU partners, and accordingly have conceded much in exchange for membership' (Haggard and Moravcsik 1993; Moravcsik and Vachudova 2002: 3; 2003). Given their inevitably strong dependency on the EU market and EU capital, the candidates preferred accepting the EU's conditions of accession to being excluded from EU membership. These include not only the adoption of the acquis communautaire but also initially lower subsidies from the EU budget than current members and transition periods on some rights such as the free movement of labour. These 'special provisions reflect the demands of narrow special interests or the concerns of voting publics in the existing members' (Moravcsik and Vachudova 2002: 10), which they could force upon the candidates thanks to their superior bargaining position. For the candidates, it was nonetheless rational to accept these conditions. The EU used transitional restrictions to exclude the new member states temporarily from benefits that are likely to affect old member states negatively. The accession negotiations on Eastern enlargement thus resulted in temporary restrictions of the free movement of labour and the phasing in of agricultural subsidies over a 10-year period.

Whereas LI theorists convincingly explain the preferences and substantive bargains that accompanied enlargement, LI is less clear about institutional choice. Given the high asymmetrical interdependence in their favour and the distributional conflicts among them, why did the member states not stick with 'association' regime that they initially negotiated with the CEE countries? The association regime enabled the potential winners of integration to intensify their economic involvement in CEE markets and, at the same time, protected the potential losers against the costs of trade and budget competition, and permitted greater protection of vulnerable sectors.

Some argue that association did not occur because member states were predominantly interested in a secure and stable neighbourhood (Skålnes 2005). This could be achieved much better through the strong incentives and ties of membership rather than through association. When the wars broke out in former Yugoslavia, the EU therefore decided to prepare for enlargement, and in the aftermath of the war in Kosovo, it expanded the membership perspective to the western Balkans. Frank Schimmelfennig (2001, 2003b) claims, by contrast, that its identity as a liberal democratic community, which is reflected in the treaty rules on enlargement and the Copenhagen Criteria for accession countries, obliged the EU to admit democratic European countries as full members if they so desire. Still, LI explains much of what we observe, even in the case of enlargement.

The European Union Today

LI theory sheds light on the most striking aspect of European integration today: its substantive and institutional stability. Despite the constitutional debacle of recent years, there seems to exist a 'European Constitutional Settlement'—a stable substantive, institutional, and normative plateau within which incremental EU policy-making is occurring. The Amsterdam, Nice, and Lisbon Treaties, unlike the Single Act or Maastricht, did not contain major substantive reforms. Instead they mark incremental movement along slow trends toward reforms within the existing constitutional structure, such as the strengthening the Council and Parliament, deepening of certain intergovernmental functions outside the first pillar, such as foreign policy and defence, and enlargement of the Union and certain policies, such as Schengen (Moravcsik 2007). Even the proposed Constitution and now the Treaty of Lisbon, despite its rhetorical grandeur, is a conservative document. The only major project in recent years has been EU enlargement.

The major reason, according to LI, is the absence of national preferences for a functional grand project, akin to the 1992 single market or the single currency, sufficient to motivate cooperation. The EU's constitutional convention in 2003 spent little time even discussing substantive reform. In areas such as social policy, centralized neoliberal reform, and immigration (Norman 2003)—attractive though they may be to philosophers as potential vehicles for legitimation (Habermas 1997). Absent a major and unforeseen exogenous shock, the EU is likely to develop incrementally, improving and reforming policies within the current confederal constitutional framework, with member states ruling by quasi-consensus and fiscal, administrative, and coercive powers decentralized to the states. Political control over the major fiscal activities of the modern state—policies like taxation, social welfare, health care provision, pensions, infrastructure, education, criminal prosecution, defence spending, and, therefore, immigration and citizenship—are likely to remain national.

Some believe this equilibrium is unstable. They charge that the EU suffers from a 'democratic deficit' that will generate a backlash from angry European citizens. LI's focus on national interest leads naturally to the contrary assessment. Checks and balances between EU institutions,

indirect democratic control via national governments, and the increasing powers of the European Parliament are sufficient to ensure that EU policy-making is, in nearly all cases, clean, transparent, effective and politically responsive to the demands of European citizens.

Moravcsik (2002: 605)

National governments still call the tune in European integration, pursuing diverse national interests, bargaining hard amongst themselves, and institutionalizing integration to retain control. In the exceptional cases where EU policy-making is salient for some subset of the population—trade policy, CAP reform, GMOs, services deregulation, immigration, constitutional reform, domestic defence reform, right down to a relatively minor issue like the recognition of Kosovo—European governments remain responsive to publics. Polls suggest that, across Europe, the EU is as or more trusted or popular than national governments. The lack of saliency of EU issues in the minds of Europeans is the main reason why they do not participate actively in European-level elections or debates (Moravcsik 2007: 41). Much of what is perceived as a democratic deficit stems from the general unpopularity of government, and from the unfortunate decision to force unnecessary public debates and referenda about a confusing constitutional reforms (Moravcsik 2006). Overall, rather than undermining the nation state, intergovernmentalists stress the role of the EU in assuring its 'survival' and 'endurance' (Hoffmann 1995: 89, 102), 'rescue' (Milward 2000), and 'strengthening' (Moravcsik 1994).

Some convinced European federalists reject this scenario. They believe that the EU must keep moving toward federal union or risk collapse, colloquially referred to as the 'bicycle theory', according to which 'you must keep moving forward lest you fall off'. This is unduly pessimistic. Every constitutional system reaches a point where it is mature, when it no longer needs to move forward to remain stable. The EU has reached that point. The EU is not a state in the making; it is the most ambitious and successful of multilateral organizations. To acknowledge this in no way diminishes its world-historical importance: the EU is the epitome of multilateral governance and, as such, its success is something that historians may well look back on for centuries as an epochal achievement.

Conclusion: Avenues for Dialogue and Synthesis

Liberal intergovernmentalism is open to dialogue and synthesis with other theories of integration. One reason why LI is open to such a synthesis is that it itself is a synthesis of rationalist theories: it combines theories of preference formation, bargaining, and institutions. Also, as we have seen, it shares elements of traditional intergovernmentalist and neofunctionalist thinking on the EU.

Synthesis is easiest where contending theories share LI's rationalist foundations and its empirical (positivist) methodological commitments. We have seen that LI's scope is much broader than it is often believed—because EU institutions are more consensual than their formal structure suggests. Still, where formal institutions matter, LI coexists well with rational-choice institutionalism, with which it shares basic theoretical and methodological assumptions (Pollack 2001, 2003, and Chapter 7 in this volume). Where historical institutionalist theory, which also shares rationalist foundations, is empirically correct—as in explaining the ECJ—it is also better seen as extension of LI than as an alternative to it.[7] This is because a reliable model of individual decisions, such as that provided by LI, is a necessary precondition for modelling the feedback of institutions on states' strategies. Without such a model, one would not know which type of feedback matters or how it matters.[8] As Caporaso (2007) points out, current HI theories (like neofunctionalist accounts) are unable to predict which interstitial changes will be undesired without such a basis. Pierson accepts LI's short-run analysis: 'At any given point in time, the key propositions of intergovernmentalist theory are likely to hold' (Pierson 1996: 126).

Yet, as the enlargement case demonstrates, LI can even be synthesized with ideational explanations borrowing from social constructivism (cf. Checkel 2001a, c; Moravcsik 2001d, e). Moravcsik states that ideological concerns and linkages to other concerns, such as geopolitics, are likely to play a stronger role when economic interests are weak and cause–effect relations are uncertain. Some argue that identity- and norm-based community effects are more likely to exert an influence on substantive outcomes and institutions if an issue has a strong constitutive or identity dimension, the norms involved have high legitimacy in the EU and resonate strongly with domestic ideas of the actors (Schimmelfennig 2003b). Constitutional politics issues as the parliamentarization of the EU and the institutionalization of human rights at the EU level are other promising areas (Rittberger and Schimmelfennig 2006).

These avenues for dialogue and synthesis should not obscure, however, the centrality of LI for the theory and explanation of European integration. There are obvious theoretical reasons why this is so. LI is parsimonious and general, using a limited number of parameters (in particular the domestic issue-specific preference structure of a few major member states) to explain the main substantive and institutional outcomes in the European integration process. It has been tested using high methodological standards, i.e. with testable alternative hypotheses using primary sources. Yet the most important reason for LI centrality is empirical: it tests out. We believe that if one examines issue by issue, there is an expanding empirical consensus that it is the strongest starting point for explaining the basic processes, and outcomes of European integration. Studies of the most consequential EU policies—CAP reform, external trade policy, free movement of people, to name a few—tend to confirm LI variables (e.g. Ludlow 2006).

The empirical dominance of national preferences, asymmetrical interdependence and credible commitments in explaining integration is obscured, in part, by the paradoxical effects of LI's role as a baseline theory. New studies are often framed against these factors. They seek to show that LI does not explain all aspects of European integration—even if often the exceptions are less significant than the rule. This creates the appearance of widespread criticism while in fact conceding LI's status as a baseline.

More insidiously, the literature betrays a selection bias in research topics away from substantively important issues (like agriculture and trade), where LI explains outcomes unproblematically, toward insignificant, exceptional and speculative issues, or secondary and hypothetical institutions. There is disproportionate attention paid to issue areas like social policy, where very little has been accomplished, as opposed to immensely important areas like agriculture, services, and trade. There are many studies of the European Parliament for every one of the massively more influential European Council. New constitutional innovations like the Open Method of Coordination (OMC) attract a broad multidisciplinary research agenda, though the OMC process has achieved—even according to strongest advocates—almost no policy outputs to date (Zeitlin and Pochet 2005).

If scholarship reflected the empirical importance of what the EU actually functions, the baseline status of LI variables would surely be clearer. Were this to be the case, the real debate would likely become more sharply focused as it should be on detailed empirical puzzles about the precise nature of the components: the precise specification of state preferences, interstate bargaining, and institutionalization. We would thus transcend what is perhaps the final vestige of the old style of EU theorizing that dominated the field in 1991: the tendency to frame debates in terms of disagreements among 'grand' theories. The purpose of social science theory, after all, is to transform philosophical debates into empirical ones. The first step is to view the contemporary EU, above all, as the result of deliberate state choice.

■ **NOTES**

1. This chapter builds on a previous version by Frank Schimmelfennig. For comments on various versions, we thank Thomas Diez, Mareike Kleine, Berthold Rittberger, and Antje Wiener. The usual disclaimers apply.

2. This is an increasingly common starting position for analysing international relations. For analyses consistent with it, see Moravcsik (1997), Fearon (1998), Lake and Powell (1999), Milner (1998), Legro (1996).

3. This is the subtitle of Moravcsik's *The Choice for Europe*.

4. This is sometimes misinterpreted as an assumption that domestic actors do not play a significant independent role in negotiations beyond the state. But multiple representation can be consistent with the rational actor model—as long as it is consistent with a preference ordering.

5. Pierson's otherwise admirable analysis simply misunderstands conventional rationalist explanations of European integration on this point. They do not assume that governments foresee the outcomes of negotiated settlements.

6. In focusing on the extent to which LI explains integration as a whole, we have deliberately set aside other criticisms. We have not, for example, addressed concerns by those who reject 'positivist' methodology altogether. Unlike non-positivists, we simply assume that theory can and should be used to understand the real world by evaluating the accuracy of causal propositions about how the EU really works. See the exchange between Diez (1999c) and Moravcsik (1999c).

7. HI theories might be linked and synthesized with other theories through scope conditions specifying their respective 'domain of application'. See Jupille *et al.* (2003: 21–2).

8. The failure to specify such a model clearly long rendered neofunctionalism indeterminate. See Moravcsik (2007).

■ **GUIDE TO FURTHER READING**

Hoffmann, S. (1995) *The European Sisyphus. Essays on Europe, 1964–1994* (Boulder, CO: Westview Press). A collection of essays by the most prominent representative of traditional intergovernmentalism.

Menon, A. (2008) *Europe: The State of the Union* (London: Atlantic). A jargon-free introduction to the EU stressing the enduring role of the member states in its everyday operation and constitutional evolution.

Milward, A. (2000) *The European Rescue of the Nation-State,* 2nd edn (London: Routledge).

A classic work by the most important post-war historian of the European integration process, who stresses its role in strengthening the post-war European state's capacity to manage globalization.

Moravcsik, A. (1998) *The Choice for Europe. Social Purpose and State Power from Messina to Maastricht* (Ithaca, NJ: Cornell University Press). This book represents the most complete outline of liberal intergovernmentalist theory and a detailed analysis of five major cases of European integration from the Treaties of Rome to the Treaty of Maastricht.

— (1993), 'Preferences and power in the European Community. A liberal intergovernmentalist approach', *Journal of Common Market Studies,* 31(4), 473–524. An earlier and shorter explication of liberal intergovernmentalism, which includes the application of 'two-level games' to European integration.

— (2002) 'In defence of the democratic deficit: reassessing legitimacy in the European Union', *Journal of Common Market Studies* (40th Anniversary Edition), 40(4), November. Defends the broad democratic legitimacy of the EU based on indirect democratic controls of various kinds.

— and Nicolaïdis, K. (1999) 'Explaining the Treaty of Amsterdam: interests, influence, institutions', *Journal of Common Market Studies*, 37(1), 59–85. Adds another case of treaty-amending negotiations to the 'Choice for Europe'.

'Review section symposium: The choice for Europe: Social purpose and state power from Messina to Maastricht' (1999), *Journal of European Public Policy* 6(1), 155–79. Unites critiques by important EU scholars and a response by Andrew Moravcsik.

Thomson, R. *et al.* (eds) (2006) *The European Union Decides* (Cambridge: Cambridge University Press). State-of-the-art analysis of EU decision-making, showing that even everyday decisions are dominated by basic preferences, voting weights, and interstate compromise.

■ STUDY QUESTIONS

1. What are the three steps of a liberal intergovernmentalist explanation of European integration outcomes?

2. How does LI differ from traditional intergovernmentalism, and which elements does it adopt from liberal IR theory? Which does it share with neofunctionalist integration theory?

3. Which kind of integration decisions does LI explain best and which steps and characteristics of European integration are less likely to be explained well? Are any decisions entirely outside the scope of LI?

4. Which current policies and institutions of the EU are most (least) in line with LI? Why?

5. Would LI currently expect a major new step of European integration? In which area would it be most likely?

6. How do LI theorists answer the critics of the EU's supposed 'democratic deficit'? Where might they nonetheless see a problem?

PART TWO

Analysing European Governance

5 Governance Approaches

B. Guy Peters and Jon Pierre

Introduction

This chapter addresses the capacity of the European Union (EU) to govern effectively. All societies require some form or another of governance, but the meaning of the concept of governance and its implications for the steering of real societies remains contested (see Pierre 2000; Tiihonen 2005). This squabbling is more than merely academic, given that the conception of governance is also to some extent normative, defining how the process *should* be undertaken as well as how it is done. In the European context the capacity to govern (Painter and Pierre 2005) also influences directly the ability of this system to maintain its progress toward greater economic and political integration.

Despite that squabbling, academic and otherwise, the fundamental argument of this chapter is that utilizing the governance perspective provides a set of important insights into European integration, as well as the capacity of the EU to fulfil the goals and dreams of its leaders, and of its citizens. We might even take the argument further, and posit that the creation of governance capacity for the institutions within the EU is the goal of much of the process of integration. European integration is to some extent an end in itself, but it may also be the means for attaining the capacity to govern a large territory with complex economic and social structures. The political process through which European policies are selected and implemented are complex, involve a number of actors, and may be less determinate even than many national policy processes (Richardson 2004). That complexity does not eliminate the capacity for effective governance, but it does reduce its probability, and that institutional design may result in unintended consequences for the capacity and legitimacy of the governing system.

What is Governance?

At its most fundamental level governance implies the capacity of a society to develop some means of making and implementing collective choices. Dror (2001) has considered governance as simply designing ways of improving the future, using collective mechanisms, or as imposing some architecture on the processes of making decisions (Parsons 2004). Another way of considering governance is the capacity to overcome collective action problems in ways that are agreed by the participants in the society. The basic logic of the governance concept, therefore, is that an effective society requires some set of mechanisms for identifying common problems, deciding upon goals, and then designing and implementing the means to achieve those purposes. This perspective is quite obviously functionalist, and rests upon the need to have some mechanisms for managing collective needs, which appear central to the maintenance and success of the social order.

Again, at a very fundamental level governance is a functional theory, assuming that societies must govern themselves, and to do so must perform certain activities. In this way governance approaches are not all that much different from the structural–functional theories used in political science in the 1960s and 1970s (Almond and Powell 1966). By positing the functions, such as goal selection mentioned above, that must be performed, and then examining what actors and institutions perform those functions governance becomes a general comparative theory that can be applied to a range of policy-making systems, including the European Union.

Taken from this broad, comparative perspective, a governance approach to studying politics is agnostic about how this fundamental steering function is performed in any society, and about who performs it. Identifying the 'who' and the 'how' of governance is an important aspect of the comparative analysis. A governance approach does not privilege public sector actors in the activity of governance. Looking analytically at the formal institutions of governing is a good place to start, but it may not be a good place to end, an analysis of governance. This openness to non-state actors (whether from the market or from civil society) is all the more important as the complexity of governing increases over time in most societies. The openness to non-state actors also can be conceptualized as important for the democratization of systems of governance.

Although we are arguing for the broader comparative perspective, some definitions of governance have contrasted governance with government, arguing that governance implies performing that steering function without the direct involvement of official governmental actors. Those who argue for 'governance without government' assume that self-organizing networks are better able to provide direction to society (Rhodes 1996; Bogason and Musso 2006) than are the clumsy, bureaucratic institutions found in the public sector. To some extent the argument on behalf of networks is empirical, noting the numerous public functions performed by non-state actors, especially in the countries of northern Europe (Marcussen and Torfing 2007). The argument is also normative, assuming that governing through networks will be at once more democratic and more effective.

Unlike some scholars working in this field, we will be considering governments as one of many potential participants in the broader processes of governance. Our view is not that of a monolithic state, however, but rather one in which the state is a highly differentiated actor with multiple components having varying degrees of autonomy (Christensen and Laegreid 2006). This conceptualization of state involvement in governance contributes to the complexity of the governance processes, adding to the already complicated picture that arises from the involvement of societal actors. Thus, rather than allowing an exclusive role for either state or society, we are conceptualizing governance as an extremely complex process involving multiple actors pursuing a wide range of individual and organizational goals, as well as pursuing the collective goals of the society.

Further, rather than assuming a stark dichotomy between government and social actors, we will emphasize that these actors often cooperate, sometimes to the point that it is difficult to separate the one from the other. For example, although the advocates of network governance argue in terms of self-organizing networks, in practice the networks may be fostered or even directly formed by the public sector (Triantafillou 2007). Governance, therefore, provides an approach to comparative politics in that researchers can examine empirical mixtures of state and society involvement, and also look at the relative success of the alternative formats.

One way out of some of the definitional issues involved in utilizing the governance concept is to use modifiers to delimit the types of governance, as well as the issues involved in governing societies. For example, any number of scholars have attempted to clarify what might be meant by 'democratic governance' (March and Olsen 1995; Sorenson and Torfing 2007; Skelcher 2005). The development of networks and other forms of linking the public sector with society are also assumed to enhance the democratic nature of governing. While the search for democratic governance has helped to understand governance more generally, it has also raised a number of important analytic questions of its own.

Scholars have also developed an extensive literature on the term 'network governance'. This term is used to describe the domination of governance processes by non-governmental actors and more specifically the dominance of social actors organized in network structures (Koopenjaan and Klijn 2006). Likewise, some scholars and practitioners have focused on the idea of 'good governance', implying largely the capacity to minimize corruption and increase transparency in the public sector (Rothstein and Torell 2008). An additional term, 'new governance', implies moving away from conventional command and control mechanisms for public intervention in economy and society in favour of 'softer' forms of intervention (Salamon 2001; Morth 2004). Much of the literature on instruments does assume (implicitly more than explicitly) that the public sector will remain the principal actor in governance and that the important change involved is in the instruments through which it chooses to intervene (see Lascoumbes and Le Gales 2004).

It is important to remember that all of the governance strategies, whether dependent upon civil society or not, are being conducted in the 'shadow of hierarchy' (Scharpf 1994). That is, even if social actors are empowered to become involved in making policy or to be involved in other forms of societal steering, those activities ultimately are being conducted in the name of the state. Because those activities involve delegation of public power (Huber 2004), if that power is abused or not used at all, then the state has the residual powers to reclaim decision-making and to exert its own control over the policy area. Advocates of informal mechanisms of governance do not like the concept of delegation, but the hierarchy of the state always remains ready if it is required.

Critiques of Governance

We have written this chapter to this point as advocates of a governance approach. Although we argue that the governance literature has added a great deal to the study of politics, the approach is not without its critics. Perhaps the standard critique is simply that governance is the proverbial 'old wine in new bottles' (Frederickson 2006). That is, governance is simply a way of packaging differently what we have known about policy and administration for decades. Likewise, the literature on the use of networks in governing builds on the well-established literatures on corporatism and the other familiar forms of interest intermediation. The critical question then is whether governance is just another academic fad, or whether there is real substance to the approach that can yield additional insights?

Discussing the critiques of governance involves defining first which of the alternative conceptions of governance the critique is addressing. For example, there are any number of critiques of the 'government without governance' approach that it tends to minimize the importance of the public sector (Marinetto 2003). These critiques address in part the empirical question of whether governing without the involvement of the public sector is possible, given the need for legitimization and for the use of public policy instruments (see also Jordan *et al.* 2005).

Network governance can be criticized because of the difficulties such systems may encounter in making decisions. While formal institutions have decision rules that can produce decisions even in the face of conflict, the more informal nature of networks may make decisions difficult. Further the decisions that are made may not advance policy very far but only be the 'lowest common denominator' (Scharpf 1988). Networks also may not be as inclusive as their advocates assume and may not advance significantly the cause of democracy in decision-making.

Finally, the emphasis on good governance, meaning primarily reducing levels of corruption, may significantly reduce the range of concerns involved in thinking about governance (Doornbos 2003). Reducing corruption in the public sector is certainly an important goal, but is only one aspect of the complex and demanding process of governing. Several major international donor organizations have stressed the importance of making the public sector more transparent and less corrupt, but have not always addressed other issues about governance, including the possibilities of including civil society actors in the political process.

Governance at Work in Europe

We have been arguing that the processes of governance with which we are concerned often involve using a wide variety of actors, many from outside the public sector itself, in order to achieve public purposes. In a policy-making system that is often perceived to be dominated by the national governments, and whose own structures are characterized as bureaucratic and formal, the use of actors from civil society might be considered somewhat unlikely. There are some more informal mechanisms for governing (Peters 2007) but these do not appear to be as numerous as in many of the member states of the EU.

The development of the Open Method(s) of Coordination (OMC) is one of the best examples of governance processes in the European Union (Borras and Jabobssen 2004; Zielonka 2007). This mechanism involves the member countries creating their own goals and benchmarks for pursuing European policies, rather than using conventional top-down means of goal setting. The initial application of the OMC was as a means of pursuing the ambitious productivity and employment goals coming from the Lisbon European Council in 2000. The EU itself did not have the means of attaining those goals, and indeed the national governments themselves could not do so. Therefore the OMC has been developed as a means of involving economic actors in designing and implementing policies. These interactions in turn involve the creation of networks of actors that resemble those functioning at the national level in many of the member countries.

Although the OMC developed to pursue the Lisbon goals is the most developed, versions of the open method have been developed in other policy areas. All these structures involve a variety of social actors from the various member states, even in areas such as justice and immigration (Caviedes 2004). Thus, the European Union has been adopting the basic 'governance' pattern in which public goals are pursued through the collaboration of a wide range of actors. The OMC is therefore also part of the general movement toward the 'new governance' in which the instruments used to implement public programmes are softer and based more on negotiation rather than the use of authority. This is in marked contrast to the use of authority in the familiar Community method of making policy.

Propositions about European Governance

With some better idea of what governance means, we then need to see how these ideas apply to the European Union, and in particular how governance relates to European integration. These are propositions that we believe to be important about this linkage, but they can also be highly contested among scholars of the EU. This degree of contestation may be in part a function of different intellectual understandings about the process (the classic distinction between neofunctionalism and liberal intergovernmentalism) as well as some of the normative debates concerning what the EU should be. We will tend to avoid the normative debates, instead focusing attention on the manner in which governance is being conducted and the implications of those styles of making and implementing public action.

Multilevel Governance

The first obvious feature of European governance is that most of the activities of making and implementing policy involve multilevel activity. The idea of multilevel governance (MLG) was developed largely in reference to the EU (Marks *et al.* 1996; Bache and Flinders 2004), although most of the features associated with this concept would be familiar to the citizens of federal states, or indeed even most unitary states. The multilevel governance model recognizes not only the existence of national governments in the EU, but also has emphasized the importance of regional governments, whether already existing regions (the German Länder, for example) or regions that have been constructed for purposes of regional policy within the EU.

Although multilevel governance is discussed as a general attribute of European governance, it is perhaps most important for understanding the implementation of European directives. The formal logic of EU governance is that the Commission has the right of initiating legislation, although in reality the agenda-setting process may be more open to influence from both national and social actors (Peters 2001). The EU has, however, little implementation capacity of its own, and therefore depends upon the member states and their components in order to be able to put policy choices into effect. The assumption is that the directives coming from Brussels will be implemented as intended.

Although it might be considered a technical aspect of implementation, multilevel governance also has a number of important political consequences. Most importantly, multilevel governance empowers, or in some instances virtually creates, regional entities with European member states. This empowerment may help to legitimate the EU, given that it involves and recognizes lower level governments which tend to have greater legitimacy (especially in multi-ethnic countries) than do national governments. In addition, the development of these relationships does provide some social and political groups which might have relatively little influence over policy in other circumstances.

The positive, democratic nature of multilevel governance should not, however, be exaggerated, and there may be some ways in which the development of complex MLG systems tend to strengthen EU and even national bureaucratic actors at the expense of subnational actors (Peters and Pierre 2004). The largely unstructured nature of many of the interactions involved in multilevel governance may appear to provide opportunities for regions or other actors outside official positions to impose priorities other than those of Brussels or even formal national actors on policy. In practice, however, such unstructured situations actors with clearly defined priorities may prevail and be able to push through those priorities. This power of the well-organized reflects the logic of the garbage can, in which the absence of priorities and procedures defined in advance leads to those with clear objectives tend to dominate over those with less clearly defined preferences (Pierre and Peters 2006).

The multilevel nature of European governance is one aspect of the complexity within this policy-making system. The existence of multiple veto points makes effective governance more difficult, and produces more need for bargaining. As Scharpf (1988) has pointed out, bargaining among the regions, or nations, in turn may produce suboptimal policy choices. The actors involved in multilevel governance may be forced to adopt solutions that correspond to the lowest common denominator among them. If unanimity is required and each actor pursues his or her own interest then bargaining will proceed until there is a decision acceptable to all, usually one not much different from the status quo. If European policy-making is to move forward, then the actors involved at the multiple levels must find some means of bargaining across issues and across time to create more positive outcomes.

Governance is Crucial for Output Legitimization

As any relatively new political entity must, and indeed as well-established political entities must, the European Union must legitimate itself. The legitimization of any political system may be problematic, but the EU faces more challenges than most in ensuring a position for itself in the governance of its constituent parts. One of the crucial legitimization challenges is the (in)famous democratic deficit (see, for instance, Follesdal and Hix 2006). That is, while operating in societies that are accustomed to institutionalized forms of democratic governing, the EU is often described as lacking effective democracy. This may be in large part because of the lack of democratic accountability of the executive, the European Commission. The European Parliament has been able to gain significant powers over policy and mechanisms for requiring some accountability of the Commission, but the characterization of the democratic deficit is still applied commonly, and perhaps appropriately, to the EU (see below).

As well as being characterized as being undemocratic, the governing style of the European Union may also be characterized as excessively bureaucratic. In contrast to the member states in which governance has been transformed by both market principles and principles of network governance, much of the output of Brussels comes in the form of formal rules made by bureaucratic organizations. Not only is the source of the regulations bureaucratic, but they often also appear to be concerned with incredibly minute details of economic life. A citizen need not be a student of von Hayek to think that the degree of curvature of a cucumber might be something that consumers could decide for themselves.

One of the fundamental weaknesses of the European Union from the perspective of output legitimization is that it addresses only slightly and tangentially some of the policy areas that have been most important for legitimating European national governments. In particular, given its economic roots, the EU has a limited role in the welfare state programmes that have been so important in post-war Europe. The role of the EU in social policy has been increasing (Daly 2006) but remains only a minor component of its policy portfolio.

European Governance Remains Undemocratic

Although the democratic deficit has been a very common characterization of European governance, and the national political systems in Europe are all democratic, the governance system within the EU remains relatively undemocratic. A democratically elected EU parliament has become more important, and procedures for co-decision on most important policy issues (Selck and Steunenberg 2004) permit greater democratic control. Likewise, comitology—the system of committees contributing to the EU policy-making process—and other mechanisms for influence from social actors permit some more direct involvement of European citizens.

The Union is currently making attempts to increase the democratic character of the European Union, through developing more parliamentary control over the executive among other means. Despite those efforts the EU remains very unlike a conventional parliamentary democracy. The OMC and other forms of involvement through the output side of the political process are also helping to democratize European politics. The style of democracy that has been developing depends more on the associative format for democracy (Hirst 1994), involving citizens through a number of channels, rather than on representative institutions.

European Governance is Highly Segmented

Almost all governing systems are segmented. The functional specialization of government organizations and programmes into the various 'stovepipes' is logical from the perspective of the capacity of those organizations to focus attention on a narrow range of problems and to bring expertise to bear on those problems, but it generates significant problems for governance when considered more broadly. Very few public programmes can perform well in isolation from other policies—agriculture, for example, needs to be related to industry (especially the food industry), environment, and health programmes. Effective governance, therefore, requires creating greater coherence and coordination across the public sector, and the capacity to govern horizontally as well as vertically (Peters 1998).

European governance is perhaps more segmented than most national systems. First, the European system's political instruments for coordination are not as effective as those of most national political systems. In national governments, political parties and governing coalitions may be able to produce some levels of coordination. Further, despite the general power of the Commission, most of the operative powers over policy reside in the individual Directorates rather than in the collectivity, also lacking strong central agencies that can impose controls (financial, personnel, etc.) across the governing system as a whole. The creation of a more established presidency in the EU, as suggested in the Lisbon Treaty, and other aspects of constitutional change may help to integrate the political system, but a high level of segmentation remains. Finally, the linkages of programmes and organizations to powerful interests in society, notably agriculture and some industries, reinforces the structural segmentation found in the system.

While the creation of policy coordination is important for effective governance, it may also have consequences for the development of the European polity. As noted above, effective governance may be important for legitimization in a governing system that does not have as effective instruments for input legitimization as do most national systems. Further, achieving several of the dominant European policy goals, e.g. competitiveness as agreed upon at the Lisbon summit, will require effective coordination. Some innovative mechanisms, notably the OMC (Borras and Jacobssen 2004), have been devised to cope with these demands, but these softer instruments may yet be inadequate for achieving the level of coordination necessary for effective governance. The result of this segmentation may be that integration may be very effective in some policy areas and less effective in others.

European Governance is Transforming

The governance arrangements of all contemporary political systems are transforming, and often transforming very rapidly (Pierre and Peters 2005), but the EU is transforming perhaps more extensively than others. This is in part because it is changing not only *how* it performs its governance functions, but also *what* it does. These two changes are linked, but should be discussed separately for analytic purposes. Indeed, sometimes the discussion of governance in the EU becomes muddled because these two dimensions of change are not seen as analytically separate.

Changing Governance Styles

Giadomenico Majone (1996) has characterized European governance as having a dominant regulatory style, and that characterization has been accepted widely. That is, the vast majority of the interventions made by the EU to steer the economies and societies of its member states have employed law as the fundamental instrument to achieve the desired results. The extensive instruments literature in policy analysis identifies regulation as one of a wide range of styles for intervention. Hood (1976) for example, discusses law as an instrument as the use of authority, while other commentators on instruments see law generally as the use of a legal stick to force action.

The EU typically operates primarily through issuing regulations that then must be implemented by the member states, with the assumption that there will be uniform implementation in all the member states, even the accession members who have less capacity to do so (Falkner *et al.* 2005). This style of governance has been effective in many ways. It has enabled the EU to steer society without developing an extensive bureaucracy of its own. The critics of the Union have delighted in referring to it as a highly bureaucratic governance system, but in reality it has had a quite small administrative system compared to its national governments (Page 1997). The style of governing may have been legalistic and bureaucratic, but carried out through a small structure. Indeed, the domination of policy-making by the specialized bureaucracies in several Directorates General (DGs) reinforces the regulatory style and empowers bureaucracies against more political forces in governing.

The legalistic, regulatory style of governing is well entrenched, but at the same time it is being transformed in a number of ways. All of these changes are having an effect on the nature of the EU system and its relationship with society and the member states. The first dimension of transformation is that the EU is becoming more directly involved with the delivery of public services. The European bureaucracy has been expanding significantly through the creation of a number of agencies, e.g. the European Food Safety Agency, analogous to the administrative agencies now found in most of the member states (see Majone 2001; Pollitt and Talbot 2004). Most of the actions undertaken by these agencies are performed through legalistic, regulatory means, but the agencies do have more capacity to intervene directly.

Even for the more conventional components of the European Commission the style of governing has to some extent become more interventionist. For example, the competition authorities within the Commission have begun to use their own powers to raid premises and to confiscate possible evidence. In the relatively recently acquired policy area of criminal justice, the use of instruments such as European arrest warrants are a further example of interventionist approaches. The limited number of employees of the EU per se will prevent there being much direct action of this sort, but still there is the sense of a greater action-orientation for EU officials, and a tendency to make European policy more directly effective within the member states. Of course, this style of intervention may be seen by some European citizens as excessively interventionist and as violating the presumed limits of the powers of the EU.

At the same time that the European governance style is becoming more extensive and more interventionist, it is also becoming less interventionist in some ways. As noted above, the emergence of 'soft law' is reducing the requirements for the DGs in the Commission to make and implement as many of their own regulations, and instead involves social actors as well as a range of other actors from the public sector in negotiating their own solutions to some policy problems facing Europe. Again, this takes place in the 'shadow of hierarchy', with the agenda to some extent determined by the EU not by the autonomous interactions of the social actors, and national actors, involved. Further, in this style of governance, compliance is not expected to be as precise as in conventional forms of European governance and there are ranges of acceptable outcomes rather than a single form.

The softening of European law and rule-making can be seen as to some extent democratizing the system, but there are also other democratizing elements. Expanding the powers of the European Parliament has been one obvious democratizing element, but there have been others. In particular, the continuing increases in the powers of comitology (Christiansen and Larsson 2007) tend to open the system to influences beyond the preferences of the bureaucrats themselves. Comitology is not without its critics and it generally does not allow the range of representation that policy networks may have at the national level in many European countries. It is, however, still an opening into the policy-making system and does permit greater influence from outside than in the past.

In sum, there are numerous 'new forms of governance' that are being implemented within the European Union and these new instruments all enable governance without the intrusive, bureaucratic style usually associated with the EU. There is, however, a different shadow of hierarchy here, as the European Commission retains its capacity to make decisions in its bureaucratic manner. The more open and democratic institutions have limited power when compared to those still retained by the Commission, so the Commission may choose to assert its powers when its members do not agree with the outcomes.

Changing Policy Issues

As well as changing the forms of intervention, the EU is also changing what it does. European governance is becoming involved directly in policy areas that once were the exclusive domain of the individual member states. The policy domain of the Union has expanded gradually since the original Treaty of Rome, but the movement into areas such as defence and foreign policy has made governance in the EU more like that of a nation state. The constitutional changes that will be implemented if the Treaty of Lisbon is adopted mean that the emerging role of a European foreign secretary becomes institutionalized and that the role of that official becomes more clearly defined in representing Europe as a whole in international forums, rather than having the individual member states involved, even if involved in a coordinated manner.

The familiar functionalist arguments about the processes of political integration also appear to be manifested in the expansion of policy domains. The increasing movement of the EU into social policy is the most obvious case of this spillover into areas that were not originally part of its policy domain. The drive to make Europe more competitive and to enhance employment opportunities that generated the OMC, discussed above, also generated some need for the EU to become more involved in social policy, and especially issues of the social costs of employment. If the social costs of employment deter firms from locating in Europe, or if there are any significant competitive advantages of one member state over another as a result of social policy and/or its costs then the EU is to some extent obliged to become involved.

The expansion of the EU into a number of consumer and safety issues has been associated with the formation of the European agencies mentioned above. This movement also reflects the functionalist logic of spillovers. The regulation and standardization of products for competition reasons very easily leads on to the standardization of products to protect consumers and to ensure safety, e.g. food safety or airline safety. The major question therefore is what degree of standardization may be required before the level of policy integration is sufficient for adequate economic and social governance.

Changing Policy and European Integration

These changes in the European governance style may have some interesting, if contradictory, effects on the continuing integration of Europe. On the one hand, these changes may create the image (correctly or not), of a kinder, gentler EU. The bargaining style evolving through the OMC and other soft law instruments weaken the possibly draconian and legalistic image of 'Brussels' and also permit greater adaptation of European policy to local circumstances. Further, despite the numerous critiques of comitology, the bargaining and representation implied in this format for policy-making also make the system appear more open and adaptable than the usual stereotype.

On the other hand, however, the increased range of policy concerns of the EU, as well as its more direct intervention in some policy areas, may create the opposite image. In some member states, the creation of the Common Foreign and Security Policy is seen as a threat to their own sovereignty in a way that many of the economic policies in the Union never had (M.E. Smith 2000). In addition, the EU has begun to exercise something like police powers in enforcing some of its other policy areas (Mastenbroek 2005), creating the appearance of a more interventionist and even more bureaucratic form of governance. This is the case, for example, in competition policy. While some inconsistency in governance styles is not uncommon, the contradictory tendencies in the EU—as a somewhat less institutionalized system of governance when compared to others—may present greater problems for citizens and for their officials.

The question then becomes if either of these types of changes and the imagery associated with them really affects the capacity of European governance to produce effective integration. On the one hand the more interventionist style might be seen by some as creating an effective governance system not dissimilar to that of many of the member countries. On the other hand, the changed style can be seen as reinforcing norms of equality across the member states and perhaps across individuals within those member states. Thus, output legitimization of the policy-making system can be enhanced by a more active European 'government'. Of course, for other observers the interventionist and perceived bureaucratic nature of these attempts to steer would only reinforce the perception of a remote and bureaucratic system.

Expansion and Governance

The expansion of the European Union from 15 to 27 members during the past decade must be seen as having profound consequences for governance within the Union.
To some extent those consequences should be obvious. Having to achieve agreement
among 27 actors rather than 15 is by nature more difficult, and when unanimity is
required may lead to the 'joint decision trap' described by Scharpf (1988). These difficulties in making decisions are exacerbated by the even greater economic and cultural
differences among the current larger group of countries. The expansion also strains the
financial resources of the EU because the majority of the new entrants are eligible for
a range of aids that will weaken the impact of those programmes on the regions in the
previous member states.

   All of that said, expansion may have had some positive consequences for governance
as well. First, although the decision-making within the Union may have some increased
complexity, there are also more options for negotiating coalitions, especially as the domain for majority voting increases somewhat. Although they might be thought of as a
natural bloc within the EU, there are a number of instances in which coalitions may be
created (Friis and Murphy 1999) that do bridge the divides among the members of the
Union. In governance terms this may mean that the decisions being made are less predictable, but that they can still be made.

   One of these has been the rather subtle expansion of the competencies of the Commission as a result of the accession criteria in the Copenhagen Treaty. Although the criteria
for accession did not by definition apply to the previous member states, many of these
became incorporated into the common pattern of governing and created more uniformity (Heidbreder 2008). This change may be especially important for some of the administrative criteria that appear to have a positive influence on public management.

   Following from the above, enlargement appears to have increased the use, and utility,
of softer policy instruments. By virtue of being less intrusive and demanding less formal
implementation capacity these instruments have been suitable to the somewhat less institutionalized political and administrative arrangements of the accession states. Further,
the less clearly defined edges of these policies have facilitated the transition from of the
new members into the relatively rigid policy regimen of the EU.

Conclusion

Although there are fundamental intellectual debates about approaches to integration in
Europe, they all point to the relevance of building governance structures. Indeed governance and integration appear to have a circular relationship. That is, effective governance may produce greater integration, while at the same time higher levels of integration
may increase the capacity to govern. These virtuous cycles could, of course, be mirrored
by a downward spiral into governance failure and disintegration. Thus, governance and

integration are inextricably bound, and the following propositions will elaborate some of those linkages.

The most fundamental question that must be asked about governance in the EU is whether or not there is adequate governing capacity within the political system not only to cope with day to day policy issues, but also to move European governance forward in ways that could steer the society and economy strategically and effectively. Further, that governance must be brought about in a sufficiently democratic form to satisfy citizens who are accustomed to highly democratic governance. If the structures of the Union are not able to be this effective and this open in the manner in which they govern, then continuing integration may not be possible.

The evidence discussed above indicates that the European Union has substantial governance capacity when it is seen from some perspectives, but limited capacity when considered from others. The EU has proven itself very effective in using the regulatory approach contained within the 'Community Method' to generate legalistic compliance from member states and entities within them, largely through bureaucratic mechanisms. This governance style was appropriate so long as the goals and policy areas involved in European governance were economic competition policy and reducing internal trade barriers. Further, this style of governance corresponds to the bureaucratic style of the EU and the dominance of the Commission in making policy. As the tasks of the Union continue to expand, the style of governing will have to adapt.

The changing tasks and the changing instruments being utilized in European governance reflect the need to use more democratic means to make and implement policy. Thus the democratization of the EU may not come through the usual means of mass politics and ministerial responsibility but rather through more indirect means on the output side of the governing process. These may not correspond to the usual understandings of political democracy, but they do increase public involvement in EU governance and may in fact open the governance system to a greater extent than a model of democratization based more on conventional parliamentary democracy.

The increased availability of democratic mechanisms for governance within the EU does not eliminate the need for effective governance. EU governance may become more democratic and that will be certainly be a positive development, but in the end output legitimization appears to remain the more crucial aspect of the activities of the EU. Several of the changes in the style of European governance may be designed to improve the implementation of programmes, but these reforms also run the risk of further disaggregating a governance system already beset by excessive fragmentation.

The above discussion should indicate that governance therefore is intimately related to the possibilities of further European integration, or to the maintenance of such integration as has been achieved. This relationship can be seen in the real world of governing but it also exists in the academic literature. As we have conceptualized the shifts occurring in how Europe is governed, as well the tasks that are being undertaken, then the governance system may become incapable of providing the type of bureaucratic governance in which it has been so skilled yet not really capable of providing the more open, flexible, and adaptive form of governance that many of the public may favour.

■ **GUIDE TO FURTHER READING**

Bache, I. and Flinders, M. (eds) (2004) *Multi-level Governance* (Oxford: Oxford University Press). Multilevel governance is a defining feature of the EU. This book looks critically at different aspects of multilevel arrangements, not least their contribution to democracy in the EU.

Morth, U. (ed.) (2004) *Soft Law in Governance and Regulation: An Interdisciplinary Analysis* (Cheltenham: Edward Elgar). Soft law is becoming an increasingly important instrument of steering and regulation, not least in the EU. This book gives an overview of changing patterns of regulation, particularly on the use of information, negotiation, and quality assessments.

Pierre, J. (ed.) (2000) *Debating Governance: Authority, Democracy, and Steering* (Oxford: Oxford University Press). This book gives an overview of theories of governance in different subfields of political science, including EU studies.

—— and Peters, B.G. (2005) *Governing Complex Societies: Trajectories and Scenarios* (Basingstoke: Palgrave). Theories of governance highlight the growing complexity of society as well as of the state. This book looks at different models of governance and specific problems of contemporary governance such as democratic accountability and legitimacy.

Scharpf, F. (1997) *Games Real Actors Play* (Boulder, CO: Westview). This is a complex and challenging book which analyses different forms of governance.

■ **STUDY QUESTIONS**

1. What does 'governance' mean? Is it a useful concept for comparative politics and for understanding the European Union?

2. What does using governance as a focus tell us about the European Union that other approaches would not?

3. The institutional complexity of the European Union makes decision-making more difficult than in many national governments. What could be done to improve the decision process and therefore improve governance?

4. Does multilevel governance in the EU provide options for participation by subnational governance or is it still dominated by Brussels?

5. What can be done to make governance in the EU more democratic?

6 Policy Networks

John Peterson

Introduction[1]

Modern democratic governance—imposing overall direction or control on the allocation of valued resources—often bears little resemblance to traditional Weberian notions of hierarchy or neoliberal ideas of delivering public services through private markets. Instead, public policies are made and delivered via some kind of hybrid arrangement involving a range of different actors, including some representing private or non-governmental institutions. Public policies, by definition, are the responsibility of *public* authorities and aim to satisfy some vision of the 'public good'. Yet modern governance, it is widely agreed, reflects a shift 'towards a sharing of tasks and responsibilities; towards doing things together instead of doing them alone' (Kooiman 1993: 1; see also R.A.W. Rhodes 1997; Pierre 2000; Mayntz 2003; A. Jordan and Schout 2006; Barber 2007; Kamarck 2007).

The term 'network' is frequently used to describe clusters of different kinds of actor who are linked together in political, social, or economic life. Networks may be loosely structured but still capable of spreading information or engaging in collective action. Academic work on networks is often vague or abstract, or both (see Peterson and O'Toole 2001; Thompson 2003), but growing interest in network forms of governance reflects how policies to regulate modern societies, cultures, and economies are all increasingly products of mutuality and interdependence, as opposed to hierarchy and independence. Linkages between organizations, rather than organizations themselves, have become the central analytical focus for many social scientists.

The term *policy* network connotes 'a cluster of actors, each of which has an interest, or "stake" in a given . . . policy sector and the capacity to help determine policy success or failure' (Peterson and Bomberg 1999: 8). Analysts of modern governance frequently seek to explain policy outcomes by investigating how networks, which facilitate bargaining between stakeholders over policy design and detail, are structured in a particular sector. Three features of European Union (EU) governance give sustenance to policy network analysis.

First, EU governance is truly *modern* governance. In this context, consider the claim of a well-known political figure about the nature of modern governance:

Most of us are conditioned [over] many years to have a political viewpoint . . . liberal, conservative or moderate. But most problems have become technical problems, administrative problems; they are very sophisticated judgments which do not lend themselves to the great sort of passionate movements which have stirred this country so often in the past.[2]

These claims were made by United States (US) President John Kennedy in 1962. In the ensuing 40-odd years, far more policy problems have become more 'technical', as well as subject to international cooperation, given the emergence of globalized markets in which goods, services capital, and people cross borders far more frequently. Technological progress has fostered more cross-border movement but also made regulation of it highly complex because it must, by definition, be cross-national.

In this context, EU policy-making resembles policy-making in other international organizations (IOs), such as the World Trade Organization or International Monetary Fund, in that much of it is extremely technical. In these and other IOs, experts who share specialized knowledge and causal understandings tend to identify and 'bond' with each other, and often seek to depoliticize the policy process. In the EU, as in other IOs, technical expertise 'can become an exclusionary device, a device that is more effective at the supranational level because representative institutions like parliaments, that can play a surveillance role by holding experts accountable, are weak' (Coleman 2001: 97; see also Radaelli 1999).

This point must be qualified when we consider the EU as a case. One of the unique features of EU governance is the formidable power of its representative parliament: the European Parliament (EP). Its emergence as a politically and legally equal to the Union's Council of Ministers in policy areas where the so-called co-decision procedure[3] applies means that the EP's members and officials are now full participants in many EU policy networks. At the same time, the EP's participation does not make most of the legislative work of the Union any less technical. Many of the Parliament's most effective members are those who are highly specialized and technically knowledgeable.[4]

A second primary feature of the EU that lends itself to policy network analysis is its status as an extraordinarily 'differentiated polity' (R.A.W. Rhodes 1997). Decision rules and dominant actors vary significantly between policy sectors, such as regional development or external trade policy. Battles for policy 'turf' are frequent and fierce, as are attempts to build high firewalls around policies in a given sector so that they cannot be altered or undone by actors from other sectors. One consequence is that EU policy networks tend to be discrete, distinct, and largely disconnected from one another, even when they preside over policies that are clearly connected, such as agriculture and environmental protection. Most have diverse memberships, extending to public and private, political and administrative, and 'European' and national (and international and subnational) actors. Many lack clear hierarchies—but the general picture is one of great diversity. The extension of the EU's competence to new areas, such as monetary and defence policy, has been accompanied by the creation of new, more diverse and anomalous policy structures. Policy network analysis helps us to describe the EU despite its 'polycentricity', or tendency to generate ever more and more dissimilar centres of decision-making and control (Peterson and Bomberg 2000). The increased power of the EP, as reflected in a quote from one of its officials, does not make the EU less polycentric: 'It is very difficult to influence the work of another committee . . . We do not normally look at what they are doing' (quoted in A. Jordan and Schout 2006: 230).

Third, EU policy-making is underpinned by an extraordinarily complex labyrinth of committees that shape policy options before policies are 'set' by overtly political decision-makers such as the college of Commissioners, Council of Ministers, or EP (Blom-Hansen

2008; Quaglia *et al*. 2008). The Union relies heavily on ostensibly apolitical committees of officials, experts and other stakeholders to surmount dissent, broker agreement, and move the policy agenda forward. EU policy formulation and implementation are usually scrutinized closely and repeatedly by national officials, via Council working groups and the arcane comitology system, with committees at different levels performing different functions and having different but overlapping memberships. Two inevitable questions arise: first, whether and how much agents representing the EU's supranational institutions are empowered by their roles as brokers of intergovernmental agreements; and, second, whether and how often 'representatives of civil society such as consumers' organizations or agricultural producers' interest groups who might have access to, or even participate in, domestic policy networks might be frozen out at the supranational [EU] level' (Coleman 2001: 97). In any event, it is clear that EU policies are significantly shaped and closely scrutinized by different kinds of officials and experts in the EU's committee system, both before and after ultimate policy decisions are taken by overtly political actors.

There exists no agreed theory of policy networks that would lead us to predictive claims about European integration or EU policy-making. Yet most analyses of the EU that employ 'policy network' as a metaphor seek to test the basic proposition that the way in which networks are structured in any EU policy sector will determine, and thus help explain and predict, policy outcomes. Nearly all contend that policy outcomes often cannot be explained by exclusive recourse to the mediation of national preferences. In order truly to *theorize* policy network analysis, more (and more thorough) case studies of the actual policy effects of governance by policy network are needed, along with a larger dose of normative thinking about how to design networks that are efficient and legitimate, particularly as the EU encroaches on progressively more and more diverse national policies (Scharpf 1999, 2002; Wallace *et al*. 2005; Bomberg *et al*. 2008).

Policy Networks and EU Governance

Policy network analysis starts with three basic assumptions. First (again), modern governance is frequently non-hierarchical. Few policy solutions are simply imposed by public authorities. Governance involves mutuality and interdependence between public and non-public actors, as well as between different kinds of public actor, not least in federal or quasi-federal polities such as the EU.

Second, the policy process must be disaggregated to be understood because 'relationships between groups and government vary between policy areas' (R.A.W. Rhodes 1997: 32). In other words, it makes little sense to talk of a 'strong state' or 'corporatist state'—let alone a 'strong' or 'weak' international organization (IO)—because states and IOs are much stronger vis-à-vis affected interests in some policy sectors than in others.

Third and finally, governments remain ultimately responsible for governance, but that is not the whole story. Before policies are set by elected political actors, policy choices are shaped and refined in bargaining between a diverse range of actors, including some who are non-governmental, all of whom have an interest in what policy is chosen. Policy networks can narrow options and shift the agenda by pursuing 'strategies that generate new political and economic forces' (Thatcher 1998: 406). Sometimes, they can go so far as to 'play a role in the determination of their own environment, with repercussions for the fit between political interests, organizational structures and economic objectives' (Thatcher 1998: 406; see also Dunn and Perl 1994; Peterson 1995b). To cite a specific example, the materialization of an EU social policy regime can be explained in part as the product of collective action on the part of an emergent social policy network to create a more favourable environment for EU intervention (see Falkner 1999; Wincott 2003).[5]

Arguably, policy network analysis is never more powerful an analytical tool than when it is deployed at the EU level. The Union is a unique polity, with no government or opposition, and powerful policy-makers who are non-elected, such as European Commissioners or members of the Committee of Permanent Representatives (COREPER). Its policy remit extends to highly technical matters of regulation, including new technologies, thus making the politics of expertise a crucial determinant of outcomes. With 27 member states, its own system of law and the capacity to impose its will on a polity of nearly 500 million citizens, the EU may seem enormously powerful, yet it is extraordinarily weak in terms of resources, and relies heavily on assets and expertise held at the national level, including in the private sector. To try to describe how the EU works without the metaphor of a network is a challenge on par with seeking to explain, under the same injunction, how international terrorists operate (see Biersteker 2002; Sageman 2004, 2007).[6]

The policy networks literature can be hard going. It features a variety of models and, confusingly, sometimes employs the same term to mean different things. For example, the Rhodes model of policy networks (see below) employs the term 'policy community' to mean a particularly tightly integrated and single-minded policy network (Marsh and Rhodes 1992; R.A.W. Rhodes 1997; Marsh 1998). Yet, elsewhere policy community is used to refer to the broader universe of 'actors and potential actors who share a common identity or interest' in a certain policy sector (Wright 1988: 606). Sometimes, works from different subdisciplines seem like islands in a stream. Keck and Sikkink's (1998) masterful study of 'advocacy networks' of activists in international politics sometimes uses terminology that is incongruous with the 'advocacy coalition' framework developed in the public policy literature primarily by Paul Sabatier (Sabatier and Jenkins-Smith 1993, 1998). Legal theorizing about network forms of governance can seem impenetrable (see Ladeur 1997). These and other alleged flaws of work on policy networks have sparked animated critiques (Borzel 1998; Dowding 2001).

The Rhodes model of policy networks has probably been employed more often than any other in the study of EU governance (see Peterson 1995a; Bomberg 1998; Daugbjerg 1999; Falkner 1999; Peterson and Bomberg 1999; Falkner 2000). Simply put, the model assumes that three key variables determine what type of policy network exists in a specific sector:

1. the relative *stability* of a network's membership: do the same actors tend to dominate decision-making over time or is membership fluid and dependent on the specific policy issue under discussion?

2. the network's relatively *insularity*: is it a cabal which excludes outsiders or is it highly permeable by a variety of actors with different objectives?

3. the strength of *resource dependencies*: do network members depend heavily on each other for valued resources such as money, expertise, and legitimacy or are most actors self-sufficient and thus relatively independent of one another?

A continuum emerges with tightly integrated *policy communities* on one end, which are capable of single-minded collective action, and loosely affiliated *issue networks* on the other, which find it far more difficult to mobilize collectively. The internal structure of policy networks is usually considered an independent variable, in that the structure of a policy network will help determine policy outcomes. Policy communities have more capacity than issue networks to steer or control the policy agenda.[7]

Policy network analysis is increasingly used to make sense of internationalized policy-making environments such as the EU. A primary aim is often to determine what interests—national or supranational—dominate bargaining within transnational net-works. The answer is usually revealed by considering two questions. First, does the policy sector in question give rise to much public sector activism? In other words, to what extent are politicians and senior public officials directly active and involved, and determined to impose their wills? Second, how much autonomy do supranational institutions have in any given sector? In the EU's case, are the Commission, EP, and Court endowed with their 'own resources' in terms of Treaty powers or funding, or are they largely dependent on national and private actors?

One of the strengths of the Rhodes model is that, despite occasional discrepancies in terminology, most other models of governance by network are compatible with it. Take, for example, the concept of 'epistemic communities' developed by Peter Haas (1992: 3) as a way to describe how policy-making can become dominated by 'network[s] of profes-sionals with recognized expertise and competence in a particular domain', particularly ones subject to internationalized policy-making. Or, consider Sabatier's (1993: 25) advo-cacy coalition framework, which holds that policy shifts usually occur when the sectoral agenda is seized by overtly political networks consisting of various kinds of policy activist, including public officials representing multiple levels of government, who 'share a par-ticular belief system' and work together over relatively long periods of time (10 years or more) to force policy change.

If EU governance is conceived as occurring within a multilevel system in which policies emerge after a fairly standard sequence of different types of decision, it is plausible to see EU governance at the subsystemic level (in space) and policy-shaping stage (in time) as largely a competition between epistemic communities and/or advocacy coalitions (some-times by competing versions of them) to steer or control policy networks, with which their own memberships overlap, in specific sectors. Sometimes, epistemic communities and advocacy coalitions may form alliances, particularly to shift the policy agenda in the direction of radical policy change as occurred, for example, when the EU embraced quite ambitious liberalization of its agricultural sector during the Uruguay Round that gave birth to the WTO in the early 1990s.

More generally, policy network analysis can help us explain why EU policy outcomes in a particular sector reflect purely technocratic rationality or, alternatively, the overtly political agenda of key actors (Peterson 1995b: 79–80; see also Peters 1998: 29–30). For example, the Framework programme for funding collaborative research has quietly expanded to become the third largest item of expenditure in the Community's budget, not least because much decision-making about precisely who gets what from the programme has been delegated to epistemic communities of researchers and scientists (Peterson and Sharp 1998: 163–87). Alternatively, highly politicized environmental policy debates over automobile emissions, packaging waste, or biotechnology can be viewed as battles between competing advocacy coalitions—broadly advocating environmental protection versus industrial interests—for influence within EU environmental policy networks.[8]

Policy network analysis often works 'best' when deployed together with other theoretical accounts of EU politics or policy-making, for two reasons. First, its explicit task of explaining subsystemic policy-shaping means that it is compatible with intergovernmentalist or neofunctionalist accounts of decision-making at the highest political levels, where 'history-making' decisions are taken which determine how the EU changes or evolves as a polity. Moreover, policy network analysis often can explain actual policy outcomes that are hard to explain using either of these theoretical accounts (which, after all, are not really theories of *policy-making*). Policy network analysis is also congruent with most institutionalist treatments of the EU,[9] particularly ones which focus on ultimate policy choices, for which authority is very much shared by the EU's institutions (Peterson and Shackleton 2006).

Second, policy network analysis adds value to alternative, meta-theoretical conceptions of EU governance. For example, the idea that sector-dedicated, mostly self-organized policy networks are responsible for a large portion of EU governance is amenable to broader notions that the Union works mostly on the basis of informal or 'network governance', in which 'political actors consider problem-solving the essence of politics and . . . the setting of policy-making is defined by the existence of highly organised social sub-systems' (Eising and Kohler-Koch 1999: 5; see also Christiansen and Piattoni 2003; Blom-Hansen 2008). Its compatibility with a theoretical portrait of the EU as a system in which actors must constantly seek to 'escape from gridlock' is obvious:

The decisional processes are obstacle-ridden, cumbersome and, to say the least prone to stalemate. This in turn gives rise to attempts to use escape routes by those actors who constitute nodes in the multiplicity of criss-crossing interactions, with subterfuge being the only way to keep policy-making going.

Héritier (1999: 97)

There is certainly plenty of anecdotal evidence to suggest that results-driven policy networks give the EU much of its (often surprising) capacity for agency. Consider, for example, the remarks of a recent French Minister for Europe: 'The thing that has most struck me since I took up this job seven months ago is precisely the capacity of an EU of 27 members, and one day more, to take decisions.'[10]

Policy network analysis also has affinities with constructivist accounts that highlight the ability of international organizations (IOs) such as the EU to generate new categories of actor and norms. Increasingly, IOs have rational and legal authority to make rules; none more so than the EU. As they make rules, IOs define international tasks (preventing the spread of AIDS in Africa), create new categories of actor ('political refugees'), and generate new norms (minority rights). They thus generate new social knowledge that can alter the interests of actors in policy-making that occurs at a level beyond the state (see Barnett and Finnemore 1999; Christiansen *et al.* 2001). For instance, EU governments have gradually come to identify their own self-interest in the prevention of 'social exclusion', with the EU hastening a shift in policy priorities in this direction and, particularly, the Commission sponsoring a new social exclusion lobby (Atkinson 2002; Bauer 2002). This example seems to vindicate assumptions that are central to the portrayal of the EU as a system of multilevel governance (see 'Evaluating policy network analysis' below): that is, the Commission retains 'virtually a free hand in creating new networks' (Marks *et al.* 1996: 359) and is often empowered by its position at the 'hub of numerous highly specialized policy networks' (1996: 355).

The Origins of Policy Network Analysis

In broad terms, the application of policy network analysis to the EU is a product of the widely shared view that the European Union is *not* an ordinary, 'garden variety' IO, but rather a system of governance in its own right. As such, leading theories of European *integration* can tell us little about the EU's processes for making *policy* (see 'The importance of policy networks for integration' below). Having emerged as the source of a large 'slice' of the total universe of all public policies in Europe, it is natural that tools developed by analysts of public policy at the national level are increasingly deployed at the EU level.

The precise origins of policy network analysis in the public policy literature are a matter of dispute. Richardson (2000: 1006) claims 'British origins of what is now termed the network approach'. Rhodes (1990: 32) concurs that 'American political science was not the major formative influence' on early work which sought to make sense of the British 'post-parliamentary' state using network analysis in the late 1970s. Yet an eclectic range of early work in the UK, US, *and* Europe on interest intermediation attempted to develop the idea of networks as an analytical concept. An important example is Heclo's (1978) spirited critique of the idea that the American policy process was subject to dynastic rule by 'iron triangles' of mutually supportive legislators, bureaucrats, and private actors. On the contrary, Heclo (1978: 102) argued, the policy process was influenced by a diverse collection of stakeholders grouped into issue networks—that is, complex networks focused on specific issues—which extended far beyond those actors with the formal power to set policy. Jordan (1981; Jordan and Schubert 1992) can claim credit for developing the idea that issue networks were one variant of network—and a rather extreme one—on a continuum ranging from very loose to very tightly integrated. The common denominator of early work on networks, which predated the EU's emergence as a true polity, was an ambition to explain how and why interests were mediated in settings that resembled neither open markets of transactions between independent entities nor hierarchies in which governments imposed control.

To make a long story short, international political developments in the 1990s—globalization, devolution (in Europe and elsewhere), and economic liberalization—gave rise to new and different forms of governance, in which power was increasingly shared horizontally. Policy network approaches became both more common in the policy literature and progressively more ambitious. No longer were its advocates content to present policy networks as mere metaphors. New attempts were made to try to theorize about them, and describe, explain, and predict policy outcomes by examining exchanges within policy networks (Peterson 1995b; Bomberg 1998; Daugbjerg 1999; Nunan 1999; Falkner 2000; Andersen and Eliassen 2001). The results were decidedly mixed, with some observers finding a widening gap between aims and achievements (see Le Galès and Thatcher 1995; Thatcher 1998).[11]

The Importance of Policy Networks for Integration

To understand the hypotheses and arguments endemic to this approach, it must be acknowledged that policy network analysis does *not* constitute a theory of political or economic integration, in Europe or anywhere else. In fact, scholars began to investigate the EU using policy network analysis in the early 1990s precisely because the time-honoured debate between intergovernmentalism and neofunctionalism, although revived in interesting new permutations (see Moravcsik 1991; Tranholm-Mikkelsen 1991; Burley and Mattli 1993), shed relatively little light on actual EU *policy*, and the complex systems that emerged for making it (Rosamond 2000: 105–13). Both intergovernmentalism and neofunctionalism were and remain macro-level theories of international relations, which are designed to describe, explain and predict the broad thrust and path of European integration as a process. Neither seek to describe, explain, or predict the policy outcomes that arise from this process.

Even proponents of policy network analysis would be hard-pressed to identify the central features—main assumptions, causal propositions, core predictions—of a 'network theory' of policy-making. Nonetheless, network analyses usually focus on one or more of three basic arguments:

1. *How policy networks are structured in discrete EU policy sectors has tangible, measurable effects on policy outcomes.* Put another way, EU policy outcomes are determined by how integrated and exclusive policy-specific networks are, and how mutually dependent are actors within them. We should expect different kinds of outcome in sectors, such as pharmaceuticals or agriculture, where tightly integrated, cabalistic policy communities are guardians of the agenda, than in sectors populated by loosely bound issue networks, such as environmental policy. One testable (although still to be proven) hypothesis is that more integrated networks will tend to block radical change in EU policies, while outcomes are far harder to predict when pre-legislative bargaining occurs within issue networks. More generally, policy networks are an independent or 'intervening' variable: 'analyses look at the ways in which network structures affect the selected aspects of the behaviour of actors and their interactions—for instance in the spread of information, strategies of actors, exchanges amongst them and policy outcomes' (Thatcher 1998: 410).

2. *Quasi-federal polities such as the EU naturally give rise to governance by policy network.* Federalism is, by nature, a method for reconciling competing values: strong yet

small government, federal standards alongside local discretion, and private sector autonomy with the provision of public goods. These values cannot be reconciled either through strict hierarchies or pure market structures. Rather, they must be reconciled through negotiation and the exchange of resources and ideas. Logically, structured but informal policy networks arise to facilitate this kind of negotiation, particularly in today's federal systems (including the EU), most of which have moved away from 'dual federalism', with ostensibly separate jurisdictions between levels of government, and towards 'cooperative federalism', in which interdependence between levels of government is accepted and even welcomed (Peterson and O'Toole 2001).

3. *Governance by policy network gives rise to management and legitimacy concerns.* Despite claims to the contrary (see Moravcsik 2002), it is commonly held that the EU suffers from both management and legitimacy deficits. The management deficit arises from the lack of incentives for any actor in non-hierarchical networks to invest in management capacities to ensure effective coordination: 'the problem is that when everyone is responsible for delivering on a particular coordinating challenge, in practice no one is' (A. Jordan and Schout 2006: xi; see also Metcalfe 2000; Weber and Khademian 2008). The legitimacy deficit results from a lack of clear rules of process, transparency or judicial review to govern informal bargaining within EU networks (see Dehousse 2002). Moreover, the technical discourse of supranational policy-making is an important reason why networks of government officials and experts are usually subject to less scrutiny than at the national level.

The 'news' that the EU governs largely by policy network is not, by any means, all bad. Informal bargaining within networks can help build consensus in a system which strives to avoid creating clear losers. Policy networks can diffuse norms of good governance, particularly to states that only recently joined the EU and whose civil services are still maturing. They can also help to ensure that private actors have a sense of ownership of EU policies. Nevertheless, the salience of the EU's management and legitimacy deficits points to the need for normative thinking about how EU policy networks should be structured, managed, and subjected to oversight and control. Complex interdependence between national and EU policy-making means that a lot of EU governance is always going to rely on exchanges within policy networks. Thus, it makes sense to design networks that can manage effectively and are part of the solution to the EU's legitimacy problem.

Evaluating Policy Network Analysis

While the EU's future is very much unwritten, there is no denying that it is a uniquely successful experiment in transnational governance. Eventually, it could emerge as:

a source of institutional innovation that may yield some answers to the crisis of the nation-state. This is because, around the process of the formation of the European Union, new forms of governance, and new institutions of government, are being created, at the European, national, regional and local levels, inducing a new form of state that I propose to call *the network state*.[12]

Castells (1998: 311); see also Nicolaïdis and Howse (2002)

Upon close examination, the 'network state' turns out to be a rather frustrating concept. Its 'actual content . . . and the actors involved in it, are still unclear, and will be so for some time' (Castells 1998: 311). What *is* clear is that EU governance occurs simultaneously at multiple levels of government, thus giving rise to multilevel governance (MLG) as a descriptive term for what the EU offers (see Bache and Flinders 2004). In theory, and at least sometimes in practice, power is distributed between the EU, national, regional and local levels according to the principle of subsidiarity: that is, the Union as a whole legislates only in areas (such as climate change or external trade policy) where policy problems cannot be solved at lower levels of government. To portray the EU as a multilevel system of governance is to assume that actors representing different levels of government are interdependent. They thus 'network' with each other to design, implement, and enforce EU rules.

Yet MLG is clearly far more prominent in some policy sectors—above all, cohesion policy—than others, such as competition policy (although even here it could be argued that the EU has shifted towards more network-type governance). MLG is probably less of a general model of EU governance now than many would have predicted in the early 1990s, when a 'Europe of the regions' seemed within reach as European integration and regional devolution accelerated simultaneously (Marks 1992; Marks *et al.* 1996). Indicative, perhaps, is Castells' (1998: 331) emphasis on the importance of the EU's Committee of the Regions (CoR) as the 'most direct institutional expression' of subsidiarity, despite general consensus 10 years after the CoR's creation that it had 'earned itself an uneviable reputation for being possibly the Union's most pointless institution' (Coss 2002: 10; Jeffery 2006).

Critique

Policy network analysis has never been short of critics (Kassim 1993; Dowding 1995; Le Galès and Thatcher 1995; Borzel 1998; Peters 1998; Thatcher 1998; Dowding 2001). It tends to be criticized on four specific grounds:

1. 'Policy network' may be a useful metaphor, but it does not constitute a model or theory.
2. Policy network analysis lacks a theory of power.
3. The literature on policy networks is often vague and caught up with insular, and purely academic debates about terminology.

'Policy Network' may be a Useful Metaphor, but it does not Constitute a Model or Theory

Many proponents of policy network analysis would accept this criticism. Most would concede that theorizing about policy networks remains at an early stage. Some would allow that while policy network analysis remains a frequent analytic device in the study of EU policy-making, it is still not a 'leading theoretical approach' in the same league as institutionalism, intergovernmentalism, and constructivism (Cowles and Curtis 2004: 305).

Nevertheless, theory-building must always start by building on metaphors which abstract from reality, and then point the analyst towards variables that may determine outcomes. Policy network analysis may remain a minority sport in EU studies in part because of two related, recent developments: increased interest in the Europeanization of EU member states and their institutions (Olsen 2002a; Featherstone and Radaelli 2003), and a growth market in new European agencies, which primarily bring together national regulators and operate at an arm's length from Brussels itself (Majone 2006b). Policy network analysis may not *answer* many important questions about European governance. However, it often points the analyst to where the answers may be found: the subterranean netherworld of officials, lobbyists, and experts, a world often quite distant from the political world of ministers and parliamentarians—and some of the most impressive work of recent years on how the EU actually generates policy has drawn on network analysis (Schout and Jordan 2005; Jordan and Schout 2006).

Policy-making in Brussels is too Fluid, Uncertain, and Over-populated with an Enormously Diverse Collection of Interests for Stable Networks to Exist or Persist

According to this view, 'EU governance is . . . best described as uncertain agendas, shifting networks and complex coalitions' (Richardson 2000: 1021). This set of circumstances is considered to be bad news for proponents of policy network analysis because:

the utility of network typologies is open to question in situations in which there is rapid change (both of institutions and actors), a lack of clear sectoral/subsectoral boundaries, complexity of decision-making and a potentially large number of actors drawn from different levels of policy formation, as claimed, for instance, to exist in European policy-making.

Thatcher (1998: 398)

Proponents of this view sometimes go as far as to question whether stable networks exist at all in Brussels. Actors may form alliances and work together on specific issues— thus the term 'issue network'—but most actors are promiscuous. Thus, once formed, networks quickly disintegrate. It is not surprising, given such fluidity, that 'case studies of EU policy-making tend to examine individual decisions rather than whole sectors or sub-sectors' (Kassim 1993: 21).

This criticism lacks credibility, for at least three reasons. First, stability of membership is a variable, not an assumption, of policy network analysis. The EU, more than most systems of governance, may give rise to loosely integrated and fluid issue networks more often than stable policy communities, especially given its recent, radical enlargement, but the matter is one for empirical investigation. Moreover, it is possible to find policy episodes—such as the 1989 directive on automobile emissions (Peterson and Bomberg 1999: 190–1) or the so-called Cardiff process launch in 1998 (Jordan and Schout 2006)— when an insecurely structured issue network managed to overcome its own fluidity and capture the policy agenda long enough to produce an outcome that would not have been predicted by pluralist or incrementalist theories. In any event, as the EU matures it is possible—perhaps likely—that 'more stable and manageable networks of policy-makers are likely to emerge' (Mazey and Richardson 1993: 4). The maze of EU committees, whose members far outnumber the total number of officials in the Council and Commission combined, is meant—perhaps above all—to provide stability to policy-making.

Second, the claim that the EU's fluidity cannot be 'captured' by policy network analysis is usually made on the basis of very little evidence. Kassim's (1993) 'sceptical view' of policy networks is based almost exclusively on evidence from the air transport sector, which is both more nationalized *and* globalized than most other European industries (and thus not very Europeanized). Richardson's (2000) dismissal of policy network analysis as over-used and inappropriate at the EU level relies mainly on secondary sources on national lobbying strategies and EU external trade policy.

Third and finally, relatively loosely constituted networks are, somewhat ironically, often more effective channels of communication than tightly integrated policy communities. The so-called 'strength of weak ties' argument holds that:

In a world of cliques of tightly knit social circles, individuals are better off investing time in acquaintances (or 'weak ties') because it is through acquaintances that cliques are bridged and that information diffuses through a policy network . . . information communicated by strong ties—within-clique communication—will tend to be redundant, and will tend to travel short distances relative to the size of the network as a whole.

Carpenter *et al.* (1998: 418–19); see also Granovetter (1973)

It may be that communication is more important as a lubricant to the policy process in the EU than in most other systems of governance. Consensus is ingrained as a norm and a vast number and diversity of policy stakeholders must typically agree before an EU policy may be set. Timing is particularly crucial in EU policy-making: the losers in policy debates (despite attempts to avoid creating any) are frequently those who are unaware of when a dossier is 'ripe' and ready for a decision, and are caught out because they lack adequate communication channels. More generally, in such a non-hierarchical system, the importance of physical presence and the cultivation of relationships appear particularly crucial to those who wish to ensure that their own interests are served, or at least not damaged, by EU policy outcomes. Consider the view of one EU ambassador on the frequent absence of the UK Prime Minister, Gordon Brown, from EU gatherings such as a ceremonial signing of the Treaty of Lisbon: 'To exert influence in the EU, you have to be present. You have to attend meetings, *network*, persuade, make the most of friendships' (emphasis added).[13]

Policy Network Analysis Lacks a Theory of Power

This criticism is a serious one, but it neglects the *interstitial* nature of policy network analysis: that is, the power of classical EU actors—particularly member governments—is not denied but it is not viewed as wholly determinant of EU outcomes.[14] Network analysis looks for explanations in exchanges that cover over the cracks or crevices that separate different levels in a system of MLG, or different sets of institutional actors in systems where multiple institutions wield a slice of power. It contends that the EU system produces outcomes that cannot be explained exclusively by recourse to the me-diation of national preferences, as is sometimes claimed (see Bueno de Mesquita and Stokman 1994). Policy network analysis is 'pitched' at a meso or subsystemic level of decision-making, and thus is entirely compatible with macro-theories of politics, such as pluralism, elitism, and Marxism (see Daugbjerg and Marsh 1998; Damgaard 2006). In the EU's case, more or less power is concentrated at the subsystemic level depending on which EU policy sector is under scrutiny: for example, a considerable amount of power for determining the Common Agricultural Policy (CAP) is delegated to the subsystemic level, while much less little power resides at this level in relation to the Common Foreign and Security Policy (CFSP). Thus, policy network analysis is likely to tell us more about how the CAP is determined than how the CFSP is made.

Consensus has become widespread that policy network analysis should be deployed within a portfolio of theories pitched at explaining outcomes at different levels of gov-ernance (see Peterson and Bomberg 1999; H. Wallace 2000; Andersen and Eliassen 2001; Peterson 2001; Bomberg *et al.* 2008). Interestingly, the plausibility of *intergovernmentalist* theories of power in EU governance is frequently conceded in such schema, as only one kind of actor—national actors—are powerful at *every* level in what has clearly evolved into a multilevel system of governance. However, most proponents of policy network analysis reject as artificial and false the dichotomy between 'intergovernmental' and 'suprana-tional governance', since virtually 'no administrative [EU] action can be developed with-out national administrative authorities being associated with it' (Azoulay 2002: 128).

The Literature on Policy Networks is Often Vague and Caught up with Insular, and Purely Academic Debates about Terminology

Sometimes, debates in the public policy literature between advocates of competing models—and especially between network analysts and their detractors—seem increas-ingly unproductive. They often focus on rather trivial questions of terminology, and can be embarrassingly self-absorbed (Rhodes 1997; Marsh and Smith 2000; Richardson 2000; Dowding 2001; Marsh and Smith 2001; Kisby 2008).[15] Still, few serious students of European integration would deny that governance by networks is an essential feature of the EU (Jordan and Schout 2006). In fact, governance by network may be becoming a steadily *more* important feature of the EU, as evidenced by the centrality to European economic policy-making of the so-called Lisbon Process over the course of over a decade (Dehousse *et al.* 2004; Groenendijk 2006; Radaelli 2007).

Application: Policy Network Analysis and Eurojust

Any survey of recent literature on EU governance will uncover a variety of analyses using policy network analysis as an investigative lens. Cohesion policy (Ansell *et al.* 1997; Ward and Williams 1997; Bache 1998; Bomberg and Peterson 1998; Bache and Jones 2000; Yesilkagit and Blom-Hansen 2007), research policy (Peterson and Sharp 1998; Grande and Peschke 1999), and the Common Agricultural Policy (see Daugbjerg 1999; Ray and Henning 1999; Coleman 2001; Ullrich 2002; Kriesi *et al.* 2006) are frequent targets of investigation via this method, not least because they are all bastions of policy-making by linked clusters of national, subnational and supranational actors and unusually technocratic procedures.

However, an illustrative case of how network analysis can help researchers to make sense of Europeanization that increasingly takes place 'beyond Brussels' are Eurojust and the European Judicial Network (Kostakopoulou 2006: 242; Thwaites 2006; Helmberg 2007). Both emerged around the time of ambitious, even historic, political agreement on closer judicial and internal security cooperation at the 1999 Tampere summit (Lavenex and Wallace 2005: 469). Eurojust was created to facilitate cross-border investigations and prosecutions in the EU, which had often proven impossible in the past. A dramatic illustration of the problem occurred when German prosecutors brought to trial four German residents who had planned to blow up a Christmas market in Strasbourg in late 2000. A number of charges—including membership of a terrorist organization—had to be dropped because it was so difficult to bring evidence and witnesses from France.

Initially, Eurojust was given only advisory powers as (literally) a network of national judicial authorities. By most accounts it worked well. By early 2008, France and 13 other member states proposed that Eurojust should be given considerably greater operational powers, such as the power to issue search and seizure warrants when investigating serious crimes.[16] Two features of this case of consolidation of network governance were particularly noteworthy. First, the European Commission had intended to propose fairly similar changes after its own report of 2007 on Eurojust, but the French and others wanted to move more quickly with rather different ideas than the Commission's, thus illustrating how the Commission's 'free hand' in the creation of new networks is not an exclusive one. Second, the Lisbon Treaty contained provisions for the setting up of a European Public Prosecutor—constituting a step-level change from the network approach of Eurojust—but requiring a unanimous vote of all 27 member states to do so. Thus, the Public Prosecutor was likely to be created in the first instance by a small number of member states using (perhaps for the first time) the EU's provisions for 'enhanced cooperation', or flexible cooperation between subgroups of states that draws on the EU's resources. It was hardly likely to be the last in a more variegated, diverse EU of 27 or more member states.

In contrast to Eurojust, the European Judicial Network (EJN) retained a highly decentralized structure, but linked national contact points in the member states and Commission to facilitate cross-border investigations and prosecutions. A key feature of EJN was a telecommunications network that established directories of information that could be searched by judicial authorities across borders. There was little question that the EJN 'fostered a tangible increase in judicial cooperation' (Kostakopoulou 2006: 242).

These examples may illustrate broader trends in European integration. We find a pattern of integration that is functional, complicated, and by no means linear. The Commission is often (even increasingly?) marginalized or plays a minor role. In an enlarged EU, subgroups of states can be expected to move things forward institutionally. Still the pattern may be viewed as having a trajectory, which itself arises from the stockpiling of reservoirs of trust and confidence over a period of years within non-hierarchical networks of actors whose affiliation and loyalty is primarily national, but which become committed to European solutions to share policy problems.

Policy Network Analysis and Enlargement

Three points are apt about how policy network analysis might help us to shed light on the EU after its radical enlargement. First, the EU-27 that arrived in 2007 is fundamentally different from the old EU-15. Yet, a number of patterns are so well established that they will persist far into future. One is that all new member states take time to adjust to the EU's unique brand of deciding by subterfuge, or 'escaping from deadlock' (see Héritier 1999); that is, essentially ignoring or subverting the formal rules and advancing the policy agenda through bargaining within informal policy networks. As such, formal accession to the EU did *not* make new member states full, 'equal' members of the European Union (see Peterson and Jones 1999). Rather, new officials, and private and non-governmental actors from new member states had to learn the rules of the game that apply to policy-specific networks, and get used to bargaining within them.

Second, there is no question that the states that joined in 2004–7 had far less mature, proficient or professional civil services compared to the EU norm. Most were relatively inexperienced participants in international organizations, and many had never encountered a Western-style lobbying system. A central issue was thus whether policy networks within an enlarged EU would be able to perform the function of disseminating norms of compliance with EU rules, despite vast disparities in levels of economic modernization (and thus economic interests) and public sector leverage in the face of private sector power.

Third and finally, it will become far more difficult to reform the EU of the future. The intergovernmental conferences (IGCs) that produced, first, the Constitutional Treaty and then the Lisbon Treaty were considered by many member governments as Europe's last shot at embracing truly meaningful reform of the Union's institutions, before an EU-27 plus emerged with far too many veto players to make it possible to change anything very important. Olsen (2002b), one of the most clever of all students of institutional change, offers a final word on networks and enlargement:

In the European Union governance takes place in polycentric, multilevel policy networks of public and private actors . . . Reformers are not omnipotent. There is no single sovereign centre with the authority and power to change fundamentally the policy order while many factors other than reformers' choices influence change. Furthermore, reform capabilities often have to be developed as an inherent part of the reform process, a key issue in many applicant countries . . . Comprehensive reforms tend to be highly divisive and European reformers face enduring differences that cannot be hidden behind apolitical rhetoric.

Olsen (2002b: 593–4)

Challenges and Prospects of Policy Network Analysis

The Contribution of Policy Network Analysis

The impact of policy network analysis on European integration theory has been significant. Yet, for the most part its significance arises from the way in which it has given theorists a language to describe and perhaps sometimes to explain—more rarely to predict—what European integration has wrought in terms of a governance system. The EU has, over time, become more eclectic as a polity as its policy competence has expanded, and more poly-centric (Peterson and Bomberg 2000). For example, contrast the highly centralized system for monetary policy with the highly decentralized system of regulating food safety or medicinal products via new European agencies (Majone 2006b; McNamara 2006). Then, consider the notion that states may develop a distinct 'policy style' (Richardson 1982), depending on how proactive or reactive, and how consensual or autocratic policy-making is. One important rationale for studying the EU using policy network analysis is that it is futile to try to characterize its policy-making process as reflecting one policy style when it incorporates so many different ones across its full range of policies.

To take the point further, it might be argued that there is great variety between EU policy networks for good reason: because a very diverse set of arrangements are needed for the EU to surmount different obstacles to cooperation in different areas of policy. Of course, governance by policy network is not without its pathologies, particularly the problem of networks being 'captured' and transformed into insular policy communities, dominated by vested interests and lacking transparency. However, policy network analysis can help us explain both continuity in EU policy outcomes, *and* the Union's (occasional, at least) capacity for policy innovation.

The main contribution of EU policy network analysis to theorizing about European integration is its emphasis on the Union's inescapable diversity and complexity. A dizzying array of different kinds of actor can claim to be a policy stakeholder in a continent-sized polity of nearly 500 million people, which incorporates a rich variety of national systems of interest representation. Transnational networks of the kind that preside over the policy agenda in the EU and other international organizations are usually seen generally to be looser and less tightly integrated than their counterparts at the national level, but the more single-minded amongst them clearly can exploit the space between the EU and its member states in pursuit of their own interests (see Josselin and Wallace 2001).

The Future Development of Policy Network Analysis

The future of policy network analysis is dependent to a considerable extent on its relative success in performing three functions.

First, can it effectively describe, explain, and even predict outcomes arising from the use of new policy methods, modes, and technologies?

In recent years, a number of new alternatives to the traditional Community method of legislating have emerged, including as the Open Method (Hodson and Maher 2001; Atkinson 2002), 'co-regulation' by private actors acting voluntarily with public regulators, and rule-making by new European regulatory agencies (Dehousse 1997; Majone 2006b). Most involve less EU legislation per se or less stringent or detailed legislation, and many seek the generic aim—highly prioritized in the post-20004 Commission under José Manuel Barroso (Radaelli 2007; Peterson 2008)—of 'better regulation', or that more clearly or efficiently achieves its stated aims. The better regulation agenda is not only a technocratic one, but also a political one designed to deliver a 'Europe of results' while acknowledging that, in the past, further political integration was often prioritized ahead of policy results (Majone 2005, 2006a).

These alternative methods all depend far more than the Community method does on *coordination*, especially between national officials and ministries, itself a far more difficult task in the under-resourced and multimodel EU than in national systems of government (Jordan and Schout 2006). However, coordination must also occur between them, EU officials, and civil society. A crucial question for future researchers is precisely what sort of interaction and overlap, with what effects, occur between domestic policy networks at the national level and Brussels-based EU networks (see Nunan 1999; Kriesi *et al.* 2006). There seems no question that there is plenty of demand for network governance, and that it may even be on the increase. Important questions remain unanswered:

precisely how will these networks emerge? How will they be structured? And how will their performance be guaranteed? As yet the emerging literature on 'new' and more networked modes of governance has not really resolved these and many other management issues.

Jordan and Schout (2006: xii)

Second, can policy network analysis generate clearer and more rigorous hypotheses about what constitutes 'success' for different kinds of network?

Long-established policy communities for whom EU policy brings benefits, and traditionally has done, might be considered successful when they are able to veto policy change. Alternatively, more recently established or emerging networks might measure their success by the extent to which they are able to force new issues onto the EU policy agenda. The success of some policy networks might be measured in terms of policy transfer, or the importation of solutions 'from the international or national policy levels, and then adopting an interpretation . . . to suit one's own context' (De Jong and Edelenbos 2007: 687). In any event, we need clearer theoretical propositions about what sort of interests are empowered by which type of policy network structures, and which find themselves disadvantaged by certain types of network, and why.

Third, is it possible to develop normative propositions about how EU policy networks can be structured and managed in order to serve the greater European good?

Thus far, most policy network analyses have generated thick description of the EU policy process, while eschewing normative propositions or prescriptions. Especially in a radically enlarged EU, future research could usefully develop overtly normative analyses of how policy networks can be constructed to help solve problems of compliance (P.M. Haas 1999), management (Metcalfe 2000; Jordan and Schout 2006), and legitimacy

(Peterson and O'Toole 2001; Montpetit 2003). In particular, the question of whether new technologies—such as the Internet—make policy networks more or less inclusive remains mostly an open one (Rethemeyer 2007).

Conclusion

We have reviewed the (disputed) origins of policy network analysis as a tool for studying the policy consequences of European integration. The most basic assumptions of policy network analysis—including *the* basic assumption that network structure partially determines outcomes—have been examined critically, along with its main arguments. More generally, we have reviewed the main criticisms of a model that has never been short of critics, and found much to criticize.

It may seem somewhat facile and predictable to conclude by calling for more theoretical development and empirical research. Yet it is worth reminding ourselves of something quite remarkable about the study of the EU: how little we still know about the internal workings of the EU (as well as most other IOs), as opposed to European integration as a broad political process. As Barnett and Finnemore (1999) argue, the theoretical lenses used to understand international cooperation between states tend to be rigidly economistic, and focused on assessing supply and demand for cooperation. Cooperation is, of course, an anomaly in an international world that is still viewed as anarchic by most international relations scholars.

Consequently, our research tends to focus on the bargains states strike to make or reshape IOs. Scholars pay very little attention to what goes on subsequently in their day-to-day operations or even the larger effects they have on the world.

Barnett and Finnemore (1999: 726)

If nothing else, the rise of policy network analysis represents a sincere effort to understand how the EU works and with what effects on the wider world. Arguably, policy network analysts are the least preachy of all types of scholar concerned with European integration because they are most willing to admit that there is much about (especially) the new, enlarged EU that we still do not understand very well.

■ NOTES

1. I am grateful to the editors, Elizabeth Bomberg, Renaud Dehousse, Richard Freeman, Grant Jordan, Laurence J. O'Toole Jr, members of the University of Edinburgh Public Policy research group, and the editors for useful comments on this and earlier drafts.

2. Quoted in Kirk Johnson, 'We agreed to agree, and forgot to notice', *New York Times Week in Review*, 6 January 2008 (available at: www.nytimes.com/2008/01/06/weekinreview/06johnson.html?_r=1andoref=slogin; accessed 26 November 2008).

3. Revealingly, the 2007 Lisbon Treaty, if ratified, would rename the co-decision procedure (which was never formally given that name) the 'ordinary' legislative procedure.

4. Indicative in this respect was the report of an EP working group on internal reform in early 2008. It observed that the increasingly frequent practice of 'informal second readings' under co-decision (thus avoiding a confrontational 'third reading' and leading to faster legislation) reflected a 'greater degree of trust and willingness to cooperate' between EU institutions, especially the EP and Council. But it also expressed 'serious concerns' about the practice's 'potential lack of transparency and democratic legitimacy' and worried that there was 'too much focus on fast-track negotiations at the expense of an open political debate within and between the institutions'. The trend for early deals 'does not increase Parliament's visibility in the public and the media who are looking for political confrontation along clear political lines and not for flat, "technocratic" debate'. See Simon Taylor, 'MEPs' quick-deal concerns', *European Voice*, 17 January 2008 (available from: www.europeanvoice.com/archive/article.asp?id=29621; accessed 3 March 2008).

5. As a caveat, we might note Moravcsik's (2005: 366) suggestion, in a critique of neofunctionalism, that 'there is little evidence' that EU intervention in this realm 'matters for policy outcomes'.

6. The latter task seems impossible. Experts agree that 'the new terrorism is increasingly networked' (Lesser 1999: 87). Consider the following prescription:

   Among the most effective strategies of defence against a global terrorist network is the development of a networked response. Transnational networks need to be mobilized, global civil society needs to be engaged and private sector financial institutions need to be employed to suppress or freeze the financial assets of terrorist networks.

   Biersteker (2002: 83)

   Or, reflect on an expert's view of progress in the 'war on terrorism': 'Now you're into a situation where there is a network of networks . . . With al-Qaeda, if you take out nodal points in the network, they will regrow' (quoted in *Financial Times*, 9–10 November 2002: 8).

7. There is dispute in the literature about whether this continuum is too 'static' and support for the idea that policy networks are dynamic structures that can change and be transformed, especially by powerful ideas (Marsh and Smith 2000; Kisby 2008).

8. Thatcher's (1998) contrast between policy network analysis and what he calls 'policy learning models', such as epistemic communities and advocacy coalitions, and his claim that 'policy network frameworks cannot simply be mixed with other approaches' are two of the less convincing points made in his otherwise thoughtful critique of policy network analysis. If we compare different approaches and concepts such as policy network, issue network, policy domaine, etc. we find that 'the fundamental principle underlying all these approaches is that relations between actors, rather than the actors' individual attributes, hold the key to explaining public policy decisions' (Knoke 1998: 508).

9. By some accounts, policy network analysis is actually a variant of institutionalism (Hall and Taylor 1996; Lowndes 1996; Blom-Hansen 1997; Peters 1999).

10. Jean-Pierre Jouyet quoted in *European Voice*, 17–23 January 2008, 12.

11. Dissent about the utility or analytical power of policy network analysis is summarized and evaluated in the section entitled 'Critique' below.

12. Emphasis in original. The astounding breadth of Castells' scholarship sometimes exposes a lack of depth of knowledge about the EU (a frequent problem for those who study the subject 'part time'). For example, Castells (1998: 314, 317) repeatedly claims that qualified majority voting was extended in the late 1980s in the 'European Council', rather than in the Council of Ministers.

13. Quoted in Tony Barber, 'Brussels' heart ponders Brown absence', *Financial Times*, 13 December 2007, 2.

14. I thank Renaud Dehousse for making this point to me.

15. As much as the authors cited here may be diligently seeking to advance or critique policy network analysis, their frequent resort to self-citation and tendencies to try to rewrite their and other

authors' places in the literature mean that a diligent postgraduate student could be forgiven for concluding that recent debates seem to have become so petty and personal that the approach itself is best avoided.

16. Judith Crosbie, 'EU member states seek more powers for Eurojust', *European Voice*, 17 January 2008 (available from: www.europeanvoice.com/archive/article.asp?id=29622; accessed 26 November 2008).

▪ GUIDE TO FURTHER READING

Jordan, A. and Schout A. (2006) *The Coordination of the European Union: Exploring the Capacities of Networked Governance* (Oxford and New York: Oxford University Press) is the best recent treatment of network governance in the EU.

Kamarck, E.C. (2007) *The End of Government as We Know It: Making Public Policy Work* (Boulder, CO and London: Lynne Rienner) is a readable analysis by a practitioner—one of Al Gore's top policy advisers—which presents government by network as one response to the policy challenges of the twenty-first century.

Keck, M.E. and Sikkink, K. (1998) *Activists Beyond Borders: Advocacy Networks in International Politics* (Ithaca, NY, and London: Cornell University Press) is one of the most impressive studies of how international politics has been transformed by the rise of transnational networks generally.

Marsh, D. (ed.) (1998) *Comparing Policy Networks* (Buckingham: Open University Press) is an edited collection of essays using policy network analysis, including several that are preoccupied with the EU.

Peterson, J. and Bomberg, E. (1999) *Decision-Making in the European Union* (Basingstoke and New York: Palgrave) uses policy network analysis to probe decision-making in a diverse range of EU policy sectors.

▪ STUDY QUESTIONS

1. What must be done to transform policy network analysis from a metaphorical tool for analysis to an actual theory?

2. Can policy network analysis generate clearer and more rigorous hypotheses about what constitutes 'success' for different kinds of network?

3. Can policy network analysis effectively describe, explain, and even predict outcomes arising from the use of new EU policy methods and modes?

4. Is it possible to develop normative propositions about how EU policy networks can be structured and managed in order to serve the greater European good?

5. Is network governance a reflection of the 'democratic deficit' in Europe and elsewhere, or is it a creative, modern solution to twenty-first century policy problems?

7

The New Institutionalisms and European Integration

Mark A. Pollack

Introduction

The European Union (EU) is without question the most densely institutionalized international organization in the world, with a welter of intergovernmental and supranational
institutions and a rapidly growing body of primary and secondary legislation, the so-
called *acquis communautaire*. Small wonder, then, that the body of literature known under
the rubric of 'the new institutionalism' has been applied with increasing frequency and
with increasing success to the study of the Union as a polity and to European integration
as a process. In fact, however, the 'new institutionalism' in social theory has evolved into
plural institutionalisms, with rational choice, sociological, and historical variants, each
with a distinctive set of hypotheses and insights about the EU. This chapter examines the
new institutionalisms in rational choice and historical analysis and their contributions to
EU studies, briefly summarizing the core assumptions of each approach before discussing
specific applications to the study of the European Union and the question of EU enlargement, and concluding with an analysis of the strengths and weaknesses of institutional
approaches to the study of European integration.

The Origins of Rational Choice and Historical Institutionalism

The new institutionalism(s) in political science did not, of course, originate in the field of
EU studies, but reflected a gradual and diverse reintroduction of institutions into a large
body of theories (such as behaviourism, pluralism, Marxism, and neorealism) in which
institutions had been either absent or epiphenomenal, i.e. reflections of deeper factors
or processes such as capitalism or the distribution of political power in a given domestic
society or international system. By contrast with these institution-free accounts of politics, which dominated American political science between the 1950s and the 1970s, three
primary 'institutionalisms' developed during the course of the 1980s and early 1990s,
each with a distinct definition of institutions and a distinct account of how they 'matter'
in the study of politics (March and Olsen 1989; Hall and Taylor 1996).

The first of these institutionalisms arose within the rational-choice approach to the study of politics, as pioneered by students of American politics. To simplify only slightly, the contemporary rational choice institutionalist literature began with the effort by American political scientists to understand the origins and effects of US Congressional institutions. During the late 1970s, rational choice scholars like William Riker (1980) noted that, in formal models of majoritarian decision-making, policy choices are inherently unstable, 'cycling' among multiple possible equilibria, with no single policy able to command a lasting majority among legislators. Yet empirically oriented scholars of the US Congress noted that the House and Senate were indeed able to agree on stable policies, raising the question of how and why such stability was achieved. In this context, Kenneth Shepsle (1979, 1986) argued that Congressional institutions, and in particular the committee system, could produce 'structure-induced equilibrium' by ruling some alternatives as permissible or impermissible and by structuring the voting and veto power of various actors in the decision-making process. In more recent work, Shepsle and others have turned their attention to the problem of 'equilibrium institutions', namely, how actors choose or design institutions to secure mutual gains, and how those institutions change or persist over time.

Shepsle's innovation and the subsequent development of the rational choice approach to Congressional institutions have produced a number of theoretical offshoots with potential applications in comparative as well as international politics. For example, Shepsle and others have examined in some detail the 'agenda-setting' power of the Congressional committees that are the linchpin of his structure-induced equilibrium, specifying the conditions under which agenda-setting committees could influence the outcomes of Congressional votes (Shepsle and Weingast 1984; Ordeshook and Schwartz 1987). Shepsle's 'distributive' model of Congressional committees has, however, been challenged by Keith Krehbiel (1991) and other scholars, who agree that committees possess agenda-power but argue that the committee system serves an 'informational' rather than distributive function by providing members with an incentive to acquire and share policy-relevant information with other members of Congress.

In another offshoot, students of the Congress have developed principal-agent models of Congressional delegation of authority to regulatory bureaucracies (and later to courts) and the efforts of Congress to control those bureaucracies (Moe 1984; McCubbins and Schwartz 1987; Cooter and Ginsburg 1996). More recently, Epstein and O'Halloran (1999) and others (Huber and Shipan 2000) have pioneered a 'transaction cost approach' to the design of political institutions, arguing that legislators deliberately and systematically design political institutions to minimize the transaction costs associated with making public policy. Although originally formulated and applied in the context of American political institutions, these approaches are applicable in other comparative and international political contexts, including that of the European Union.

By contrast with the formal definition of institutions in rational choice approaches, sociological institutionalism and constructivist approaches in international relations (examined in detail by Thomas Risse in Chapter 8 of this volume) define institutions much more broadly to include informal norms and conventions as well as formal rules, and they argue that such institutions 'constitute' actors, shaping the way in which actors view the world. Moreover, by contrast with rational choice models, in which actors are regarded as strategic utility-maximizers whose preferences are taken as given, sociological institutionalist accounts often begin with the assumption that people act according to a 'logic of appropriateness', taking cues from their institutional environment as they construct their preferences and select the appropriate behaviour for a given institutional environment. In the case of the EU, sociological institutionalist and constructivist scholars have examined the process by which EU and other institutional norms are diffused and shape the preferences and behavior of actors in both domestic and international politics (Risse, Chapter 8 this volume).

Historical institutionalists (HI), finally, took up a position in between the two camps, focusing on the effects of institutions *over time* (Thelen 1999; Pierson 2000, 2004). By contrast with the rational choice approaches discussed above, HI scholars generally reject 'functionalist' explanations for institutional design. In such functionalist explanations, political institutions are assumed to have been deliberately designed by contemporary actors for the efficient performance of specific functions, such as the provision of policy-relevant information or the adoption of expert and credible policies, and little or no attention is paid to historical legacies. In contrast with this view, historical institutionalists argue that institutional choices taken in the past can persist, or become locked in, thereby shaping and constraining actors later in time. Institutions, it is argued, are 'sticky', or resistant to change, both because of the uncertainty associated with institutional design, and because national constitutions and international treaties can create significant transaction costs and set high institutional thresholds (such as a supermajority or unanimous agreement) to later reforms (Pollack 1996: 437–8).

In perhaps the most sophisticated presentation of this strand of historical–institutionalist thinking, Paul Pierson (2000, 2004) has suggested that political institutions and public policies are frequently characterized by what Pierson calls 'positive feedbacks', insofar as those institutions and policies generate incentives for actors to stick with and not abandon existing institutions, adapting them only incrementally to changing political environments. Insofar as political institutions and public policies are in fact characterized by positive feedbacks, Pierson argues, politics will be characterized by certain interrelated phenomena, including: *inertia*, or *lock-ins*, whereby existing institutions may remain in equilibrium for extended periods despite considerable political change; *a critical role for timing and sequencing*, in which relatively small and contingent events that occur at *critical junctures* early in a sequence shape (that is, provide the institutional context for) events that occur later; and *path-dependence*, in which early decisions provide incentives for actors to perpetuate institutional and policy choices inherited from the past, even when the resulting outcomes are manifestly inefficient. With regard to the last concept of path dependence, perhaps the most influential notion in recent historical-institutionalist work, Pierson cites with approval Margaret Levi's definition:

Path dependence has to mean, if it is to mean anything, that once a country or region has started down a path, the costs of reversal are very high. There will be other choice points, but the entrenchments of certain institutional arrangements obstruct easy reversal of the initial choice. Perhaps the better metaphor is a tree, rather than a path. From the same trunk, there are many different branches and smaller branches. Although it is possible to turn around or to clamber from one to the other—and essential if the chosen branch dies—the branch on which a climber begins is the one she tends to follow.

Levi (1997: 28), quoted in Pierson (2000: 252)

Note that theories such as Pierson's and Levi's, while rejecting equilibrium analysis, typically adopt assumptions about actors and their preferences that are fully consistent with those of rational choice theory (North 1990; Pierson 2000, 2004). For this reason, this chapter does not consider historical institutionalism as a distinct and competing school of thought, but rather as a particular variant of rational choice theory emphasizing the importance of time, feedbacks, sequencing, and path-dependence in the study of politics.

By and large, the 'first generation' of historical institutionalist work has been more effective in explaining continuity (often in the face of exogenous shocks) than in explaining institutional or endogenous source of change (as in the original neofunctionalist theory, which posited spillover as the primary engine of the integrative process). For this reason, both historical institutionalist and rational choice theorists have devoted increasing attention in recent years to the challenge of theorizing the sources of both continuity and change in political life. Within historical institutionalism, a growing second-generation literature has focused on the central claim that existing institutions and policies may produce not only positive feedbacks that support existing institutions and policies, but also negative feedbacks that create pressures for institutional and policy change. Existing institutions and policies, in this view, may have perverse effects that can gradually undermine social or political support for them (Streeck and Thelen 2005; Hall and Thelen 2006). Welfare-state programmes, for example, may be structured such that the value of benefits erodes, and this benefit erosion in turn may lead to a decline in public support for those programmes—a clear negative feedback in an issue area long characterized by positive feedbacks and stability (Immergut 2006).

Within rational choice theory, a similar approach is taken by Avner Greif and David Laitin (2004), who provide a formal model of institutional change in which feedbacks from institutions can either strengthen and reinforce existing institutions, or conversely undermine them. Self-reinforcing institutions, in this view, are those that change the political environment in ways that make the institution more stable in the face of exogenous shocks. Self-undermining institutions, by contrast, are those that change the environment such that a previously stable institutional equilibrium is undermined; these institutions 'can cultivate the seeds of their own demise' (Greif and Laitin 2004: 34), producing not stability but increasing pressure for change with the passage of time.

Perhaps most importantly, such rational choice and historical institutionalist work has gone far beyond the now-familiar claims that political institutions are path-dependent or 'sticky'. Instead, this literature tells us, political institutions and policies can produce *varying* effects over time, depending on the characteristics of the institution or policy in question and the types of feedback effects it generates. For example, some institutions, such as national constitutions, involve considerable start-up costs, generate adaptive effects among large numbers of people, and can be changed only by a large majority of parliamentarians and the electorate, and should therefore generate positive feedbacks and path-dependent behaviour. By contrast, however, other institutions or public policies may involve lower fixed costs, fewer adaptive effects, and lower institutional barriers to wholesale reform, and in these cases institutions and policies may be changed easily, with little or no evidence of historical legacies or path-dependence. And in still other cases, existing institutions and policies—including, possibly, European integration—may produce negative feedbacks and become self-undermining over time.

In theory, therefore, historical institutionalism and its component concepts such as feed-back effects and path-dependence offer the prospect, not just of claiming that 'history matters', but of explaining how and under what conditions historical events do—or do not—shape contemporary and future political choices and outcomes.

Applications to the Study of the European Union

Within the past decade, all three new institutionalisms have been adopted by students of European integration, with results that have been reviewed extensively elsewhere (Jupille and Caporaso 1999; Dowding 2000; Aspinwall and Schneider 2001; Pollack 1996, 2007). Rational choice institutionalist analyses of the EU arguably date back to the late 1980s, with Fritz Scharpf's (1988) pioneering work on 'joint-decision traps' in the EU and other federal systems, and continued into the 1990s and 2000s with work by George Tsebelis, Geoffrey Garrett, and others who sought to model in rational choice terms the origins and above all the workings of EU institutions. Simplifying considerably, we can say that rational choice analyses have examined all three of the major functions of government at the Union level:

1. legislative politics, including decision-making within the Council of Ministers as well as the ever-changing legislative role of the European Parliament;
2. executive politics, i.e. the delegation of executive powers to the European Commission and other agencies, and their exercise of those powers; and
3. judicial politics, specifically the European Court of Justice's role vis-à-vis EU member governments and national courts.

The remainder of this section briefly discusses each of these bodies of literature, with special attention to the first question of executive politics, followed by

4. a brief discussion of historical institutionalist approaches emphasizing joint-decision traps, lock-ins, and European integration as a path-dependent process.

Legislative Politics

Without doubt the best-developed strand of rational choice theory in EU studies has focused on EU legislative processes. Drawing heavily on theories and spatial models of legislative behaviour and organization, students of EU legislative politics have adapted and tested models of legislative politics to understand the process of legislative decision-making in the EU. This literature, as Gail McElroy (2007) points out, has focused on three major questions: legislative politics within the European Parliament; the voting power of the various states in the Council of Ministers; and the respective powers of these two bodies in the EU legislative process.

The European Parliament (EP) has been the subject of extensive theoretical modelling and empirical study over the past two decades, with a growing number of scholars studying the legislative organization of the EP and the voting behaviour of its members (MEPs), adapting models of legislative politics derived largely from the study of the US Congress. The early studies of the Parliament, in the 1980s and early 1990s, emphasized the striking fact that, in spite of the multinational nature of the Parliament, the best predictor of MEP voting behaviour is not nationality but an MEP's 'party group', with the various party groups demonstrating extraordinarily high measures of cohesion in roll-call votes. These MEPs, moreover, were shown to contest elections and cast their votes in a two-dimensional 'issue space', including not only the familiar nationalism/ supranationalism dimension but also and especially the more traditional, 'domestic' dimension of left–right contestation (Hix 2001). Still other studies have focused on the legislative organization of the EP, including not only the party groups but also the Parliament's powerful committees, whose members play an important agenda-setting role in preparing legislation for debate on the floor of Parliament (Kreppel 2001). Perhaps most fundamentally, these scholars have shown, the EP can increasingly be studied as a 'normal parliament' whose members vote predictably and cohesively within a political space dominated by the familiar contestation between parties of the left and right (Tsebelis and Garrett 2001a; Hix *et al.* 2007).

By contrast with this rich EP literature, the rational choice literature on the Council of Ministers until recently focused on the relatively narrow question of member-state voting power under different decision rules. In this context, a number of scholars have used increasingly elaborate formal models of Council voting to establish the relative voting weights—and hence the bargaining power—of various member states under various qualified majority voting (QMV) voting formulas. The use of such voting-power indexes has led to substantial debate among rational choice scholars, with several scholars criticizing the approach for its emphasis on formal voting weight at the expense of national preferences (Albert 2003). In recent years, however, the study of legislative politics in the Council has undergone a renaissance, driven in part by lively theoretical debates among rational choice, constructivist, and other scholars, and in part by the increasing public availability of Council voting records and data-sets such as the Decision-making in the European Union (DEU) project (Thomson *et al.* 2006). This thriving literature has produced new theoretical conjectures, and new qualitative and quantitative empirical tests, on issues such as the relative power of EU member states in the Council; the coalition patterns among member states within the Council (which appear to break down largely on geographical or north–south lines); the Council's remarkable (and, for traditional legislative-politics models) puzzling tradition of consensus decision-making, rather than minimum-winning coalitions; and the as-yet uneven evidence for the socialization of national officials in the Council and its subsidiary committees and working groups (for an excellent review see Naurin and Wallace 2008 and the chapters in that volume; see also Mattila 2004; Hayes-Renshaw and Wallace 2006; Thomson *et al.* 2006).

Third and finally, a large and ever-growing literature has attempted to model in rational choice terms, and to study empirically, the inter-institutional relations among the Commission (as agenda-setter) and the Council and Parliament, under different legislative procedures. Over the course of the 1980s and the 1990s, the legislative powers of the EP have grown sequentially, from the relatively modest and non-binding 'consultation procedure' through the creation of the 'cooperation' and 'assent' procedures in the 1980s, and the creation and reform of a 'co-decision procedure' in the 1990s. This expansion of EP legislative power, and the complex nature of the new legislative procedures, has fostered the development of a burgeoning literature and led to several vigorous debates among rational choice scholars about the nature and extent of the EP's and the Council's respective influence across the various procedures. The first of these debates concerned the power of the European Parliament under the cooperation procedure. In an influential article, George Tsebelis (1994) argued that this provision gave the Parliament 'conditional agenda-setting' power, insofar as the Parliament would now enjoy the ability to make specific proposals that would be easier for the Council to adopt than to amend. Other scholars disputed Tsebelis's model, arguing that the EP's proposed amendments would have no special status without the approval of the Commission, which therefore remained the principal agenda-setter. This theoretical debate, in turn, motivated a series of empirical studies which appeared to confirm the basic predictions of Tsebelis's model, namely that the Parliament enjoyed much greater success in influencing the content of legislation under cooperation than under the older consultation procedure (Kreppel 1999).

A second controversy emerged in the literature over the power of Parliament under the co-decision procedure introduced by the Maastricht Treaty (co-decision I) and reformed by the Treaty of Amsterdam (co-decision II). In another controversial article, Tsebelis (1997) argued that, contrary to common perceptions of the co-decision procedure as a step forward for the EP, Parliament had actually *lost* legislative power in the move from cooperation to co-decision I. By contrast, other rational choice scholars disputed Garrett and Tsebelis's claims, noting that alternative specifications of the model predicted more modest agenda-setting power for the EP under cooperation, and/or a stronger position for the EP in co-decision. Here again, quantitative and qualitative empirical analyses have provided at least tentative answers to the question of EP influence across the various legislative procedures, with the most extensive study suggesting that the EP has indeed enjoyed greater legislative influence under co-decision I than under cooperation, largely at the expense of the Commission (Tsebelis *et al.* 2001a). In any event, the Treaty of Amsterdam subsequently simplified the co-decision procedure, creating a genuinely bicameral co-decision II procedure.

To some observers, these debates have verged on scholasticism, focusing more on model specification than on the empirical reality of legislative decision-making, and coming around to empirical testing relatively late in the day (Crombez *et al.* 2000; Garrett *et al.* 2001). Taken as a whole, however, the debate over the EP's legislative powers, like early work on the internal organization of the Parliament, has both clarified the basic theoretical assumptions that scholars make about the various actors and their preferences, and motivated systematic empirical studies that have generated cumulative knowledge about the EU legislative process.

Executive Politics

The study of EU executive politics is not the exclusive preserve of rational choice scholars (Tallberg 2007). Neofunctionalists and intergovernmentalists have been debating the causal role of the executive Commission for decades, and the Commission has been studied by sociological institutionalists, by students of political entrepreneurship, and by normative democratic theorists. Nevertheless, rational choice institutionalism (RCI) and principal-agent analysis have emerged over the past decade as the dominant approach to the study of the Commission and other executive actors such as the European Central Bank and the growing body of EU agencies. These studies generally address two specific sets of questions. First, they ask why and under what conditions a group of (member-state) principals might delegate powers to (supranational) agents, such as the Commission, the European Central Bank, or the Court of Justice. With regard to this first question, rationalists like Moravcsik (1998), Majone (2001), Franchino (2002, 2004, 2007), and Pollack (2003) have drawn from the theoretical literature on delegation in American, comparative and international politics in order to devise and test hypotheses about the motives of EU member governments in delegating specific powers and functions to the Commission and other supranational actors.

Simplifying considerably, such transaction-cost accounts of delegation argue that member-state principals, as rational actors, delegate powers to supranational organizations primarily to lower the transaction costs of policy-making, in particular by allowing member governments to commit themselves credibly to international agreements and to benefit from the policy-relevant expertise provided by supranational actors. Despite differences in emphasis, the empirical work of these scholars has collectively demonstrated that EU member governments do indeed delegate powers to the Commission, the European Central Bank, and the Court of Justice largely to reduce the transaction costs of policy-making, in particular through the monitoring of member-state compliance, the filling-in of framework treaties ('incomplete contracts'), and the speedy and efficient adoption of implementing regulations that would otherwise have to be adopted in a time-consuming legislative process by the member governments themselves (Moravcsik 1998; Pollack 2003; Franchino 2002, 2004, 2007). By contrast with these positive results, however, scholars have found little or no support for the hypothesis that member states delegate powers to the Commission to take advantage of its superior expertise (Moravcsik 1998; Pollack 2003). Similarly, the same studies generally concede that transaction-cost models do a poor job of predicting patterns of delegation to the European Parliament, which appears to have been delegated powers primarily in response to concerns about democratic legitimacy rather than in order to reduce the transaction costs of policy-making.

In addition to the question of delegation, rational choice institutionalists have devoted greater attention to a second question posed by principal-agent models: what if an agent—such as the European Commission, the Court of Justice, or the European Central Bank—behaves in ways that diverge from the preferences of the principals? The answer to this question in analysis lies primarily in the administrative procedures that the principals may establish to define *ex ante* the scope of agency activities, as well as the oversight procedures that allow for *ex post* oversight and sanctioning of errant agents. Applied to the European Union, principal-agent analysis therefore leads to the hypothesis that agency autonomy is likely to vary across issue areas and over time, as a function of the preferences of the member states, the distribution of information between principals and agents, and the decision rules governing the application of sanctions or the adoption of new legislation. By and large, empirical studies of executive politics in the EU have supported these hypotheses, pointing in particular to the significance of decision rules as a crucial determinant of executive autonomy (Pollack 1997, 2003; Tallberg 1999, 2000; Tsebelis and Garrett 2001b).

Much of this literature on delegation and agency focuses on the rather arcane question of *comitology*, the committees of member state representatives established to supervise the Commission in its implementation of EU law. For rational choice theorists, comitology committees act as control mechanisms designed by member-state principals to supervise their supranational agent (the Commission) in its executive duties. In this approach, member government preferences are assumed to be fixed, the aim of comitology is control rather than deliberation, and the rules governing a committee matter in determining the discretion of the Commission in a given issue area. More specifically, rational choice analysts have analysed the differences among the three primary types of comitology committees—advisory committees, management committees, and regulatory committees—noting that, in formal models of executive decision-making, the Commission is least constrained under the advisory committee procedure, and most constrained under the regulatory committee procedure, with the management committee procedure occupying a middle ground (Steunenberg *et al.* 1996). Under these circumstances, rationalists predict, EU member governments will prefer and select comitology committees designed to maximize their expected utility by producing favourable 'policy streams' in a given issue area; and they will carefully calibrate the autonomy or responsiveness of the Commission through the selection of specific comitology procedures (Pollack 2003; Franchino 2000).

By contrast with this rationalist view of comitology as a control mechanism, Christian Joerges and Jürgen Neyer (1997a, b) draw on Habermasian accounts of deliberative democracy as well as constructivist analysis in political science to argue that EU comitology committees provide a forum in which national and supranational experts meet and deliberate in a search for the best or most efficient solutions to common policy problems. In this view, comitology is not an arena for hardball intergovernmental bargaining, as rationalists assume, but rather a technocratic version of deliberative democracy in which informal norms, deliberation, good arguments, and consensus matter more than formal voting rules, which are rarely invoked.

Comitology, then, emerges as a key area in which rationalist and constructivist theorists provide competing accounts and hypotheses on a common empirical terrain, which offers the unusual prospect of direct, competitive empirical testing. Unfortunately, as I have argued elsewhere (Pollack 2003), testing such hypotheses requires researchers to deal with serious methodological challenges, including the measurement of elusive concepts such as 'deliberation' (for constructivists and sociological institutionalists) and 'autonomy' and 'control' (for rationalists). Faced with these difficulties, students of comitology have pursued two distinct research strategies to test hypotheses about the significance of EU committees. First, as Franchino demonstrates in his landmark book (2007), the decision to delegate powers to the Commission, as well as the choice of comitology procedure and other oversight mechanisms, are systematically influenced by institutional and environmental factors including the degree of conflict within the Council, the degree of conflict between the Council and the Commission, and the decision rules governing the adoption of legislation (i.e., voting rules in the Council), and the varying role of the European Parliament (see also Dogan 2000; Pollack 2003; Franchino 2002, 2004). This careful and systematic selection of comitology committees suggests, in turn, the differences in comitology procedures do indeed matter for subsequent policy outcomes.

Second, moving from the delegation to the post-delegation stage, other scholars have undertaken process-tracing case studies of Commission behaviour under comitology, allowing the observer to establish the respective preferences of actors such the Commission and the member governments and examine the process of committee decision-making in practice. Among rational choice analysts, Schmidt (1997) and Pollack (2003) have engaged in such case-study analysis, in areas such as the liberalization of telecommunications and electricity, merger control, the management of the Structural Funds, and the negotiation of the Uruguay Round. Their findings, although tentative, suggest that member governments do indeed use comitology committees as instruments of control, and that Commission autonomy and influence vary as a function of the administrative and oversight procedures adopted by the Council. By contrast, however, Joerges and Neyer's (1997a, b) empirical research in the foodstuffs sector, although not reported in the form of a case study, de-emphasizes the control functions of comitology in favour of the emergence of deliberative interaction among delegates in scientific advisory committees. These disparate results suggest the need for further empirical work, and careful case selection, to determine the extent of, and the conditions for, the use of comitology committees as a means of control or a forum for deliberation, respectively.

In sum, the rational choice, principal-agent approach has indeed come to dominate the study of the Commission and other executive actors in the past several decades. This principal-agent literature, like other rational choice approaches, can be criticized for its focus on a particular set of (albeit very important) questions about the relationship between principals and agents, and for its neglect of other equally important questions, such as the internal workings of the Commission. Furthermore, as Simon Hix (2007: 149–50) has argued, the traditional PA assumption that the Commission is an outlier with particularly intense preferences for greater integration may be misleading in the post-Maastricht era where the EU has already placed markers in nearly every area of public policy. Nevertheless, principal-agent models have provided a theoretical framework to ask a series of pointed questions about the causes and consequences of delegating executive power to EU actors, and they have directed scholars' attention to factors such as transaction costs, information asymmetries, and the operation of formal rules and administrative law, that had been neglected or indeed ignored by earlier studies.

Judicial Politics and Legal Integration

In addition to the lively debate about the nature of EU executive politics, rational choice institutionalists have also engaged in an increasingly sophisticated research programme into the nature of EU judicial politics and the role of the European Court of Justice in the integration process. Writing in the early 1990s, for example, Geoffrey Garrett first drew on principal-agent analysis to argue that the Court, as an agent of the EU's member governments, was bound to follow the wishes of the most powerful member states. These member states, Garrett argued, had established the ECJ as a means to solve problems of incomplete contracting and monitoring compliance with EU obligations, and they rationally accepted ECJ jurisprudence, even when rulings went against them, because of their longer-term interest in the enforcement of EU law (Garrett 1992). In such a setting, Garrett and Weingast (1993: 189) argued, the ECJ might identify 'constructed focal points' among multiple equilibrium outcomes, but the Court was unlikely to rule against the preferences of powerful EU member states, as Burley and Mattli (1993) had suggested in a famous article drawing on neofunctionalist theory.

Responding to Garrett's work, other scholars have argued forcefully that Garrett's model overestimated the control mechanisms available to powerful member states and the ease of sanctioning an activist Court, which has been far more autonomous than Garrett suggests. To simplify considerably, such accounts suggest that the Court has been able to pursue the process of legal integration far beyond the collective preferences of the member governments, in part because of the high costs to member states in overruling or failing to comply with ECJ decisions, and in part because the ECJ enjoys powerful allies in the form of national courts and individual litigants, the ECJ's 'other interlocutors' which refer hundreds of cases per year to the ECJ via the 'preliminary reference' procedure of Article 234 (Weiler 1994; Mattli and Slaughter 1995, 1998; Stone Sweet and Caporaso 1998; Stone Sweet and Brunell 1998; Alter 2001). In this view, best summarized by Stone Sweet and Caporaso (1998: 129), 'the move to supremacy and direct effect must be understood as audacious acts of agency' by the Court. At the same time, however, they argue that:

judicial politics in the EC is not easily captured by [principal-agent] imagery. The Court's constitutionalization of the treaty system produced profound structural changes. Among other things, it reconstituted relationships among the ECJ, national judges, and private and public actors at the national and transnational levels. Often enough, the impact of the Court's rule-making is to effectively constrain member-state governments, both individually and collectively. The P-A framework is ill-equipped to capture these dynamics.

Stone Sweet and his collaborators are undoubtedly correct in their assertion that a simple principal-agent model of member government-ECJ relations cannot constitute a satisfactory theory of EU legal integration, since the ECJ must necessarily address other actors, including the individual litigants who bring cases as well as the national courts that are responsible for submitting and applying the bulk of all contemporary ECJ decisions. By the same token, however, no satisfactory theory of EU legal integration can *omit* the principal-agent relationship between the member governments and the ECJ, since it is this relationship that sets the bounds of ECJ discretion through the adoption and amendment of the treaties and through the threat or use of control mechanisms such as legislative overruling and non-compliance; and indeed, rational choice approaches to the ECJ have gradually become more complex, and have been subjected to greater empirical testing, in response to critics (Garrett 1995; Garrett *et al.* 1998; and Kilroy 1999).

More recently, as Lisa Conant (2007) points out, the literature on the ECJ and legal integration has increasingly moved from the traditional question of the ECJ's relationship with national governments, toward the study of the ECJ's other interlocutors, including most notably the national courts that bring the majority of cases before the ECJ, and the individual litigants who use EU law to achieve their aims within national legal systems. Such studies have problematized and sought to explain the complex and ambivalent relationship between the ECJ and national courts, as well as the varying litigation strategies of 'one-shot' litigants and 'repeat players' before the courts (Mattli and Slaughter 1998; Alter 2001; Conant 2002). These and other studies, influenced largely (although not exclusively) by rational choice models, have demonstrated the complexities of ECJ legal integration, the interrelationships among supranational, national, and subnational political and legal actors, and the limits of EU law in national legal contexts.

Unintended Consequences, Joint-decision Traps, and Path-dependence

Thus far, we have looked at the executive, judicial and legislative politics of the European Union through the standard lenses of rational choice theory, in which institutions are either: (1) independent (or intervening) variables that explain how institutions shape policy outcomes—what Shepsle (1986) calls 'structure-induced equilibria'; or (2) dependent variables created and maintained by rational actors to perform certain functions for the actors that created them (Shepsle's 'equilibrium institutions'). Implicit or explicit in such accounts is the notion that institutions, once created, are indeed 'sticky' and persist over time; yet the functionalist assumption that institutions are indeed *chosen* to perform certain functions is seldom tested empirically, and little attention is usually given to the specific question of how institutions evolve and shape political outcomes over time. Thus, despite the substantial contributions of rationalist approaches to our understanding of the EU, much of the rational choice literature on the EU arguably underemphasizes the central point of the early neofunctionalist literature, namely the concept of European integration as a *process* which does indeed unfold over time, often as a result of the unintended consequences of early integration decisions that become difficult for the EU's constitutive member states to control or overturn.

For these reasons, EU scholars have turned increasingly to historical institutionalism in an effort to understand temporal aspects of European integration, including phenomena such as feedback effects, lock-ins, and path-dependence (see e.g. Scharpf 1988; Bulmer 1994; Pierson 1996; Armstrong and Bulmer 1998; and the authors in Cowles *et al.* 2001). In a pioneering article, for example, Fritz Scharpf (1988) argued that the institutional rules of certain joint decision-making systems, such as German federalism or the European Union, lead to what he called 'the joint decision-trap', in which a given institution or policy, once instituted, tends to remain in place, rigid and inflexible, even in the face of a changing policy environment. Such joint-decision traps, Scharpf specified, were particularly likely in institutions characterized by three interrelated rules: intergovernmentalism (as opposed to federalism or supranational decision-making); a voting rule of unanimity (as opposed to majority); and a default condition in which a policy or institution would persist (as opposed to being terminated) in the event of no agreement. Under these specific conditions, Scharpf argued, policies such as the EU's Common Agricultural Policy could become entrenched or locked-in, even in the face of ever-growing agricultural surpluses or other pressures, as long as a single member state remained able to block policy or institutional reforms. On the other hand, Scharpf implied (albeit without elaboration) that a change in any of these three rules—for example, a move to supranational or majoritarian decision-making, or a change in the default rule providing that policies be terminated unless periodically reauthorized—could alleviate the joint-decision trap and allow for ready adaptation of existing institutions to changing circumstances.

Similarly, Pierson's (1996) study of path-dependence in the EU seeks to understand European integration as a process that unfolds over time, and the conditions under which path-dependent processes are most likely to occur. Working from essentially rationalist assumptions, Pierson argues that, despite the initial primacy of member governments in the design of EU institutions and policies, 'gaps' may occur in the ability of member governments to control the subsequent institutions and policies, for four reasons. First, member governments in democratic societies may, because of electoral considerations, apply a high 'discount rate' to the future, agreeing to EU policies that lead to a long-term loss of national control in return for short-term electoral returns. Second, even when governments do not heavily discount the future, unintended consequences of institutional choices may create additional gaps, which member governments may or may not be able to close through subsequent action. Third, Pierson argues, the preferences of member governments may change over time, most obviously because of electoral turn-over, leaving new member governments with new preferences to inherit an *acquis communautaire* negotiated by, and according to the preferences of, a different government. Given the decision rules of intergovernmentalism and unanimity emphasized by Scharpf, however, individual member governments are likely to find themselves 'immobilized by the dead weight of past initiatives' (Pierson 1996: 137). Fourth and finally, Pierson argues, EU institutions and policies may become locked-in not only as the result of change-resistant institutional rules from above, but also through the incremental growth in political support for existing, entrenched institutions from below, as societal actors adapt to and develop a vested interest in the continuation of specific EU policies. In the area of social policy, for example, the European Court of Justice has developed a significant jurisprudence on gender equality that certainly exceeds the original expectations of the member governments. Rolling back these unexpected consequences, however, has proven difficult, both because of the need for a unanimous agreement to overturn an ECJ decision in this area, and because of the domestic constituencies (e.g., working women) with a vested interest in the maintenance of the *acquis*.

Looking beyond these pioneering works by Pierson and Scharpf, most historical institutionalist analyses of the EU have emphasized positive feedbacks, in which an initial integrative act can lead to functional spillover (Haas 1958), gaps in member-state control (Pollack 2003), gradual accretion of institutional forms and actors (Thatcher and Coen 2008), long-term socialization of elites (Checkel 2005) and the negotiation of informal agreements that become entrenched and are subsequently codified after the fact (Farrell and Héritier 2005). While these works offer us important insights about the development of European integration over time, their most important contribution is not the idea that institutions are 'sticky'—which is a generic and rather banal institutionalist claim—but rather their statements about the *conditions* under which we should expect feedback effects and path-dependent behaviour. In Scharpf's analysis, for example, lock-ins occur only under a specific set of decision rules; in other areas, joint-decision traps may be avoided insofar as existing institutions and policies either expire (hence their default condition is *not* the status quo) or can be amended by supranational decision or by qualified majority (breaking the logjam of unanimous intergovernmental decision-making). Similarly, while Pierson calls our attention to the prospects of micro-level adaptations to EU policies and institutions, and hence increasing returns, not all EU policies create such effects, and we should therefore expect variation in the stability and path-dependent character of different EU policies and institutions. To take only one example, the EU's

Structural Funds might at first glance seem to be a classic candidate for a joint-decision trap and path-dependent behavior, like the Common Agricultural Policy. By contrast with the CAP, however, the Structural Funds must be reauthorized at periodic intervals by a unanimous agreement among the member states, and this 'default condition' of expiration, together with the uneven pattern of reliance on the Structural Funds across member states and their citizens, allows EU member states to reform the funds more readily, and with less incidence of path-dependence, than we observe in Treaty reform or in the Common Agricultural Policy. Finally, the notion that EU institutions and policies might have negative or self-undermining feedback effects has been explored less systematically, yet the Union's long constitutional crisis and the long-term decline in public support for further integration suggest that negative feedbacks should be the focus of greater attention in future studies of institutional change.

The New Institutionalisms and EU Enlargement

The enlargement of the European Union has posed multiple challenges to EU policymakers, and multiple research questions to students of European integration (Wallace 2000b; Schimmelfennig and Sedelmeier 2002). Simplifying slightly, we can say that the bulk of the recent scholarship focuses on four primary questions raised by the current enlargement of the EU:

1. Why did the European Union decide, during the course of the 1990s, to enter into enlargement negotiations with as many as 12 new members, despite the obvious budgetary and institutional challenges this would pose for the members of the EU?

2. How can we account for the subsequent negotiations between the European Union and the individual candidate countries, including the preponderant bargaining power of the Union but also its occasional willingness to enter into compromises with the candidate countries?

3. What effects, if any, has the European Union and its promise of eventual membership had on the process of political and economic reform in the candidate countries, particularly the former communist countries of central and eastern Europe? And

4. What effects is the projected enlargement of the Union from 15 to as many as 27 members likely to have on the institutions and policies of an enlarged EU?

Simplifying once again, it seems fair to say that sociological institutionalist and constructivist scholars have devoted greater attention than either rational choice or historical institutionalist scholars to the first two questions, while historical institutionalists have devoted somewhat greater attention to the process of reform in central and eastern Europe, and rational choice institutionalists have applied their familiar tools to projecting the impact of enlargement on the institutions of an EU of 27 or more members.

With regard to the first and second questions on the EU's decision to accept membership applications from and negotiate membership agreements with the new democracies of central and eastern Europe (CEE), a number of sociological institutionalist and constructivist scholars argue that the conduct of the EU's member governments at the very least presents a puzzle for rationalist accounts of European integration. In this view, rational choice theory cannot explain why and how EU member governments have, gradually and somewhat grudgingly, embraced the goal of EU enlargement despite the substantial financial costs of enlargement (particularly for countries like Spain which fear the diversion of EU structural and agricultural aid to the less developed CEE states). Such decisions, it is argued, cannot be explained except with reference to the acceptance of common norms and common standards of legitimacy, according to which the Union cannot reject pleas for membership from neighbouring countries that credibly invoke 'European' values such as democracy and free markets (Sedelmeier 2000; Fierke and Wiener 1999). In an interesting twist on this essentially constructivist argument, Schimmelfennig (2001) argues that while rational choice calculations of material interests can explain member-state preferences on enlargement, their reluctant decision to enlarge represents a case of rhetorical entrapment in which governments, having professed allegiance to a set of common Community norms, were then constrained to live up to those norms in their public behavior. Indeed, Schimmelfennig's argument occupies an intermediate space between rationalist and constructivist (or sociological institutionalist) analyses, since the informal norms of democracy and free markets do not appear to 'constitute' the EU's member governments, but rather to act as external constraints for governments concerned about the reputation on the international scene. Finally, it is worth pointing out that the sociological institutionalist account is not uncontested; indeed, as Andrew Moravcsik and Milada Vachudova (2003) have pointed out, the issue-specific material interests of EU member governments provide at the very least a good first-cut set of predictions about their behaviour in the enlargement negotiations, and the relative success of rationalist and constructivist accounts of those negotiations remains a matter for further empirical research.

Turning to the third major question posed by enlargement—namely, the effects of the EU on the policies and institutions of the applicant countries—we find arguments associated with all three variants of the new institutionalism. A number of scholars, drawing on the influential 'Europeanization' literature within the EU (Cowles *et al.* 2001; Börzel and Risse 2007) and on the early literature on post-Communist transitions (Stark 1992), adopt an historical-institutionalist perspective, noting the path-dependent nature of national institutions and national policies, and underlining the variation in the acceptance and transposition of EU norms by candidate countries, each of which has integrated new elements of the acquis communautaire in line with its own distinct national traditions (Jacoby 2004; Vachudova 2005). Other scholars, writing in a constructivist or sociological institutionalist vein, acknowledge the importance of historical legacies but emphasize the constitutive power of EU and international norms for the elites of the newly democratizing countries of central and eastern Europe, arguing that international social learning and the diffusion of legitimate norms has played a central role in the transition from communist to 'European' politics and policies in each of these countries (Checkel 2005; Epstein 2005; Gheciu 2005). A third set of theorists, drawing from rational choice institutionalist scholarship, have articulated a distinctively rationalist set of causal mechanisms, whereby explicit EU 'conditionality' provides rational incentives for domestic actors to undertake reforms in anticipation of the credible perspective of EU membership (Kelley 2004; Schimmelfennig and Sedelmeier 2005b; Vachudova 2005).

In the most extensive effort to test these competing theories, Frank Schimmelfennig and Ulrich Sedelmeier led a team of researchers who sought explicitly to test alternative rationalist and constructivist hypotheses about the effect of EU membership on the new member states in central and eastern Europe (Schimmelfennig and Sedelmeier 2005a). Drawing on previous rationalist and constructivist work, they derived three distinct models of the mechanisms driving the Europeanization of the candidate/new member countries of central and eastern Europe. The first, 'external incentives' model was derived from rational choice models of bargaining, focusing on the asymmetrical bargaining power of the EU and its applicant states and in particular on EU 'conditionality', namely the EU's insistence that candidate countries apply the acquis communautaire as a prerequisite to membership. Against this rationalist model, the authors put up two competing constructivist or sociological institutionalist accounts—a 'social learning' model predicated on a 'logic of appropriateness' and focusing on the socialization of state and civil-society actors in the target countries, and a 'lesson-drawing' model in which dissatisfied governments in central and eastern Europe actively seek out and import EU practices, with the Union itself playing an essentially passive role.

Schimmelfennig and Sedelmeier's findings, based on a series of case studies cutting across multiple countries and multiple issue-areas, provide striking support for the external incentives model. While various studies in the larger project found some instances of socialization and/or lesson-drawing in the absence of conditionality, the authors conclude that, on balance, 'the external incentives provided by the EU can largely account for the impact of the EU on candidate countries'. Observed variations in rule adoption, moreover, are explained in large part by the independent variables hypothesized in the external incentives model, including most notably a credible membership perspective and clear political conditionality (Schimmelfennig and Sedelmeier 2005b: 210–11). Other recent studies employ varying theoretical frameworks and focus on different aspects of the Europeanization process, but here too the general finding is that explicit and credible political conditionality is the most important source of EU leverage and policy change in the new and candidate countries, with socialization and lesson-drawing having a much weaker and more variable impact (Jacoby 2004; Kelley 2004; Vachudova 2005; Schimmelfennig 2005; Zürn and Checkel 2005).

Fourth and finally, the recent enlargement of the EU to 27 (and possibly more) member states raises significant questions about the operation of EU institutions and policies, and rational choice institutionalist analysts have active in theorizing the effects of enlargement and of the 2001 Treaty of Nice (designed in large part to prepare for enlargement) on the distribution of voting power among member states, as well as the member states' collective ability to reach agreement on new policies. Specifically, a number of rational choice models based on the provisions of the Treaty of Nice hypothesized that the likelihood of reaching agreement *decreased* in an enlarged, post-Nice EU (largely because of the raising of the QMV threshold from 71.2 per cent of all weighted votes to 73.9 per cent), while the relative voting weight of each of the individual members will also decrease as their numbers increase; larger member states, however, would benefit disproportionately from the Nice reforms in an enlarged EU (Baldwin *et al.* 2001; Bräuninger and König 2001; Felsenthal and Machover 2001). These hypotheses have received mixed support in the very early studies of the newly enlarged EU of 25 or 27. On the one hand, one of the most striking features of the Treaty of Nice is the extent to which the methods of rational choice scholars were in fact replicated by the delegations to the Nice European Council, where negotiators reportedly brought calculators to assess the impact of proposed institutional changes on their respective voting weights. In this case, more than any other, rational choice analysts can reasonably claim not only to have accurately depicted, but also to have influenced, the decision-making characteristics of EU member governments in the process of European integration. On the other hand, however, preliminary studies of EU institutions and legislation in the enlarged EU suggest that the core institutions (Commission, Council, EP, and ECJ) have continued to function effectively despite the shock of the 2004 'big-bang' enlargement, and that the EU's legislative output has continued to grow unabated after as well as before enlargement (Dehousse *et al.* 2007; Thomson 2007; Wallace 2007). Analysing and explaining the workings of EU institutions after enlargement remains as one of the most significant research challenges in today's EU.

Conclusion

Over the course of the past decade, the new institutionalisms—including sociological institutionalism and constructivism as well as the rational choice and historical variants analysed in this chapter—have arguably become the dominant approaches to the study of European integration. Moreover, despite the differences among them, all three institutionalisms offer substantial advantages over the traditional neofunctionalist and intergovernmentalist theories of European integration, in three ways. First, whereas the old neofunctionalist/intergovernmentalist debate was limited almost exclusively to EU studies, new institutionalist analyses draw explicitly from and can in turn contribute to the development of general theories of politics. Indeed, the rational choice and historical institutionalist theories reviewed in this chapter share basic assumptions and approaches not only with each other, as I have argued, but also with a wide variety of rationalist theories of EU politics (e.g. Moravcsik 1998), comparative domestic politics (Hix 2005), and international politics (Milner 1998), and the theoretical compatibility of these cases in turn allows for comparison with relevant domestic and international cases outside the EU.

This observation points to a second advantage, namely that institutional analyses generally challenge the traditional distinction between international relations and comparative politics, and indeed we have seen that the basic concepts of institutionalist analysis are applicable both at the 'international' level of the EU and at the level of member states, where the mediating impact of domestic institutions can help explain patterns of Europeanization among current member states and applicant countries.

Third and finally, all three institutionalisms have advanced considerably over the past two decades, in terms of both theoretical elaboration and empirical testing. At the start of the 1990s, for example, the rational choice institutionalist literature on the European Union was in its infancy, concerned primarily with the elaboration of formal models in the absence of empirical testing. Since then, however, rational choice scholars have made real progress in both the specification of formal models and the gathering of new data to test them. Historical institutionalist accounts, by contrast, have been slower to move beyond the concepts of lock-in and path-dependence as broad metaphors for the integration process, but here too recent work has begun to refine the theory into distinct, testable hypotheses. In that context, the primary challenge for rational choice institutionalists consists in the specification of new and more accurate models of EU institutions, and the testing of those models through a range of empirical approaches including qualitative as well as quantitative analysis; while for historical institutionalists, the primary challenge is to specify and test more precise hypotheses about types of institutions likely to generate positive or negative feedbacks, the mechanisms of path-dependence, and the impact of temporal factors on the path of European integration.

Despite their multiple strengths and promise, finally, a careful balance sheet reveals two potential weaknesses of rational choice and historical institutionalism as those approaches have been defined in this chapter. First, both varieties of institutionalism are essentially mid-level theories, concerned largely with the effects of institutions as intervening variables in EU politics. As such, neither theory constitutes in and of itself an adequate theory of European *integration*, the ultimate causes of which typically remain exogenous to the theory. Historical institutionalism has begun to address some of these questions, examining the ways in which initial integrative acts *may* create unintended consequences and lead to and endogenous, path-dependent process of integration, but even in such accounts the root causes of integration may be external to the theory itself. Here again, however, the compatibility of rational choice and historical institutionalism with other rationalist theories of politics offers the prospect of linking mid-level analysis of EU institutions with broader theories that might explain the integration process more fully. Second, the rational choice approach to the EU is based on a highly restrictive set of assumptions about the nature of actors and institutions—assumptions that have been fundamentally questioned by sociological institutionalists and constructivists, who believe that rational choice theory is blind to the most important constitutive and transformative effects of EU institutions on the preferences and identities of the people who interact with them. To the extent that EU institutions do indeed have such effects—an empirical question which begs continuing research—rational choice institutionalists may be systematically underestimating the importance and impact of the European institutions that are their primary object of study.

■ GUIDE TO FURTHER READING

Aspinwall, M. and Schneider, G. (eds) (2001) *The Rules of Integration: Institutionalist Approaches to the Study of Europe* (New York: Manchester University Press). This is an edited volume featuring a number of institutionalist analyses of the European Union, with an excellent introduction by Aspinwall and Schneider.

Franchino, F. (2007) *The Powers of the Union: Delegation in the EU* (New York: Cambridge University Press). A theoretically and empirically rigorous analysis of the delegation of powers to EU institutions and member states, which explores in detail the determinants of member state decisions to delegate powers to the Union.

Hix, S., Noury, A.G., and Roland, G. (2007) *Democratic Politics in the European Parliament* (New York: Cambridge University Press). A comprehensive analysis of legislative politics in the European Parliament, based on the most extensive database of roll-call votes over the history of the EP.

Jupille, J. and Caporaso, J.A. (1999) 'Institutionalism and the European Union: beyond international relations and comparative politics', *Annual Review of Political Science*, 2, 429–44. Another
excellent review of institutionalist analyses to the European Union, emphasizing the promise
of institutionalism as an approach capable of overcoming the gap between comparative politics and international relations.

Hall, P.A. and Taylor, R.C.R. (1996) 'Political science and the three new institutionalisms', *Political Studies*, 44(5), 936–57. An excellent review article, summarizing the basic assumptions
and arguments of what the authors call the 'three new institutionalisms' in political science:
rational choice, historical, and sociological.

Naurin, D. and Wallace, H. (eds) (2008) *Unveiling the Council: Games Governments Play in Brussels* (London: Palgrave). A cutting-edge collection of scholarship on the Council of Ministers,
drawing on a range of theoretical perspectives and a wealth of new qualitative and quantitative empirical data.

Pierson, P. (2004) *Politics in Time: History, Institutions, and Social Analysis* (Princeton, NJ: Princeton
University Press). The best and most comprehensive statement of historical institutionalism,
emphasizing the importance of feedback effects and path-dependence in political life.

Pollack, M.A. (2003) *The Engines of European Integration: Delegation, Agency and Agenda-Setting in
the EU* (New York: Oxford University Press). An extended rational choice institutionalist discussion of delegation to, and agency and agenda-setting by, supranational organizations.

Schimmelfennig, F. and Sedelmeier, U. (eds) (2005) *The Europeanization of Central and Eastern Europe* (Ithaca, NY: Cornell University Press). A superb comparative analysis of the impacts of the
EU in the new member states and candidate countries of central and eastern Europe, pitting
a rationalist 'external incentives' model against competing explanations drawn from other
theoretical approaches.

■ STUDY QUESTIONS

1. What are the various strands or versions of 'the new institutionalism' in political science, and what
assumptions or approaches characterize each of these three strands? How do institutions 'matter' in
producing political outcomes, according to each of these approaches?

2. Is historical institutionalism a distinct body of theory with specific predictions about the path of
European integration, or is it simply a halfway house between the other two 'institutionalisms'?
What, if anything, does a distinctly historical–institutionalist approach add to our understanding of
the integration process?

3. How does rational choice institutionalism account for the delegation of powers to supranational
actors such as the Commission, and for the subsequent role of the Commission in the integration
process? What are the advantages of such an approach vis-à-vis traditional theories of European
integration, and what criticisms of rational choice approaches might you offer?

4. What issues and research questions are raised by the recent enlargement of the EU from 15 member
states to 27 (and possibly more)? How effective is rational choice institutionalism, or indeed the
other variants of the new institutionalism, in answering these various questions?

5. What, at the end of the day, are the strengths, and the weaknesses, of rational choice and historical
institutionalism in the study of European integration?

8

Social Constructivism and European Integration

Thomas Risse

Introduction

Social constructivism reached the study of the European Union (EU) in the late 1990s. The publication of a *Journal of European Public Policy* special issue in 1999 marks a turning point in this regard (Christiansen *et al.* 1999; but see Jørgensen 1997). Social constructivism entered the field of EU studies mainly as a 'spillover' from the discipline of international relations, but also because of profound misgivings among scholars about the rather narrow focus and sterility of the debates between neofunctionalism and (liberal) intergovernmentalism. Research inspired by social constructivism contributes substantially to European integration studies, both theoretically and substantially. This chapter proceeds in the following steps. First, I introduce social constructivism as an approach to the study of European integration and a challenge to more rationalist approaches such as liberal intergovernmentalism, but also versions of neofunctionalism. Second, I take a closer look at the question of European identity as a particular subject area to which research inspired by social constructivism can contribute. Third, the chapter discusses constructivist contributions to the study of EU enlargement. I conclude with remarks on the future of European integration research inspired by social constructivism.

Social Constructivism as an Approach to European Integration

There is considerable confusion in the field of European studies as to what precisely constitutes social constructivism and what distinguishes it from other approaches to European integration. As a result, it has become fairly common to introduce constructivism as yet another substantive theory of regional integration, such as liberal intergovernmentalism (Moravcsik 1993; see also Chapter 4 of this volume by Moravcsik and Schimmelfennig) or neofunctionalism (E.B. Haas 1958; see also Chapter 3 of this volume). It should be emphasized at the outset that social constructivism as such does not make any substantive claims about European integration. Constructivists may join an intergovernmentalist reading of interstate negotiations as the central way to understand the EU. They may equally join the neofunctionalist crowd, emphasizing spillover effects and the role of supranational institutions (see e.g. E.B. Haas 2001), and constructivists could certainly contribute to the study of the EU as a multilevel governance system and to an institution-alist interpretation of its functioning (see Chapters 5 and 7 of this volume).

It is equally misleading to claim, as some have argued, that social constructivism sub-scribes to a 'post-positivist' epistemology (how can we know something?), while conven-tional approaches are wedded to positivism and the search for law-like features in social and political life. Unfortunately, terms such as 'positivism' are often used as demarca-tion devices to distinguish the 'good self' from the 'bad other' in some sort of discipli-nary tribal warfare (for an excellent discussion of this tendency in international relations theory see Wight 2002). However, if post-positivism means, first, a healthy scepticism toward a 'covering law' approach to social science irrespective of time and space and instead a striving towards middle-range theorizing, second, an emphasis on interpretive understanding as an intrinsic, albeit not exclusive, part of any causal explanation, and, third, the recognition that social scientists are part of the social world which they try to analyse: double hermeneutics see Giddens (1982), then—is anybody still a 'positivist' (to paraphrase an article by Legro and Moravcsik [1999]; for an excellent introduction to con-structivist research strategies see Klotz and Lynch [2007])? In sum, positivism and post-positivism is not what distinguishes social constructivism from rational choice. Rather, an epistemological divide between those who deny the possibility of intersubjectively valid knowledge claims, on the one hand, and those who stick to more or less conventional methods in the social sciences, on the other, is increasingly salient within the construc-tivist field itself. It is epistemology rather than ontology (what is the nature of things?) that distinguishes more radical from more moderate constructivists (see Chapter 9 by Ole Wæver in this volume; also Wiener 2003; for different epistemological positions compare the articles in Checkel 2005 with Diez 2001; Manners 2007).

Defining Social Constructivism

So what then is 'social constructivism' (for the following see e.g. Adler 1997, 2002; Fearon and Wendt 2002; Wendt 1999; Christiansen *et al.* 2001)? It is a truism that social reality does not fall from heaven, but that human agents construct and reproduce it through their daily practices—Berger and Luckmann called this 'the social construction of reality' (Berger and Luckmann 1966). While this is a core argument of social constructivism, it does not provide us with a clear enough definition. Therefore, it is probably most useful to describe constructivism as based on a social ontology which insists that human agents do not exist independently from their social environment and its collectively shared systems of meanings (culture in a broad sense). This is in contrast to the methodological individualism of rational choice according to which '[t]he elementary unit of social life is the individual human action' (Elster 1989: 13). The fundamental insight of the structure-agency debate, which lies at the heart of many social constructivist works, is not only that social structures and agents are mutually codetermined. The crucial point is that constructivists insist on the mutual *constitutiveness* of (social) structures and agents (Adler 1997: 324–5; Wendt 1999: ch. 4). The social environment in which we find ourselves, defines (constitutes) who we are, our identities as social beings. 'We' are social beings, embedded in various relevant social communities. At the same time, human agency creates, reproduces, and changes culture through our daily practices. Thus, social constructivism occupies a sometimes uneasy ontological middleground between individualism and structuralism by claiming that there are properties of structures and of agents that cannot be collapsed into each other (see also Adler 1997).

This claim has important, if often overlooked, repercussions for the study of the European Union. The prevailing theories of European integration—whether neofunctionalism, liberal intergovernmentalism, or multilevel governance[1]—are firmly committed to a rationalist ontology which is agency-centred by definition (see E.B. Haas's recent interpretation of neofunctionalism in Haas 2001). This might be helpful for substantive empirical research, as long as we are primarily in the business of explaining the evolvement of European institutions. If institution-building and, thus, the emergence of new social structures are to be explained, agency-centred approaches are doing just fine. Here, a constructivist perspective will complement rather than substitute these approaches by emphasizing that the interests of actors cannot be treated as exogenously given or inferred from a given material structure. Rather, political culture, discourse and the 'social construction' of interests and identities matter.

Take the debate on the future of the European Union as it has evolved from the 1990s onwards. Do the German and French contrasting visions of a future European political order reflect some underlying economic or geopolitical interests? If this were the case, we would expect most French politicians to plead for a federalist vision of the EU, since France should be obviously interested in binding a powerful Germany as firmly as possible to Europe. In contrast, most German contributors should embrace a 'Europe of nation states', as a means to gaining independence from the constraining effects of European integration. Thus, an emphasis on material power as well as economic or security interests would mis-predict the positions in the current debate. Those positions, however, can be explained as reflecting competing visions of a good political and socio-economic order which are deeply embedded in the two countries' contrasting domestic structures and political cultures (for empirical evidence see Jachtenfuchs 2002; Jachtenfuchs *et al.* 1998).

Yet such an emphasis on ideational, cultural, and discursive origins of national preferences complements rather than substitutes an agency-based rationalist account. 'Soft rationalism', which takes ideas seriously, should be able to accommodate some of these concerns (see e.g. Goldstein and Keohane 1993; Moravcsik 1997). The more we insist that institutions including the EU are never created from scratch, but reflect and build upon previous institutional designs and structures, the further we move away from rational choice approaches, even of the 'soft' variety. The issue is not so much about path-dependent processes and 'sunk costs' as emphasized by historical institutionalism (Pierson 1996), but about institutional effects on social identities and fundamental interests of actors. Thus, a constructivist history of the EU would insist against liberal intergovernmentalism in particular, that we cannot even start explaining the coming about of the major constitutional treaties of the union without taking the feedback effects of previous institutional decisions on the identities and interests of the member states' governments and societies into account. Finally, such a rewritten history of the

EU would focus on the ongoing struggles, contestations, and discourses on how 'to build Europe' over the years and, thus, reject an imagery of actors including governments as calculating machines who always know what they want and are never uncertain about the future and even their own stakes and interests (see, for example, Parsons 2003 against Moravcsik 1998).

The differences between constructivism and a liberal intergovernmentalist approach to European integration are, thus, pretty clear as the latter is usually based on a rationalist ontology that takes actors' preferences as given. It is less clear, though, how constructivism differs from neofunctionalism. On the one hand, neofunctionalism constitutes an actor-centred approach to European integration (see E.B. Haas 1958, 2001; for a discussion see Risse 2005). It starts with egoistic utility-maximizing actors who cooperate to solve some collective action problems. At some point, the functional logic takes over (spillover) leading to further integration. On the other hand, neofunctionalism also talks about normative integration, the 'upgrading of common interests', and the shift of loyalties (identities) from the national to the supranational levels. This latter language implies some constitutive effects of European integration on the various societal and political actors. If European integration is supposed to transform collective identities, we have moved beyond a narrow rational choice approach and toward a much 'thicker' understanding of institutions, as Ernst Haas himself has recognized (see e.g. E.B. Haas 2001; E.B. Haas and P.M. Haas 2002). In sum, there are aspects to neofunctionalist accounts that resonate pretty well with a constructivist focus on the constitutive rather than the purely regulative impact of norms.

Agency, Structure, and the Constitutive Effect of Norms

The constructivist emphasis on the mutual constitutiveness of agency and structure becomes even more relevant for the study of European integration, the more we focus on the *impact* of Europeanization on the member states and their domestic policies, politics and polities. Recent work on European integration has started to look at the various ways in which the integration process itself feeds back into the domestic fabric of the nation states (e.g. Cowles *et al.* 2001; Kohler-Koch and Eising 1999; Héritier *et al.* 2001; Börzel and Risse 2007). Thus, European integration studies increasingly analyse the EU as a two-way process of policy-making and institution-building at the European level which then feed back into the member states and their political processes and structures. It is here that the difference between the methodological individualism emphasized by rational choice, on the one hand, and the constructivist focus on the mutual constitutiveness of agency and structures matters a lot.

The reason can be found in the way in which social constructivists conceptualize institutions as social structures impacting on agents and their behaviour. Rationalist (or 'neoliberal' in international relations jargon, see Keohane 1989) institutionalism views social institutions including the EU as primarily constraining the behaviour of actors with given identities and preferences. These actors follow a 'logic of consequentialism' (March and Olsen 1989, 1998) enacting given identities and interests and trying to realise their preferences through strategic behaviour. The goal of action is to maximize or to optimize one's interests and preferences. Institutions constrain or widen the range of choices available to actors to realize their interests. The EU's liberalization of telecommunications markets, for example, broke up state monopolies while empowering foreign companies to penetrate the markets of their competitors.

In contrast, social constructivism and sociological institutionalism emphasize a different logic of action, which March and Olsen have called the 'logic of appropriateness':

> Human actors are imagined to follow rules that associate particular identities to particular situations, approaching individual opportunities for action by assessing similarities between current identities and choice dilemmas and more general concepts of self and situations.
>
> March and Olsen (1998: 951)

Rule-guided behaviour differs from strategic and instrumental behaviour in that actors try to 'do the right thing' rather than maximizing or optimizing their given preferences. The logic of appropriateness entails that actors try to figure out the appropriate rule in a given social situation. It follows that social institutions including the EU can no longer be viewed as 'external' to actors. Rather, actors including corporate actors such as national governments, firms, or interest groups are deeply embedded in and affected by the social institutions in which they act.

This relates to what constructivists call the *constitutive* effects of social norms and institutions (Onuf 1989; Kratochwil 1989). Many social norms not only regulate behaviour, they also constitute the identity of actors in the sense of defining who 'we' are as members of a social community. The norm of sovereignty, for example, not only regulates the interactions of states in international affairs, it also defines what a state *is* in the first place. Constructivists concentrate on the social identities of actors in order to account for their interests (e.g. Wendt 1999, particularly ch. 7; also Checkel 2001a). Constructivism maintains that collective norms and understandings define the basic 'rules of the game' in which they find themselves in their interactions. This does not mean that constitutive norms cannot be violated or never change, but the argument implies that we cannot even describe the properties of social agents without reference to the social structure in which they are embedded.

Consequently, the EU as an emerging polity is expected not just to constrain the range of choices available to, say, nation states, but the way in which they define their interests and even their identities. EU 'membership matters' (Sandholtz 1996) in that it influences the very way in which actors see themselves and are seen by others as social beings. Germany, France, Italy, or the Netherlands are no longer simply European states. They are EU states in the sense that their statehood is increasingly defined by their EU membership. The EU constitutes states in Europe insofar as it maps the political, social, and economic space enabling private and public actors to define their interests and go about their business (Laffan *et al.* 2000; Jönsson *et al.* 2000; see also Risse 2009). EU membership implies the voluntary acceptance of a particular political order as legitimate and entails the recognition of a set of rules and obligations as binding. This includes that European law is the 'law of the land', and, thus, a constitutional order 'without constitution', at least for the time being (Weiler 1995; Shaw 2001b). Thus, constructivists emphasize that the EU deeply affects discursive and behavioural practices, that it has become part of the 'social furniture' with which social and political actors have to deal on a daily basis. Such a view implies that EU membership entails socialization effects (Checkel 2001b, 2005). At the very least, actors need to know the rules of appropriate behaviour in the union and to take them for granted in the sense that 'norms become normal'.

Constructivist emphasis on norm-guided behaviour and constitutive rules does not imply, however, that norms are never violated. Any study of the implementation of the *acquis communautaire* shows that compliance rates vary significantly among member states and across issue areas (Börzel 2001; Börzel *et al.* 2007). Acceptance of a social and political order as legitimate might increase compliance rates with the law. However, we all occasionally run a red light. Does this mean that we do not accept the rule as binding and valid? Of course not. We can infer from the communicative practices of actors whether or not they consider a norm as legitimate. Do they try to justify their behaviour in cases of rule violation? Do they recognize misbehaviour and offer compensation?

Communication and Discourse

The emphasis on communicative and discursive practices constitutes a final characteristic feature of social constructivist approaches. If we want to understand and explain social behaviour, we need to take words, language, and communicative utterances seriously. It is through discursive practices that agents make sense of the world and attribute meaning to their activities. Moreover, as Foucault reminds us, discursive practices establish power relationships in the sense that they make us 'understand certain problems in certain ways, and pose questions accordingly' (Diez 2001: 90). And further, '[a]lthough it is "we" who impose meaning, "we" do not act as autonomous subjects but from a "subject position" made available by the discursive context in which we are situated' (ibid., referring to Foucault 1991: 58).

There are at least three ways in which the study of communicative practices has recently contributed to our understanding of the European Union. First, some scholars have started applying the Habermasian theory of communicative action to international relations (Habermas 1981, 1992a; Müller 1994; Risse 2000). They focus on arguing and reason-giving as an agency-centred mode of interaction which enables actors to challenge the validity claims inherent in any causal or normative statement and to seek a communicative consensus about their understanding of a situation as well as justifications for the principles and norms guiding their action, rather than acting purely on the basis of strategic calculations. Argumentative rationality means that the participants in a discourse are open to be persuaded by the better argument and that relationships of power and social hierarchies recede in the background. Argumentative and deliberative behaviour is as goal-oriented as strategic interactions, however the goal is not to attain one's fixed preferences, but to seek a reasoned consensus. As Keohane put it, persuasion 'involves changing people's choices of alternatives independently of their calculations about the strategies of other players' (Keohane 2001: 10). Actors' interests, preferences, and the perceptions of the situation are no longer fixed, but subject to discursive challenges. Where argumentative rationality prevails, actors do not seek to maximize or to satisfy their given interests and preferences, but to challenge and to justify the validity claims inherent in them—*and* are prepared to change their views of the world or even their interests in light of the better argument.

Applied to the European Union, this emphasis on communicative action allows us to study European institutions as discourse rather than merely bargaining arenas allowing for deliberative processes to establish a reasoned consensus in order to solve common problems. Joerges and Neyer in particular have used this concept to study the EU comitology (Joerges and Neyer 1997b; Neyer 2002), while Checkel has emphasized persuasion and social learning in various settings of the EU and other European institutions (Checkel 2001b). Göler has examined deliberative processes at the EU's Constitutional Convention (Göler 2006; see also Kleine and Risse 2007; Risse and Kleine 2007).

The second way in which discursive practices have been studied in the EU does not so much focus on arguing and reason-giving, but on discourse as a process of meaning construction allowing for certain interpretations while excluding others (see also Chapter 9 this volume). In other words, this work focuses on discursive practices as means by which power relationships are established and maintained. Who is allowed to speak in a discursive arena, what counts as a sensible proposition, and which meaning constructions become so dominant that they are being taken for granted? Rosamond's work on European discourses on globalization has to be mentioned here as well as Diez's study of the British discourse on European integration (Rosamond 2001; Diez 1999b, 2001; see also Larsen 1999).

The latter work is related to the more radical versions of social constructivism mentioned above which conclude from the 'linguistic turn' in international relations (cf. Milliken 1999; Fierke 2002; Wiener 2003) that claims to knowledge in the social science have to be considered as rather questionable. However, these distinctions should not be exaggerated. When it comes to actual empirical research, most scholars of 'discourse analysis' still use rather conventional methods of qualitative content analysis to make their points (compare Larsen 1999; Marcussen 2000; Jachtenfuchs *et al.* 1998; Marcussen *et al.* 1999; for a general argument see Klotz and Lynch 2007).

A third way in which communicative practices have recently become the focus of attention for EU scholars concerns the emergence of a transnational European public sphere. Over the past 10 years empirical studies, particularly media analyses, investigated the extent to which we can observe the gradual Europeanization of national public spheres (see e.g. Kantner 2004; Pfetsch 2004; Trenz 2006; Van de Steeg 2006; Fossum and Schlesinger 2007; Koopmans 2007; Meyer 2007; Sifft *et al.* 2007; for an overview see Risse 2009). In this context, Eder and Kantner have suggested that the ability to communicate meaningfully across borders depends crucially on the extent to which the same issues are debated at the same time with similar frames of reference or meaning structures (Eder and Kantner 2000). Transnational contestation and politicization of European issues only become possible if we share frames of interpretation so that we understand each other. In a way then, the emergence of a transnational public sphere is a social construction par excellence. It only exists insofar as participants in the debate discuss European issues of common concern thereby creating a transnational community of communication (Risse and Van de Steeg forthcoming).

The Three Contributions of Social Constructivism

In sum, there are at least three ways in which social constructivism contributes to a better understanding of the European Union. First, accepting the mutual constitutiveness of agency and structure allows for a deeper understanding of Europeanization including its impact on statehood in Europe. Second and related, emphasizing the constitutive effects of European law, rules, and policies enables us to study how European integration shapes social identities and interests of actors. Third, focusing on communicative practices permits us to examine more closely how Europe and the EU are constructed discursively, how actors try to come to grips with the meaning of European integration and how they develop a European public sphere.

In the following, I apply these rather abstract arguments to the question of European identity, which is highly relevant for the construction of Europe in both political and analytical terms.

The Social Construction of European Identity

The Contested Nature of European Identity

Most people agree that a viable and legitimate European polity requires some degree of identification in order to be sustainable, but European identity is a contested idea.[2] Many people still discuss the relationship between European and national identities in zero-sum terms. They follow *essentialist* concepts of collective identities, taking cultural variables such as membership in ethnic groups as a given which then develop into national identities during the process of nation-building. If the causal connection between 'culture' and 'identity' is seen as a one-way street, there is not much one can do about this and supranational or post-nationalist identities are almost impossible. Collective identities will firmly rest with the nation state as the historically most successful connection between territory and people. French will remain French, while British remain British, and Germans remain Germans. 'Euro-pessimists' challenge the prospects for further European integration on precisely these grounds. They argue that a European polity is impossible, because there is no European people, no common European history or common myths on which collective European identity could be built (see Kielmansegg 1996; Grimm 1995).

Yet we know from survey data and other empirical material that individuals hold multiple social identities. As a result, people can feel a sense of belonging to Europe, their nation state, their gender, and so forth. It is wrong to conceptualize European identity in zero-sum terms, as if an increase in European identity necessarily decreases one's loyalty to national or other communities. Europe and the nation are both 'imagined communities' (Anderson 1991) and people can feel as part of both communities without having to choose some primary identification. Analyses from survey data suggest and social psychological experiments confirm that many people who strongly identify with their nation state also feel a sense of belonging to Europe (Duchesne and Frognier 1995; Martinotti and Steffanizzi 1995; Citrin and Sides 2004; Hooghe and Marks 2005).

This finding is trivial for scholars studying collective identities, but it nevertheless has important implications for the political debates about Europe and the nation state. Take the debates about the future of the European Union. Many people still hold that Europe lacks a demos, one indicator being the lack of strong identification with Europe in mass public opinion. Yet 'country first, but Europe, too' is the dominant outlook in most EU member states, and people do not perceive this as contradictory. Moreover and more importantly, the real cleavage in mass public opinion is between those who exclusively identify with their nation (exclusive nationalists), on the one hand, and those perceiving themselves as attached to both their nation and Europe (inclusive nationalists), on the other hand. Interestingly enough, citizens from the new eastern European member states do not differ much in their attitudes toward European identity from their counterparts in 'old Europe'. In addition, Citrin and Sides as well as Hooghe and Marks have demonstrated that that the individual willingness to support further European integration increases quite dramatically from the former to the latter group (Citrin and Sides 2004; Hooghe and Marks 2005; see also McLaren 2006). They argue, therefore, 'that creating support for a stronger European state does not require a European identity that dominates national identity' (Citrin and Sides 2004: 175). In other words, the European polity does not require a 'demos' that replaces a national with a European identity, but one in which national and European identities coexist and complement each other. This is a significant empirical finding that speaks directly to the debate on the future of the union.

Most scholars working on collective identities today have abandoned essentialist conceptualizations of social identities, but embrace versions of social constructivist reasoning (see e.g. Giesen 1993, 1999; Eder and Giesen 1999; Cederman 2001). From this perspective, the connection between cultural variables such as ethnic belongings or religious or ideological affiliations, on the one hand, and collective identities, on the other, is more historically contingent, tenuous, and subject to constructions and reconstructions. Accordingly, social identities contain, first, ideas describing and categorizing an individual's membership in a social group or community including emotional, affective, and evaluative components. Common Europeanness, for example, could constitute such a community. Second, this commonness is accentuated by a sense of difference with regard to other communities. Individuals frequently tend to view the group with which they identify in a more positive way than the 'out-group', but a sense of collective European identity is always accompanied by the need to differentiate 'Europeans' from 'others', be it Soviet Communism during the Cold War, Islamic fundamentalism, or Anglo-American laissez-faire capitalism.

'Europeanness' and National Identities

Thus, there might be much more 'Europeanness' enshrined in national cultures and, hence, a much stronger collective European identity than is usually assumed. This identification process might encompass a much longer—and probably also more contested—history than the 40 years of European integration (see below), but we need to go beyond the rather simple insight that European and national identities can go together.

The question is how multiple identities relate to each other. First, identities can be *nested* or layered, conceived of as concentric circles or onions, one layer above the next. My identity as a Rhinelander is nested in my German identity, which is again nested in my Europeanness. Second, identities can be *cross-cutting*. In this configuration, some, but not all, members of one identity group are also members of another identity group. Some women might feel a strong gender identity, but only a subgroup of them might also identify with Europe, while the latter group also encompasses women without a strong sense of gender identity.

There is a third way of conceptualizing the relationship between European and other identities that people might hold. We could call it the 'marble cake' model of multiple identities. Accordingly, the various components of an individual's identity cannot be neatly separated on different levels as both concepts of nestedness and of cross-cutting identities imply. What if identity components influence each other, mesh and blend into each other? What if my self-understanding as German inherently contains aspects of Europeanness? Can we really separate out a Catalan from a European identity? Or take the major European party families. From the 1950s on, Christian Democratic parties in continental Europe were at the forefront of European integration. Europeanness has always been a constitutive component of post-Second World War Christian Democratic ideology originating from the inter-war period. The same holds true for modern Social Democrats in Europe. It is interesting to note that the turn toward accepting capitalism and the social market economy which the German Social Democrats experienced in the late 1950s, the French Socialists in the early 1980s, and British Labour in the 1990s, went hand in hand with a strong identification with European integration (although conceptualized in different ways) in each of these cases. Today, Europeanness forms a constitutive part of modern Social Democratic ideology (for details see Marcussen *et al.* 1999; Risse 2001).

Contested Meanings of Europe and the EU

What does it mean in substantive terms to identify with Europe and the EU? A most important corollary of the marble cake concept concerns the content of what it means to identify with Europe. Different groups might fill it with different content. Indeed, a longitudinal study of political discourses about Europe among the major parties in France, Germany, and Great Britain revealed that the meaning of Europe varied considerably (Marcussen *et al.* 1999). For the German political elites, 'Europe' and the European integration meant overcoming one's own nationalist and militarist past. The French elites, in contrast, constructed Europe as the externalization of distinct French values of Republicanism, enlightenment, and the *mission civilisatrice*. While French and German political elites managed to embed Europe into their understandings of national identity, the British elites constructed Europe in contrast to their understandings of the nation, particularly the English nation.

Yet elite discourses on Europe and the EU appear to converge on a vision of European identity that encompasses the values of modernity and enlightenment. 'Unity in diversity' as well as democracy, human rights, the rule of law, and social market economy (as opposed to laissez-faire capitalism) are constructed as what is special about the EU. Thus,

European institutions and European elites deliberately try to construct a post-national civic identity in the Habermasian sense (Habermas 1994, 1996a), and this modern and post-national European identity seems to resonate with mass public opinion. The 'inclusive nationalists' who show some degree of identification with Europe also share the modern values. The more people identify with Europe, the less xenophobic and the more positive toward Eastern enlargement they are (Citrin and Sides 2004; Bruter 2005; McLaren 2006). Education, income, and (left) ideology all have a positive impact on levels of attachment to Europe.

Thus, modern and post-national values have become constitutive for the EU, as you cannot become a member without subscribing to them. As the enlargement debates show, the self-description of the EU and the dominant discourses surrounding it have moved quite a long way toward building a polity and going beyond simple market integration (see also Laffan *et al.* 2000). The EU as an active identity builder has successfully achieved identity hegemony in terms of increasingly defining what it means to belong to 'Europe' (Laffan 2004). EU membership has significant constitutive effects on European state identities. States in Europe are increasingly defined as EU members, non-members, or would-be members. Their status in Europe, and to some degree also worldwide, depends on these categories. There is no way that European states can ignore the EU, even such devoted non-members as Switzerland.

In this sense, the EU has achieved identity hegemony in Europe. In the context of Eastern enlargement, central and eastern European (CEE) states want to 'return to Europe', as if they were currently outside the continent. When Italy prepared itself for entering the Euro zone, the main slogan was 'entrare l'Europa' (entering Europe!) as if Italy—one of the six founding members of the European Community—had ever left it (Sbragia 2001). In these contexts, Europe is used synonymously with the EU. To the extent that people identify Europe with the EU, this would be a remarkable achievement of 40 years of European integration. If Europe and the EU are used interchangeably, it means that the latter has successfully occupied the social space of what it means to be European. One could then not be a 'real' European without being an EU member. The EU increasingly fills the meaning space of Europe with a specific content.

However, and in sharp contrast to the modern image of Europe that the EU wants to convey, we can also see the emergence of an alternative vision of European identity—'fortress Europe' (see particularly Checkel and Katzenstein 2008). This conceptualization of European identity emphasizes Europe's cultural heritage, a common history, and a grounding in a Christian–Judean culture (see also Bruter 2005 on Europe as a 'cultural entity'). In this context, Europe and the EU are constructed as exclusionary entities that are only open to white Christians while hostile to foreigners, immigrants, and—particularly—to Islam. This counter-vision of Europe as an exclusionary construct is increasingly being promoted by Eurosceptical and right-wing populist parties which are on the rise across the EU (on Euroscepticism see e.g. Hooghe and Marks 2007). It resonates with 'exclusive nationalist' attitudes identified in mass public opinion which also correlate strongly with hostility toward immigrants and foreigners (Citrin and Sides 2004).

The counter-vision of 'fortress Europe' has recently become salient in two transnational debates. First, there is a European-wide concern about immigration and the influx of extra-EU foreigners (see Lahav 2004). Second, the debate on the potential Turkish

EU membership is replete with references toward competing visions of Europe (see e.g. Wimmel 2006; Yavuz 2006; McLaren 2007; Goren and Nachmani 2007; Madeker 2008). On the one hand, the vision of modern Europe would, of course, open the doors to Turkish accession, as long as Turkey complies with the Copenhagen criteria of democracy, human and minority rights and the rule of law. On the other hand, 'exclusive Europe' cannot accept Turkey into the EU, because it is a predominantly Muslim country. Europe's cultural identity is constructed in essentialist terms in the anti-Turkish discourse and resembles what Eisenstadt and Giesen have called primordial identity constructions (Eisenstadt and Giesen 1995). While these are still social constructions, they resemble ethno-nationalist identities in the sense that they cannot be changed. As a result, the door to Turkish EU membership would remain closed for good.

These latter remarks also show another feature in the construction of collective identities. Social identities not only describe what it means to be member of a community, they also connote the boundaries of the group, i.e., who is 'in' and who is 'out' (Neumann 1996a, b). As a result, we can infer quite a bit about the substance of European identity, if we know more about the European 'others'. For fortress Europe, the out-group is pretty clear: it is Islam as well as non-white foreigners.

In contrast, modern, enlightened, and post-national Europe has 'fuzzy boundaries', since this identity construction cannot rely on clear cultural and/or geographical borders. Where does 'modern Europe' end? Why should Poland be 'in', while neighbouring Ukraine remains 'out'? Why accept the western Balkans, at least in principle, but rejecting Turkey? And what about the southern Mediterranean countries?

In fact, Europe is already characterized by overlapping and unclear boundaries. The European Economic and Monetary Union with the single currency encompasses 13 of the currently 27 EU member states. The European Single Market, which includes the European Economic Area (EEA), encompasses some non-EU members such as Norway. 'Schengenland' with its absence of internal border controls, has even more complicated borders, since it includes the non-member Norway, but not the EU member Great Britain.

Moreover, the 'other' of modern and post-national Europe is very much context-dependent. In the discourse centring around the European welfare state and the European social model, we find repeated references to the US and to Japan as European 'others' (Rosamond 2001). The discourse about the EU's foreign and security policy as a civilian or 'normative' power also constructs the US as its 'other' (cf. Diez 2005; Sjursen 2006a). In the German discourse on the future of European integration, Germany's own past of militarism and nationalism constituted the European other against which the European integration project was to be built (Risse 2001). In a similar way, many of the new central and eastern European member states constructed their own Communist past as the 'European other'. In sum, modern Europe has many 'others' that are referred to and represented in context-dependent ways. This does not mean at all that anything goes, but it warns us not to reify the concept of European identity and to fix its meaning once and for all.

This short survey of current research on European identity demonstrates how one would approach a crucial issue for the future of Europe from a social constructivist perspective. Four points need to be reiterated here. First, questions such as European identity, which are usually bracketed by conventional approaches to European integration, assume centre stage in a constructivist account. This shows how a particular perspective serves as a theoretical lens with which to look at questions which are normally overlooked or under-theorized by other theoretical perspectives. Second, the sociological institutionalist account adopted here allows for highlighting the constitutive effects of Europeanization on people's social identities. The EU not only increasingly regulates the daily lives of individuals in various respects; it also constitutes 'Europe' as a political and social space in people's beliefs and collective understandings. Third, studying questions of European identity highlights the importance of analysing the discursive construction of meanings mentioned above. European identity is not a given, nor does it fall from heaven: it is a specific construct in time and space whose content actually changes depending on the social and political context in which it is enacted. Fourth, the increasing contestation and politicization of European identity with competing visions of modern Europe versus fortress Europe reminds us that social identities are unlikely to remain fixed for a long period of time. Rather, they are frequently contested and subject to political controversies. The EU's identity is no exception.

The Enlargement Puzzle from a Social Constructivist Perspective

One criticism of research on European identity concerns the 'so what?' question. The discussion above explored European identity as the 'dependent variable' (to use conventional social science language), but does it actually matter in terms of explaining observable outcomes in European integration? At the end of the day, political scientists want to account for political processes and outcomes and a constructivist focus on collective meaning constructions only makes sense if it helps us to understand these processes. Thus, I now use European identity as an explanatory factor to account for a crucial issue in European integration, namely eastern enlargement.

The Eastern enlargement of the European Union has not only represented a major challenge for the EU itself, but also a puzzle for conventional theories of European integration. As Schimmelfennig has convincingly demonstrated (Schimmelfennig 2003a, b), liberal intergovernmentalism offers a plausible first-cut explanation for the association agreements of the CEE countries with the EU. However, EU *membership* for the CEE countries is an entirely different story. The membership preferences of CEE countries were pretty clear: representation in EU policy-making processes was to be preferred over simple association agreements. Moreover, CEE countries expected some security benefits from EU membership (in addition to their NATO membership). Yet all of this does not explain why EU member states—including Germany—decided in favour of EU enlargement. As Schimmelfennig shows, a majority of EU member states should actually have been opposed to enlargement (including France and all southern European states; see Schimmelfennig 2003a, b; also Sedelmeier 2005; Sjursen 2006b). Yet, the 1993 Copenhagen

European Council agreed 'that the associated countries . . . shall become members of the European Union' and formulated conditions of admission. As Sedelmeier shows in detail (Sedelmeier 2005), members of the European Commission in particular served as norm entrepreneurs pushing and cajoling EU members into a commitment in favour of enlargement. How can this decision be explained?

Schimmelfennig uses a sociological institutionalist account to argue that the EU constitutes a liberal community of states committed to the rule of law, human rights, democracy, and to social market economy. His argument resonates with the concept of security communities based on a collective identity of its member (see e.g. Adler and Barnett 1998; for the original argument see Deutsch *et al*. 1957). Since the values of the community constitute its members, the members undertake a normative obligation toward 'states that share the collective identity of an international community and adhere to its constitutive values and norms' (Schimmelfennig 2001, 58–9). Therefore, these states are entitled to join the community.[3]

In other words, the collective identity of the EU as a liberal community explains the eastern enlargement puzzle to a large degree. Rhetorical commitment to community values entrapped EU member states into offering accession negotiations to the CEE and other eastern European countries despite the initial preferences against enlargement. Schimmelfennig's analysis represents a clever attempt to combine a constructivist account emphasizing constitutive norms and collective identities with a rationalist explanation focusing on narrowly defined egoistic interests. Fierke and Wiener push this analysis one step further by using speech act theory to show how Western states including EU members had committed themselves during the Cold War to welcome a free and democratic eastern Europe into the western Community. Their work on EU and NATO enlargement shows how normative commitments acquire their own dynamics as social rather than material capabilities (Fierke and Wiener 1999).

Yet two theoretical puzzles remain, one for rationalism, the other for constructivism. The rationalist puzzle concerns the problem how one can assume rational actors with pre-social (egoistic) preferences, on the one hand, who are—at the same time—embedded in the social structure of a community affecting their collective identities via constitutive norms, on the other hand. A rationalist ontology has a hard time accounting for constitutive norms presupposing a social structure in which actors are embedded. The constructivist puzzle concerns the fact that constitutive norms might affect actual behaviour of actors to only a limited degree. The EU's collective identity might explain the enlargement decision as such, but not the bickering of the member states during the actual negotiations with eastern European countries (for details see Sedelmeier 2005). A rationalist account such as liberal intergovernmentalism seems sufficient to account for the EU's behaviour in and the outcome of the actual enlargement negotiations, as Schimmelfennig argues (Schimmelfennig 2003a). When it comes to paying a price for one's collective identity in terms of offering beneficial conditions to new members, the EU looks more like an exclusive club dictating the terms of accession to new members. In sum, the EU's collective identity, which explains the 'if and when' of EU Eastern enlargement, appears to be largely decoupled from the EU's behaviour in the actual negotiations.

Conclusion

This chapter has tried to make three points. First, I presented a short overview on social constructivism as a distinct research programme and tried to show what it contributes to the study of European integration. Second, I used the question of European identity to illustrate empirically social constructivism 'at work'. Third, I presented a constructivist account of the EU's Eastern enlargement in order to demonstrate that an identity-based explanation is better able to account for the enlargement decision itself than conventional theories of integration such as liberal intergovernmentalism.

My overall conclusion is that the arrival of a social constructivist research programme at the study of the EU was long overdue. It is all the more remarkable that this research has quickly left the stage of meta-theorizing and concern for ontology and epistemology behind and has now entered the realm of concrete empirical work dealing with real puzzles of European political life. Thus, social constructivist research on the EU has quickly entered the realm of 'normal social science'. It is, of course, ultimately up to the readers of constructivist work to decide whether their claims contribute to the accumulation of our knowledge about the EU. Most empirical work from a constructivist perspective engages alternative explanations and demonstrates its claims against competing hypotheses.

So, what remains to be done? My concluding remarks centre around the lack of a social constructivist theory of European integration on a par with, say, liberal intergovernmentalism, as Moravcsik has called for (Moravcsik 2001a). It is true that social constructivism has not generated a set of mid-range propositions that could compete with conventional integration theories such as neofunctionalism or liberal intergovernmentalism. Checkel's efforts to develop a constructivist theory of socialization processes in Europe probably come closest to such an attempt (see e.g. Checkel 2001b, 2003).

Should we strive for yet another stylized theory of integration offering a comprehensive account of European integration, this time from a constructivist perspective? And can we reasonably expect one to emerge from constructivism? As argued above, social constructivism does not represent a substantive theory of integration, but an ontological perspective or meta-theory. Constructivist insights might be used to generate theoretical propositions, e.g., on collective identity constructions, their causes and their effects on the integration process. Sociological institutionalism as the constructivist-inspired version of institutionalist research can be used to generate hypotheses about the impact of Europeanization on domestic change which can then be tested against or supplemented with more rationalist accounts of institutional effects (Börzel and Risse 2003, 2007). However, a full-fledged constructivist theory of regional integration is probably not on the cards.

Moreover, we do not need another theory of European integration resting on a single logic of social action and interaction. As the *Handbook of European Union Politics* demonstrates (Jorgensen *et al.* 2007), the theoretical fistfights in the study of European integration are over—they have never interested scholars of comparative politics or public policy as much as students of international relations anyway. If it is indeed true that there is more than one social logic of action and social rationality, our theories need to take this insight into account. I have argued above that we need to distinguish the rational choice logic of consequentialism from the sociological institutionalist logic of appropriateness and that both are different from the logic of arguing. Yet real actors in the real world of the EU tend to combine various logics of action in their behaviour. They pursue egoistic interests—embedded in a society constituting their collective identities. They argue about the right thing to do—in order to pursue some goals and to solve collective action problems.

As a result, theories of European integration should strive to integrate the various logics of social action and resulting propositions about human behaviour in order to figure out in which ways they complement each other and where they offer competing accounts. Constructivist reasoning contributes to this endeavour by emphasizing processes of social action such as rule-following and meaning construction through reason-giving which rational choice accounts mostly bracket.

▉ NOTES

1 Whether 'multi-level governance' represents a full-fledged theory of integration or rather an analytical framework to study it, remains unclear (see contribution by Jachtenfuchs and Kohler-Koch in ch. 5 of the first edition of this volume; also Hooghe and Marks 2001).

2 The following discussion is partly based on Risse forthcoming. See also Checkel and Katzenstein 2008; Herrmann *et al.* 2004.

3 A similar argument could be made with regard to the 2004 EU decision to open accession negotiations with Turkey. At the time, the vision of modern and post-nationalist Europe clearly prevailed over those favoring a more exclusionary EU. Yet, the Turkish case also shows in contrast to Eastern enlargement that the negotiations themselves are clearly hampered by the lack of consensus on membership among the EU countries. This lack of consensus is strongly influenced by the contested nature of European identity when it comes to whether Turkey is 'in' or 'out'.

▉ GUIDE TO FURTHER READING

Adler, E. (2002) 'Constructivism and International Relations', in *Handbook of International Relations*, edited by W. Carlsnaes *et al.* (London: Sage), 95–118. This article represents a good overview of the core arguments and debates of social constructivism.

Checkel, J. T. (ed.) (2005) 'International Institutions and Socialization in Europe'. Special Issue of *International Organization* (Cambridge: Cambridge University Press). This edited volume uses sociological institutionalism to examine how exposure to European institutions has or has not had socializing effects on actors. It is a prime example of theoretically informed empirical work inspired by social constructivist insights.

—— and Katzenstein, P. J. (eds) (2009) *European Identity* (Cambridge: Cambridge University Press). This edited volume challenges the prevailing view of European identity as related to modernization and enlightenment. The authors argue that European identities are increasingly politicized and challenged, due to Eastern enlargement and the emergence of populist parties on the left and the right.

Christiansen, T. *et al.* (eds) (2001) *The Social Construction of Europe* (London: Sage). This edited volume demonstrates in an exemplary fashion what social constructivism has to contribute to the study of the European Union.

Risse, T. (2009) *We the European Peoples? Identity, Public Sphere, and European Democracy* (Ithaca, NY: Cornell University Press). This book presents an overview of what we know about the Europeanization of collective identities and public spheres from a variety of disciplinary and methodological perspectives.

Sedelmeier, U. (2005) *Constructing the Path to Eastern Enlargement: The Uneven Policy Impact of EU Identity* (Manchester: Manchester University Press). This book provides another prominent example of 'applied social constructivism'. It discusses the EU's Eastern enlargement using theoretical insights from both rationalist and sociological institutionalism.

Wendt, A. (1999) *Social Theory of International Politics* (Cambridge: Cambridge University Press). This book by one of the most prominent American international relations theorist introduces the core features and arguments of social constructivism.

■ STUDY QUESTIONS

1. What is social constructivism, and what is its contribution to the study of European integration?
2. How does social constructivism's emphasis on constitutive analysis relate to the study of Europeanization?
3. What are the different ways in which communicative practices can be studied, and how does this relate to the analysis of European integration?
4. What is 'European identity', and how can we study it?
5. What can social constructivism contribute to the explanation of the EU's enlargement?

PART THREE

Constructing the European Union

9 Discursive Approaches

Ole Wæver

Introduction

Within the study of European integration, discourse analysis has begun to make its presence felt, although it has hardly gained a clear profile as either contender for the position as one of the leading schools or as a distinct interpretation of 'the nature of the beast' (Risse-Kappen 1996). It should initially be observed that the editors have been perceptive in designating this branch 'discursive approaches'. Within international relations (IR) in general, the heading would almost certainly be 'postmodernism' or 'post-structuralism', with discourse analysis seen as one of the (non-)methods used by 'post-ies'. Possibly, it is a sign of the position of European integration studies (EIS) between IR and political science, that the higher independent profile of discourse analysis within political science influences the study of European integration. Or it is because EIS, compared to IR, has a more European profile. It is characteristic of the American intellectual scene that postmodernism has become established as a 'school' with extreme views and with a role as combatant within IR, whereas European IR has been more pragmatic about including postmodernism and discourse analysis as an approach to the study of international politics (Wæver 1998a). This chapter will not use discourse analysis as a pretext for a general rehearsal of postmodern attacks on the mainstream: it will report on work done by way of discursive approaches to the analysis of European integration and discuss their value and limitations.

Two different categories of work fit the heading discursive approaches. One consists of the relatively limited number of works that try to develop discourse analysis as *a theory of European integration*. The other is the vast field of studies *based on discourse analysis* that take up key questions in the field of European integration, but are not conceived of as 'general integration theory'. The latter show up within subfields and policy areas (see e.g. Wæver 1996c; Rosamond 1999; Burgess 2000; McDonald 2000; Wodak and Weiss 2000; Hay and Rosamond 2002), but they are too diverse to be covered systematically in this chapter, and examples will be presented in the context of the general theories, where they fit. Thus the attempts to develop discourse analysis as a general theory are used as a structuring device for the chapter. It should be noted that this presents a picture that is much more logically structured than the experience on the ground where practitioners of discourse analysis will often feel that they simply analyse some European subject of interest. In the section entitled 'Three approaches in European integration discourse theory' I will focus on three distinct 'schools' or 'programmes'.

The concept of discourse analysis is used in linguistics and in various parts of the humanities for a great variety of things (e.g. for studies specifically aimed at analysing oral communication), but in political science, IR, and EIS, it most often has connotations of French conceptions of discourse that refer back to the work of Michel Foucault, Jacques Derrida, and others. When developed as a general theory of politics and society, one of the main reference points is the theory of Ernesto Laclau and Chantal Mouffe (1985). Most of the studies covered in this chapter are explicitly situated within this context of works, and the general presentation of 'what is discourse analysis?' in this chapter will therefore concentrate on this type. Nonetheless, the three research programmes or approaches to be discussed will often do very different things and reach possibly quite opposite conclusions. This is because discourse analysis has entered EIS less committed to a particular substantive position towards European integration than some of the approaches covered in the other chapters of this book. Instead, discursive approaches can be seen as either a methodology (discourse analysis) and therefore compatible with quite different theoretical approaches, or as a theoretical approach that had been developed in other disciplines and has then been applied in EIS in different ways.

Discourse Analysis in the Study of European Integration

The Basic Idea(s)

What does it mean to focus on discourse? Why would one do that? What difference does it make vis-à-vis other approaches? What are the implications for the kind of questions one can and cannot ask? What is 'discourse'? How is it studied?

Discourse analysis looks for structures of meaning. 'Things' do not have meaning in and of themselves; they only become meaningful in discourse. As a consequence, it is problematic to ground one's analysis in 'given' subjects or objects because both are constituted discursively, and one should therefore study this process of constitution first. *Objects* of knowledge might be said to exist independently of language, but when they enter into human, social life, they need to be categorized and conceptualized if they are to make sense. The *subjects* of knowledge and action, similarly, are constituted in many different ways—and have been so throughout history—for example, as 'man', 'reason', 'civilization', 'the nation', or 'the word of God'. Neither things nor subjects and their intentions are given by themselves. We therefore have to cut into the discursive webs that provide meaning to such concepts. Discourse analysis does this.

One of the central concepts of this approach is obviously discourse. Discourse can be defined as *a system that regulates the formation of statements* (cf. Foucault 1972; Dreyfus and Rabinow 1982; Bartelson 1995: 70; Wæver 1996a; Torfing 1999). In the context of EIS, it is usually assumed that the most important discourses are political discourses. Consequently, many studies focus on the delineation of what can meaningfully be said in a given political arena. This can very well be different from private views, and thus discourse analysis should be clearly distinguished from cognitive approaches, which analyse what people perceive and think. If cognitive approaches sometimes use public texts these serve as indicators for perceptions, thoughts, and beliefs, raising all kinds of problems regarding the validity of discourse as a source of knowledge about people's minds (see, among others, Bonham *et al.* 1987). Discourse analysis focuses attention on discourse as interesting in itself. It is not an indicator for something else and thus questions about whether 'they really mean what they say' are irrelevant. A discourse analysis tries to find the structures and patterns in public statements that regulate political debate so that certain things can be said while other things will be meaningless or less powerful or reasonable.

The relationship between discourses and actors is complicated. On the one hand, discourse is 'prior' in the sense that subjects are not given outside discourse and it is only from within discourse that certain subject positions are opened up from which one can speak. On the other hand, discourses only exist and are reproduced and transformed through practice. This amounts to what Thomas Diez (1999a: 603) has called 'linguistic structurationism' with reference to Anthony Giddens' view of the mutual dependence between structure and agency (see Giddens 1984). Indeed, it is becoming increasingly common to see discourse analysis as divided into agent-focused and structure-focused approaches, respectively focusing on the power of discourse and the power of actors in discourse (Holzscheiter 2005). The conception of discourse in this chapter is more aligned to the 'structural', Foucauldian side of this, whereas the actor-focused one typically draws on (often Habermasians versions of) speech act theory (Risse 2000; Crawford 2002).

Another aspect of the relationship between actors and discourses is whether actors are fully in the grip of discourses. Many discourse analyses give this impression when explaining a particular political position directly by discursive structures. This is problematic, because such analyses slide into the cognitivist position where discourse regulates the *consciousness* of actors, whereas the study of political discourse should focus on discourse as placed *in-between* actors. Thus actors need to be conceptualized as having at least the possibility of acting strategically in relation to discourse—both in relation to how they shape a political position in relation to a given discursive position and in how they try to transform the discursive structure itself (Wæver 1996a, 2005; L. Hansen 2007).

Discourse analysis does not claim that discourse is all there is to the world, only that since discourse is the layer of reality where meaning is produced and distributed, it seems promising for an analysis to focus on it. Discourse does not stand apart from 'reality'. On the one hand, it is hard to conceive of any meaningful concept of a reality about which we can talk if one excludes discourse and thereby meaning. On the other hand, where would discourse exist if not embedded in reality in the sense of actions, materiality, and institutions?

If one wants to predict policy it is necessary to make two more specific assumptions about discourse: inertia, and constraining effects on political options. A popular view of politicians is that they say anything that suits their immediate interest, pay no attention to what they said the day before and feel free to change it tomorrow. However, most people who have studied political discourses have been surprised about how coherent and systematic political language is. Political speech is not only a short-term justification of this or that decision but also a struggle over the resources for future battles that reside in the structuring of public discourse. Therefore, discourse analysts are often more interested in *how* a politician argues than *what* they say. Whether they argue for or against a specific decision is less interesting than what they do to the general political language and therefore to long-term possibilities enabled and constrained by this language.

Philosophical Roots

What traditions does discourse analysis draw on philosophically and how does this matter?

Discourse analysis of the kind I discuss here has post-structuralist roots. This does mean influence from e.g. Heidegger's analysis of how the 'Western metaphysics' is deeply imbedded in our whole vocabulary. There are Anglo-American ways to get to post-structuralism too, notably radical pragmatism such as Richard Rorty, but the most influential route leads from figures like Martin Heidegger and Friedrich Nietzsche via amongst others Michel Foucault, Jacques Derrida, Jacques Lacan, and Gilles Deleuze to formulations by Laclau and Mouffe, William Connolly, and Judith Butler, who locate themselves more explicitly in the field of political theory.

This pedigree means that if one is interested in engaging in meta-theoretical discussions *pro-et-contre* discourse analysis, or if one wants to address the deeper questions of methodology within discourse analysis, it is helpful to study these sources in order to get a sense of the mode of thinking within post-structuralism. For instance, the Heideggerian inspiration actually implies that structures of meaning are abundantly stable and hard to escape—quite contrary to the popular image of post-structuralism as 'scepticism' regarding 'secure knowledge'. However, the field of discursive approaches has matured sufficiently to make it possible to take the analytical frameworks provided by discursive approaches and apply them, just as lot of researchers doing neorealist, rational choice or Marxist analysis read only the relevant IR theorists, while their leading theorists—and their critics—have (hopefully) based their work on more extensive studies of the original texts.

With an inspiration from structuralist linguistics, discursive approaches generally assume that meaning rests within systems of differences. However, where structuralism ends in a static system of 'codes' that explain how meaning *works*, how a culture is structured conceptually, post-structuralism—most clearly articulated by Derrida—points out how ultimately the closure of meaning is *impossible*. No system of meaning can fall fully into place—it will always be unfinished and unstable, containing an excess of meaning that it cannot pin down unequivocally. In any system of meaning, one sign refers to another. Discourses try to establish something as a 'transcendental signified', as that which we can point to as ultimate ground (e.g. God, reason, the nation, or evolution), but nothing *is* just itself—it too makes sense only by reference to something else, and on we go in the eternal play of signs (Derrida 1978 [1967]). It should be noted that Derrida points to both the impossibility of closure and the constant longing for the fixity and security of any such ultimate basis. This is what Laclau and Mouffe (1985) build on in their influential theory of discourse. Partial fixations of political meaning are constantly attempted and make up much of the dynamics of politics, but any such attempt always has a loose end, an opening for a possible rearticulation. When the concept of 'democracy' is articulated within a social-democratic discourse, for instance, there is an attempt to fix its meaning in a particular way. This however is a futile project: the concept will always include a surplus of meaning that enables a competing articulation of democracy, for instance into a neoliberal discourse—it will remain 'essentially contested' (Connolly 1983).

This form of discourse analysis includes an element of structuralism in that the analysis will try to discern patterns or structures in discourse that are the precondition for specific political statements. It thus needs to have some conception of the whole, of what characterizes a particular epoch or a particular setting in order to analyse the 'condition of possibility' for a particular statement. While such an analysis might very well show how different discourses compete in a particular setting, it will need to have some idea of the overall conceptual landscape.

In contrast, there are also forms of discourse analysis that typically draw more directly on operational ideas from linguistics—e.g. metaphors or euphemisms—and show how particular tropes are used in discourse (e.g. Chilton 1996; Straehle *et al.* 1999). Journals such as *Discourse and Society*, *Journal of Language and Politics*, and *Discourse Studies* typically publish this kind of work. It will often be more attentive to the micro-features of texts than what I have discussed above, and it can show how, for example, Delors used one family of metaphors while Santer and Prodi have used metaphors drawn from other contexts; or it can trace particular powerful metaphors such as 'the European common house' (Chilton and Illyin 1993; see also Drulak 2006). Studies also relevant to European politics have analysed linguistic avoidance strategies in Jacques Chirac's pre-Iraq war interview transcripts (Anchimbe 2008) and 9/11 analyses' use of proverbs and sayings (Gándara 2004). But what does this mean? Such analysis typically provides less of a picture of the whole, and therefore, it is often on the one hand convincing—because well documented—and on the other hand not very good at leaving a major imprint on more general debates. In the future it would probably be advisable for discourse analysis to try to integrate these two sides, i.e. use more disciplined and precise ways of analysing texts while contextualizing these in more general, 'structuralist' interpretations that offer tools for interpreting the findings.

One school within discourse analysis that tries to bridge this gap is the so-called 'critical discourse analysis' spearheaded by Norman Fairclough (1992, 1995; Chouliaraki and Fairclough 1999; cf. Titscher *et al.* 2000; Wodak and Krzyzanowski 2008).[1] It stretches from the micro to the macro level in texts. A weakness of this approach is the limited integration of the different elements and the tendency to resort to intuitive laundry lists of important questions to ask to a text—and it has been used relatively little in IR and EIS so far, although this is beginning to change, first by researchers publishing in specialized discourse journals picking up IR and 'Europe' questions and more slowly finding its way into IR and European studies conferences and journals (see e.g. Pfister 2007; Wiener 2007, 2008).

When and How Discourse Analysis Entered Political Science, IR, and European Integration Studies

Discourse analysis has had strikingly different fates in political science and IR. In political science, the discourse theory of Laclau and Mouffe in particular gained a certain niche prominence. In IR, in contrast, post-structuralism has gained a surprising prominence—and paid a price. During the 1980s, the two main rivals within IR, realism and liberalism, transformed themselves into neorealism and neoliberalism respectively. In doing so, the gap between them was narrowed significantly. In particular, both approaches subscribed to the same rationalist ideal of science. The resulting debate between the two theories about how rational egoists act, including the debate over relative and absolute gains left space for the next 'great debate' to emerge between this almost consensual, rationalist 'neo-neo' position and a radical challenger of this position—which became post-structuralism (see Wæver 1996b). During the 1990s, a more moderate constructivism then began to occupy the middle ground between rationalism and post-structuralism (see Adler 1997). Among the costs for post-structuralism of this unlikely prominence was a radicalization and turn towards the meta-level where it became absorbed by debates about the discipline as such, while more operational elements like discourse analysis were downplayed.

The debate between rationalism and post-structuralism was not directly transferred into EIS, where the main debate took place between liberal intergovernmentalism and multilevel governance. Post-structuralist interpretations of the EU were rare—at least within EIS. While discourse analysis was applied here and there, only gradually did it coalesce into a candidate for independent treatment (cf. Diez 1999a, 2002).

Although discursive approaches in EIS have not been developed around a specific core argument on Europe, there are some recurrent themes. One is 'there is not one Europe but many'. Those who study Europe as a 'fact' naturally assume there is one Europe, but analysing discourse points to the role of competing 'Europes' (Wæver 1990; Stråth 2000b). A second argument, often indirect or implicit, is against interpreting the EU in state terms—be it in terms of intergovernmentalism or as a new and bigger state. Instead, it is proposed, the EU resembles a network or postmodern empire. This argument follows from a deconstruction of existing discourses and thus is based on discourse analysis, but it stems at least as much from general arguments in postmodern IR and therefore it will not be dealt with in this chapter (but see Diez 1996, 1997, 1998; Börzel 1997). A third core argument is that European questions are tied in with other issues—not primarily due to cause–effect connections or strict logical implication, but because of the rela-tional nature of language, which means that concepts are valorized in relation to each other. This, however, begs the question of what other issues to emphasize: gender, socio-economic divisions, national traditions, social cosmologies, or yet other possibilities. This is exactly one of the main issues on which the different 'schools' within Euro-discourse analysis differ.

Three Approaches in European Integration Discourse Theory

This section covers three examples of bodies of work that have each operationalized dis-course analysis in a particular way in order to make it speak to European integration. Even if one is clear on how one defines discourse analysis, it is not clear how to take the step from there to an analysis of European integration, and especially at what level it should be applied: specifically on 'European' discourses that transcend national confines, or on national discourses on Europe, or with a particular conceptual focus? In what fol-lows, I have selected three approaches, primarily because they have been among the most prominent and influential, and secondarily because they are complementary in terms of the choices they make on basic questions.

Governance and Political Struggle

A notable body of work adopting, albeit often implicitly, a discursive approach has grown around the concept of (multilevel) governance. It is organized around different concepts of legitimizing European governance, inspired by Beate Kohler-Koch and developed by Markus Jachtenfuchs, Sabine Jung, and Thomas Diez (see Jachtenfuchs 1995, 2001, 2002; Jachtenfuchs *et al.* 1998; Diez 1999a, b, 2001; Jung 1999). To label this a programme or approach does not imply a fixed and unison subscription to one set of assumptions. It is rather a school in the sense of being an interconnected stream of works stretching from Kohler-Koch's role in triggering this kind of work without doing herself discourse analysis as such (cf. Jachtenfuchs and Kohler-Koch 1996; Kohler-Koch 2000) over the individual and joint work by Jachtenfuchs, Jung, and Diez in the mid-1990s to their separate directions of development. In the work of this group of authors, the political battle lines are not located primarily between nation states or for and against integration as such but between different socio-economic models, which again rest of a number of wider suppositions of almost cosmological nature. This approach thereby installs the main research issues squarely within politics in every sense of the term.

The most programmatic article from the research group (Jachtenfuchs *et al.* 1998) makes the case for 'polity ideas' as a particularly important category of ideas to be emphasized within the general battle for supplementing rational choice studies of interests with a thorough study of ideas. Polity ideas are normative ideas about a legitimate political order. In practice, the authors study political party documents in Germany, France, and the UK to reconstruct elements of polity ideas, based on 180 different subcategories within a general analytical scheme built around participation, output, and identity as possible dimensions of legitimacy. Another element in the approach is to establish four ideal–typical polity ideas, two based on the modern state (one where it is carried through the nation states, ie. intergovernmentalism, and one where the state is the EU, the federal state), and two beyond statehood (output-legitimized 'economic community', and 'network' legitimized by participation and identity). When tracking the debates in the three countries, one major finding is the relative continuity over time, another is the consistency within parties united by the same ideology, while national context accounts for the rest of the variation.[2]

Diez has later (1999b, 2001) elaborated this analytical scheme in ways that make it live up to the standards of discourse analysis more fully. His key concept is 'discursive nodal points' inspired by Laclau and Mouffe (1985). He treats European governance as one such nodal point through which various core conceptions of politics are drawn together in a seemingly coherent worldview and their meaning thereby stabilized. Thus, while Diez continues to use the four-pronged typology from the collective work, the different polity ideas are now linked to various metanarratives that capture developments in 'deeper' concepts like politics, progress, and the economy.

One of the strengths of this approach is that it offers a way to handle a problem characteristic of much discourse analysis: change. Diez's elaborate scheme offers a way to conceptualized degrees of 'translatability' between discourses, and this explains how easily one discourse can change or not change into another (Diez 1999b).

Another advantage is that this approach with its predefined list of elements offers instructions as to how to read and what to look for. This part of the analysis therefore comes close to living up to methodological standards as pronounced from more traditional corners. It is not an impressionistic interpretation of a limited number of texts, but a quasi-automated cataloguing of a high number of texts. Thus, the actual 'coding' of the material might be reproducable by others and there is a quite systematic empirical data-set against which to assess the macro-interpretations. Methods for computer-supported, quantitative text analysis exist and have been used in IR (e.g. Alker 1996), and it is not impossible to imagine something similar being used for parts of an analysis like the search in this school for 'elements'.

Among the problems that mark the general 'governance' approach (see also Chapter 5), and, although to a lesser degree, Diez's later work are:

- The use of ideal types is 'un-discursive'. It goes against the basic idea of discourse analysis where no categories are universally valid: different discourses construct concepts and ideas differently, and therefore, it is surprising to see ideal types derived from general overarching considerations and then used as boxes into which discourses fit, although in fairness to Diez, he addresses this issue and claims that such ideal types are used to make explicit the context from which he is writing (see Diez 1999b).

- The approach downplays national context. At first, this may sound like a good move, because it wants to transcend traditional limitations from state-centric approaches, but thereby it also downplays the interconnectedness of different discourses that are defined mutually in relation to each other, e.g. British Conservatives very likely develop their position in relation to Labour and this is usually more important than family connections to other conservative parties. Rivals share traits either directly or in inverted form. However, as we will see in the following section, to take the opposite approach creates the opposite problem and points back to the value of Diez's approach.

If the story about Europe of this first group of authors should be summed up, it must be: Europe is politics. The main battle lines go between different general political orientations and relate to choices about other issues that are generally seen as political (e.g. socio-economic models), and the form of this struggle is about *legitimacy*, also a classical political category. As we will soon see, the two other approaches take us gradually into battles further removed from the openly political, even if they surely want to argue that this is politics, too: first a theory that links Europe primarily to concepts of nation and state; secondly an approach that brings out hidden political investments in concepts like 'heading', 'crisis', and 'concept'.

Foreign Policy Explained from Concepts of State, Nation, and Europe

A relatively distinct approach posits the configuration of concepts of nation, state, and Europe as the basis for building theory of discourse as layered structures able to explain foreign policy options for a given state. This approach is more traditional than many other discursive approaches in its focus on *national* spaces of political debate and in its explicit ambition to *explain* (which some post-structuralist discourse analysts remain sceptical about). It has been marketed less as a theory of European integration than as a general bid for a theory of foreign policy, but all its main contributions have been on European states and often on EU member states' European policy, and the theory includes an explicit suggestion for how to analyse the interplay between on the one hand national discursive struggles among competing articulations of national traditions and on the other hand the process (or not) of European integration. Authors in this group include Ulla Holm (1992, 1997), Henrik Larsen (1997a, b, 1999, 2000), Iver B. Neumann (1996a, b, 2001, 2002), Lene Hansen (1997, 2001), Işıl Kazan (1994), and Ole Wæver (1990, 1991, 1995, 1996a, 2005; see also Wæver *et al*. 1991)—but see closely related works by Haahr (2003), Merlingen (2001), Parsons (2000), Banerjee (1997), Kadayifei (1996), and Ruggie (1997).

The central idea of this approach is to see how the general lines of foreign and European policy are based on different concepts of Europe and how these in turn are made possible by articulating differently concepts of state and nation. It is assumed that each country has a particular basic problematique of state and nation such as the French state-nation and the German concept of the romantic nation and the power state. The main positions in each country can then be characterized by the way they choose among the few available ways of relating to this concept. This is depicted in a model of layered structures inspired by Kenneth Waltz's concept of international structure (Waltz 1979). At the deepest level is the basic national concept of state-nation, at the second a purely relational conception of where the state/nation is in relation to Europe (internal, external, doubled, etc.), and at the third level are different concepts of Europe. The layered conception defines a way of studying stability and change because from any specific point, one can see possible changes as being more or less radical, and therefore more or less likely, depending on whether they happen at the third, the second or the first layer. Similarly, it is an important characteristic of a political situation whether the main rivals are within the same box or represent the different main options at, for instance, the second layer.

State, nation, and Europe are chosen because they are we-concepts, identities we hold simultaneously and which therefore have to be articulated with each other. European identity is not studied as a potential replacement for national identity, but because each nation's 'vision of itself' today includes a concept of Europe.

Thus this approach is not just a method for studying discourse, it is a theory of foreign policy. It is necessary for any political leader to be able to make sense of the big question of 'where are we heading', i.e. to be able to tell narratives of the nation/state, where it is coming from and where it is going. These increasingly include concepts of Europe as a way to project for example 'Germany' or 'France' into the future. European integration is only stable to the extent that the key countries can make sense out of their own future within a discourse that includes the current European project (see Wæver 1994, 1995, 1996a, 2005, 2000). These discourses do not at all have to be identical between countries; they only have to be compatible. Thus, French policy has to be *discursively* compatible with the basic French concept of state-nation, while it has to be *politically* compatible with German policy in particular. While this approach allows for interesting links to classical realism, the study of diplomacy and the question of translations and mediation among countries (Kissinger 1957; Wæver 1995, 2005), it is weak on the possibility of an emerging European public sphere where discourses leave their national confines and meet directly on a European arena.

In contrast to the first set of authors, this approach therefore emphasizes the mutual dependence of (very different) domestic competitors. The German political debate, for instance, may be stable in itself because the leading political rivals share a commitment to deepen European integration because their state-nation concepts would become 'homeless' without such deepening. Yet radical change is possible in Germany because this German constellation is dependent on a certain momentum at the European level and thus on the internal stability of French policy, which is much more doubtful. This school has mainly been carried forward by pro-European researchers in Eurosceptical countries like Norway and especially Denmark, and can be seen as a warning about the fragility of European integration and the need for taking serious the national peculiarities of Europe debates.

The theory can usefully be compared to social constructivist theories of foreign policy that describe how a certain policy and self-conception is institutionalized—as typically in a number of studies on German foreign policy (e.g. Banchoff 1999; Berger 1996) that explain why German foreign policy remained relatively stable after the end of the Cold War and did not turn more aggressive, as predicted by structural realism (Mearsheimer 1990). These studies put forward arguments as to why a given policy has been sedimented, but they have no 'deep structure' to explain why *both* this *and* some radically different positions are available. Consequently, this kind of social constructivist analysis has difficulties understanding change (cf. Legro 2007) and is often forced to fall back on material structure. Identities and other social constructions explain inertia, not change. In contrast, the theory of layered discursive structure can account for even abrupt change because it follows from a change one level down the trunk of the tree structure and out onto another branch.

Because there are no ideal types, this approach faces a question about how to *find* discourse! How do you know a discourse when you meet one? And how do you avoid a circular argument where you first find a discourse in the texts and then you prove its importance and explanatory relevance—because it is (still) in the texts? Usually, the way out is sought in some form of combination of diachronic and synchronic analysis. In a first (synchronic) step, a wide selection of texts are read, not only of politicians but also of influential intellectuals. The aim is to get as clear an understanding as possible of the inner logic of a particular discourse which is ultimately an analytical construct but justified empirically by a first reading of texts. This establishes the structure that is to be used in a second (diachronic) step, studying political processes in more detail, focusing on the moves made by leading politicians, which are interpreted on the basis of the discourses as conceptualized in the first phase.

Again, some sociological constructivist work, especially by Thomas Risse's research team at the European University Institute (Risse *et al.* 1999; Marcussen 1999; Marcussen *et al.* 1999) seems closely related because it includes a very similar reading of concepts of Europe in different national contexts as shaped by the different traditions of state and nation. While this work as such is presented in Chapter 8 of this volume, it should be possible to point out mutual advantages and disadvantages:

- The approach is vulnerable to the criticism that discourse floats freely, that it is 'all discourse', lacking an explanation of where discourses come from. Thus it will generally be seen as progress when Risse and other constructivists include a sociological explanation for the institutionalization and de-institutionalization of ideas. In particular the 'ideational life cycle' (see, for instance, Marcussen 1998) is an interesting explanatory model in this respect.

- The sociological school in turn is very limited in its analysis of national traditions. These works do not get to the inner properties of ideas because they do not include a structural–linguistic component. Like the above-mentioned social constructivist work on foreign policy it focuses on the social explanations for the sedimentation of a particular idea, and can (externally to itself) explain its stability and change, but not how it relates internally to rival concepts in the national debate (see Legro 2007).

Other problems with the state-nation discourse theory are:

- The central place of national settings. The theory does allow for a European ('Brussels') scene as an overlapping layer (Wæver 1994), but this is secondary to the basic construction in terms of national spaces. In this sense, it turns the problem of the governance school upside down. While the latter emphasizes ideological orientations first and underplays national connections, the state-nation approach privileges national context over socio-economic orientation.

- It is quite traditional in its causal conception of discourse as explanation for policy. It is structuralist more than post-structuralist and therefore misses the inner dynamics of language, the paradoxes and tensions within language as emphasized by, for example, Derrida and Lacan. The discourses become too static, stable, and self-identical, whereas a more fully post-structuralist analysis would emphasize the inherent tensions within any move towards coherence and thus their ironies and strange effects.

The European Project as Productive Paradox

A third—and in this case more loosely connected—body of work analyses the project of European integration itself, often using texts from the EU system and/or more general developments in the public debate related to Europe, such as history books or the interventions of intellectuals. The focus here is on the way the integration project as such is conceptualized, what kind of identity it projects, how this interacts with more general changes in the European polity regarding legitimacy, history, medialization, concepts of citizenship, and politics (examples include Pocock 1991; Schlesinger 1991; Derrida 1992; Delanty 1995a, b; Burgess 1997a, 2001; Johansen 1997; Stråth 2000a, b; Rytkønen 2002; Joenniemi 2003; Diez 2004; Stavrakakis 2005).

One advantage of this school is that it is often more strongly linked to general philosophical points from especially Derrida's deconstruction, because it focuses on the inner dynamics of *one* attempt to structure discourse. A danger of the two first schools is to depict language as too controllable, as a tool used in power games. Rationalist scholars underestimate language by treating it as a transparent media of representation and communication; but many social science post-structuralists might underestimate the particular features of language by treating it as a transparent media of power, purely a tool for politics. A more radical deconstructivist would instead want to emphasize how language plays games with actors. As mentioned, systems of signification never fully close up and fall into place—they retain always paradoxes, open ends, and impossibilities. The more insistently an actor tries to repress unpleasant elements, the more likely this is to show up in peculiar forms elsewhere in the text (Derrida 1974 [1967]; Wæver 1989). If one wants to depict, for example, a policy as 'unpolitical' and technical, this demands a grounding in some transcendent reference. Otherwise, it remains based on signs referring to signs referring to signs and thus openly a political choice. A transcendental grounding, in contrast, produces a forceful justification outside the text—but it has to be secured by operations internal to the text, and this will haunt the text through the effects of the moves necessary to do this grounding.

Interestingly, there seems to be a contrast between work on the United States (US) which tends to develop into rather monolithic, Foucault-inspired stories of how the identity needs of the US state has demanded continued production of self–other images and foreign threats (Campbell 1992), whereas the EU invites deconstruction, Derrida-inspired stories about ambiguity and ironies. In Derrida's own book on Europe (1992 [1991]), for instance, he underlines the simultaneous necessity to be responsive to the call for Europe and at same time opening up Europe to its Other, to avoid closing it down as being identical to itself. Exactly because we (in the early 1990s Europhoria) move under the banner of a 'Europe' we don't really know the meaning of, it becomes a politics of anticipation rather than precedent. Thus, the analysis can investigate critically attempts to define European identity through cultural essentialism (cf. the critique in Delanty 1995b) while it also shows how another kind of paradoxical political identity is created that avoids classical pitfalls.

It is only possible to develop Europe if one remains attentive to rather philosophical questions. Derrida develops his conception of European culture by way of the general argument that 'what is proper to a culture is to not be identical to itself, . . . to be able to take the form of a subject . . . only in the difference with itself' (1992: 9; emphasis added). When drawing on the concept of Europe, one has to also take on the Europeanness of the concept of concept (Burgess 2001). This shows how philosophical this can become, and sometimes it therefore almost stops being discourse analysis—because it is unclear what is actually read and the analysis turns into philosophical argument as such.

A specific advantage of this school is the possibility to link form and content, to study the position of media and culture and thus identity not only as object but also as practice (Schlesinger 1991; Burgess 1997b; Johansen 1997; Delanty 1998). In particular the electronic media are changing both in their expression and in their organization in relation to states, and the nature of identities produced and reproduced in dominant media are likely to change as well. It is common to note how national identity is about a glorious past and a heroic future, but the present is also conceived in a specific way. According to Benedict Anderson (1991), the modern nation is structured around an understanding of compatriots living simultaneously even if distant from oneself. Therefore its emergence depended on both epistemic innovations like 'homogenous empty time' and the single-point perspective and on technologies of communication with print and the novel later reinforced by newspapers, telephone, and radio. What kinds of political communities are likely to thrive in a media world fragmented into multiple TV channels filled with hyperreality and constant live-ness?

Many other contributions can be presented as reflections on what kind of identity Europe might be constructing. Traditional approaches typically ask what European identity is and thus they end up talking identity talk themselves (Europeans are united by their commitment to the Enlightenment, but divided by confessions, etc.). Discourse analysis helps us to understand *how* identity is constructed, and quite different mechanisms have to be investigated. Most of the existing work on this issue connects identity to the question of legitimacy: does the European project necessitate a form of legitimacy which in turn demands a political identity (A.D. Smith 1992; García 1993; Howe 1995; Laffan 1996; Kostakopoulou 1997; Beetham and Lord 1998; Banchoff and Smith 1999; Hansen and Williams 1999)? If yes, how much can this be a *political* identity in contrast to more ethnic identities in the nation states (Habermas 1992a; Kelstrup and Wæver 1993; Hassner 1997)?

Deconstruction here shows its value and discourse analysts question the questions traditionally asked and expose the terms of debate. Hansen and Williams (1999) have shown how this debate assumes a contrast between technical rationality and myth, whereas instrumental rationality has been the key myth in the self-understanding of the EU. Another typical deconstructive move is to show how the debate takes for granted a connection between identity, legitimacy, and polity that is transferred from the nation state and its heyday. A critical analysis of the debate itself opens a space for thinking the possibility of a different kind of legitimacy, one that is not a question of identity (cf. the first school discussed above, particularly Jachtenfuchs 1995). Thirdly, the impasse reached by much of the traditional debate, that cultural identity is both impossible and necessary, can be taken beyond logical contradiction to a dynamic understanding of the paradoxical nature of identity (Burgess 1997a; Stavrakakis 2005): identity is not being but always longing and desire, and thus European identity politics can be grasped through an analysis of passions of politics and identification.

Another possibility for constructing European identity is by contrast to some external 'Other'. Much discourse analysis has therefore investigated whether Europe is built through a negative casting of Japan, Turkey and/or Islam, Russia or maybe increasingly the US (Kostakopoulou 1997; Neumann 1998, 1999; Pocock 1991; Behnke 2000; Stråth 2000a, b). Studies often find that the EU does this to a surprisingly limited degree given the historical centrality of this road to identity. The limited use so far might be explained by the complex nature of the EU, where its de facto variable geometry prevents a 'digital' logic of total contrast and leads to a more nuanced 'analogue' model of multiple differentiations (Neumann 1998). Another explanation could be the centrality of its 'magnet function' as spatial ordering of the wider Europe and therefore a necessity to avoid exclusionary logic (Wæver 2000). Discourse analysts face an important research task here of sorting out contradictory findings that sometimes claim strong Othering, sometimes its striking absence. Superficial registration of negative adjectives has to give way to more structural analysis of texts to see if 'Radical Others' *carry* their meaning or not. Another form of advancement of this approach is to move from radical others to the 'almost-European other' (Rytkønen 2002)— immigrants and Euro-Islam within, eastern Europe and Maghreb externally to the EU.

Discourse analysts often look at Europe through its margins and borders. Where mainstream studies focus on the core of Europe with the assumption that it is the most influential and therefore most important, some discourse analysts follow the postmodern advice to look at the seemingly unimportant, exceptional, and atypical. Since it is in these places that the *boundaries* of Europe are lived, they might actually shape Europe more strongly than the normality at the centre (Boym 2000; Parker 2002; Browning and Joenniemi 2004).

A fourth form of identity rests on temporal instead of spatial differentiation. Europe is defined in relation to itself but along the axis of past, present, and future: Europe's violent past is the defining Other, and the necessity of integration in the present is given by the need to avoid that a return of power-balancing gives Europe a future too much like its past (Wæver 1996c; Buzan *et al.* 1998: ch. 8). Although this argument has clearly been central to the integration project, it is not clear whether the most far-reaching interpretations of this as an identity project (den Boer *et al.* 1995 [1993]: 202–10) are still valid. If rupture is stressed very strongly, Europe is built on a dialectical usage of history and therefore builds identity without injecting any positive essence into its own history. A negative essence combined with a commitment to break away from this would be a promising way to build an identity not prone to self-righteousness. However, this is probably a too-idealized view of the EU (Diez 2004). One way to get to a more nuanced understanding of the European mix of self-celebration and self-negation is for discourse analysts to engage with the history of the European idea (Hay 1968; Pocock 1991; den Boer *et al.* 1995 [1993]; Delanty 1995a; Malmberg and Stråth 2002; Pagden 2002).

Discourse analysis of the emerging European identity can draw on studies of the cultural and identity policies of the EU. The strategy of especially the Commission in relation to the creation of European cultural identity has clearly changed over the years. The late 1970s and the 1980s particularly were marked by a straightforward hunt for the symbols of the nation state: flag, anthem, passport, examples of cultural and historical uniformity (see the Copenhagen declaration of 1973 and most clearly expressed by the Adonnino Committee in 1985). The early 1990s saw a change to a policy emphasizing much more that the identity of Europe *is* its pluralism, its variation (Pantel 1999; Delgado Moreira 2000). Subsidies in the cultural area shifted from Eurosymbolism to local variation. This project still has the potential to weaken national identities by breaking up their uniformity and harmonization, not by integration from above but through fragmentation from below. Studies of this particular policy area could benefit from more systematically combining classical policy analysis and the 'type 3' discourse analysis on the plays of identity, difference, responsibility, and text (Diez 1995, 1997; Stråth 2000a, b; Stavrakakis 2005).

The story told about Europe in this third 'school' is usually related to the question of essentialism and culturalism. It can have a negative twist, especially when it studies the policies of Othering, or a more positive tone when it tries to construct Europe as a discourse that lives up to the high demands of post-structuralists for an open-ended, other-respecting and ethical politics. Europe is here included on the list of concepts—with justice, responsibility, and emancipation—that Derrida has invested with the dual logic of being both a call for political response and at the same time indeterminate, impossible to fulfil, never to be realised in any specific form and thus a source of constant challenge and demand for us to live up to ethical demands.

Comparing the Three Programmes

The most obvious difference between the three programmes or approaches is in terms of the main 'unit' of discourse. The third approach takes Europe at large as its arena and posits one or a few general (dominant) discourses as representing the integration process. At the other extreme, the second approach claims a prominence of national discursive spaces and therefore structures its map of competing discourses as competitors within national systems (tied together in three-like structures of depth and surface in each nation) and interacting mostly in a rather exterior way amongst the nations. On this axis, the first occupies the middle position because it takes in some respects Europe as one arena where the same basic discourses compete and travel across borders, but it often organizes its studies around the analysis of national debates, and it is interested in explaining, understanding or problematizing national policies on Europe. Since the first approach stresses discourses across nations, while the second has everything channelled through foreign policies, the two can be seen as the discursive manifestations of multi-level governance (see Chapter 5 this volume) and intergovernmentalism (Chapter 4 this volume) respectively. In other words, there is a parallel to debates elsewhere in EIS, in that one of the main choices the student of European integration is confronted with is whether to approach Europe via national policies or by looking directly at the European project as such, 'its' discourses and institutions.

Enlargement

When approaching enlargement with discursive approaches, two large fields of research immediately open up. The first one that follows from previous work is self–other constructs either between a Western (current EU) self and Eastern (new members) other or between the enlarged EU and non-Europe. To the extent that eastern Europe figured in the set of differences that defined EU-Europe, redefinition of identity has to take place. This challenge has been aggravated by the way the *process* of enlargement negotiations have offered west Europeans lots of chances to define themselves vis-à-vis the 'not yet fully' European east. After the new members joined, such differentiations have become very dangerous to integration if reproduced within, and so increasingly, the next layer of potential candidates (above all, Turkey) occupy the empty position and discourse thereby continues, together with new discursive figures, for example more radical Othering of Russia, although this has not become as predominant a feature of European identity discourses as some new member states would have wished (Neumann 1998, 1999).

The second option answers one of the questions that non-discursive approaches find most interesting: the rationale or justification for enlargement—why did the EU decide to do something so costly and cumbersome? Here, the best answer from within or close to discourse analysis comes from *speech act theory*, which is currently emerging within IR as a middle ground between constructivism and post-structuralism (cf. Buzan *et al.* 1998: ch. 2; Fierke and Wiener 1999; Williams and Neumann 2000). In relation to enlargement both Fierke and Wiener (1999) and Schimmelfennig (1997, 2003b; see also Chapter 4 by Moravcsik and Schimmelfennig in this volume) show how speech acts (or 'rhetorical action' in Schimmelfennig's terminology) can explain the paradox of an enlargement process that does not seem to be in the self-interest of member states. Just as with other acts, those done with words create unintended effects including commitments and moral obligations that are hard to get out of. More generally since they are *acts* they *change* reality (not only comment on it). Thus, words are not only derivatories in relation to politics, they often *are* politics.

Discourse analysis ought to be applied also to the *nature* of the enlargement process, especially its relative technocratization. A whole machinery is constructed to handle the negotiations and this rests on a specific construction of 'enlargement' as an issue and problem—an attempt to depoliticize the decisions about whom to accept through an 'objective' evaluation. Where much literature just ridicules the thousands of pages produced on each country and the naivety of the non-political assumption, discourse analysis could handle the more interesting question of how (and why) supposedly 'objective' and 'apolitical' interpretations are produced politically.

The three approaches presented above each lead to specific research agendas:

1. Governance studies will look at the competition between different models of legitimization, in the 'old' EU 15 and in the 'new' member states, in the relations between them and thus especially at the changing balance and possible internal redefinition due to enlargement. Legitimacy by efficiency has become more difficult with enlargement, but the grand historical rationale is given new life by the role of the EU in healing Europe's division and by allegedly extending the zone of peace (Friis and Murphy 2000).

2. The state-nation approach can study the new member states according to its standard procedure, but will probably focus on how the main powers redefine their concept of Europe so that it encompasses enlargement, that is, how is enlargement tied into their state-nation-Europe constellations? It is widely assumed that Germany has a special stake in Eastern enlargement, but should that be understood primarily in terms of material interests or a particular form of Europe? Has enlargement put increasing pressure on the French debate because state, nation, and Europe fitted better together with a more tight and action-oriented EU?

3. The third, 'depth-discursive' approach will surely engage in the already mentioned rethinking of external and internal differentiations and 'others'. Enlargement also recasts questions of responsibility and ethics (see, on Turkey, the discussion in Diez 2007). Who is to make decisions on who can join the EU? What would be legitimate grounds to decide membership?

Conclusion

Three final questions should be addressed:

First, what is the relevance of discursive approaches to other approaches? The most immediate overlap is to social constructivism where several studies demonstrate that there is a broad contact zone, and to governance approaches, where some of the literature, for instance on multilevel governance, is discursive in form. Other connections might also be cultivated. The state-nation approach could make links to liberal intergovernmentalism because they share the tendency to channel politics through states, not directly as transnational processes, while they give competing explanations of 'preference formation'. The legal and constitutional debates (e.g. Weiler 1999; Wind 2001) could also team up with discourse studies because legal analysis is often language-oriented, but its in-depth study of one type of discourse could be more systematically imbedded to a more systematic understanding of the more general discourses.

What is the status and standing of discursive approaches? Much has been done within this approach, but it is often quite dispersed and often not seen as part of EIS. However, a few efforts are relatively concerted (those discussed as 'schools' here), and it is for discourse analysts to push these forward.

Finally, what are the challenges for the immediate future? Many internal debates are needed, not least on methodology (cf. Milliken 1999; Malmvig 2002; Walters 2002; Hansen 2007; Baker *et al.* 2008; Wiener 2008). The debates on methodology promise to become a dynamic field (which is probably surprising to most critics who see this as anti-method). There is a widespread sense that it is time to be more disciplined and self-reflective about how discourse analysis is done. The meta-theoretical debates could be influenced by general developments within IR theory, but it is probably more likely that the relative autonomy of EIS means that discourse analysis within this field will continue to develop along a separate path. Finally, it might be necessary to address some of the tensions that have run through this article stemming from the duality of discourse analysis as theory and as methodology.

Thus discourse analysts within EIS face the dual challenge of simultaneously becoming better in order to speak to the other theories within the field and explain what discursive approaches can contribute, while engaging in complex internal debates on methodology and analytical strategy that necessarily demand specialized terminology and attention to the more exotic philosophical roots of these approaches. Discourse analysts will need to pay close attention to language—not least their own.

▓ NOTES

1. Several of the books from critical discourse analysis (CDA) are written in the style of 'manuals' in how to do discourse analysis. This is much rarer for the macro-oriented type inspired by Foucault and especially Laclau and Mouffe, which often leaves students uncertain about how to actually practise it. An important exception is Hansen (2007), which presents very detailed and concrete suggestions for operational procedures. It deserves its place in the Guide to further reading, but its empirical subject is not EU-oriented enough for that.

2. For a more recent analysis updating empirically what metaphors, images, and topoi are applied for representing and explaining the European Union as a unique political space, see Oberhuber *et al.* 2005.

▓ GUIDE TO FURTHER READING

Derrida, Jacques (1992 [1991]) *The Other Heading: Reflections on Today's Europe* (Bloomington, IN: Indiana University Press). Probably the key instance of a deconstructivist reading of the concept and project of Europe. It transcends simplistic notions of self-other construction to investigate the intricate play of otherness within the European venture. And it provides a challenging reflection on the ethical requirement raised by 'Europe'.

Diez, Thomas (1999) 'Speaking "Europe": the politics of integration discourse', *Journal of European Public Policy*, 6(4), 598–613. Diez makes a general case for the value of discourse analysis in European studies. This is done by way of three 'moves' of increasing radicality: J.L. Austin's theory of speech acts introduces a performative view of language. Michel Foucault's concept of discourse as the locus of power moves politics as well as the constitution of subjects more fully into language. Jacques Derrida's deconstruction builds on a concept of language even further removed from the ideal of communication and more in terms of technique which allows for e.g. analyses of nodal points, metanarratives, and translatability. Throughout the article uses examples from European studies to show the relevance of the different aproaches.

Jachtenfuchs, M. *et al.* (1998) 'Which Europe? Conflicting Models of a Legitimate European Political Order', *European Journal of International Relations*, 4(4), 409–46. A wide-ranging article that is simultaneously programmatic and based on large empirical material. In a study mostly of political party documents in Germany, France, and the UK, the authors show the importance of 'polity-ideas', i.e. normative ideas about a legitimate political order. Four basic ideal types are derived logically, and the article shows how large data work can be synthesized in a discourse-based approach.

Malmberg, M. and Stråth, B. (eds) (2002) *The Meaning of Europe* (Oxford: Berg). This book contains a number of perceptive analyses of different concepts of Europe in different countries. It is not based on a shared form of discourse analysis, neither is it explicit about method, but it contains studies on many of the themes that future discourse analysts are likely to continue working on.

Wæver, O. (2005) 'European integration and security: analysing French and German discourses on state, nation, and Europe', in D. R. Howarth and J. Torfing (eds), *Discourse Theory in European Politics: Identity, Policy and Governance* (Basingstoke: Macmillan), 33–67. This is a theory- and methodology-centred presentation of the 'concepts of state-nation-Europe' type of discourse analysis in European studies. France and Germany are the main empirical illustrations. The chapter is relatively detailed on practical questions such as 'what to read', 'how much is enough?', and the relationship between diachronic and synchronic analysis, and it presents the tree-shaped structure of depth levels used in this approach.

■ STUDY QUESTIONS

1. Why is the analysis of discourses on European integration important?
2. What is the relationship between discourses and actors in the European integration process?
3. What are the three main strands of discourse theory in European integration studies, and how do they differ?
4. What role do concepts of state and nation play in the European policies of member states and membership candidates?
5. How is the 'other' linked to European identity?

10 Gender and European Integration

Birgit Locher and Elisabeth Prügl

Introduction

Gender politics seem to have been high politics for European states. Curtailing access to abortion rapidly emerged as a priority for governments after the end of communism, and gay rights are stirring up tempers in new European Union (EU) member states. Although communist governments put women's equality on their banner little seems to remain of egalitarian sentiments in eastern European polities after the communist demise. Women have lost jobs, positions in government, and degrees of control over their bodies. A new regime, the European Union, appears to promise relief under a Western model substituting neoliberal equality in an integrated Europe for the lost socialist equality. Where the communist state failed in the end, the EU apparently offers a better future—of egalitarian gender relations in conjunction with a European economic space and political unity. In it the urgency states brought to curtailing women's independence has been replaced by a gradual, low politics approach of lobbying, legislating, litigating, and gender mainstreaming in order to advance equality.

The origin, shape, and the effects of this approach are a main subject of feminist research on the European Union. Feminists ask: what kinds of gender equality policies does the EU pursue? How did they get on the agenda? What kinds of feminist and masculinist politics hinder and promote these policies in the EU? And what are the consequences of these politics? These seem purely empirical questions but, we will argue, they have theoretical ramifications. Feminist research starts from an ontological proposition, i.e. that gender is a basic organizing principle of the social and political world. This presumption is made explicit in research probing the ways in which gender is inscribed in the diverse policy fields of the EU. Questions such as 'what are gendered effects of EU policy-making?', 'what are underlying normative assumptions of distinct policies?', and 'is the EU patriarchal?' become relevant in this perspective. In addition, feminists critically reveal gender biases in concepts and categories of mainstream theories on European integration. In order to overcome given conceptual limits, feminist research probes and amends theoretical approaches in novel ways: by focusing on particular constellations of feminist activism, it reveals hidden aspects of European integration and gives voice to subjugated knowledges. By focusing on gendered structures, it makes visible mechanisms engaged in the reproduction and amelioration of patriarchal domination.

Gender Approaches and Feminism

Traditionally concerned with equality between women and men, feminist research has moved from focusing on women and men as equivalent categories to studying gender, i.e. the way in which women and men, femininity and masculinity relate to each other, the way in which 'masculine constructions depend upon maintaining feminine ones—and vice versa' (Peterson 1992: 9). In gender approaches, women and men, femininity and masculinity thus do not exist in isolation from each other, but, instead, are mutually interdependent. As a relation, gender ceases to function as a causal variable that can deliberately be included or excluded in an explanatory model, but becomes an integral part of social phenomena such as the European integration process. Gender analysis is social analysis in that it describes the way gender informs social relations and probes the meanings of femininity and masculinity in social contexts. Gender is thus not static: its meanings and the particular state of gender relations are created and perpetuated through the interactions of various actors in diverse contexts. Analysing the underlying mechanisms as well as premises involved in the (re-)production of existing gender arrangements is at the centre of a feminist research programme that conceives of gender as a critical category for analysis.

Gender approaches to studying European integration make an ontological claim, that is that gender matters when probing European integration. European integration is part of a sociopolitical world that is fundamentally structured by understandings of femininity and masculinity and contributes to reconstructing these understandings. Gender approaches assume that one can only fully understand and explain large parts of the European integration process with the help of a gender-sensitive perspective—that is through an analysis that also focuses on the (re-)construction, malleability and functionality of gender in the making of Europe and on the norms, ideas, discourses, and practices that sustain and advance the process. Conversely, European integration constructs gender in new ways, i.e. it newly produces mutually constitutive understandings of masculinity and femininity.

Cynthia Weber (2001: 89) has suggested that taking gender as a viewpoint challenges conventional accounts as partial and incomplete by questioning not only the scope and range of common theories but also their very concepts and categories. In her review of European integration theories from a gender perspective, Annica Kronsell (2005) provides a trenchant illustration of this effect. She shows how intergovernmentalism fails to consider power relations within the state, obscures the gendered boundaries between private and public, conceptualizes power as masculine, and fails to appreciate the relation of women's interests to national interests. While neofunctionalism and multilevel governance theories tend to be more amenable to including feminist concerns, they fail to account for the dominance of some groups over others, conceal hierarchies among institutional levels and actors, and have been blind to the tendencies towards 'homo-sociability' i.e. the preference for the company of the same sex in governance networks. A gender perspective thus reveals significant yet hidden aspects, driving forces, and unaccounted effects of the European integration process.

In addition to providing a framework for analysis and critique, a gender approach also offers a methodological lens. Feminists have argued that all knowledge is interested and all truth situated. Accordingly, all research implies a viewpoint. Unlike most analysis, feminist analysis makes this viewpoint explicit and self-consciously grounds itself in the knowledges of particular standpoints, such as the standpoints of different feminist movements. This allows feminist researchers to offer a critical perspective that reveals knowledge and practices as gendered and gives a voice to those not typically heard in the interpretations of European integration. It also allows feminists to approach research as collective and democratic, an exercise in knowledge creation not limited to the privileged position of academics, but validating everyday and activist interpretations and points of view (Ackerly *et al.* 2006).

Not all gender analysis of European integration is feminist research in this sense. Some gender analysis focuses on illustrating the way gender operates, some on making visible processes that have been hidden, some on validating subordinated knowledges. There also is a tradition of feminist research that seeks to provide a better understanding of the EU by making visible the variables that influence its gender equality polices. Thus, there is no such thing as 'a gender theory' or 'a feminist theory' on European integration, at least not in a narrow sense of a coherent set of theoretical propositions outlining causal mechanisms and factors contributing to and accelerating the European integration process. Indeed, unlike classical approaches such as neofunctionalism and intergovernmentalism, gender perspectives do not constitute substantive theories of European integration. As a consequence gender perspectives cannot be placed vis-à-vis these scholarly traditions for immediate comparison. However, feminist approaches do shed light on *how* the EU is integrating by providing an understanding of the way gender is structuring integration and the way integration has structured gender relations.

In this review of feminist approaches to the European Union, we include a broad range of perspectives. The way in which gender matters has been the topic of a diverse body of scholarship steeped in varied disciplinary traditions, asking different questions, employing multiple methodologies, and arriving at diverse answers. Much of this scholarship probes the EU's gender equality policies through standard social science methods, exploring the causes of policy adoption and implementation, and frequently painting the EU as a feminist ally. Gender constructions enter the explanations of some, but not all of this scholarship. A smaller body of studies employs a critical feminist standpoint probing constructions of gender in EU policies and critiquing the effects of these constructions. Our purpose is to show that acknowledging gender in the European construction project enriches the understanding of European integration by making visible an under-appreciated social reality. We illustrate the contribution that gender and feminist analysis can make by presenting empirical case studies on trafficking in women and the Common Agricultural Policy (CAP) as well as by discussing EU enlargement from a gender perspective.

Gender Approaches and European Integration

One of the more astonishing aspects of European integration has been the creation of an EU gender equality regime encompassing a variety of soft law instruments in addition to treaty provisions, directives, and court rulings (Hoskyns 1996; Hantrais 2000a;

Mazey 2002; Ellina 2003; Berghahn 2004). The regime has been built in stages, shifting approaches and expanding in scope over time. Scholars have described a three-stage movement from a focus on equal rights and treatment, to positive action, to gender mainstreaming, i.e. the consideration of gender differences in all areas of policy-making and programming, from the stage of planning to implementation (Rees 1998; Mazey 2001; Booth and Bennett 2002). While originally focused narrowly on non-discrimination in European labour markets, the scope of the regime has expanded over time. It now includes measures enabling workers to better reconcile work and family, a pregnancy directive, a parental leave directive, directives on part-time and temporary work, and a directive on non-discrimination in the provision of services (Hantrais 2000b; Hoskyns 2000; Walby 2004).

Explaining Gender Equality Policy

Why have governments adopted gender equality policies at the EU level when they sometimes did not have similar commitments at the national level? Feminists have sought to answer this question employing the tools introduced in the range of theories presented in this book. Intergovernmentalism and rationalism have been used to explain the original placement of Article 119 in the Rome Treaty as an outcome of the French interest in levelling the economic playing field by extending its national legislation to the European level (Hoskyns 1996; van der Vleuten 2007). Intergovernmentalist arguments have also surfaced in explaining various innovations in European gender equality policies, such as gender mainstreaming, as outcomes of the accession of the Nordic countries (Liebert 1999). Equally, the accession of new eastern European member states has been used to explain a slow-down in EU activism in the field of gender equality (van der Vleuten 2004). Constructivist arguments on norms have been used to explain the EU engagement in the area of trafficking in women (Locher 2007).

Supranationalist arguments have appeared in the form of historical institutionalism suggesting that the codification of equal pay in Article 119 (now 141 EC) generated path-dependent developments. Short-term government interests in the 1950s led to long-term unintended consequences, i.e. EU leadership in gender equality policy (Pierson 1998; Ellina 2003). The Commission acted autonomously to advance gender equality by taking advantage of qualified majority voting, creating the European Women's Lobby (EWL), and strategically employing the gender gap in EU support to advance gender equality policy in the 1990s (Abels and Bongert 1998; Liebert 1999; Abels 2001; Ellina 2003). The European Court of Justice played a crucial role in moving gender equality forward (Egan 1998), and feminist legal studies often draw on 'integration through law' approaches (Flynn 1996; Lundström 1999; Shaw 2000). More broadly, supranational rule-making on gender equality (and other domains) has entailed a combination of litigation and civil society mobilization (Cichowski 2007). Or, in a similar recent formulation that combines supranational and subnational agency, governments have seen themselves outmanoeuvred in a pincer movement from above and below (van der Vleuten 2007).

Although these explanations resemble those of traditional theories of European integration, feminist approaches rarely stop there. The feminist movement has been crucial to bringing gender equality to the EU agenda, and gender analyses of the EU draw on theories of social movements and advocacy networks that can account for the activism of feminist lawyers, advocates, and policy-makers. Thus, a key contribution of feminist approaches to European integration has been to theorize activism, the power of framing, and the 'opportunity structures' for movement activism, i.e. the conditions that enable movement effectiveness. Gender equality policies may have an unintended outcome from the perspective of governments, but not from the perspective of feminist activists.

Movement activism—both EWL lobbying and grass roots organizing—was crucial to reviving Article 119, broadening the gender policy agenda, and raising issues of racial diversity (Hoskyns 1996; Cichowski 2007; van der Vleuten 2007). The EWL has played a key role in such activism and has worked strategically to develop a 'transnational feminist interest' consisting of non-controversial goals among its diverse national member organizations (Helfferich and Kolb 2001). Gender equality policies changed over time in response to such activism, leading to gender mainstreaming as 'an attractive form of "policy succession"' (Mazey 2002: 20). Such activism has operated in the context of 'opportunity structures', including on the one hand the interests of the European Commission and the Court, and on the other hand the rise of neoliberalism. Within these opportunity structures, activists developed new policy frames that over the years moved away from social legislation while also broadening its scope. Gender analyses make visible the potency of shifting frames and the way in which notions of femininity and masculinity are reconstructed as women are constructed as equal (in labour market policy), as different (in gender mainstreaming), or as victims (in anti-trafficking policy).

If the EU has constituted an opportunity for advancing gender equality policy, national gender constructions frequently have appeared as an obstacle to their implementation. National-level institutions upholding the male breadwinner norm and the norm of the family as a care giver have functioned as 'needles' eyes' through which European-level policy prescriptions need to pass, sometimes leading to a distortion of their intent (Ostner and Lewis 1995). The difficulty has not been the same for all member states but, in Mazey's words, 'national policy styles beget a dense "hinterland" of detailed programmes, policies and institutions and it takes a very long time for EU institutions and policies to permeate and change this hinterland significantly' (1998: 145). The extent to which EU policies fit domestic institutions thus makes a difference in the speed with which EU prescriptions are implemented. So do 'mediating institutions', such as equality agencies or labour tribunals and the quality of state–society relations (Caporaso and Jupille 2001). In addition, state projects matter, such as building democracy in post-authoritarian Spain or the protection of the family in Italy (Calloni 2003; Valiente 2003).

Scholars studying the process of implementation have emphasized the relationship of institutions and activism and highlighted in particular the importance of legal mechanisms in reconstructing gender regimes in Europe (Cichowski 2007). For example, legal pressure from the EU was crucial to generating public debate and elite learning in Germany (Berghahn 1998; Liebert 2002: 252; Kodré and Müller 2003). Somewhat unexpectedly, European Court of Justice (ECJ) rulings condemning compulsory maternity leave and quotas are changing the meaning of gender equality in Sweden, traditionally considered a pioneer on gender equality (Sunnus 2003). In contrast, movement activism seemed to be central in other contexts of implementation. While the British government opposed EU social policy initiatives, British feminists participated in the formulation of gender equality norms at the EU level and mobilized around the domestic implementation of these norms (Sifft 2003). The British case illustrates that the distinction between processes of policy formulation and policy implementation cannot be upheld. Advocates in networks often operate in a two-way process, using the EU to advance domestic agendas in a way described by Margaret Keck and Kathryn Sikkink (1998) as a 'boomerang pattern'. Kathrin Zippel (2004) further develops this metaphor in her study of the incorporation of sexual harassment into the amended Equal Treatment Directive of 2002 to identify a 'ping-pong effect', in which advocates bounce an issue back and forth between national and regional levels.

Literature on adopting and implementing gender equality policy thus identifies a number of mechanisms that reconstruct gender relations in the EU (litigation, mobilization, framing, elite learning), while emphasizing in particular the role of legal and movement activism. Because this literature seeks to explain EU policies, it tends to paint the EU as a champion of gender equality and governments as laggards. In contrast, gender approaches that focus on a broad range of EU policies and on the socio-economic order that they produce tend to be more critical of the EU's feminist credentials and probe the way gender organizes power in EU policies and practices.

The Reproduction of Gender in EU Policies and Practices

Critical approaches to studying the European Union frequently conceptualize the EU as a regulatory body, a set of regimes, a socio-economic order, or as a 'postmodern state', i.e. a decentred authority structure that codifies and/or modifies existing power relations (Caporaso 1996; Sauer 2001b). They understand the EU as a superstructure regulating economic production and reproduction, the result of political struggles between social forces, and the institutionalization of masculinist interests. They propose that meanings of gender are deeply inscribed not only in society but in public policies and the organization of political life. Because the male has long served as the norm in the political arena, characteristics associated with masculinity have become hegemonic: they are thoroughly enmeshed in political institutions and support patriarchal cultural practices. The EU's focus on the neoliberal market project can be understood as validating and constructing rational, autonomous, economic man as the hegemonic type of masculinity (cf. Connell 1998: 15; Kronsell 2005: 1033). Gender mainstreaming is intended to make visible such gender constructions in EU policies in order to counteract the disadvantage they produce for women and men who do not live up to the hegemonic ideal.

The EU formulated its gender equality policies in parallel to its efforts to eliminate trade barriers, first in Europe and increasingly also internationally in the context of WTO negotiations. Feminists have shown that its policies of market liberalization have entailed a liberalization of gender orders, including a movement from dependency to individualization made possible by a flexibilization of labour. Liberalization may have meant superficial gender equality, but has left unresolved the issue of care labour:

Despite its private seclusion, the reproductive work of the Fordist period was at least socially recognized. Now, with the flexibilization and informalization of the labour markets, child rearing has, once again, become an economic and social externality.

Young (2000: 95)

The emphasis on individual choice and the interpretation of non-discrimination as being treated like a man have produced a gender equality policy in tune with deregulation (Ostner 2000). ECJ rulings invariably led to a less favourable treatment of women in instances where they previously were treated preferentially (e.g. equalizing working hours, night work, and retirement age) and governments have used equalization arguments to justify cutbacks (e.g. eliminating 'husband-only' benefits). No politics of redistribution substituted for the cuts enabled by these interpretations.

Care politics and women's insertion into the European labour market became a topic when the EU's Lisbon strategy on employment creation called for enabling workers to better reconcile work and family. Feminists have long demanded a more equal sharing of domestic and care work. However, increasingly, the language in EU texts has shifted from one of 'sharing' family responsibilities to one of 'reconciling' work and family. This shift has served to legitimize the flexibilization of labour relations, create a secondary feminized labour market and leave unchanged the distribution of unpaid labour in the family (Stratigaki 2004). The European employment strategy in this way has amounted to the creation of a new social model in which women enlarge the workforce by taking flexible and part-time employment while there is no serious engagement with issues of child care and family-friendly hours (Threlfall 2005). To the extent that these matters are discussed, they are framed no longer as a matter of equality policy but as a matter of active labour market policy or an effort to 'render the family more "employment-friendly"' (Ostner 2000: 38).

The EU's policy on reconciling work and family is intended also to address the 'demographic time bomb', i.e. an ageing population combined with low fertility rates. Making it easier for women to combine work and family is designed to enable women to bear and raise more children (Duncan 2002). Furthermore, the 1992 Pregnant Workers Directive and the 1996 Parental Leave Directive can be interpreted as 'policies to ensure the stability of population numbers and the future viability of the welfare state' (Guerrina 2002: 52).

In these interpretations, the European Union contributes to key functions of the state—ensuring the organization of production and reproduction—and it does so in a way that constructs gender subordination in a new way. It recreates gender divisions of labour by inserting women into the common labour market as flexible workers while ensuring that they remain available for unpaid care work. The EU reveals itself as a new form of the patriarchal state. Yet the EU is no unitary polity (nor has the patriarchal nation state ever been as unitary as the label may suggest). The juxtaposition of the EU's gender equality policy with its gendered labour market policy suggests internal diversity. Gender mainstreaming, i.e. taking into account differential effects on women and men in all policy actions, has further made visible the degree to which gender constructions in the EU differ according to issue areas and in different sites of the decentred state.

Gender mainstreaming has been implemented in a highly uneven fashion. Those Directorates General (DG) that have 'historically been interventionist in character, and relatively open to consideration of social justice issues' (Pollack and Hafner-Burton 2000: 440), such as the structural funds and DGs charged with employment and development policy, have been receptive to gender mainstreaming. By contrast, the most strongly neoliberal DGs, including those focused on competition policy, have resisted gender mainstreaming. So have DGs in important areas such as agriculture, environment and transport, and in foreign policy (Braithwaite 2000; Woodward 2003: 75).

The unevenness of implementation may point towards the fact that gender constructions form part of a larger set of discursive commitments in different issue areas. Labour
relations are gendered very differently in agriculture, manufacturing and in the services
sector. Different gender constructions may characterize not only different productive sectors, but different policy fields. The fact that gender mainstreaming resonates differently
in different DGs points in this direction. Similarly, the continued diversity of local gender
regimes throughout the EU is a testament to the internal diversity of gender constructions in the postmodern state.

Our two case studies illustrate the diversity of EU gender constructions. They also show
that EU gender orders have morphed in parallel with integration, both when the EU
has consciously adopted policies to reduce gender subordination and when it has implemented other policies. They thus illustrate the two types of feminist approaches we have
reviewed above—one that seeks to explain policy adoption and implementation and one
that probes the EU's gender equality project in relation to other state projects. They also
illustrate two distinct contributions of feminist approaches to understanding European
integration—i.e. the significance of feminist agency and the importance of understanding the EU as a site of gender construction.

'Best Cases': Trafficking and CAP

The two case studies we discuss in this section focus on (1) the emergence of the EU
policy on trafficking in women and (2) the gender assumptions guiding the Common
Agricultural Policy.[1] The adoption of a policy on trafficking illustrates how supranational
opportunity structures combine with feminist activism and the deployment of powerful frames to explain the construction of new understandings of gender. The analysis of
the CAP shows how gender constructions are subordinated to state projects of creating
a common market and modernizing agriculture. Our gender analysis makes visible how
European integration efforts have included conscious and unconscious modifications of
European gender orders.

EU Policies Against Trafficking in Women

The emergence of the EU policy on trafficking in women is particularly well-suited to illustrate the relevance of a feminist understanding of agency for explaining EU gender equality
policies (see Locher 2007). Starting from the puzzle that despite the existence of trafficking
in women since the 1970s, it was only in the second half of the 1990s that the 'slave trade'
became an issue on the political agenda of the EU, different factors need to be singled out
to explain policy change. In this case, a 'velvet triangle'[2] of EU femocrats and feminist
politicians, academics and experts, and non-governmental organizations (NGOs) came
together in a powerful feminist advocacy network and put the issue on the EU agenda.
The velvet quality of the triangle refers to the fact that most of the involved actors operate in a male-oriented environment resembling the 'velvet ghettos' of the business world

(Woodward 2001: 35). Depending on their formal position, their particular experience and background, actors of the velvet triangle are endowed with specific skills and types of knowledge. Whereas academics and experts possess technocratic knowledge comparable to that of epistemic communities, femocrats and feminist politicians as insiders are endowed with a particular procedural knowledge concerning the norms, rules and procedures of the institutions they are part of, whereas NGOs are characterized through testimonial knowledge emerging from their contact with grass-roots movements and local actors (Keck and Sikkink 1998: 19). Combining different experiences, backgrounds and distinct types of knowledge, the triangle of actors was able to advance potent policy frames evoking bodily violations and the slave trade in a context of opportunity to generate EU action.

Exogenous events such as the Dutroux scandals in Belgium opened up a 'window of opportunity' to take action. The entry of Nordic states into the EU also benefited the cause. In addition, major institutional changes, such as the creation of the Third Pillar and the provisions in the Amsterdam Treaty, provided opportunities to push trafficking on the agenda. Importantly, the case shows the relevance of constructivism to understanding gender politics in the European Union: gender equality frames are normative and changing; and their resonance with other norms in the international context (such as women´s rights or human rights) facilitates their adoption. International events such as the World Conference on Human Rights or the Beijing Conference gave these norms credibility and accelerated their trickling down not only to the national, but also to the European level.

The study is a striking example of the explanatory power of a feminist constructivist approach for EU policy-making. Utilitarian approaches are neither able to explain the timing of the policy invention, nor can they account for the EU's specific approach to trafficking. From a utilitarian perspective it is hardly obvious why the traditional migration and criminality frames applied to trafficking were broadened to include a new human rights and women's rights perspective and an anti-violence approach that implied costly policy programmes. With no additional benefits, but behavioural constrains and internal sovereignty losses the policy change is not comprehensible from a utility-maximizing point of view. Changing constructions of gender in advocacy frames combined with feminist activism provide a more ready and plausible answer.

The Common Agricultural Policy and Gendered Reform

Built on a commitment to preserve family farming, the EU's common agricultural policy has cemented a rural gender order based on the subordination of women. Patriarchal family constitutions, entailing male inheritance and constructing farming as masculine, characterize family farming throughout Europe. Government policies, including the CAP, are built on this gender order and perpetuate it through policies that target 'the farm' and fail to problematize power relations within the farming family. Common market policies and modernization programmes have contributed to reproducing a patriarchal gender order while shaping it in new ways.

A common market based on high, guaranteed prices has long formed the core of the CAP. The gender bias in this policy has recently been made visible by an assessment of the implementation of gender mainstreaming in the EU's structural funds, in which the Commission found that:

The majority of funding [in the European Agricultural Guarantee and Guidance Fund] concerns the agricultural sector where women are underrepresented. Actions are primarily focused on farms and their beneficiaries are the farm owners. The fact that only one out of five farm owners is a woman reduces the possibility for women to benefit directly from these projects. Farmers' wives and female employees are ignored by this kind of funding.[3]

The bias towards rewarding men in agriculture is likely aggravated by the fact that the barely 20 per cent of farms managed by women in the EU tend to be disproportionately small. Because price supports reward those who sell more, they disproportionately benefit large farm owners. Recently, responding to liberalization pressures in WTO negotiations, the EU has begun to eliminate price supports and substituted them with direct payments to farmers. While on the surface this change entails no gender effects—the target continues to be the farm owner—it is eyed wearily by some spouses of farmers. Previously they could claim that their labour contributed to the product from which the farm earned income, and they could lay claim to some of this income. But direct payments are based on heads of cattle or acreage of land—owned typically by men—and hide the basis on which women could lay claim to payments.

Policies of modernization and rural development were a second aspect of the CAP, delegated mostly to member states but gaining salience at the European level. These policies have sought to increase efficiency through specialization, mechanization, and farm growth. As farms specialized they typically eliminated women's income from the direct marketing of eggs, milk, jams, and other minimally processed foods. Furthermore, the more farms mechanized, the more production became men's work and women became flexible labourers supporting the needs of specialized production. Modernization policies thus reinforced price policies which empowered men. Price policies funnel money to male farmers to distribute to the rest of the family while modernization further constructed men as 'the farmer' and women farmers as 'wives' engaged in ancillary production activities.

The global pressure to liberalize European agriculture has brought back to the fore the importance of diversifying rural economies and farm incomes, recalling women's production and service skills. The EU's 2005 rural development regulation formulates diversification and improving rural quality of life as one of three goals.[4] European rural development efforts are now seeking to revive direct marketing and on-farm processing of regionally typical products, in conjunction with developing tourism and the rural services industry. Women in agriculture are still not approached as farmers, but as entrepreneurs who can help create a flourishing countryside. Rural women are constructed as uniquely suited to developing the services sector. Unequal gender relations remain pervasive in European agriculture as CAP funds continue to favour male farmers. While the introduction of direct payments may define women entirely out of farming as agriculture income gets divorced from labour input, rural development policies increasingly define mostly low-paid services as the realm of new rural femininity.

The cursory review of the CAP shows that it has participated in the construction of rural gender identities in Europe. Policies of modernization and high prices functioned to construct farmers as male and empowered them as business owners and breadwinners. At the same time, they constructed 'spouses' as female and moved them out of production into ancillary work and housework. Recent policy reforms, including the substitution of direct payments for high prices and policies of diversifying rural incomes, have further removed women from agricultural production and constructed them as rural service providers.

The Case of Enlargement

Enlargement provides a good case study for further illustrating how gender perspectives make visible hidden aspects of the integration process, because granting full membership to new candidate countries involves 'a highly complex policy process through which the external becomes internal' (Bretherton 2002: 15). Consequently, there is much more at stake than the formal adoption of the acquis communautaire and its translation into different national legal systems. Questions of identity—shifting notions of 'us' and 'them'—of sovereignty and of implicit or explicit norms and normative orders become equally relevant. While the EU pushes legislative progress in the area of gender equality on the national level, the enlargement process also functions as a site where power operates and new hegemonies are established. EU enlargement involves constructing gender relations by advancing distinct normative ideas of gender orders. Gender perspectives shed a different light on the rather mixed and contradictory effects of the enlargement process in the new member states.

Gender Equality in the Negotiation Process

When discussions about enlargement began, gender equality had already been a firmly established and officially promoted norm of the EU. With the Amsterdam Treaty gender equality and non-discrimination became guiding legal principles of the Union that were laid out in a number of new articles extending the old Article 119 on equal pay. The new Article 3(2), for example, obliged the Community in all its activities to 'aim to eliminate inequalities and promote equality between men and women'. For the first time the EU was given a sound juridical base for pursuing gender issues in any sector, not just in employment policies. As Steinhilber (2002: 2) points out, the EU Commission Strategy Paper (2001–2005) confirmed the Treaty's provisions by conceiving gender equality 'as an integral part of any social, economic and democratic development'. Given this strong legal background and the EU's public commitment, there were high expectations that gender equality would constitute a key principle in accession negotiations.

Negotiations focused on a total of 31 chapters, including Chapter 13 on Employment and Social Policy which contained all EU legislation on gender equality. However, despite treaty commitments to address gender equality in *all* EU activities, during the accession negotiations such issues were only dealt with in the context of Chapter 13 and were from the very beginning limited to the equal treatment of women and men in the field of employment and social policy (Steinhilber 2002). It appears that the favoured policy concept was one that understood gender equality as a particular policy field rather than a guiding principle for all policy areas. In contrast to the major paradigm change in gender politics that has taken place at the EU level years ago with the introduction of gender mainstreaming (see above), the enlargement negotiations represented a step back to the old and narrow gender equality approach that had dominated the Union for many decades.

The European Parliament, in particular the Women´s Rights Committee, frequently demanded greater efforts to place issues of gender equality higher on the agenda during the accession negotiations (Steinhilber 2002: 3). It had support from the European Women's Lobby, representing women's organizations from the EU member states. Both bodies shared a particular interest in promoting an understanding of gender equality that went well beyond a liberal approach of non-discrimination. In addition, a great number of women's organizations in western and eastern Europe considered the enlargement process to be a great opportunity for more gender equality. They hoped that the EU could be an ally in order to fight the gender backlash that most of the central and eastern European (CEE) countries had witnessed after the communist demise (Lohmann 2005; Steinhilber 2002). Women's and human rights organizations placed issues such as reproductive rights, particularly access to abortion (most notably in the case of Poland), rights to sexual self-determination, such as the protection of gay rights, and the fight against the dramatic increase of trafficking in women high on their agendas. Moreover, activists expected that the EU would advance the economic and political rights of women in the CEE countries, as the end of communist rule not only swept women out of parliaments and political office, but also led to a severe deterioration of their economic status (see e.g. Funk and Müller 1993; Ruminska-Zimny 2002).

Despite these various efforts gender issues did not receive much attention during the negotiation process. There was impressive feminist activism, but a powerful velvet triangle could not be established. Feminists lobbied the two parties at the table, representatives of the EU and delegations from the candidate countries; but in both women were severely under-represented (Steinhilber 2002: 4). This was problematic because women generally tend to be more open to gender equality issues and the absence of influential allies is an obstacle for successful lobbying. Within the EU at the time of the accession process there was a lack of powerful femocrats in high positions, particularly the Commission, who could have influenced the design and process of the enlargement negotiations. On the other side of the table, civil society organizations in CEE countries, particularly the women's movement and feminist NGOs, struggled hard to gain access to their national governments with varied, but often limited success (e.g. Lohmann 2005). Obviously, there was a great degree of feminist activism at different levels, but no functioning velvet triangle that could influence the accession negotiations to advance a more progressive gender equality approach.

Confined to Chapter 13, arguments in support of gender equality were limited and marginal. Critical issues such as violence against women, women's sexual and reproductive rights as well as trafficking in women, an issue that has been high an the EU's agenda from the mid-1990s onwards, could hardly be covered within this limited approach to gender equality. Even though annual progress reports for some countries—Poland for example—cited gender equality as 'critical', 'precarious', or as an 'area of concern', no visible consequences resulted. A key problem was that there were no clear and comprehensive indicators providing objective criteria for assessing progress; thus, no systematic analysis of the legal and de facto progress of the candidate countries in the area of gender equality took place (Bretherton 2002; Steinhilber 2002: 3).

Not surprisingly, a number of scholars (e.g. Bretherton 2002; Steinhilber 2002; Krizsán and Zentai 2006) have described the enlargement process as a 'lost opportunity' with respect to developing a comprehensive gender policy. Case studies of candidate countries are somewhat more nuanced. They report an impressive *de jure* harmonization of legislation in the candidate countries, but bemoan the dearth of enforcement. For example, Hungary made legal progress in the first stage of accession but with very limited consequences for political practice.[5] Only in mid-2003 and close to the time of full membership did a somewhat more policy-oriented approach appear concerning the way gender equality issues were handled between Hungary and the EU (Krizsán and Zentai 2006). In Poland the 1997 elections caused a policy shift towards a 'transitional backlash' against the social and political advancement of women (Titkow 1998: 29). While the Commission's 1999 progress report noted this development and expressed concern, the subsequent failure of the Polish government in 2000 to make any progress in implementing women's rights legislation did not lead to a slow down of the accession process (see Bretherton 2002: 9–11). Despite significant feminist mobilization, an organized opposition to EU gender equity law and its close ties to a government of the right delayed gender equality legislation (Anderson 2006). In contrast, in the Czech Republic there was less feminist mobilization but also little right-wing opposition. The country adopted a gender equity law a year earlier than Poland, but de facto enforcement of rights proved to be a problem here as well (Anderson 2006).

In sum, the EU's emphasis in the enlargement process was on the promotion of the formal, legal requirements of the EU gender-related *acquis*. Indeed, there was a uniform emergence of legislation across the CEE countries in the late 1990s and early 2000s designed to secure equal opportunities in the workplace, to guarantee equal treatment in social security benefits and to protect employees from sex discrimination (Anderson 2006: 101). Yet contrary to its rhetoric and the expectations of feminist politicians and activists in the old and new member states, the EU did not live up to its commitment to gender mainstreaming. The lack of a comprehensive understanding of gender equality has been detrimental to an extension of women's rights to include political, reproductive, and sexual rights in addition to economic and social rights. Indeed, looking beyond the negotiation process, one can argue that the EU has helped produce new gender orders in CEE countries based on liberal understandings of disembodied citizens and workers and exporting a particular construct of hegemonic masculinity.

Exporting Hegemonic Masculinity

In the 1990s the European Union sought to extend its regional and international influence more actively (see also Bretherton 2002: 2). To this end Agenda 2000 explicitly pointed out that a declared goal of the EU was to 'promote values such as peace and security, democracy and human rights, defend its social model and establish its presence in world markets' (European Commission 1997: 27). The Treaty of Lisbon, in an even more pronounced fashion, spelled out core values and principles of the Union such as democracy, the rule of law, human rights and fundamental freedoms, respect for human dignity, and the principles of equality and solidarity—principles that constituted the normative basis upon which the EU's new outreach strategy was built.

Gender equality was among the declared values of the European Union fostering expectations, particularly among feminist activists, that in the process of moving from the EU 15 to the EU 27 gender equality policies in the sense of gender mainstreaming would play an important role. The lack of a velvet triangle may explain why this expectation was not met, as demonstrated out above. Another and complementary way to explain the failure is to probe the masculinist commitments of existing EU institutions and policies. Despite its progressive equality rhetoric the EU has institutionalized hegemonic masculinity: i.e. its institutions have been dominated by men and constituted on norms associated with masculinity (Kronsell 2005). Similarly, its policies have institutionalized norms that privilege particular forms of masculinity. Kronsell (2005: 1033) points out that most of the gendered practices of the EU and its member states emerge from well-established, highly institutionalized yet hidden norms. She argues that from a feminist viewpoint, the EU institutions can be considered as institutions of hegemonic masculinity in which 'distinct cultural norms and institutional power . . . mutually support a particular masculinity' (Kronsell 2005: 1033).

Viewed from such a perspective, the lost opportunity for progressive gender politics in the enlargement process appears even less puzzling. In the contest of values, gender equality in a broad understanding appears as subordinate vis-à-vis other values emerging out of a situation of hegemonic masculinity. The liberal institutional order that the EU represents and the market liberalization that it champions can be interpreted as expressions of such a hegemonic masculinity (Kronsell 2005: 1033). Liberalism hides masculine norms behind assumptions of genderless rational choosers and equally rights-bearing citizens. Yet, as feminist economists and political scientists have shown, the notion of an autonomous subject is profoundly gendered in that it fails to account for relations of dependency and connection that are particularly pronounced for women in their roles as carers. Insofar as EU policies adopt liberal presumptions—as for example in the neoliberal market model—its prescriptions for the making of a single market and a political union reproduce masculinist commitments (see also Bretherton 2002: 14). These commitments became particularly visible in the use of inherently gender-biased indicators for assessing candidate countries' development toward market economies that greatly underestimated women's contribution to national economies when, for example, they did not take into account unpaid work, predominantly done by women (e.g. Stratigaki 2004; Threlfall 2005; van der Molen and Novikova 2005; Anderson 2006). The institutionalization of masculinity in EU institutions and policies thus explains the lack of commitment to gender equality and mainstreaming during the accession negotiations and the failure to critically assess the gendered effects of privatization and market opening.

Yet there are diverse gender regimes operating at the EU level, not least in the different Directorates General of the Commission (see above). The institutional culture of a particular DG encompasses the degree to which male experiences are the norm and the degree to which masculine norms become guiding principles for policy-making. DGIA which coordinated the EU's enlargement prior to the reorganization of the Commission was one of the few DGs which had no officer responsible for gender mainstreaming and did not participate in the Commission's internal mainstreaming processes (Bretherton 2002:

15). In contrast, in DGV (later renamed DG Employment and Social Affairs) gender mainstreaming was a well-established principle, but the DG was rather weak and undergoing
major internal reorganization, which contributed to the low priority of gender issues in
the enlargement process. As Bretherton (2002: 16) concludes, 'in relation to enlargement,
gender mainstreaming was thus a casualty, not only of the inhospitable internal culture of
DGIA, but also of the bureaucratic politics of intra-Commission rivalry'. Obviously, DGs
using a neoliberal framework enjoy more prestige and power than others (cf. Pollack and
Hafner-Burton 2000: 447). As a consequence, during the enlargement process the meaning of gender was not only downplayed, but the EU also uncritically exported masculine
norms and values via the neoliberal market principle into the candidate countries.

This is highly problematic as economic transformation has disproportionately hurt
women. It appears that the new market economies institutionalize gender biases and reinforce existing inequalities. Research and statistical data have shown that the labour market transformation process in the CEE countries has exacerbated gender inequalities (e.g.
UNICEF 1999). Discrimination and strong occupational segregation for example characterize labour markets in the Baltic republics. Labour markets in Estonia, Lithuania, and
Latvia have exposed 'how the "happy marriage" of a neo-liberal economic framework and
neo-conservative gender ideology is in reality a restatement of women´s political, social,
and economic disempowerment' (van der Molen and Novikova 2005: 147–8). Steinhilber
points out that the transformation of the agricultural sector in some CEE countries is de-
teriorating women's economic opportunities and increasing poverty among rural women
(2002: 5). In addition, CEE efforts to comply with convergence criteria for the Economic
and Monetary Union have had disastrous consequences for the social infrastructure in
new member states with negative effects on women (Steinhilber 2002: 6–8), aggravating
'the already grave consequences of tight fiscal policies and social restructuring which
characterized the decade of the 1990s'.

Thus, the EU's validation of hegemonic masculinity in the process of enlargement has
had highly problematic effects for women. In failing to question existing economic policy
instruments and in failing to problematize thoroughly gendered outcomes, EU enlargement has amounted to the expansion not only of a European economic space, but also of
a patriarchal European gender order.

Conclusion

European integration must be understood to entail a decisive reorganization of gender
relations. Gender approaches reveal this hidden dimension of the European integration
process. As political authority is reorganized in Europe, gender relations are the subject
of intense contestation. The EU's explicit commitment to gender equality and justice
circumscribes this contestation. As a decidedly novel feature of modern state policy this
commitment has received deserved attention, but more implicit, patriarchal commitments remain in the institutionalization of hegemonic masculinity and in the way in
which the EU organizes its economic space. These commitments are made visible in research that looks at European integration through a gender lens.

Gender approaches also provide an understanding of the potency of gender constructions in producing particular outcomes, such as the policy on trafficking. Gender becomes
a force in European politics in the frames advanced by social movements, the arguments
of lawyers, the administrative interventions of gender mainstreaming personnel in
dispersed sites, but perhaps most importantly in velvet triangles of activism. As agents
of integration, activists, lawyers, and bureaucrats construct gender to promote equality
and justice in old and new ways. Studying the way in which gender operates to support
diverse agendas in European integration enriches the understanding of how the European
integration process moves forward.

This effort, however, faces challenges. Like other research in European integration studies, feminist researchers are steeped in their own disciplines and their research is informed
by disciplinary outlooks. Thus, approaches that explore the construction of gender in the
EU tend to be more salient in international relations and international political economy,
while feminists in comparative politics tend to focus more extensively on gender equality
policies. Studies of agency in networks—often informed by sociological literature—begin
to bridge the divide between research that focuses on gender constructions and that
which focuses on policy processes. Such studies can show how gendered constructions are
reproduced (for example in agricultural policy networks) or changed (for example through
activist networks). They can also link EU politics to local, national, and international
levels, describing a field of global governance embedded in diverse discourses of gender,
partly reinforcing each other, partly contesting each other. The relationships of agency at
different levels and their embedding in different opportunity structures presents a weakly
explored frontier of feminist research.

Little progress has been made in mapping the diversity of gender regimes in a way that
overcomes the state-centric literature on the issue and relates gender constructions at
different administrative levels and/or different geographical scales. One way to address
the fluidity and multiplicity of such constructions in the EU is to bring to bear feminist
state theories on conceptualizations of the EU as a postmodern state (e.g. Sauer 2001b).
As such, the EU institutionalizes compromises between gender and other social forces
throughout Europe, compromises that are the result of cross-cutting struggles. Conceiving of the EU in this way recalls that the rules institutionalized by the EU are the outcome
of political agency.

Studying networks and state-like regimes can anchor an understanding of gender construction in the European Union that brings to the fore both feminist and masculinist
agency and its role in challenging and reproducing gendered structures.

■ NOTES

1. For a more extensive treatment of these cases see Locher (2007), Prügl (2004), and Prügl (2009).
2. Alison Woodward (2001) in her original concept of the 'velvet triangle' refers to the women's movement as the third type of actor. Describing feminist activism in the context of trafficking the term
   non-state actors was preferred over the women's movement not only because the latter has become
   more formal and professional, but because other non-state actors, such as human rights NGOs, have
   joined forces to promote and implement the anti-trafficking norm.

3. Communication from the Commission to the Council, the European Parliament, the European Economic and Social Committee and the Committee of the Regions. Implementation of gender mainstreaming in the Structural Funds programming documents 2000–2006. COM/2002/0748 final, item 3.1.3.

4. The other two goals pertain to continued modernization and environmental sustainability.

5. Surprisingly in Hungary the role of the EU concerning the implementation of gender equality policy was much less prominent than the role of the Beijing process which brought about the development of a national strategy and the establishment of the first Hungarian gender equality agency (see Krizsán and Zentai 2006).

■ GUIDE TO FURTHER READING

Hoskyns, C. (1996) *Integrating Gender: Women, Law and Politics in the European Union* (London: Verso). A classic text that traces the development of the EU's gender equality policy, emphasizing in particular women's agency.

Kronsell, A. (2005) 'Gender, Power and European Integration Theory', *Journal of European Public Policy,* 12(6), 1022–40. A comprehensive critique of theories of European integration from a feminist perspective.

Marx Ferree, M. (ed.) (2004) 'Gender politics in the EU: feminist discourses and policy debates'. Special Issue of *Social Politics* 11(1), 1–145. A series of articles exploring engaged feminist politics in the EU and probing the social construction of meaning in EU discourses.

Ostner, I. (2000) 'From equal pay to equal employability: four decades of European gender policies', in M. Rossilli (ed.) *Gender Policies in the European Union* (New York: Peter Lang), 25–42. Argues that EU gender equality policies have developed within a framework of negative integration and regulatory policies designed to remove market barriers and increase marketization.

Van der Vleuten, A. (2007) *The Price of Gender Equality: Member States and Governance in the European Union* (Aldershot: Ashgate). Provides a detailed history of the adoption of European gender equality policy in Germany, the Netherlands, and Britain and offers a rationalist explanation for why governments have adopted these costly policies.

■ STUDY QUESTIONS

1. How do gender approaches differ from theories that seek to explain the causes of European integration? What contribution do gender approaches make to understanding the process of integration?

2. What is gender? What claims do gender approaches make with regard to the ontology of European integration?

3. What is a feminist understanding of knowledge? How do non-feminist and feminist understandings differ?

4. What are the two main approaches to probing gender in the European integration process identified in this chapter? What are the different questions that they seek to answer?

5. According to the two approaches introduced here, what explains (a) the adoption of gender equality policies and (b) the reproduction of gender in the EU?

11 Normative Theory and the EU: Between Contract and Community

Richard Bellamy with Claudia Attucci

Introduction

The 'normative turn' among European public policy makers and scholars of the European Union (EU) is usually linked to the difficulties experienced in ratifying the Treaty of Maastricht (Bellamy and Castiglione 1997, 2003; Bellamy 2006a). Of course, there had always been European idealists who were driven above all by the desire to rid the continent of war by creating some sort of European federation (Spinelli and Rossi 2006 [1944]). Paradoxically, however, the pursuit of peace and foreign policy more generally, despite enjoying broad popular support as potential pan-European initiatives, have tended to be secondary concerns—the indirect result of the EU's primary objective of enhancing European prosperity. Moreover, this latter goal was mainly pursued by stealth by political and business elites through technocratic decision-making in key economic policy areas—the so-called Monnet method. Its justification was primarily utilitarian and functional, with the process largely intergovernmental. It was also hugely successful. As a result, policy-makers assumed a 'permissive consensus' among the citizens of Europe for European integration. That assumption ceased to hold as the geographical reach, direction, and impact of the integration process rose to greater prominence with the collapse of communism and the step change effected by the Single European Act and the moves towards the creation of a single market. Indeed, the introduction of the status of Union citizenship in the Maastricht Treaty had in some ways been a response to signs that the passive acquiescence of citizens could no longer be taken for granted. That fear seemed confirmed by the Treaty's initial rejection by a Danish referendum, the 'petit oui' offered by an unprecedented French referendum, and its troubled passage through the British Parliament.

In many ways, the problems that beset the ratification of Maastricht, followed by the shock of Ireland's initial rejection of the Nice Treaty, presaged the even greater tribulations that afflicted the Constitutional Treaty. Yet in this respect the failure of the proposed Constitution could be regarded as ironic, for its framers had conceived it as the culmination of a series of post-Maastricht attempts to tackle the issue of the EU's perceived lack of normative legitimacy. Some commentators and politicians have argued that this perception was simply mistaken and the error lay in raising such matters in the first place. They were an unnecessary departure from the central economic purposes of the EU, and consequently called for an undesirable degree of popular endorsement and involvement. They contend the EU should stay clear of areas liable to require inevitably contentious normative legitimation. Instead, it should stick to its core business of promoting Pareto-efficient improvements that enhance the functioning of the member state economies by increasing market efficiency and correcting for its failures with regard to certain public goods, such as the environment (Moravcsik 1993, 2002; Majone 1996, 1998). We concede there is an element of truth in this view (Bellamy 2006b). Nevertheless, other commentators rightly note that the reaction to Maastricht revealed how even measures linked to market-improving policies can be controversial and create calls for more popular consultation and normative legitimacy. On the one hand, economic policy and the role of the market within it are not uncontroversial and can have knock-on effects for welfare and other social policies. Not everything the EU does gets viewed as—or in fact is—a Pareto improvement. On the other hand, the institutional structure of the EU has gradually developed an internal dynamic of its own that to some degree is independent of the inter-governmental structures designed to render it accountable to the elected politicians of the member states. As a source of quasi-state power with a not inconsiderable, if occasionally exaggerated, influence on domestic policies, there is a natural desire on the part of citizens to be assured that it cannot abuse its authority and is responsive to their concerns (Bellamy 2006c, d; Føllesdal and Hix 2006).

Consequently, the question of the EU's normative legitimacy remains a live policy issue and not just a matter of academic concern. Roughly speaking, two broad approaches have been adopted towards the problem, both in the literature and in practice. The first stresses the justice, as opposed to the efficiency and productiveness, of outcomes and the structures that lead to them (e.g. Van Parijs 1997b). By contrast, the second stresses the processes by which decisions are made and the degree to which citizens can be said to identify with them and each other (e.g. Føllesdal 2006a). Neither approach entirely ignores the concerns of the other. However, the one tends to read process through outcomes, the second outcomes through process. While outcome theories have been predominately contractarian and adopted a 'rationalist' ontology, process theories have tended towards the communitarian and employed an 'interpretative' ontology (Taylor 1995; Dobson 2006)—with a number of theories, arguably like the EU itself, hovering tantalizingly betwixt and between (Bellamy and Castiglione 1997). Yet both kinds of theory prove indeterminate as to what the character of the EU should be, since both rest on questionable empirical assumptions as to the likely results of adopting particular policies or institutions.

A European Contract?

The Social Contract Tradition

Social contract theory emerged within Europe during the seventeenth century more or less alongside the development of the modern state and recognizably modern socio-economic and political relations. Two features of these new relations proved particularly important in promoting the growth of states: the rise of the market via the regulation of labour and commercial transactions through freedom of contract, and the need to handle religious and ideological conflicts.[1] The disembedding of individuals from traditional social hierarchies to become freely acting economic agents, combined with the possibility that these agents would recognize different and occasionally conflicting moral authorities, created the need for a central political authority with a monopoly of coercive power that was capable of imposing collectively binding rules on all. For if all individuals are liable to view their obligations towards others from quite different and often competing perspectives as a result of their pursuing short-term self-interest or divergent, and possibly quite subjective, moral codes, then a need arises for a single power able to offer an authoritative and consistent view of the rules of social life so that everyone knows where they stand with regard to others. However, while such a centralized political body came to be regarded as necessary to provide the personal security required for an economy and society based on a market in labour and goods to flourish and prosper in conditions of political and religious disagreement, it was also seen that it constituted a potential evil that had to be justified to those subject to it, with its authority and power limited by what was justifiable. The superior organizational capacity of modern states, and the increased wealth the commerce and industry of their members placed at their disposal, gave them an unprecedented ability to police their subjects and to engage in war against each other. The idea of a social contract offered a conceptual tool whereby citizens could be said to endorse and limit the new-found coercive power of the state.

The standard starting point of social contract theory is to imagine what life would be like without a coordinating political authority—a condition described in the classic texts as the 'state of nature' (Hobbes 1996 [1651]; Locke 1988 [1680–90]; Rousseau 1968 [1792]). Although later theorists mostly disputed the contention of the seventeenth-century philosopher Thomas Hobbes that human existence would be 'nasty, brutish and short' (Hobbes 1996, ch. XIII) as overly pessimistic, all conceded that as soon as social interaction became unavoidable our existence would be highly uncertain unless there were settled rules to regulate our social behaviour and a political authority to uphold them. Limited resources and the fact that humans are neither angels nor omniscient meant that conflicts—many inadvertent—between different individual activities were inevitable. Without some agreed method and authority for resolving these disputes, a dangerous anarchy would result, in which the strong ruled over the weak. The idea of a social contract then becomes a way of modelling the terms under which individuals might be expected to subject themselves to a political authority, including the sorts of processes that would be available to control it and the outcomes its rules and regulations ought to promote. The underlying intuition is that a just political and legal system would be one that free and equal individuals could be expected to unanimously consent to because it offers fair and equitable mechanisms and rules for securing and promoting their interests and preventing it threatening them. This argument does not necessarily rest on any actual consent by citizens to generate their obligation to obey a just state. For many theorists in this tradition it is sufficient that a political society's arrangements are such that we could imagine that all citizens might have hypothetically consented to it. The idea of a contract is simply a device for thinking about what social and political arrangements and principles treat people equitably and justly.

While not inherently liberal, the notion of a social contract has come to encapsulate a number of the key tenets of liberalism: notably, that individuals are rational and purposive beings, among whom there is no ascribed status, and that the rules of any political society should therefore be publicly justifiable as being consistent with showing them equal concern and respect as autonomous agents. As such, it appears to embody the liberal ideal of the state as a neutral and impartial facilitator of the interactions of free and equal individuals. According to this view, the state's aim should be to allow each citizen to maximize their potential by limiting possible harmful mutual interferences and promoting public structures and goods from which all gain, without itself seeking to develop a goal that is other than that of the contractors themselves. Of course, there is considerable controversy about which policies best promote this ideal and the social, economic, and political institutions most likely to sustain it. There is a wide variety of contractarian theories among contemporary political philosophers, offering different views of the motivations of human beings and what they might be said to contact to (e.g. compare Rawls 1971; Gauthier 1986; Scanlon 1998). However, the ideal itself is now broadly endorsed in some form or other by the vast majority of citizens and politicians in all European democracies—indeed, in all democratic states worldwide.

To the extent that the EU has taken over certain aspects of the facilitating role hitherto performed by the member states, it seems appropriate to extend to it the same justificatory criteria that social contract theorists have applied to the state. Thus, a number of theorists have employed a contractualist approach to discuss such issues as EU citizenship, the case for majority rule and federal arrangements within the EU, and the nature of an EU constitution (Føllesdal 1997, 2001, 2006a; Lehning and Percy 1997). Doing so, though, encounters three important objections to the contractarian approach, if not to the liberal ideal per se. First, as we noted, the social contract originated as a way of legitimating the state. That raises the issue of how far it is appropriate to apply it to an institution that is at best state-like, but which cannot claim to be an encompassing political community in the traditional manner of a nation state—not least because its authority is shared with, and to a large extent dependent on, the member states. Second, if the EU is best characterized as a form of intensive interstate cooperation rather than as a quasi-state, how does that affect the terms of the liberal social contract—is it in this case between individuals, the member states or the European peoples? Third, as we noted, the contract was in some respects a response to diversity of belief, both religious and political. Even if the ideal behind the contract is shared, though, how far can the terms of any given contract be said to be justifiable to all? The issue of whether we should see the liberal ideal as 'outcome' or 'process' enters at this point. As we noted, contract theorists tend to take an 'outcome' view. They see the contract as the product of a hypothetical agreement between rational agents which sets the goals a political system should secure. However, such arguments risk a certain circularity, whereby the conclusions of the theorist are read back into the presuppositions of the hypothetical contractual situation. They also beg the question of who exactly the contractors are. If it can be shown that there can be valid disagreements about the terms and nature of the contract, then we may need to think about the kind of 'process' that might resolve them. In doing so, we shall have to think not just about the justice of the EU's institutional structure, but also its authority and legitimacy with regard to those it seeks to act for and upon. In other words, we may need to look at how the EU is actually interpreted and seen by those subject to it, rather than as how a certain sort of idealized rational agent might view it.

Who Contracts, How and to What? Rawls and the Problems of Contractarian Thinking for the EU

John Rawls's Two Principles of Justice

All three of the issues raised above with regard to contractarian thinking have been levelled at, and partially addressed by, the most prominent recent contractarian political philosopher, John Rawls. Rawls's books *A Theory of Justice* (1971), *Political Liberalism* (1993), and *The Law of Peoples* (1999) tackle the topics respectively of justice within a liberal democratic nation state, the difficulty of motivating political agreement among those who reasonably disagree within a multicultural society, and justice between states. Each has been taken as offering a slightly different contractarian model for the EU, depending on whether it is seen as akin to a nation state, as a new breed of pluralist multi-state federal polity, or as an intergovernmental arrangement. His work, therefore, offers a convenient way of exploring the contribution of contractarian thinking to the normative dilemmas confronting the EU.

A Theory of Justice sought to update the social contract tradition and provide a normative justification for a radical version of the social democratic state with its combination of civil liberty, equal opportunity, and social justice—values upheld, in that order, by Rawls's two principles of justice. Just as earlier social contract theorists had employed the fiction of a state of nature to imagine the circumstances that might motivate agreement to establish a political society and generate consensus around the sorts of principles of justice that could legitimately guide its functioning, so Rawls employed an imaginary 'original position' for similar purposes. By placing his imagined contractors behind a 'veil of ignorance' and depriving them of any knowledge of their abilities, religious views, family or social advantages, whether they were likely to be poor or rich, a member of the racial or religious majority or minority, and so on, Rawls sought to model a situation that might generate principles that would be regarded as fair and equitable by all, regardless of their social position, views or circumstances. He contended that in such a situation, people would opt for an 'equal right to the most extensive total system of equal basic liberties compatible with a similar system of liberty for all' (his first principle), on the one hand, and the arrangement of social and economic inequalities so that they resulted from conditions of a fair equal opportunity and benefited the least well-off (his second principle), on the other hand. He also argued they would prioritize liberty over social and economic equality (Rawls 1971: 60ff).

Rawls's theory clearly offers a plausible reading of the 'liberal ideal' yet has been subject to a torrent of criticism even from within the liberal camp with regard to both the success of his justification for his two principles and their substance. We shall address these criticisms below only to the extent they are relevant to the application of his theory to the EU. It is also important to note that Rawls's theory was aimed at established liberal democracies, such as his native United States and the member states of the EU. As we shall see, it is doubtful that Rawls himself would have thought his two principles applied to the EU (Rawls and Van Parijs 2003). However, it is worth noting that to do so would involve a major step change in its current competences, requiring that it offer European-wide mechanisms for ensuring that basic political and civil liberties, such as the right to vote and hold office, freedom of conscience and religion, and the right to hold property, are protected, and that the distribution of wealth and income across the EU is such that it is to everybody's advantage. Hitherto, these have not been primary concerns of the EU, although indirectly many of its activities impinge on both. So far as the first principle is concerned, the EU's main rationale has been to promote a limited set of liberties—namely, freedom of movement, services, labour, and capital and non-discrimination in their enjoyment—across all the states within the Union. True, it has gradually developed political and judicial mechanisms for making and overseeing decisions related to foster-ing these market freedoms, which have occasionally had positive implications for certain other, non-market, uses of these liberties by European citizens. However, the primary responsibility for the protection and exercise of the fuller range of civil and political liber-ties has remained with the member states. To the extent they have a European-level obli-gation to implement them, it stems from their membership of the Council of Europe and adherence to the European Convention of Human Rights (ECHR), both preconditions for EU membership, rather than their belonging to the EU per se. Moreover, unlike them, the EU is not a signatory of the ECHR—although it is now planned that it does so. Similar caveats apply to the EU's promotion of the second principle. Although fostering a single European market is believed to make the member state economies more competitive and boost both wealth and employment, it aims at Pareto-efficient improvements rather than maximizing the lot of the least well-off. Structural funds are given to the least favoured regions, but in order to raise market competitiveness and efficiency overall. Again, welfare and social security remain primarily a member state responsibility.

While it can be argued that the EU has aided the member states to foster Rawls's two principles, undoubtedly helping Spain, Greece, and Portugal and now the countries of the former Soviet bloc in their transition to democracy, there are also tensions between the primacy the EU places on the market freedoms and the protection of certain other liberties, on the one hand, and the promotion of social and economic equality, on the other. There are also many differences and potential conflicts between the ways the mem-ber states understand the two principles. It is not clear how a contractarian approach might resolve these difficulties—not least because some of them might be regarded as challenging the very enterprise. In particular, they raise important questions concerning who contracts with whom, why (or for what purpose), how (or with what motivation), and to what.

Who Contracts? The Cosmopolitan Critique

With regard to the first question of who contracts, at least four scenarios seem possible. First, we could see the EU as a unitary state (Vibert 1995, 2002; Morgan 2004), with the contractors all long-term EU residents. Second, we could see the EU as a federal state, with the contractors those currently designated as EU citizens, who also possess citizenship of a member state (Lehning 1997). Third, we could see the EU as a limited contract between the member states as representatives of their respective peoples (Føllesdal 1997, 2001, 2006b). Fourth, we could see the EU as part of a cosmopolitan scheme of justice resulting from a contract between all individuals in the world (Pogge 1997). Rawlsians of different kinds have endorsed some version of all four. Rawls himself seems to have come down in favour of either the third or the second. The reasoning behind Rawls's position highlights some of the issues involved in deciding the scope of any contractarian account of justice. In particular, Rawls draws attention to the way who contracts has implications for the other questions of why, how, and to what.

Rawls believed different regulative principles apply to different sorts of entities, even if all these different principles could be constructed as the product of different kinds of contract (Rawls and van Parijs 2003). So, the principles regulating personal conduct among individuals are different to those regulating private organizations towards their members, and those that regulate the domestic affairs of states with regard to their citizens are distinct from those that regulate interstate relations. As we noted, Rawls followed the classic theorists of the social contract tradition in taking the state as the locus of his principles of justice. Like his predecessors in the contractarian tradition, Rawls reasoned that the relationship between citizens and a state is of a particularly demanding and comprehensive nature. It involved recognizing the legitimacy of the state's claim to sovereign power as necessary to provide the collective goods needed for an orderly social life, and obeying and actively collaborating with state institutions and fellow citizens to maintain and sustain that power. Moreover, people cannot avoid living in a state if they are to lead reasonably secure lives but have very limited possibilities for choosing which one. These three qualities of a state—its sovereignty, the need to obey and collaborate with it, and its unavoidability—create obligations, both to fellow citizens and state institutions, of a kind that require justification in terms of justice. Note, though, that even within a state Rawls's two principles only apply to what he calls the 'basic structure of society'—the framework of public rules regulating social life that the state exists to uphold and that all citizens must collaborate with and help sustain. His prioritizing of liberty stems in part from his not requiring individuals to pursue just outcomes in their private transactions. Indeed, the second principle only applies to state welfare and taxation policies regarding the life chances of different classes of people rather than to individuals (Rawls 1971: 7ff). In other words, he advocates an egalitarian state, not that we adopt egalitarianism as a personal moral code.

Some cosmopolitans have criticized him on this point. These cosmopolitans view separate sovereignties as inconsistent with the moral imperative to create a common system of institutions, if not necessarily a world state, capable of promoting global standards of justice (Beitz 1979; Pogge 1989, 1994, 2002; Kuper 2004). However, unlike them, Rawls did not believe the principles of justice stem from duties of equal concern to our fellow human beings as such, with a consequent need to create institutions that might be capable of establishing a framework for global justice. We have pre-political humanitarian duties not to harm others and to aid and rescue those in dire distress, which naturally devolve on states as well, but these fall far short of the duties of justice that arise only from the historically contingent associative political obligations between citizens in a particular state. Rawls believed that even the distributional responsibilities that rich states have towards poorer, 'burdened' ones are duties of assistance, not of justice (Rawls 1999: 106ff). Likewise, the principles regulating relations between states are less demanding than those that apply to their domestic arrangements.[2]

What does all this mean for the EU? One implication is that on Rawls's account the EU only becomes an object of considerations of justice to the extent it exercises sovereign authority of a kind analogous to a state. It is unclear how far that is currently the case. Formally, at least, the EU remains a treaty-based international organization controlled by sovereign states, which may leave it should they so choose—albeit it at some cost, and which is empowered by them to pursue a limited number of mutually agreed goals. Moreover, though EU decisions have a direct impact on individual citizens, it has no real coercive power of its own—it relies on the active cooperation of member state institutions to implement its policies. Nevertheless, the European Court of Justice (ECJ) operates as a supranational institution with which domestic authorities are obliged to comply, while the European Parliament gives EU citizens a partial direct input into EU decision-making. In other words, the EU has certain state-like characteristics, producing pressures for it to acquire a degree of democratic legitimacy and some obligations to promote socio-economic justice. Yet to the extent it retains its character as a voluntary organization between independent parties to pursue common interests, it lacks the authority and justification to be considered a full site of justice between citizens.

The halfway position of the EU poses problems for both theory and practice. At various times, member state constitutional courts have raised the issue of whether an EU decision, even if backed by an ECJ ruling, could be disallowed on the grounds that it undermined domestic arrangements for promoting justice. In a famous ruling on the legitimacy of the Maastricht Treaty, the German Federal Constitutional Court argued that since the EU was not a sovereign state, the Court retained the right to decide if any EU decision or policy exceeded the justifiable competence of the EU in conflicting with the domestic constitutional order. This argument was challenged by the ECJ, which contended that it alone had the competence to decide questions of the competence of the EU. Rawls never commented directly on this issue, but evidence exists to suggest that he would have sided with the German Court—indeed, that stand seems the most consistent with his position. For on his account, the EU would have to acquire a clear sovereign power to gain responsibility for issues of justice—something it currently lacks and which he doubted it ought to obtain.

How We Contract: The Communitarian Critique

The question of how we contract comes in here. As we noted, Rawls contends citizens of already existing sovereign states have relations of justice that they do not have with the rest of humanity. However, though criticized by cosmopolitans on this point, he also found himself taken to task by communitarian thinkers who tend to make a not dissimilar defence of the nation state. They argued that Rawls's contractarianism as presented in *A Theory of Justice* abstracted individuals from the social relations and cultural practices that provide the context of individual choice, shaping how citizens of a given society relate to each other and understand the content and scope of justice. In certain respects, that critique proves misplaced. In restating his thesis in *Political Liberalism*, Rawls made clear that his theory applied not to abstract individuals but citizens of liberal democratic states who shared its basic goals. Against communitarians, he still contended the right, or principles of political justice, could be separated from any given conception of the good—indeed, this possibility was what made a multicultural political society achievable.

In such a society, he claimed, groups holding different conceptions of the good could subscribe to the same view of justice to govern the public sphere for different, if overlapping, reasons. Nonetheless, he not only accepted but positively welcomed that over time citizens will internalize and shape these principles in distinctive ways that reflect certain shared aims and develop a national consciousness, including an especial sense of social solidarity with their co-nationals. In fact, in his one work touching on international justice, the *Law of Peoples*, he makes the various societies of peoples, bound by common institutions, cultural 'sympathies', and a commitment to justice, the moral units of international ethics, with equality of respect being owed between them rather than individuals or states (Rawls 1999: 3, 23).

Rawls believed that any decision for two or more liberal democracies to form a federal union must be decided by these peoples 'by an election in which in each society the decision whether to unite is thoroughly discussed' (Rawls and Van Parijs 2003: 7). These peoples must also choose among a range of 'reasonable' liberal political conceptions of justice. In other words, for Rawls the creation of a federal Europe could not be justified on the grounds that it would realise conditions of equality that can be modelled in a hypothetical contract—it would require something more like an actual contract between European peoples. As Percy Lehning has suggested, in a piece written before the *Law of Peoples* appeared, as with Rawls's account of a multicultural society, the best way of conceiving a shared federal conception of justice from a Rawlsian point of view would be as an 'overlapping consensus' between the various peoples of the European Union—a common constitutional language, to which they relate for slightly different but congruent reasons, without giving up their historic cultural identities as French, English, and so on (Lenhing 1997). Indeed, a number of theorists speculated that the EU constitution, and particularly the Charter of Fundamental Rights, could be seen in just these terms (La Torre 2002; Attucci 2004, 2006). That said, Rawls himself seems to have been concerned these identities would only be able to truly express themselves if they retained their 'separate political and social institutions, historical memories and forms and traditions of social policy' (Rawls and Van Parijs 2003: 9). In this case, anyway, he seems to have made a distinction between multiculturalism, which usually results from immigration, and multinationalism, which tends to consist of territorially concentrated historic political communities that have been absorbed by conquest into a state. The former may conceive of themselves as having hyphenated identities, the one personal and social, the other public and civic—as in Italian-American. The latter may prefer to express their civic identity in separate institutions, as has been the gradual trend in even well-established multinational Unions such as the UK, where Scottish-British has become more contested than, say, Muslim-British.

What Do We Contract To? The Libertarian Critique

So far we have not commented on the final question—namely, what the contractors might agree on. Rawls's theory has also been criticized on the grounds that the substance of what is agreed to fails to realise his declared aim of treating individuals with equal concern and respect. Perhaps the most powerful argument of this nature has come from libertarian critics who take issue with certain aspects of Rawls's view of society as a scheme of social cooperation between citizens. Rawls seeks to distinguish between the advantages or disadvantages individuals receive from favourable circumstances, which he contends nobody should benefit or suffer from, and those that result from their own choices, for which they are responsible. He contends the 'difference principle'—that part of the second principle that says distributions should be such that they benefit the least well-off—offers a logical response to that distinction so long as liberty and equal opportunity are prioritized. Neoliberal libertarians counter that individuals have certain antecedent self-ownership rights, which includes the right to whatever endowments they have, and so should be left to freely employ and benefit from them so long as they do not interfere with the equal right of others to do likewise (Nozick 1974; Vibert 2002, 2007; Barry 2004). Of course there are problems about how to deal with the many undoubted coercive transactions of the past, such as those involving the lands of indigenous peoples in areas colonized by Europeans, but if these could be rectified then the redistribution sanctioned by Rawls's difference principle would be illegitimate. Put in contractarian terms, proponents of this view argue a contract should be seen not as a model of fair terms of reciprocity set behind the veil of ignorance, as Rawls portrays it, but as a scheme for mutual advantage between real people relative to the disadvantages of the state of nature. So conceived, it becomes a mechanism for ensuring that no tax or other potentially redistributive proposal could be passed except with unanimous consent, thereby ensuring only measures where the benefits outweigh the costs, however they are distributed, can be adopted, and so—on this measure—treat all equally. According to this view, the well-endowed are never likely to regard the difference principle—or any other substantively egalitarian proposal—as a mutually advantageous scheme.

By contrast, so called left-wing post-libertarians argue that the problem lies with the difference principle failing to realise fully Rawls's aim for an endowment-insensitive, ambition-sensitive scheme. One influential group have proposed that all individuals receive a 'stake' or 'basic income' in order to provide individuals with equal resources or opportunities (Van Parijs 1995, 1997a). Whereas neoliberal libertarians argue that natural resources should be available for all to appropriate on an equal basis, left-wing libertarians suggest all individuals ought to be viewed as being entitled to an equal rent from these resources. Moreover, some suggest that many of the resources available to us to exploit are socially created but not the product of any individual, such as job opportunities, and that the rent from these should also be fairly distributed. Though these schemes appeal to similar egalitarian liberal intuitions to Rawls, he rejects them nonetheless on the grounds that entitlement to an unconditional grant might allow the indolent to free-ride on the effort of others, thereby undermining the reciprocity he sees as inherent to the welfare contract.

Here is not the place to consider the pros and cons either of these criticisms or Rawls's response to them. We wish merely to highlight why both critiques could offer attractive images of the EU. The EU has sometimes been characterized as a neoliberal, free market project—indeed, Rawls himself apparently saw it in this light. That view somewhat mischaracterizes the reality—as the criticisms of the EU by neoliberals attest. However, it is certainly true that its prime rationale has been to remove barriers to pan-European market competition and has often appealed to mutual advantage, rather than fair terms of reciprocity, as the incentive to do so. While EU-sponsored health and safety and environmental regulations reveal that the result has not been unbridled competition, the measures undertaken to equalize competitive opportunities for workers and firms fall far short of what a liberal egalitarian such as Rawls would desire. On Rawls's account, that shortfall stems from the EU not being a state whose citizens owe each other fairly strong duties of reciprocity as members of a politically regulated scheme of social cooperation. The danger Rawls feared, but that neoliberals are likely to welcome, was that seeking to transfer welfare to the EU level might disembed these feelings of mutual obligation from well-established social and political networks without recreating them on a pan-EU scale.

Arguably the left libertarian proposal of an unconditional Eurogrant—a basic income paid to all permanent adult residents deriving from an EU-wide tax on energy, cross-border commercial transactions, or some other area reflecting an EU competence—overcomes this difficulty. According to its proponents, such a measure need not be seen as competing with member state welfare programmes but as an EU-generated addition to them that derives from the additional opportunities European integration offers to the appropriately resourced. Moreover, its basis—according to the account given—can be attributed either to an entitlement to natural resources analogous to the neoliberal libertarians, or to an equalization of the resources that make equal opportunity possible. Once again, though, the Rawlsian concern is that this scheme assumes the very solidarity it seeks to economize on to work. At best—as in arguments for negative income tax, the neoliberal version of the scheme—it might be used as an argument for only helping the least well-off achieve a basic minimum, offering in the process a huge subsidy to employers of low-cost labour.

A Rawlsean Europe?

In presenting this overview of how Rawls's theory might relate to the EU, we do not wish necessarily to endorse it. Rather, the aim is simply to illustrate the diversity of possible contractarian views of the EU and the assumptions they rest on. However, two points in the analysis above merit stressing, for they inform what follows. The first relates to the cosmopolitan and communitarian critiques of Rawls. As we have seen, the one views Rawls as over-emphasizing the importance of national political communities, the other of not emphasizing them enough. So far as the EU is concerned, Rawls seems vindicated to the extent that support for EU-wide social policy is considerably lower than it is for areas of traditional intergovernmental cooperation, such as trade and foreign policy. Sociologically, at least part of the explanation may lie in the degree to which a commitment to welfare rests on feelings of reciprocity that are likely to be stronger within smaller, historic communities than a large and recent association of historically distinct and (in the recent past) often warring communities. In fact, Rawls's own proposal is considerably more radical than most welfare states, which aim less at distributive equality than a more relative equalizing of social standing, a view that appears to enjoy greater popular support. Leaving to one side whether such a move would be either likely or desirable, it would seem that for social policy beyond a market-improving kind to be plausible for the EU some fuller sense of a European social solidarity may be a necessary precondition.

The second point concerns the very fact of disagreement. Many contractarians argue that the principles emerging from the putative contract ought to be entrenched in a judicially protected constitution so as to ensure that all policy conforms to it. The argument is that these principles are fundamental to the justice and legitimacy of a political association—they are what make it reasonable for all to accept their obligations under it—and need to be put beyond political contestation. However, this view assumes that we can regard these principles as above the disagreements that legitimately animate normal democratic politics, and that the judiciary are more liable to uphold them than democratically elected politicians. A number of theorists dispute the first claim on normative grounds and the second claim on empirical ones (Bellamy 2007). In fact, Rawls accepts, though many within this tradition do not, that his second principle can be subject to political bargaining if the liberties covered by the first principle are secured. As we have seen, though, it is perfectly possible to respect something like the liberal ideal that lies behind both principles, as all the member states do, and yet differ about which interpretation is best, what policies most effectively secure them, and where and among whom a given view ought to prevail. After all, the two main cleavages in modern democratic politics are those between left and right, on the one side, and centre and periphery, on the other—divisions that place the issue of 'why' we contract into the realm of normal political debate and that turn on, respectively, the potential for differing answers to the questions of 'what' we contract to and with 'who'. For example, both issues informed the conventions to draft the Charter of Rights and the Constitutional Treaty (Bellamy and Schönlau 2004a, b). In these cases, 'how' we contract cannot be a hypothetical exercise, because different citizens are likely to offer different views of what it entails. Instead of seeking to define which outcomes best offer citizens an equal opportunity, we need an equitable process that allows them an equal say in determining and revising how best to secure an equal liberty. It is to the prospects and pitfalls for a democratic, process-based, approach for the EU that we now turn—looking, in particular, how far this too assumes the existence of an already existing political community or demos.

A European Community?

In this section we shall review three approaches, all of which emphasize the centrality of democracy and have informed normative assessments of the democratic credentials of the EU. We start with the writings of Jurgen Habermas, probably the most important political theorist to explore the normative questions raised by the EU. Habermas offers a strong case for the creation of a democratic federal European welfare state (Habermas 1998, 2001a, b). Unlike cosmopolitans in the contractarian tradition, he seeks to ground his argument in the requirements of the democratic process within Europe rather than by appealing to hypothetically derived principles of justice. Yet, as we shall see, he remains open to the communitarian objection that his arguments overlook the ways these processes are embedded within the different national communities of the member states and are as much a hypothetical idealization of his own preferences as the contractarian thinkers he seeks to distance himself from. It is to these communitarians that we then turn to explore their contention that a European political community is unlikely and potentially undermines democracy at the national level. Though both Habermas and communitarians claim an affinity with republican thought in grounding their views in the collective autonomy or self-government of the demos, the third group of theorists to be examined adopt an explicitly republican position—though of a somewhat different kind to theirs. They base their argument on freedom as non-domination and their advocacy of democracy on its link with political equality rather than autonomy. They dispute the plausibility of communitarian views of national identity in a pluralist and interconnected world, seeing the EU as a mechanism for dispersing power between different states and other communities in ways that check the capacity of different groups and entities to dominate others in securing those collective goods that are only available through international cooperation.

Habermas and the EU as a Post-national Constitutional Federation

The requirements of a democratic political order lie at the heart of the theory of Jurgen Habermas. He argues that any legal order must be consistent with what he calls 'the democratic principle' (Habermas 1996b). This norm decrees that 'only those statutes may claim legitimacy that can meet with the assent of all citizens in a discursive process of legislation that in turn has been legally constituted' (Habermas 1996b: 110). However, to be legitimate in its turn, such a legally constituted discursive process must respect civil, legal, and social rights. On Habermas's account, these rights are implied by, and so are constitutive of, the process of democratic self-legislation. They provide the basis for the private and public autonomy necessary for citizens to deliberate on a free and equal basis with each other. Yet Habermas does not wish thereby to argue that the establishment of such a system of rights is a moral requirement demanding the creation of a certain sort of legal and political order. That argument would be incompatible with his claim that rights are essentially legal in nature and produced through democratic processes. This point is more than just conceptual. He regards moral claims unmediated by democratic law as both ungrounded and as contradicting our status as autonomous agents. In a disenchanted world, appeals to morality as such are like appeals to God—beyond human reason and apt to produce disagreements that appear little more than the assertions of opposed subjective wills and as such generative of intractable conflicts. It is only as authors and addressees of a common system of law that we are in a position to collectively decide the terms of our association in ways that can be discursively settled. Consequently, rights can only be legitimately invoked within the context of such a system. Applying this thesis to the EU, Habermas has contended that it leads to support for an EU federal polity grounded in a pan-European constitution, incorporating a Charter of Rights giving expression to all three sets of democratic rights, and calls for a much more extensive role for both welfare rights and the European Parliament than currently exists in the EU (Habermas 2001b).

Putting to one side the adequacy of Habermas's general theory of democratic legitimacy, it is unclear even in its own terms that it has the implications for the EU he claims. As we noted, he wants to avoid the argument adopted by some cosmopolitans of invoking certain moral rights to justify the establishment of an appropriate international legal and political order, of which the EU would be but a component. However, he argues that the transformation of the EU into a constitutional democratic federation is a step on the way to realizing

an obligatory cosmopolitan solidarity [whereby the] form of civil solidarity that has been limited to the nation state until now has to expand to include all citizens of the Union, so that, for example, Swedes and Portuguese are willing to take responsibility for one another.

Habermas (2001a: 99)

How is such a proposal possible without employing the very moral arguments he seeks to avoid? Habermas rests his case on a number of arguments that are as much empirical as normative, all of which are open to question.

Most straightforwardly, perhaps, he notes that the EU already is a legal and political order that appeals to, yet in his view fails to meet, democratic standards of legitimacy. On this argument, the conventions on the Charter of Rights and the Future of Europe, and subsequent referenda and parliamentary debates within the member states, were consistent with the democratic principle in being democratic processes that sought to establish a democratic system of rights and an appropriate set of institutions at the EU level. Of course, the difficulty with this argument is that the Constitutional Treaty failed to be ratified, attracting at best tepid support even in those countries that passed it. The commonest reaction was indifference, with a significant degree of outright opposition across Europe. Habermas and his supporters have responded by arguing that the failure lay in the proposals not going far enough so as to involve an explicit commitment to a European social market economy. However, this argument also rests on highly questionable empirical assumptions.

On the one hand, Habermas contends that the current market focus of the EU tends to reinforce many of the negative effects of globalization, undermining the capacity of states to regulate the economy in ways consistent with high levels of social spending and protection. On the other hand, he maintains that these same forces have eroded national collective identities and with it the sense of solidarity between co-nationals. He claims the solution lies in creating a new form of civic solidarity at the European level based on a form of constitutional patriotism focused on his three sets of democratic rights. Yet neither of the assumptions underlying this proposal proves warranted.

There is little empirical support for the argument that economic globalization and the market promoting policies of the EU inevitably produce either rising levels of unemployment in those sectors exposed to international competition, or erode the revenue base and support for welfare spending. In fact, the general trend remains that the more developed and competitive economies become, the higher their levels of employment and welfare spending. Those countries experiencing difficulties—such as Germany, France, and Italy within the EU—have done so largely because of the specific structures of their welfare states and a failure to implement appropriate reforms. As the example of Denmark shows, much can be done at the domestic level to adapt welfare systems to change so as to maintain high levels of both productivity and social protection. Meanwhile, opinion polls show little support for the EU taking responsibility for welfare.[3] Issues relating to socio-economic rights, insofar as they involve health, welfare, and education, all have a low Euro-legitimacy, with 65 per cent or more of European citizens regarding these as exclusively national responsibilities. The areas enjoying high Euro-legitimacy are either those tied to market-building, such as freedom of movement (including gender equality), competition policy, currency matters, and structural funds for disadvantaged regions, or polices that have a clearly transnational dimension and where international cooperation secures a genuine public good for all member states, such as environmental protection, the fight against drugs, foreign trade, and relations with other states more generally.

His claim that a European political identity might substitute for an eroding national collective identity is similarly suspect. Again, opinion polls consistently show the second to be much more robust than the first. Whereas 89 per cent of European citizens usually declare themselves attached to their country and 87 per cent to their locality, only 58 per cent feel attached to the EU, while the depth of that attachment is considerably stronger at national and local than the European level. A mere 3 per cent of citizens generally view themselves as 'Europeans' pure and simple, with barely 7 per cent saying a European identity is more important than their national one. By contrast, approximately 40 per cent describe themselves as national only and a further 47 per cent place nationality above Europeanness. True, at a very abstract level there is a general commitment to the sort of democratic values Habermas endorses across all of Europe, but that is very different to a pan-European enthusiasm for a European democracy. On the contrary, it is perfectly compatible with a fear that developing a democratic welfare state at the EU level would undermine such values at the national level where they are more solidly embedded. Even if we were to accept that nationalistic sentiments were eroding and giving way to a constitutional patriotism as a source of solidarity, a further argument would be needed to suggest why such patriotism should be located at the EU rather than the member states' level.

An unequivocal case for a cosmopolitan legal and political order seems only possible by making the sort of moral appeal to rights that Habermas seeks to avoid. Yet for communitarian advocates of national solidarity, such as David Miller, such appeals will only yield a commitment to humanitarian aid and the mutual recognition of the right to self-determination of other nation states—arrangements far short of a European federation. At least part of the reason for this limitation derives from the very plurality and diversity Habermas contends his procedural approach respects. As the variety of democratic and constitutional systems within the EU attests, a commitment to democracy is consistent with significant variation on which rights should be promoted, why, and how. Far from national cultures ceasing to be important, the trend within all the member states is for territorially concentrated minority national groups to seek, and largely obtain, ever greater devolution of such matters to semi-autonomous subunits. In other words, the spread of constitutional and democratic values has not produced either a consensus on what these values entail or a concern to institutionalize them in ever-more encompassing political units. Quite the contrary—the opposite has occurred. It is to the normative justifications of this development and its implications for the EU that we now turn.

The National Limits to the EU

For a number of theorists, among them David Miller (1998, 2000), Claus Offe (2000, 2003), Fritz Scharpf (1999), and Dieter Grimm (1997), the lack of a common identity grounded in a shared nationality constitutes the chief block to the vision of the EU Habermas seeks to defend. Though all the above named broadly share Habermas's social democratic politics, they dissent sharply from his belief that extending such arrangements to the EU would be the best mechanism for their preservation within the member states. On the contrary, they believe it would undermine them.

Their reasoning is as much functional and sociological as normative. They argue that both democracy and welfare depend on a high degree of trust and solidarity which is unlikely to be found at the EU level. Trust is required because, as with any collective good, democracy and welfare are open to abuse by free-riders. Citizens may not bother performing their civic duties, such as voting, if they believe others will do so for them.

Welfare is similarly open to abuse: contributors may attempt to avoid paying their share of taxes, letting others foot the bill, while recipients may engage in fraud or not bother seeking work or improving their health, say. This problem is exacerbated because many of the collective goods supported by social democratic states are only quasi-public goods in the technical sense—that is, they are goods where, unlike measures to improve air quality, say, or to defend against a foreign invasion, it is possible for individuals to make private arrangements from which they can exclude others from the benefits. As a result, the rich may abandon the state schooling and health systems, employ private security firms and so on and seek a reduction in personal taxes. They may use targeted lobbying and litigation to promote their interests rather than participating in the more collective mechanisms of party politics, where they must compromise with the views of others in the formulation of a programme of government that reflects common rather than factional needs. Of course, such arrangements may prove more expensive in the long run—not least through creating social and economic problems with knock-on effects even for the well-off. However, such goods are always open to collective action problems whereby individuals seek to offload the costs of their provision on to others. Escaping such dilemmas requires not just trust in everyone else to do their bit, but a degree of solidarity—a willingness to support arrangements that may appear (or even be) suboptimal personally but are optimal for the community as a whole.

Social psychologists have found that trust and solidarity are far more likely among people who share a common identity and have a history of regular interactions with each other that are likely to extend into the future. The more diverse and the larger the social group, the less likely these qualities are. Thus, these thinkers argue that democracy requires not just good procedures grounded in a set of irreproachable democratic rights but also a demos—a group of people who feel an attachment to each other and share a public culture—including languages and a media in which they can collectively communicate and debate. Only then will minorities not fear tyrannous majorities because political disagreements will always be tempered by a degree of equal concern and respect born of trust and solidarity. As a result, political losers will not dispute the legitimate authority of the winners to implement polices they rejected. Likewise, such a political community will be far more likely to promote not just win–win Pareto-improving measures but also redistributive policies of a zero-sum character. Indeed, this will partly be true because more homogenous communities are more likely to adopt majoritarian voting and feel less need for counter-majoritarian veto points, which—contrary to the intentions of some of their proponents—favour the status quo and are less egalitarian, thereby hindering progressive change.

Miller has argued that nation states are not just instrumentally better suited to these tasks but in certain respects normatively more appropriate as well (Miller 1998). For a start a national demos is able to interpret and develop the system of democratic rights in ways that reflect its distinctive traditions, values, and concerns. Votes simply count for less in large units, thereby weakening electoral accountability, while diversity is likely to be greater, increasing the likelihood of the tyranny of the majority. Most importantly, though, the autonomy and identity of individuals has been mainly fostered within the national political community and reflects the political choices they have made. It has been the cooperative efforts of fellow citizens, not least in their support for the public structures of social and economic life, such as schools, the health and welfare systems and so on, that have enabled members of this society to make the best use of their abilities. A primary obligation of reciprocity, therefore, is owed to co-nationals. After all, countries differ considerably in terms of what public services they prioritize, how much tax is paid, the way the economy is structured and so on. Why should a country that has put in place policies that have produced economic growth and high public spending subsidize a country that has made other choices—possibly with less success? On this reasoning, cosmopolitanism conflicts both with pluralism and our duties towards our fellow citizens.

It might be thought that the solution would be to create a European 'national identity' on a par with that of the member states. Indeed, there have been periodic attempts to appeal to common European values and shared history in this way and to provide the EU with the symbolic trappings of a nation state—notably the flag, anthem, and passport. However, as debates about references to Christianity in the preambles to the Charter of Rights and then the Constitutional Treaty revealed (Bellamy and Schonlau 2004a, b; Schonlau 2005; Weiler 2003), European values are highly contested—indeed, the history of Europe is one of conflict over just such issues. Moreover, these differences are already well embedded in the separate national traditions. Meanwhile, the very size and linguistic diversity of Europe militates against a shared political culture. In fact, far from the different European national cultures coming together in a synthesis, the trend is in precisely the opposite direction with a growing demand from minority national groups for ever greater political autonomy at the substate level.

Obviously, multiculturalism is forcing national and subnational public cultures to become more diverse, while globalization constrains national political, economic, and social policies. Yet the one has not led to post-nationalism nor has the other completely undermined the capacity for nation states to respond. Miller tends to see the EU as necessarily detracting from the national political community of the member states, diluting their political cultures and placing something far inferior in their place. However, others have seen it as a mechanism for preserving those very virtues, while adding the capacity to tackle problems that can only be resolved through their acting in concert. Such arrangements might be consistent with Miller's argument if they were seen as purely voluntary agreements between states that had been appropriately legitimized through domestic democratic procedures. Even if formally this is the position, though, there are clearly pressures that make such cooperation necessary, while once in existence the EU partly takes on a life of its own that exerts its own influence. It is to the normative implications of this situation that we now turn.

Betwixt and Between the National and the Supranational

Although there have been numerous descriptive accounts of the 'multilevel' character of the EU, with its mixture of regional, national, transnational, and supranational elements, there have been fewer attempts to provide this mix with a normative rationale. The tendency has been to see this situation as normatively unstable and likely to either return to a system of nation states or progress towards some form of European federation. However, a group of influential analysts have argued that the combination is coherent so long as the member states and the EU are seen as sharing rather different kinds of competence that requires distinct types of legitimation.

A view developed in different ways by Fritz Scharpf (1999), Giandomenico Majone (1996), and Andrew Moravcsik (1993, 2002), these figures contend that although the EU lacks a demos and the consequent degrees of trust and solidarity needed to support a democratic welfare state, these qualities are unnecessary for the regulatory tasks it undertakes. These aim at Pareto improvements and, having no redistributional effects—at least long term—do not require electoral endorsement or accountability. Indeed, direct democratic control might undermine rather than ensure the equity, efficiency, and effectiveness of their conception and implementation. In part, this is because these are highly technical matters with low electoral salience, where broad agreement exists as to the goal to be achieved. They are also often areas where there is a small and diffuse benefit to the public but particular sectors that stand to gain or lose a great deal, and hence have a stronger incentive than the public at large to lobby and apply political pressure to secure their preferred outcome. In such cases, the danger is not of democracy producing a tyrannous majority so much as myopia and indifference on the part of the general public leading to politicians paying too much attention to unrepresentative minorities with a capacity to make a fuss. Depoliticizing such decisions helps secure the public good. Moreover, a degree of political control remains in that member states control the structure of the EU through the negotiation of the treaties, and the effective requirement for super majorities not only to endorse these major changes but also most directives due to the need for the endorsement of both the Council of Ministers and a majority of MEPs in the European Parliament. As a result, a pan-European democratic consensus forms the ultimate foundation of the EU.

We noted above that both Habermas and communitarians such as Miller relate their arguments to republicanism rather than liberalism. They do so because they associate republican thinking with democracy as a form of collective self-rule. In Habermas's post-nationalist argument, a system of democratic rights secures self-rule by establishing the basis for private and public autonomy. In Miller's nationalist argument, nation states secure self-rule by allowing a national demos to govern itself. However, arguably both are flawed because unless one assumes a normative consensus on the preconditions of autonomy (in Habermas's case) or complete identification with the national community (in Miller's case) there will always be trade-offs between personal autonomy and involvement in a collective decision. As R.P. Wolff famously pointed out, for democracy to be a true system of self-rule for all citizens would require an implausible degree of agreement among them as to the suitability of all common policies to meet their joint and several needs (Wolff 1970). It might appear that in seeking to depoliticize so much, the arguments of Scharpf, Moravcsik, and Majone are unpromising candidates for a republican theory. However, Philip Pettit (1997) has proposed an alternative basis for republicanism in the concept of freedom as non-domination. On his account, non-domination is secured so long as no person or body is able to exert arbitrary interference over another—that is, can act at will to impose their own interests on others. The archetype of domination is the relationship of a slave to a master. Even if the master is benevolent, he always has the power to oblige his slave to follow interests other than his own and that can influence the slave's behaviour as much as actual interference would. The overcoming of domination requires not so much self-rule as a system of governance in which all are treated with equal concern and respect. Domination is overcome through formulating policies that view all as on a par with each other and entitled to an equal hearing. Although democratic control can be a mechanism for holding rulers to account in such a way that they act for their principals rather than themselves, it is not a failsafe mechanism. In circumstances such as those remarked on above, it may involve an arbitrariness of its own in which relevant views do not get due consideration. If democracy is seen as being not just rule 'by' but also 'for' the people, then sometimes democratic 'outputs' are better realised without democratic 'inputs'. Dispersing power so as to uphold the rule of law, so that like cases are treated alike, and protect against either tyrannous majorities or over-influential minorities, so all views get treated equitably, can be more effective ways of guarding against domination than electoral accountability. Meanwhile, the supra-majoritarian consensus that we noted ultimately lies behind so much EU decision-making offers a further democratic safeguard that policies reflect the public good rather than sectional interests. For consensual decision-making makes it more likely that the measures that pass will either be those all agree are conducive to general prosperity and well-being, or can gain wide acceptance as reasonable exceptions.

Some of these ideas have been explicitly applied to the EU by Bellamy and Castiglione (1997, 2000; see too Bellamy and Warleigh 1998 and Bellamy 2003). They have argued that the danger of arbitrary interference is increased in a globalizing and interconnected world, where the activities within and by a state can have a huge impact on the citizens of other states, and individuals find themselves increasingly needing to work and trade across borders and to deal with international, transnational, and multinational bodies and corporations. From this perspective, the multilevel structure of the EU offers a mechanism for dispersing power so that states can more effectively hold each other in check and cooperate with other states on an equitable basis to provide collective goods no longer available to citizens at the national level. In their view, the guiding principle of a non-dominating scheme should be mutual recognition and the search of fair compromise agreements on matters of common concern. To a degree, the status of European citizenship offers a good example. It is grounded in the different citizenship practices of the various member states but provides for these states to accord mutual recognition of an appropriate set of rights to those citizens engaged in cross-border activities, so that they are not penalized or discriminated against as 'foreigners'. However, the full acquisition of the entitlements enjoyed by the citizens of another member state requires that the European citizen gradually take on the burdens of national citizenship and shows a willingness to reciprocate by contributing to national public goods. Consequently, it neatly embodies the betwixt and between character of the EU, being less than a federal status and more than a national one, which deals with the space in between states relating to their increasing interaction with one another (Bellamy 2008b).

Nevertheless, Bellamy and Castiglione have been more critical of the depoliticizing mechanisms of the EU than Pettit and those authors whose writings might be assimilated to his argument. In particular, they see technocratic decision-making, on the one hand, and the EU's complex, consensual democratic arrangements, on the other, as undermining political equality. By contrast to Pettit (2004) they see equality in democratic decision-making as the fairest means for ensuring their non-dominating character. They believe it is only when citizens' arguments are presented on equal terms, and there are encouragements for each to align their views with those of others, that decisions are likely to be seen as equitable both as to their making and their substance. Majoritarian decision-making in the context of a competitive party system achieves this result reasonably well at the domestic level. One person one vote and majority rule satisfy the criteria for a fair input, while the need for competing parties to build coalitions of voters between a variety of minority groups creates incentives for equitable out puts as well (Bellamy 2007, 2008a). However, the size, diversity, and fragmented public sphere of the EU has meant that such a system has failed to develop at the European level. European elections tend to be 'second order' and fought on domestic issues, with European parties being no more than parliamentary groupings. In such a situation, the quasi-consociational decision-making between member states may be justified but it reduces accountability, because it becomes hard to identify who has been responsible for particular decisions, and undermines electoral fairness, because it gives extra weighting to smaller sectional interests and the status quo. As a result, such mechanisms are unlikely to promote anything but win–win policies, and even then may only do so by buying off opposition. Meanwhile, technocratic decision-making need not be as impartial as assumed. Not only are technical decisions often contested both normatively and empirically, but also the possibilities for regulatory capture are increased by the closeness of EU regulation to various 'stakeholders'— notably business and unions. The EU's habit of consulting with civil society organizations more often increases than counteracts the problems of the over-representation of 'insider' groups, as does the increased use of litigation as a mechanism for influencing the regulative process. Consequently, contrary to Pettit's assumptions depoliticization may actually increase the very dangers he seeks to overcome (Bellamy 2006d, 2009). Yet there seems little prospect of overcoming the necessity for using such mechanisms. As a result, there may well be democratic limits to what the EU may legitimately seek to undertake—limits that it seems right that citizens should be able to control and monitor through their national parliaments (Bellamy 2006c). The result may be a somewhat fragmented EU of different speeds and functions according to how far a given member state believes it necessary to cooperate with others.

Conclusion

Normative issues have become ever more salient within the EU as it develops competences that have standardly required democratic legitimation within states. Yet, how far it should take on these competences in the first place is as normatively contested as the degree to which it is able legitimately to do so. We have surveyed a range of normative positions, noting how each rests on a set of empirical assumptions. In our view, the most convincing are those that make sense of the EU's character as 'betwixt and between' the nation state and a supranational institution, mixing contractarian and communitarian elements in the process. For these accounts accord with the reality of an institution that has the potential to add to national citizenship without undermining it. The EU is a symptom of the enhanced globalization of social and economic processes and the need for states to attend to the effects of their policies on each other and to control much activity that can otherwise escape domestic democratic control. But many policies continue to be rightly located within states as related to the cooperation and interactions taking place between national citizens. The normative challenge of the EU, therefore, consists in not undermining these state-centred practices while providing appropriate mechanisms for tackling those issues that these arrangements cannot or do not cope with, and doing so in ways that accord citizens a like degree of equal concern and respect to that achieved by domestic democratic systems.

As our review of normative theories reveals, in many respects identifying this issue as *the* normative challenge is in itself a key normative question. Contractarian or neo-contractarian cosmopolitans and post-nationalists tend to underestimate or even deny the value of state-centred practices except as functionally convenient mechanisms for realizing universal principles of justice that apply to all humans equally. By contrast, communitarians view universal principles of justice as only having real purchase within the context of a national culture of shared values and practices of a kind unlikely to develop at the EU level. Our claim is not simply that neither of these approaches makes much sense of the reality of the EU's betwixt and between nature, but also that they neglect the normative as well as the practical justification of this situation. Cosmopolitans and post-nationalists tend to be dismissive of the ethical force arising from the particular attachments the citizens of member states have to each other as participants in an ongoing set of continually renegotiated contractual relations within established practices of self-government. These relations pre-empt and are in tension with many cosmopolitan and post-nationalist demands for global justice. Yet while communitarians fully acknowledge the force of these national bonds, they have been mistaken in their turn for ignoring both the degree they are challenged by global forces and the extent of our obligations to secure similar forms of national self-government elsewhere.

Enlargement

In many respects enlargement illustrates both the appeal of this approach and the difficulties it faces. On the one hand, the decision to allow in so many member states from the former Soviet bloc, notwithstanding the budgetary and institutional problems such a move would pose, illustrates the ability of EU norms to triumph over pure national self-interest. On the other hand, it would be mistaken to see such norms as reflecting a cosmopolitan or post-nationalist perspective that denies or overrides state concerns. The 15 pre-2004 enlargement member states have wished to guard many of their privileges, disappointing many of the expectations the new countries had had from membership of the Union, while the 10 new members from the former Soviet bloc have been understandably ambivalent about yielding too much of their hard-won state sovereignty. However, enlargement can be portrayed as an act of solidarity between European democratic states. The consolidation of democracy within the former dictatorships of Spain, Greece, and Portugal constitutes one of the EU's great successes, and the welcome accorded to the new democracies of central and eastern Europe derived in part from the desire to achieve a similar success there. Of course, this policy was not entirely disinterested since consolidating democracy in the region would improve the security of the existing member states. Yet it can also be related to a normative commitment to accord an equal right for the citizens of these states to enjoy a similar system of self-government to that enjoyed by their own citizens. To the extent enjoyment of such rights in a globalizing world depends on cooperation between states, both to reap the benefits of their positive externalities—such as trade—and to diminish the harms of their negative externalities—such as pollution— then the EU can be seen as an appropriate cosmopolitan mechanism for supporting the communitarian ties of its member states.

Nevertheless, enlargement poses an undoubted challenge to the democratic credentials of the EU itself. It has added not only to the size but also the diversity of the EU, making democratic control even harder to establish and exercise at the EU level as a result. Finding appropriate policies to address this difficulty, therefore, is likely to prove even more daunting and be at the heart of EU policy for the next decade and more. Yet a strategy that recognizes the legitimacy of that diversity and seeks to promote democracy—including the discussion of EU affairs—at the member state level seems likely to have greater success than one that seeks to replace member state democracy with EU level democratic institutions. In sum, a cosmopolitan contract between national political communities to cooperate in non-dominating ways offers both a practically plausible and a normatively attractive future for the EU.

■ NOTES

1. The theory of the social contract is standardly linked to the works of Hobbes (*Leviathan* 1651), Locke (*Two Treatises on Government* 1680–90), and Rousseau (*The Social Contract* 1762), and associated respectively with the development of the European Westphalian model of state sovereignty, the rise of parliamentary power with the Glorious Revolution in England, and the Republican movement that led to the French Revolution.

2. Though this argument is only implicit in much of his published work (e.g. Rawls 1993: 12, 1999: 23) he made it explicitly in a letter responding to Van Parijs's defence of global justice (Rawls and Van Parijs 2003).

3. Figures here and in the next paragraph come from Eurobarometer 60, 62, 67.

■ GUIDE TO FURTHER READING

Bellamy, R. and Castiglione D. (2003) 'Legitimising the Euro-polity and its regime: the normative turn in EU studies', *European Journal of Political Theory*, 2(1), 7–34. An influential account of why normative reasoning is inescapable when attempting to theorize the EU.

Føllesdal, A. (2006) 'Survey article: the legitimacy deficits of the European Union', *Journal of Political Philosophy*, 14(4), 441–68. A survey and assessment of different views of the EU's legitimacy or lack thereof.

Dobson, L. and Føllesdal, A. (eds) (2004) *Political Theory and the European Constitution* (London: Routledge). A collection highlighting the normative issues at the heart of the debate on the constitution.

Weale, A. (2006) *Democratic Citizenship and the European Union* (Manchester: Manchester University Press). A normative exploration of the nature of citizenship and its potential role within the EU.

Bellamy, R. (2006) 'Still in deficit: rights, regulation and democracy in the EU', *European Law Journal*, 12(6), 725–42. A critical normative examination of those who believe the EU's democratic deficit can be overcome or does not exist.

■ **STUDY QUESTIONS**

1. Some normative theorists have argued the terms of any EU treaty should be guided by those principles that could be agreed to in an international social contract. What are the key debates concerning who might contract, how, and to what, and how might these disagreements affect the scope and terms of any treaty?

2. How do different normative positions relate to different policy proposals on the EU constitution, such as the status of the Charter of Rights, the supremacy and direct effect of EU law, and voting weights in the Council of Minsters?

3. Which normative theory, if any, best captures the current status of Union citizenship? Which normative view offers the most attractive view of how it might develop in the future—and why?

4. What normative grounds might be given for (a) believing there was a democratic deficit in the EU, and (b) denying any such deficit?

5. To what extent does the plausibility of any of the different normative views of the EU depend on the empirical correctness of a given theory of European integration?

12 Critical Political Economy

Alan W. Cafruny and J. Magnus Ryner

Introduction

Since the Marshall and Schuman Plans, the European Union (EU) has made its most significant advances in the economic sphere. Because these advances so evidently have taken place through political means, one would have thought that the study of European integration naturally lends itself to a political economy approach. Yet EU scholars have been slow to embrace political economy. Their reticence is all the more striking given the emergence of international political economy (IPE) as a subfield of international relations, which offers a variety of linkages to the problems of European integration.

Nevertheless, in recent years, political economists—including those working in the critical-theoretical tradition—have made important contributions to EU studies. We begin this chapter by situating the belated arrival of political economy in integration studies within the context of the division of the social sciences in the late nineteenth century. We then suggest that the crisis of the Bretton Woods system served to revive the study of political economy through the establishment of a subdiscipline of IPE and discuss critically the key strands of political economic analysis as they were imported into the study of the EU. Finally, we analyse from the perspective of critical political economy the causes and consequences of the economic and monetary union as a case where such an approach seems particularly useful, and Eastern enlargement for the purpose of comparison with the other chapters in this volume.

The Disciplinary Split and European Integration Theory

Classical political economy, which enjoyed a century-long golden age following the publication of Adam Smith's *Wealth of Nations* (1776), represented a unified conception of social science. However, as a result of the rise of neoclassical economics at the end of the nineteenth century, the social sciences fragmented into separate disciplines (economics, sociology, and political science), each of which offered an alternative set of assumptions about society that eschewed the intellectual radicalism of classical political economy.[1] Neoclassical economics severed the link between production and power that was central to Marxism, but also to classical political economy. It dealt summarily with the problems of classes and surplus by abandoning them. Identifying its concern as the allocation of scarce resources, it restricted its view to exchange relations between 'households' and 'firms' abstracted from the social structure. Coinciding with the emergence of the 'social question' in Europe, the demise of political economy was more than a scholastic concern. The explosion of unprecedented material wealth alongside impoverishment produced by industrial capitalism threatened the very foundation of social order. Sociology acquired a reformist ethos and an analytical abstraction that separated social relations from both production and power. 'Social relations' referred to something that existed between 'individuals' whose social existence as such was taken for granted, in contradistinction to 'economic' and 'political' relations. The 'density' of these ties determined the degree of orderliness (integration) of society and the potential for 'social consensus'. Finally, 'political science' was defined narrowly in terms of 'power in government'. Economic and social relations were displaced to the 'environment', without serious questions being asked about how power relations in the 'environment' constrain 'government'.

Thus when the time came to make sense of European integration in the 1950s and the 1960s, the fragmentation of the social sciences had, for the most part, long since been institutionalized. The limited horizons of each exerted great influence over the theories that were deployed to understand Europe's novel experiment. Alan Milward and colleagues (1993) have pointed to the unacknowledged ideological dimension of social scientific theories used to make sense of European integration. There was, moreover, a coincidence of the problematic and central assumptions of these theories and the United States (US) State Department's Cold War Atlanticist and 'corporate-liberal' foreign policy paradigm in the 1950s (see also van der Pijl 1996: 272–86). This paradigm was concerned with consolidating US interests by reconstructing Europe in the image of the US. Pluralist theories of a self-sustained, piecemeal, European integration, themselves based on the systems theory of David Easton's (1953) political science and Talcott Parsons' (1951) sociology, lent intellectual credibility to this policy stance. Neofunctionalist IR theory and the fusion of Keynesianism with neoclassical economics resonated with a particular way of posing policy problems.

This 'modified liberalism' rested on a particular managerial–administrative conception of rationality, defined as the 'conscious and systematic application of legitimate controls on conduct' (Lowi 1979: 21) in production and technology, in exchange and commerce, in social control, and in administration. Questions are raised about whether such a 'visible hand' can be maintained within the strict confines of administration understood as 'formal adaptation of means to ends' (Lowi 1979: 21) without degenerating into the arbitrary exercise of power. For liberals, the solution lies in the very social differentiation studied by sociologists: a rationally organized society generates a complex set of checks and balances that prevent particular ideologies, special interests, and protracted social conflicts from dominating in public life (Lowi 1979: 21). This conception resonates with the vision of a European state-system that is dissolving through spillover into an overarching polity or multilevel entity: social and political integration has to follow economic integration to maintain order (social equilibrium as opposed to merely economic equilibrium) in a process whereby politics is simultaneously functionally differentiated, integrated, and 'supranationalized'.

Hence, the concept of integration in the aforementioned sense is not entirely innocent. It implies that economic integration (the realm of economics) and social and political integration (the realm of international relations) are a priori idealized as the 'rational' and 'general', which can be distinguished from the 'irrational', 'special interests', and the realm of power politics that were associated with the old European interstate and inter-imperialist system (Cox with Sinclair 1996: 60–84). The question becomes one of whether it is warranted to be optimistic that the parochial inter-state power politics can be transcended by the rationality of integration. Most political science theories of European integration, including its recent political–sociological variants, such as social constructivism (see Chapter 8), are caught up in the particularities of this problematic. This is quite obviously the case with Karl Deutsch's communications theory (1957) and Ernst Haas's neo-functionalism (1964b: especially 47–50, 1968: especially xv–xxii), but it is also apparent in recent neo-institutionalist 'multilevel governance' works (see Chapter 5). Simon Hix directly invokes Easton in the title of his *The Political System of the European Union* (1999) and constructivism primarily derives its concepts from sociology (van Apeldoorn *et al.* 2003: 26–32). Even Stanley Hoffmann's (1966: 862–63, 872–3, 889–901) emblematic critique of Haas from a realpolitik perspective was caught up in the 'pessimism–optimism' terms of debate, as he gloomily observed the resurgence of French nationalism in Gaullist form.

While political scientists sought to elucidate the conditions under which a politics of rationality could emerge, the economic questions of the Common—and later the Single—Market, were for the most part left to the specialized domain of economists. Given the disciplinary remit of economics, this tended to rule out concerns with the social power relations and interests constitutive of the European economy. Most of this literature takes its cue from international trade theory and Ricardo's concept of comparative advantage, but sanitized from his class analysis, concerned as it was with the elimination of land rent. On the basis of concepts such as trade creation, diversion, and deflection, the literature is concerned with 'Pareto-optimal'[2] welfare benefits but also with the costs associated with a regional customs union within a broader multilateral and progressively liberalizing international trade regime (Viner 1950; Bhagwhati and Panagariya 1996; Balassa 1997). Central in this context is the particular value assigned inter alia to the economies of the division of labour, competition, scale, and knowledge diffusion. All these economies were central to the Cecchini Report (European Commission 1988) that articulated the rationale for the single market. In the field of monetary affairs, the question of the pros and cons of fixed exchange rates and ultimately monetary union hinged on the trade-offs between transaction and adjustment costs in what is recognized not to be an 'optimal currency area' (e.g. De Grauwe 2003).[3]

The (Re-)turn to Political Economy

The premise that the old European interstate and imperial system was arbitrary, irrational, and served the parochialisms of powerful special interests, is by no means objectionable. To be sure, studies such as those referred to in the previous section that are concerned with the transcendence of such politics were (and remain) eminently worthy. The problem is rather that the paradigmatic framework tends to obscure considerations of the power relations and (possibly arbitrary) special interests that are constitutive of Atlanticism and European integration itself. These problems became too salient to ignore as the American grand design began to unravel in the latter part of the 1960s, culminating in the collapse of the Bretton Woods system in 1971, making the political dimensions of international economic affairs and the economic sources of political conflicts evident.[4] Similar and related developments occurred at the European level, starting with the 1965 Empty Chair crisis but continuing with the collapse of the Werner Plan, the problematic attempts to create a European zone of monetary stability through the 'Snake in the Tunnel', creeping non-tariff barriers, and debates over the Common Agricultural Policy (CAP).[5] Conflicts intensified in the context of the stagflation crisis and sharpened class conflicts between 1968 and 1974. All this called for the analysis of the material conditions of existence of the 'corporate–liberal' foundations of Atlanticism and its possible replacement in changing conditions. In this context, political economy analysis was rediscovered.

IPE as the Politics of International Economic Relations

Developments from the late 1960s through the 1980s presented the specialized disciplines of international relations and international economics, including the study of European integration, with a number of anomalies. IPE emerged in no small measure as an attempt to deal with them. As we will show below, the most influential strand of IPE has been fundamentally shaped by the so-called neorealist/neoliberal synthesis in IR. As such it can be described as the study of 'politics of international economic relations'.

Considerations of power relations in economic affairs return to the fore in the politics of international economic relations through its recognition of the contribution of realism and mercantilism. It returns to a basic insight of Hamilton and List that because security cannot be taken for granted in international economic affairs the cosmopolitan principle of comparative advantage cannot be unconditionally embraced. Because security depends on a balance of power that is inherently relational, Pareto-optimal absolute gains (see note 2) are insufficient in the consideration of international economic relations. States must also seek to maximize relative power and hence relative gains. It is the distribution of specialization in the international division of labour that matters. Units will seek to maximize their prospects for competing in strategic sectors that are easily convertible into power and/or that ensure relative gains through higher than average rates of productivity and value added. Realists consider this question primarily with reference to the external balance of power of states. However, some also consider the importance of relative gains for internal security as high productivity growth increases the possibility for Pareto-optimal distributive bargains between classes, sectors, and groups *within* states. According to several realist political economists, American hegemonic decline in the 1970s and the 1980s made such mercantilist considerations increasingly important and this helps to explain the disintegrative dynamics of the period (e.g. Krasner 1976; Gilpin 1981; Calleo 1982; Grieco 1990).

Realist IPE was not without its own anomalies, not least of which was the correlation between purported American hegemonic decline and the increase of economic cooperation on the basis of cosmopolitan–liberal principles. This has given purchase to Robert Keohane's (e.g. 1984, 1986) institutionalist synthesis of neorealism and liberalism in the form of regime theory. Whilst recognizing the importance of power politics, Keohane argued that the beneficial effects of regimes (such as absolute gains generated by comparative advantage) make the costs of exiting regimes too high when a hegemon declines. Hence a politics of 'complex interdependence' (Keohane and Nye 1977) survives the end of hegemony as the institutional dynamics of the regime achieves autonomy from the structure of its creation.

The influence of Keohane on IPE can hardly be overestimated. This is not the least illustrated in IPE-inspired attempts to make sense of the SEM and the EMU. Most of these attempts conceive, qua Keohane, of some sort of balance of power and interest interaction and regime-institutional dynamics. 'Supranationalists' such as Wayne Sandholtz and John Zysman (1989) assign critical importance to the realist question of *relative gains*. In their account, Europe can no longer rely on spin-offs for productivity catch-up that serves as the basic impetus for the relaunch. Conversely, the liberal intergovernmentalist Andrew Moravcsik (1998: see Chapter 4 this volume) confirms the staying-power of liberalism when he asserts the importance of *credible commitments*. Debates about how to explain the SEM and the EMU take place *within* regime theory, turning on the more fine-grained and pragmatic question about whether supranational actors exercise autonomous authority in the political process. Conclusions that the process is multilevelled (e.g. Marks *et al.* 1996; Armstrong and Bulmer 1998) are perhaps the ultimate consequence of this mode of reasoning.

Questions can be raised, though, about the extent to which these approaches overcome the discipline-specific blind spots that warranted the return to political economy in the first place. When it became apparent that the SEM and Maastricht Treaty could not be explained satisfactorily on the basis of state interests in the international system, Moravcsik turned to the pluralist political sociology to derive state preferences from the 'inside' of political systems. But pluralist accounts based on the assumption of state neutrality overlook structural relations of power between capital and labour (van Apeldoorn 2002: 39–41) (hence not explaining why it is, as he acknowledges, big business that dominates domestic bargaining outcomes). More cognisant of particular interests that underpin these bargains is Jeffry Frieden's (1991) analysis, which comes closest to returning to a classical political economy analysis in the Ricardian tradition. Rather than grounding his 'two-level' analysis in pluralist politics, Frieden traces the particular sectors that are favoured by the agreements. Similarly, Fritz Scharpf (1996) has highlighted the systemic bias in terms of substantive policy outcomes of a system based on negative integration and prone to joint decision-making traps. Whilst such analyses have their merits, the fundamental social structures of society remain obscure in them as well (Talani 2000; van Apeldoorn *et al.* 2003: 28–9). There is also a tendency to idealize liberal principles and mechanisms and to apply these as a yardstick upon which one can measure the special interests of other principles and motivations.

A European Variety of Capitalism?

Alan Milward and colleagues (1993; see also Milward 1992) have offered an alternative historical–realist account based on the motivations of European policy-makers. From this perspective, European integration was not about abandoning the nation state but, rather, 'rescuing' and recasting it towards new social purposes. Western European nation states were so weakened after the Second World War that they 'more or less had to re-create themselves as functional units' (Milward *et al.* 1993: 4). This could only be done by drawing on the assistance offered by the US and transferring certain functions and competences to the nascent European Coal and Steel Community (ECSC) and European Economic Community (EEC). However, the sharply circumscribed range of policy competences transferred to the supranational level were only conceded as long as states were 'able to assert the priority of a national interest' (Milward *et al.* 1993: 4–5). Western European nation states, in many respects, became *more* powerful than ever before as they embarked

on unprecedented programmes of intervention in economic and social life with the express purpose of shaping and controlling their national destinies. Concepts such as 'the mixed economy' and 'the welfare state' reflect the recognition of this historical reality.

Milward *et al.* (1993: 5)

It is against this backdrop that a different perspective on European political economy has emerged, which has been concerned with the particularities of the European variety of capitalism. This is a political economy that does not take liberal conceptions of economics as the universal standard, but which argues that in certain instances dynamic economies associated with technological change and/or coordination can be accomplished by intervention and even restrictions of the market logic rather than allowing the free-play of markets. Empirically, this literature invokes French *dirigisme*, Germanic corporatism, and Scandinavian integration of welfare and economic policy. List's and Colbert's mercantilism is an important source of inspiration, but so is the work of Schumpeter, Myrdal, Gerschenkron, Shoenfeld, and Hirschmann. This perspective is also associated with the works of two French industrialist-intellectuals: Jean-Jacques Servan-Schreiber (*The American Challenge* 1969) and Michel Albert (*Capitalism Against Capitalism* 1993), who popularized the concept of 'Rhineland capitalism'.

These works positively emphasize the economic principles that Rhineland capitalism represents: monopolistic financial relationships between 'housebanks' and corporations may contradict the impeccable neoclassical principles of allocation of the stock market, but deliver instead longer time-horizons in productive investment and capacities of coordination through 'voice' rather than 'exit', which in turn facilitate productivity-enhancing technological change. Centralized trade unions, engaging with employers' associations in centralized bargaining over wages and work conditions, are integrated into this productivity bargain, ensuring labour's support for technological change in exchange for higher social wages and social protection underwritten by productivity growth. This variety of capitalism has endowed European states with broad repertoires of macroeconomic, industrial, and labour market tools, which have eased the trade-off between economic growth and equality objectives compared to the Anglo-American world. This is the ideal type of Rhineland capitalism which, with variations, has operated in at least the continental western member states of the EU (see e.g. Lehmbruch and Schmitter 1979; Zysman 1983; Katzenstein 1978, 1984; Streeck 1992; Hall and Soskice 2001).

From this perspective, the debate about European integration has asked whether integration undermines the operation of the socio-economic mechanisms of the Rhineland model or whether it enhances it. By the late 1960s, Servan-Schreiber (1969) was ambivalent. He observed that American multinational corporations had seized many of the investment opportunities that the Common Market represented, and that in fact Community institutions inadvertently facilitated an American colonization of the leading sectors and commanding heights of the emerging European economy. In some respects this was to the benefit of the European consumer as it countered the rent-extraction of national monopoly groupings. However, Servan-Schreiber feared the undermining of a European autonomous base for high value-added competition and the strategic development of products and processes. For him, the American challenge required a more consistent adaptation of a Rhineland capitalist European model, where rents were productively reinvested and where the benefits of these reinvestments were distributed in adequate amounts to workers and consumers. While few would subscribe to Servan-Schreiber's mercantilist–federalist position quite as unequivocally today, the concern about the implications of the Single Market for the Rhineland model has been revisited, and many do take the view that the expansion to a Single Market on the basis of 'negative integration' [6] comes at the price of the progressive undermining of the Rhineland mechanisms. It is especially the integration into Anglo-American-dominated global financial markets (e.g. Story and Walter 1997) that is mentioned, or the effects of mutual recognition on voice-based networks. The latter has been the subject of a remarkable piece by Schmitter (1997) who, drawing on his expertise in both corporatism and integration, has synthesized a 'variety of capitalism' perspective with neofunctionalism. Schmitter asks if the problems posed by mutual recognition for what he calls the intermediary institutions of the Rhineland model are likely to lead to spillover towards a pan-European Rhineland model. Whilst the prospect of a formal politics in that direction is slim (e.g. Streeck and Schmitter 1991), he explores the prospects for an informal spill-over in the field of standard-setting. Ultimately he concludes on a pessimistic note that the requisite element of politicization is missing.

These pessimistic conclusions are far from uncontested. Drawing on the historical–institutionalist idea of path-dependence, Martin Rhodes (2002) and Ronald Doré (2000) suggest that the EU's rhetoric of creating a modified European 'social model' fit for the age of globalization has more purchase than the pessimists conclude. Colin Hay (2000, 2004) agrees, but argues from a constructivist perspective that it is important to differentiate between structural–functional and contingent–ideational forces. He categorizes Europe's restrictive macroeconomic stance as a contingent–ideational force, which has been more detrimental to Europe's social model than the putative objective structural forces associated with globalization.

Critical Political Economy

The politics of international economic relations perspective on IPE begins to develop a certain critical distance from the corporate–liberal Atlanticist design upon which European integration was based. The 'varieties of capitalism' literature broadens the critical framework by throwing a spotlight on the strategies that were deployed in a European setting to maintain a competitive advantage in the vanguard sector of the international economy, and to the distributive implications of these strategies. These contributions represent a significant return to political economy concerns with the co-constitution of production and power that provide the material foundations of social order. Nevertheless, from a critical perspective they represent only a partial return to considerations of the historically specific conditions of social relations of production. Whilst the 'varieties of capitalism' perspective is concerned with the social foundations of economic institutions and distributive relations between groups, it is essentially functionalist because it studies social relations exclusively from the point of view of how they serve to reproduce economic institutions.

Neo-Marxism

Although Servan-Schreiber highlighted socio-economic power relations, his work also curiously assumes a high degree of state autonomy and, hence, voluntarism. Why should one assume that European federalism was a realistic option, especially one that challenged American supremacy? What were its preconditions? Moreover, Servan-Schreiber's account of socio-economic power is descriptive, with a tendency to underestimate problems associated with class compromise between labour and capital. For Ernest Mandel, corporatist cooperation would deprive European workers of the strike weapon, the essential tool for advancing their interests. Furthermore, the *dirigiste* strong state that Servan-Schreiber envisaged had historically never been associated with anything but the power of monopoly capitalism, binding workers into a relationship of subordination in a highly commodified and bureaucratized society (see also Panitch 1981).[7] Monopoly capitalism was also associated with imperialism, fascism, and two world wars (Mandel 1968: 103–17).

From such a point of departure, Mandel conceived of European integration as expressing capitalist dynamics at a particular stage of development. Where others saw a distinctive European variety of capitalism, Mandel perceived a monopoly capitalist essence. Was this stage of development conducive to a transcendence of European inter-imperialist rivalry? Deploying the concept of *uneven development*—describing the effect of the increasingly problematic profitable deployment of capital—Mandel's answer was affirmative. The post-Second World War 'absolute dominance' of US capital, facilitating trade and investment on the transatlantic as well as European level, had organized a broader sphere for individual national capitals. As this dominance waned, Mandel anticipated growing inter-imperialist rivalry between amalgamated European capital and American capital in competition for spaces of profitable deployment. Although the Common Market was central to the US grand design, it was facilitating capital accumulation on a continental scale, setting the stage for US–European rivalry.

Nicos Poulantzas's account (1974: 161–9) was closer to that of Servan-Schreiber. Although European capital had its own base for accumulation, it was nevertheless becoming more dependent on American capital as a result of US foreign direct investment in leading sectors. Poulantzas also noted the growing significance of US-centred money—capital, which at the time was beginning to affect the terms of access to credit. Finally, the prominence of US capital in Europe determined a whole series of corporate 'practices, know-how, modes and rituals to do with the economic sphere' (Poulantzas 1974: 164). He proposed the concept of 'interior bourgeoisie' to describe a European capital that was not *comprador*[8] or wholly dependent on the United States but nevertheless increasingly articulated with American capital and its distinct social formation and power bloc (Poulantzas 1974: 164–7). The result was a complex disarticulation of autonomous European circuits of capital. This tendency made it harder for European states to perform their functions as 'factors of social cohesion'; that is, to mediate Europe's distinct class compromises and ideological constructions of political subjectivity that distance politics from overt class rule (e.g. Poulantzas 1975).

Mandel and Poulantzas have greatly influenced subsequent critical theorists and the debate concerning the balance of transatlantic unity and rivalry (e.g. van der Pijl 1984; van der Pijl and Holman 2003; Cafruny and Ryner 2007). In many respects, Mandel's approach to European integration synthesizes the interpretations of neofunctionalists and realists. With the latter, he shares a keen awareness of power politics and interests that inhere in states and markets, and his assessment of US decline echoes hegemonic stability theory.

However, his perspective on power and interest is dialectical and informed by a keen appreciation of societal transformation in a historically specific mode of production. With the neofunctionalists, therefore, Mandel foresees a qualitative transformation of the European state system, albeit through a different set of dynamics. Mandel's analysis oscillates between transcendence of inter-imperialist rivalry in Europe and continuity in the transatlantic sphere. Poulantzas addresses this latter question more satisfactorily—and indeed presciently—in his analysis of the interiorization of capitalist social relations on terms that structurally subordinate Europe to the United States (Ryner 2007). His conception of Euro-American interdependence echoes themes from the work of Keohane. However, Poulantzas pays much more attention to power relations within interdependence as well as the implications for social classes.

Regulation Theory and the Neo-Gramscians

Marxist analyses have sought to describe and explain the power relations that are constitutive of the integration process itself. As such, they have rejected idealist accounts whilst still being open to the transformative potentials of European integration. However, classical Marxist studies have consistently over-estimated the actualization of crisis tendencies and have not grasped qualitative variations within capitalism over space and time. In the early 1980s, it became clear that capitalism was *not* collapsing but that it *was* undergoing profound qualitative transformations. Regulation theory emerged as an alternative account, conceiving of a variety of qualitative configurations of capitalism, with profoundly different social implications.

Alain Lipietz (1987) has characterized regulation theorists as 'rebel sons' of two parents. As 'sons' of structuralist Marxists they learned that the social relations of capitalism have to be reproduced, but emphasis on reproduction forgets that these relations can at any time generate a crisis because of the inherent contradictions of capitalism, thereby directing our attention to the particularities of regulatory practices that counteract these tendencies. As 'sons' of the managerial cadres charged with regulating the French economy (such as Servan-Schreiber and Albert), they adopted a reformist ethos. At the same time, however, their acute sense of history led them to emphasize the transience and contradictions underlying macroeconomic models as representations of aggregate behaviour.

From its double rebellion, regulation theory developed a more concrete and historical–conjunctural analysis of the post-war 'Fordist' phase of capitalism. Phases of capitalism are characterized by particular regimes of capital accumulation, defined by specific production technologies that enable a particular 'solution' to the contradictions of capitalism. Semi-automation and mechanics, applied through the conveyor belt, provided the Fordist basis for productivity increases, enabling the expanded reproduction of capital. At the same time, this highly scale-dependent system solved its realisation problem through the *ex ante* integration of mass consumption with mass production. Particularly important was a historic compromise between capitalist managers and labour, allowing collective bargaining in exchange for acquiescence to managerial change at the workplace, even if this implied an increased tempo and deskilling of work. Pioneered in the United States in the 1920s, Fordism was 'exported' to western Europe and adapted with variations after 1945, through the Atlanticism of which European integration was an essential component.

In order to stabilize, regimes of accumulation require enabling institutional frameworks or modes of regulation. Keynesian demand management, welfare state expansion, collective bargaining regimes, and practices designed to deepen and extend consumer market relations such as advertisement were essential components of the Fordist mode of regulation. All of these practices served to integrate mass production and mass consumption. In short, all the practices and developments associated with modified liberalism, including European integration, balanced the requisites of openness for the expansion of mass production and national closure required for interventionist economic policy.

According to regulation theory, the crises of the Bretton Woods system and European integration in the 1960s and 1970s express a deeper crisis in Fordism. By the late 1960s, Fordism had reached its frontier of productivity expansion as the scope for conveyor-belt rationalization was exhausted. Productivity growth declined and price-setting, macroeconomic policy, and raw material price increases resulted in stagflation as the attention of policy-makers increasingly shifted to price stability (Aglietta and Orléan 1982; Lipietz 1985). Disintegrative conflicts over economic management in Europe and across the Atlantic reflected a disjuncture between accumulation regimes and regulation modes in crisis, and uncertainties with how one might deal with these.

Nevertheless, this crisis opened up new economic possibilities deriving from computer-based cybernetic automation and information technologies. Regulation theorists do not subscribe to a determinist reading of this situation. In principle, a variety of post-Fordist strategies designed to break down information bottlenecks and deploy cybernetic general purpose machines in order to adjust production to demand without productivity losses can be imagined. Following the variety of capitalism literature, regulation theory argues that diversified quality production on the basis of social-democratic, labour-inclusive, codetermination practices provides the basis of a viable post-Fordist future (compare Streeck 1992 with Leborgne and Lipietz 1988). However, regulation theory argues that the particular mode of regulation that is being promoted by a Single Market based on negative integration and a monetarist EMU is biasing developments in favour of a neoliberal post-Fordism (e.g. Grahl and Teague 1989, 1990; Lipietz 1989; Boyer 2000; Grahl 2001).

Regulation theory represents a fruitful synthesis of the neo-Marxist and variety of capitalism literatures. However, despite its emphasis on regulatory practices and historical contingency, regulation theory has difficulty accounting for the power-laden process through which one constellation of accumulation regimes and regulation modes is replaced by another. Neo-Gramscian theory usefully complements regulation theory in this regard (Bieling and Steinhilber 2000; Bieler and Morton 2001; Cafruny and Ryner 2003). Bastiaan van Apeldoorn's (2002) study of the critically important role of the intellectual leadership served by the European Roundtable of Industrialists (ERT) for the formation of the Single Market is exemplary. Taking his cue from Gramsci's 'relations of force' analysis (1971: 181) and van der Pijl's (1984) analysis of Atlantic Fordism in the post-war period, van Apeldoorn shows how the inner workings of the ERT constituted European transnational capital around a unified neoliberal project that was successfully advanced to policy-makers. Van Apeldoorn highlights the inherently political and ideological nature of the process as mercantilist and social democratic alternative conceptions were ultimately displaced in a process that assigned leadership to transnational finance-led capital fractions. Still, elements of mercantilism and social democracy remained at the margins as compensatory elements, providing for a broader-based class compromise and appeal. Van Apeldoorn's analysis works as an account of how an elite accumulation strategy is formed, but it probably overstates the supranational dimensions in the formation of broader inter-class social hegemony, and understates the continued importance of nationalism, the nation state and interstate relations in that regard. Hence, in our own analysis, we propose a synthesis of neo-Gramscian analysis with Poulantzas' work (itself inspired by Gramsci) as accounted for above (Cafruny and Ryner 2007: 18–21).

Economic and Monetary Union

Money and finance have played a central role in the transformation of European and transatlantic politics during the last two decades. International monetary relations often serve 'as a metaphor for general political economic relations in the world system' (Calleo 2003: 43). Hence, the analysis of the origins and implications of EMU spotlights the strengths and weaknesses of integration theories.

Neofunctionalists have pointed to the causal significance of spillover resulting from economic cooperation. Integration in one area produces a demand for integration in others, providing a basis for the establishment of supranational institutions. Hence, the European Commission identified functional linkages between the SEM and EMU (Padoa-Schioppa 1988). Gains already generated by the single market and capital liberalization could not be fully realised unless accompanied by monetary union. Moreover, in the absence of a single currency, the problem of competitive devaluations would increase as a result of greater openness, thereby placing the single market in jeopardy.

Yet it is far from clear that there was a necessary functional linkage between the internal market and monetary union, or that the possibilities for trade creation had been exhausted within the framework of the single market and national currencies, as indicated by the performance of Sweden and the United Kingdom. Furthermore, the euro has not generated sufficient pressures for a spillover into fiscal transfers and a single fiscal policy. Finally, the extravagant claims of proponents of monetary union concerning the impact of the EMU on European growth rates have been undermined by its constitutional design: a monetarist European Central Bank (ECB) and a succession of intergovernmental pacts mandating fiscal orthodoxy. Realists have argued that member states have adopted the single currency as a matter of rational self-interest. These interests have included a desire to challenge US dollar hegemony and France's determination to anchor a unified Germany to the West and to wrest a degree of control over monetary policy from the Bundesbank (e.g. Andrews 1993). Where national interests are insufficient to explain the policies of member states, they are supplemented (as noted above) by conceptions of national preference formation based on domestic interest groups or sectors (Moravcsik 1998; Frieden 1991). A focus on domestic politics and economics clearly helps explain national preferences and the bargaining among member states. Yet the emphasis on formal decision-making in these accounts does not adequately address the underlying socio-economic content of EMU or conflicts and contradictions posed for European society.

Finally, constructivists have focused on the role of agency and ideas, viewing the construction of ideas as prior or supplemental to interests, narrowly conceived. Kenneth Dyson (2000) and Kathleen MacNamara (1998; see also Abdelal 2007) have pointed to the growing 'consensus of competitive liberalism' (Dyson 2000: 30) among elites as a result of the crisis of Keynesian economics. Thomas Risse and colleagues have taken the argument further. Arguing that member states adopted diverging positions vis-à-vis EMU, the crucial factor was neither material interests nor economic ideas, but rather the development of a collective identity around the symbolism of EMU, which was adopted 'irrespective of its rationality' (1999: 148). These studies highlight the role of agency and the extent to which a sense of 'Europeanness' mobilized support for EMU. However, approaches which sever material interests from ideology are problematic. Advances in European integration are assumed to be evidence of collective European identity. However, the concept of identity is difficult to operationalize. Moreover, it cannot explain how and why policies were adopted in particular historical conjunctures (Talani 2003) and why integration is limited to certain policy arenas. Even if constructivists acknowledge the interrelations between material and social realities, they run the risk of taking ideas as given rather than explaining their co-constitution with interests. As we show below, the actual workings of the monetary union have been suffused with distributional conflicts and covert mercantilism.

A critical political economy analysis of EMU starts with the crisis of the Bretton Woods system and its impact on the Fordist mode of regulation in western Europe. Western European countries experienced growing instability through their exposure to speculative attacks on the dollar. Whilst the catalyst for regional monetary cooperation was the danger that France's post-1968 inflationary policies posed to the CAP, the broader objective of these cooperative attempts throughout the 1970s was to preserve the terms of the Fordist settlement at both the national and intra-regional levels by insulating Europe from the disruptive effects of dollar instability. These embryonic forms of monetary cooperation predated the single market, but the failure to construct a zone of regional monetary stability on an intergovernmental basis demonstrated the difficulties of maintaining fixed exchange rates within the consensual framework of the post-war settlement when the costs of adjustment arising from uneven development could not be passed on to strongly entrenched working classes.

The Maastricht Treaty was signed in a very different sociopolitical climate. After the failure of France's nationalist strategy from 1980–82, when France unsuccessfully pursued policies of nationalization and national Keynesianism, transnationalizing European capital sought a decisive departure from the post-war settlement. By then, working class power had steadily eroded after two decades of high unemployment, globalization, and the nascent incorporation of the former Soviet bloc economies into transnational capitalism. Already in 1985, the ERT had called for a single currency. Its proposal, *Reshaping Europe* (1991), bore remarkable similarities to the Maastricht timetable for EMU (van Apeldoorn 2002; Carchedi 2001).

EMU served, alongside the SEM, as the linchpin of 'disciplinary neoliberalism', the defining feature of Europe's re-launching (Gill 1998). In contrast to the McDougall Report of 1977, which had envisioned a monetary union buttressed by a substantial community budget and macroeconomic policies designed to promote full employment, the Maastricht criteria and successive fiscal pacts have firmly subordinated macroeconomic policy to short-term global financial markets. Given the monetarist remit of the ECB, flexible labour markets or structural reforms are offered as the cure for 'eurosclerosis' and the only means of maintaining the stability of the monetary union. The EU increasingly replicates the Anglo-US model of labour flexibility and capital market liberalization (even as it rejects its emphasis on macroeconomic promotion of growth). Yet flexible labour markets and capital mobility exacerbate low growth and high unemployment through 'competitive austerity' (Albo 1994: 148–57) among the constituent units, as each unit reduces domestic demand as part of its export-oriented production strategy, wherein wage increases and benefits are kept below productivity growth. There are winners and losers, but the overall effect has been economic stagnation and intra-European mercantilism. For example, as a result of the 'employer's offensive' (Kinderman 2005), the share of wages in German GDP declined significantly between 1998 and 2005, whereas it increased significantly in France and Italy. By 2003, Germany had overtaken the US as the world's largest exporter in total terms; in 2004, German companies exported approximately $1 trillion of products, equal to the combined exports of Britain, the Netherlands, and France (Cafruny and Ryner 2007: 68–9). Within the eurozone, Germany continues to register substantial trade surpluses with virtually all of its trading partners. The German strategy of 'competitive austerity'—representing an effective competitive devaluation—has been deeply problematic for other member states, especially Italy and France, and has imposed substantial fiscal and social pressures throughout the eurozone:

It is no exaggeration to state that Germany has followed a policy of 'beggar thy neighbor' reminiscent of similar policies in the 1930s. As a result, it has exported its problems to the other eurozone countries, which are likely to retaliate.

De Grauwe (2006: 13)

Yet even in Germany wages have stagnated, and poverty and inequality have increased significantly over the last decade.

European elites maintain that post-Maastricht neoliberal integration policies are compatible with the social- and Christian-Democratic variants of Europe's social model. Yet 'competitive austerity' places growing pressures on the welfare state. As trade union and mass party membership declines, populism and far-right parties and movements flourish, diminishing support for European integration (Cafruny and Ryner 2007: 87–103).

The neoliberal design of EMU is undermining the European social model and the possibility of partially decoupling from reliance on the US economy. Nevertheless, the euro has made significant inroads on the international reserve currency status of the dollar. The status of the dollar as international reserve currency has been called into question (Galati and Wooldridge 2006; Lim 2006). Euro-denominated notes, coins, and bonds in circulation now exceed those in dollars. Foreign currency reserves held in euros increased from 18 to 25 per cent, while the dollars share fell from 70 to 65 per cent between 1999 and 2007 (*Financial Times* 2007: 8). Yet the aforementioned structural limitations of EMU as a 'fragile regime' (De Grauwe 2007: 1) and its inability to generate a self-sustaining growth model in the context of massive trade and investment interdependence suggest a note of caution concerning the putative challenge of the euro. The thesis of euro–dollar rivalry overlooks the massive structural problems of the eurozone that arise from a lack of cohesion. Absent a political or budgetary foundation for monetary union, the neoliberal remit of the ECB inevitably produces uneven development and mercantilism. In many respects, what Poulantzas (1974) called the 'interiorization' of US capital has been reproduced by Europe's neoliberal path to monetary union. EMU in its present form is not likely to insulate Europe from the growing travails of the US and world economy.

Enlargement

The Eastern enlargements of 2004 and 2007 represented a significant new development for the EU. They have dramatically increased the disparity in levels of economic development across the Union, virtually nullifying the possibility of almost any cohesion policy (Dunford and Smith 2000; Holman 2006), but they have also propelled the EU into a new economic arena, greatly enhancing Europe's growth prospects but also re-inforcing Europe's geopolitical dependence on the United States by incorporating 'new European' states closely allied to Washington (Cafruny and Ryner 2007: 108–17). Liberal intergovernmentalists have sought to explain these recent enlargements in terms of national interests and relative power of existing member states and candidate countries and domestic and sectoral interests (Moravcsik and Vachudova 2003). The relative weakness of the candidate countries accounts for their acquiescence to substantial economic and social costs imposed by draconian terms of accession, but it is assumed that over the long term the benefits will outweigh the costs.

Constructivists have asked why the member states of the EU would themselves agree to sustain significant costs to enable Eastern enlargement. Given the asymmetries in bargaining position, and the availability of alternative arrangements short of full membership, they argue that the agreement to enlarge cannot be explained exclusively through material factors or rational interests (Schimmelfennig 2001; Diez 1999c; Fierke and Wiener 1999). Some scholars working within this school of thought point to the causal significance of European identity: only a community such as the EU, based on norms of inclusion and solidarity, would be willing to make the sacrifices necessary for enlargement. In addition, the logic of rule-following—itself a function of discourse and the 'social construction of interests'—establishes strong imperatives for implantation of compliance criteria on the part of both accession states and existing members (Schimmelfennig and Sedelmeier 2002; Wiener 2006).

From a critical political economy perspective, both of these approaches contribute important insights into the enlargement process. At the same time, however, they do not provide a comprehensive explanation for enlargement because they do not adequately address substantive socio-economic power relations (see especially Agnew 2001; Bieler 2002; Bohle 2006). Assessments of costs and benefits reflect prior theoretical assumptions about the interests of various groups and classes within society. Assumptions that eastern European member states will close the development gap are based on comparative advantage conceptions that are implausible, at least in relations between highly unequal units. Enlargement has been shaped not only by states but also by European and global capital. Realist and constructivist approaches have tended to focus on the development of institutions, *forms*, and rhetorical bases of interactions but have overlooked the structural power of capital and underlying social purposes of arrangements. Finally, the emphasis on solidarity does not adequately explain the power relations between member and candidate states. Enlargement has resulted in nominal equality but has also served to reproduce the power of transnational European capital over the new member states. Full Union membership played an important role in facilitating market discipline and the penetration of western capital on a scale that might otherwise not have been possible. Nominal equality also had an important compensatory function for populations whose standard of living declined precipitously due to enlargement. The widespread disenchantment with the 'Washington consensus' in Latin America and Asia has found little echo among eastern European elites or populations that have strongly embraced neoliberalism and membership in NATO and the EU.

The community norm of solidarity undoubtedly played an important role in mobilizing public opinion behind the decision to admit the eastern European states to full membership. Yet in practice the norms—in cohesion policy, free movement of labour, Justice and Home Affairs (JHA) *acquis*, and agricultural assistance—have been violated in ways that are unprecedented in the history of the EU. Indeed, 'the impact of solidarity on the EU's enlargement policy is weaker at the level of substantive policy-making than at the start of the enlargement process' (Jileva 2004: 18–19). The absence of solidarity— and the concomitant persistence of nationalism—have been most notable in two crucial sectors: energy and money. The most powerful member states have established bilateral ties with Russia at the expense of new member states (Leonard and Popescu 2007). The ECB and the Commission have rigidly applied Maastricht criteria to central and eastern European applicants to EMU even as they have repeatedly acquiesced in the bending or even abandonment of stability pact rules for the 'old' member states.

Underlying the political economy of enlargement is the structural power of European and US capital. Although the Commission took the lead in the negotiation with candidate countries and implementation of the enlargements, the ERT played a 'pivotal' role, just as it had with the EMU:

Of the crucial issues that have dominated the ERT's agenda since its formation in 1983, eastward enlargement is on a par with the creation of the single market in the 1980s and of the single currency in the 1990s.

Bohle (2006: 71; see also Carchedi 2001; van Apeldoorn 2002)

The structural power of US and European capital was reinforced through the exercise of US geopolitical power. The dual track enlargements of NATO and the EU served to entrench the power of transnational business interests across Europe, linked to the US and the neoliberal project. Europe's political dependence on the US has thus marginalized forces in 'core Europe' that favour alternatives to neoliberalism (van der Pijl 2001; Cafruny and Ryner 2007).

Policy towards the new member states was based on two pillars: shock therapy and foreign investment (Ivanova 2007). Existing trade and industrial linkages based on the Soviet-led Council for Mutual Economic Assistance were broken; the state was recast drastically to reduce redistributive and investment functions. Unprecedented structural adjustment could be induced through rapid privatization, price liberalization, and the penetration of foreign capital. Foreign aid was used to facilitate the sale of state assets to foreign investors. Crucial to this process were the activities of the European Bank of Reconstruction and Development (EBRD): initially conceived of as a purely European institution with currency and debt management responsibilities, it became open to US capital and was given a highly restricted remit to support private sector and foreign-funded projects. The contrast between the EU's policy towards central and eastern Europe and the Marshall Plan is striking:

Financial assistance to Eastern Europe has largely been of a symbolic nature and was never meant to play a significant economic role. It is quite obvious that massive amounts of foreign aid coupled with debt relief would have been inconsistent with the strategy of maximizing profit opportunities for foreign investors and Western credit agencies. Moreover, the meager aid that was made available was disbursed in a way which secured that the bulk of it went into the pockets of Western firms and consultants for capitalism, with the whole enterprise amounting to a symbolic 'Marshall Plan of advice'.

Ivanova (2007: 363)

According to the neoliberal paradigm, foreign direct investment should have engendered balanced industrial development, productivity gains, and export-led growth, tapping into abundant pools of skilled labour. In reality, adherence to market principles has exacerbated the acute problems of post-socialist transition. It has led to a model of accumulation based on cheap labour and trade-dependence on western Europe, especially Germany. Strategic sectors of the central and eastern European economies, including banking, telecommunications, and utilities, have been privatized and sold to Western firms.

The new member states have borne significant social costs of this structural adjustment. Social inequality has increased dramatically while high levels of unemployment have persisted. Despite rapid growth, standards of living have fallen precipitously (Dunford 2005). Only Slovenia recovered its pre-transition level on the UN human development index by 2005 (Ivanova 2007: 372). In 2007, Romania and Bulgaria remained well below the level of 1989 (United Nations Development Program 2008; Lisbon Council 2007). Many central and eastern European economies have become heavily exposed to borrowing in foreign countries and vulnerable to global financial disorder by virtue of massive current account deficits. By 2004, debt service payments accounted for 25 per cent of Hungary's, 27 per cent of Croatia's, and 35 per cent of Poland's exports (Ivanova 2007: 369; see also *The Economist* 2007; Wagstyl 2008). The accession process that started with the

Copenhagen Agreements has accordingly resulted in increasing disillusionment of citizens of new member states with EU economic policy (European Bank for Reconstruction and Development 2007).

Finally, enlargement has served to reinforce market discipline throughout the Union—either through migration, outsourcing, or competitive taxation policies. German corporations have become especially dependent on outsourcing (Lorentowicz *et al.* 2002). As Daimler Chrysler CEO Jürgen Schrempp noted in collective bargaining with IG Metall, the German metal works union: 'We were very clear in the talks: We said, "We have Poland. We have Hungary. We have the Czech Republic"' (quoted in Boudette 2004: 1). In the UK, the fear of unemployment as a result of eastern European migration and outsourcing has reduced the bargaining position of labour (Blanchflower and Shadforth 2007). Whereas expansion was defended in terms of solidarity, stability, and convergence, the reality has been the acceleration of uneven development.

Conclusion

This chapter has explored the contribution of political economy to the study of European integration. We began by situating EU studies within the context of broader trends in the social sciences. Seeking to understand the nature and limits of integration, political scientists tended either to remain within the sphere of power politics (intergovernmentalism) or to propose an implicitly normative template under which the arbitrary exercise of power could be checked by rational administration (functionalism). At the same time, the 'economics of integration' became a specialized domain for (neoclassical) economics. The crisis of the Bretton Woods system—with its concomitant destabilizing impact on European politics—exposed the limitations of these approaches. By throwing a spotlight on the political dimensions of international economic affairs, the crisis revived international political economy. It also reinvigorated comparative political economy, as it became important to understand the nature of European varieties of capitalism on their own terms.

Because it seeks to situate the political world within the broader structure of social power relations, critical political economy relates developments in the EU to the constraints and opportunities of capitalism. Hence, it focuses on the socio-economic content of policies and developments and distinguishes between two very different projects of integration: the modest or 'shallow' European initiatives of the post-war Fordist era, characterized by an 'embedded liberal' social content and the 'deeper' neoliberal integration of the post-Fordist era. Supranational institutions and ideas have not been, in themselves, the most important factors driving European integration. Rather, they have played a decisive role only to the extent that they have successfully articulated the interests and strategies of the dominant national, regional, and transatlantic social forces.

We hasten to add, however, that between critical political economy and alternative theoretical perspectives that insist on the causal primacy of ideas and institutions there is much room for dialogue. The emphasis on structure does not imply that structures can exist outside the beliefs and practices of agents or that the strategies of agents are not important. Nor does it propose a form of reductionism whereby institutions take on a purely passive role as expressions of class or group interest. Rather, it assumes that agents are always situated in structural relationships that give them a partial view of the terrain on which they operate and partial capacities to shape institutions and structures.

From the perspective of critical political economy, the contemporary predicament of the EU does not arise naturally from a crisis of integration per se or the growing pains that might inevitably be expected to arise as the Union enlarges and governance is gradually shifted from the nation state to supranational institutions. Rather, Europe's contemporary predicament results from the internal contradictions and limitations of a neoliberal post-Fordism, wherein European capitalism is interiorized in a subordinate way with American capitalism. Critical political economy helps to illuminate the nature and scope of this predicament with respect to monetary union and enlargement. Neither initiative has given rise to deepening political integration and substantive solidarity. Nor have these initiatives overcome Europe's chronic problems of slow growth and uneven development. Yet this analysis does not imply that a return to national state strategies represents a viable alternative. To be sure, Europe possesses the abstract potential to translate its undoubted economic resources, critical mass, and productive self-sufficiency into a more dynamic growth trajectory and reinvigorated social citizenship. But current arrangements prevent monetary policy from supporting any sort of fiscal policy (whether through an expansion of the European budget or coordination of the national budgets) or an effective 'Marshall Plan' for central and eastern Europe through a radically beefed-up European Investment Bank and greatly expanded structural fund. These are firmly entrenched in the treaties and would require unanimity to be changed even as the problems generated by the EMU in its present form are fragmenting rather than uniting the member states. Since the Maastricht Treaty, Europe's leaders have managed to maintain the cohesion of the euro-zone—and the expanding Union—through flexibility, selective enforcement, exhortation, and the absence of viable alternatives. As regional and global economic turbulence increases, the ability of these leaders to sustain cohesion will be tested.

■ NOTES

1. What follows is a summary of Wolf (1997: 8–10).

2. This is based on an abstract-analytical construct by Vilfredo Pareto. It refers to exchange whereby all parties in the exchange are better off compared to their situation prior to the exchange. It should be noted that Pareto optimality is concerned exclusively with absolute gains in welfare at the aggregate level. It is not concerned with whether some have gained much more than others (relative gains). Neoclassical economics holds that market forces and free price-formation ensure that all potentially Pareto-optimal exchanges are realized and that non-Pareto-optimal exchanges are avoided.

3. An optimal currency area requires that quantities of commodities and factors of production (such as labour and capital) are mobile enough to respond to asymmetric shocks, whereby either supply or demand conditions change in favour of one locale over another. In neoclassical economic theory, in the absence of these conditions, flexible exchange rates serve as shock-absorbers that make it easier to macroeconomically adjust (combat inflation or unemployment, for instance) locales to the new situation. This makes it far from straightforward that the reduction of transaction costs, which a single currency no doubt implies, necessarily results in Pareto-optimal outcomes.

4. The Bretton Woods system of international monetary affairs is generally considered to be the linch-pin of post-Second World War Atlanticist modified liberalism. This was a fixed exchange rate system with currencies pegged to the US dollar, which in turn was pegged to gold. The fixed exchange rates provided a stable framework for the expansion of trade, but it also contained administrative mecha-nisms, such as the interstate network of the IMF, that would support currencies in case of exchange rate turbulence and mutual recognition of capital and exchange rate controls, which enabled states to pursue macroeconomic policy. The system presupposed US capacities to underpin the system, which were progressively undermined in the 1960s.

5. The Empty Chair crisis of 1965 is generally seen as breaking the integrationist momentum that com-menced with the Schuman Plan. French President Charles de Gaulle called the Commission's bluff in a conflict over taxation power. The outcome was the Luxembourg Compromise which affirmed the right of states to exercise veto in the Council of Ministers on matters of fundamental national interest and reined in the power of the Commission vis-à-vis nation states. The collapse of the Werner Plan of European monetary union in the early 1970s added further to disintegrationist ten-dencies and clearly reveals the link between European integration and Atlanticism. The Werner Plan was meant to build on the edifice of Bretton Woods and could not survive its collapse. The 'Snake in the Tunnel' represented a set of more modest attempts to limit the variation of exchange rate between European currencies that ultimately failed because of differences in macroeconomic doctrine and circumstances. Nevertheless, the Snake was in many respects a precursor to the European Monetary System (EMS) and the EMU, which proved more successful in the subsequent era of a permissive neoliberal consensus.

6. Negative integration is the type of integration that occurs when states agree to cease to intervene in social and economic affairs (for instance, the increase of trade resulting from the removal of tariffs). This is in contrast to positive integration that denotes common policies (such as the Common Agri-cultural Policy).

7. Monopoly capitalism is a key concept of Marxist theories of imperialism and was developed by Hilferding, Bukharin, Lenin, and others in the early part of the twentieth century, on the basis of the observation that market competition among small units was being replaced by concentration and imperfect competition between oligopolies that tended to give way to trusts and monopolies. These tended also to break down the liberal formal separation between the state and the economy as overt influence by the monopoly capitalist on the state became increasingly apparent. In Marxist theory, this is seen as inherent in the dialectical development of capitalism as it expresses the development of the forces of production coming into contradiction with the social relations of production of the market system, generating crisis tendencies such as the outbreak of the First World War (and eventu-ally also the Second World War).

8. 'Comprador bourgeoisie' refers to dependent development in the Third World, where merchants are the dominant class, and with their interests primarily geared towards selling raw material commodi-ties on the world market with little interest in developing an independent productive base in the domestic social formation.

■ GUIDE TO FURTHER READING

Bieler, A. and Morton, A. (2001) *Social Forces in the Making of New Europe* (London: Palgrave). Drawing upon neo-Gramscian theory the authors analyse the rise of neoliberal social forces in Europe.

Cafruny, A. and Ryner, M. (2007) *Europe at Bay: Neoliberal Hegemony and Transformation in Europe* (Boulder, CO: Lynne Rienner). The authors argue that the internal contradictions of the EU's neoliberal project and continuing subordination to the United States greatly diminishes prospects for European economic development and political unity and autonomy.

Cafruny, A. and Ryner, M. (eds) (2003) *A Ruined Fortress? Neoliberal Hegemony and Transformation in Europe* (Lanham, MD: Rowman and Littlefield). This anthology presents research on
the theory and practice of Europe's neoliberal project by leading scholars of critical political
economy.

van Apeldoorn, B. (2002) *Transnational Capitalism and the Struggle over European Integration*
(London: Routledge). The author explores the role played by transnational European capital—
spearheaded by the European Roundtable—in the EU's 'relaunching'.

——, Horn, L., and Drahokoupil, J. (eds) (2008) *Contradictions and Limits of Neoliberal European
Governance: From Lisbon to Lisbon* (London: Palgrave). This anthology analyses the contradictions and tensions arising from European integration.

■ STUDY QUESTIONS

1. What factors account for the re-emergence of political economy during the 1970s?

2. Assess how critical political economy draws upon insights from neo-Marxism, the 'varieties of
    capitalism', and 'politics of international relations' literatures.

3. Most theoretical approaches assume that EMU is a force for greater European regional integration
    and solidarity. Yet critical political economy suggests that EMU generates simultaneously forces
    leading to disintegration and integration. Trace and assess the mode of reasoning that leads to this
    conclusion.

4. Why are critical political economists less sanguine about the benefits of Eastern enlargement for the
    'new' European member states?

5. Assess the advantages and disadvantages for the study of the EU of the interdisciplinary (or better,
    post-disciplinary) approach that critical political economy represents.

13 Taking Stock of Integration Theory

Antje Wiener and Thomas Diez

Introduction

This volume sought to achieve two goals. First, it was compiled to assess the state of the art in European integration theorizing. To that end, we brought together a group of scholars who are able to present and reflect upon the core theoretical contributions that have been developed since the early stages of analysing European integration and governance. The second goal of the book was the generation of a critical discussion about the object and process of theorizing European integration as such. To that end, the choice of contributions reflects the variation in disciplinary context, historical stage of theorizing, and the comparative dimension of approaches. This analytical dimension of the book is sustained by the 'best' and 'test' case scenarios. While authors did not necessarily apply these precise terms, all chapters demonstrate how their respective approaches work best, and then turn—sometimes with a little less enthusiasm—to comment on how their theoretical approach would address the issue of European enlargement (see e.g. 'easy' and 'difficult' cases in the contribution by Moravcsik and Schimmelfennig). That is, all contributors have been asked to comment on their respective approaches' value added when applied to the issue of European enlargement. Based on this pattern, it is now possible to compare the chapters and test the robustness of each approach. This second revised and expanded edition of *European Integration Theory* is able to base the comparative assessment on more detailed references to the now completed round of massive, primarily eastern European enlargement.

This concluding chapter brings the past-present-future theme running through the book as well as through each contribution, to a close. In the remaining sections we offer first a historical overview over the type and focus of each theoretical approach to European integration developed by the contributors (past); second, we develop a comparative assessment of the respective strengths and weaknesses of each approach according to the definitions of 'theorizing' and 'integration' developed in the introductory chapter (present); and third, we critically consider the first edition's outlook on constitutional development and identify current challenges that lie ahead (future).

We argue that the different theoretical perspectives developed in the eleven contributions to this volume demonstrate an emerging robustness of European integration theory. The variation in approaching the respective 'test cases' of European enlargement reveals the need for both rigorously prescriptive and normative approaches to European integration.

The discussion of approaches covered primarily in the third part of this book demonstrates that until recently, core constitutional issues had been receiving relatively less analytical attention than approaches that seek to capture and sometimes explain institutional and regulatory processes. The latter are more closely explored in the first and second part. Yet core constitutional issues include social facts or soft institutions such as for example values and norms, identity or normative standards such as legitimacy, equality, or equal access to participation. They determine the quality of emergent transnational political orders (March and Olsen 1998; Olsen 2002a).

Since the 1990s, a 'political and intellectual stampede to embrace the idea of a constitution for Europe' (Weiler 2002: 563) has swelled and ebbed away again. To be sure, the 'constitution is no longer a taboo' in integration discourse (Pernice 2001: 3–4). The constitutionalization of the Treaties has become an accepted policy objective for a while now[1] and an expression of a perhaps short-lived constitutional turn in the EU. However, with the French and Dutch 'no' votes in their respective referenda on the Constitutional Treaty, this highpoint of constitutionalism in Europe has come to a rather abrupt, if not entirely unexpected, end. Nonetheless, at the time of writing there is still some leverage for ratification of a quasi-constitutional treaty in the form of the Lisbon Treaty, or an amended version, as one potential outcome at this stage of the EU's constitutional process.

Venturing into the constitutional turn meant engaging with the process of integration through deepening more directly. It has generated results that have been unwelcome to those who had praised the constitutional convent as a prime example of democratic deliberation and transparency. Yet the language of constitutionalism has raised concerns with many European voters, and created a new opportunity for Eurosceptics. Together these political forces have been able to pull the brakes of deepening and to return to the probed and slow, if cumbersome, process of gradual treaty revisions instead of bold constitutional change. The pressure of constitution-building has thus raised the stakes of transnational politics. While it did not turn into the make or break of the project of European integration (as we speculated in the first edition), it has revealed gaps in the constitutional and political structure of the EU as a polity, especially with a view to establishing equal access to participation for all members, i.e. old and new states as well as directly elites and other citizens. For example, learning, accessibility, and democratic legitimization remain to be addressed more fully, and—importantly—based on shared discussions with the new member states.

Over the first 50 years supranational European integration evolved from the pre-integration time of cooperation under anarchy, a long period of cooperation towards integration, a long but largely invisible period of constitution-building towards a new phase in which the European Union is taking on a more active role in international politics. Thus, during the first decade of the twenty-first century the European Union has taken on a substantial role as a civilian or, as some would argue, 'normative' power on the world stage. This is a surprising turn, when compared to the policy documents of the 1970s when the search for a 'European identity' and the EU's role as an 'actor in world politics' was on (for summaries, see e.g. Dinan 2006; Wiener 1998, ch. 3 of that volume). In light of the world economic crisis and the Cold War politics that structured most of the world's international relations at the time, the then European Economic Community's influence was rather minimal. The turn towards the EU's emergent impact on world politics as a 'normative power' (Manners 2002, 2006) is less surprising in light of the mosaic of integration theories presented in this book. For example, the discussion of normative standards, the role of identity, the input of routinized procedures and policy practices which is presented pretty much across the board of this book's contributions, allows for a comprehensive understanding and for concise explanations of this change in the EU's role within the wider global context.

The following sections first offer a comparative assessment of the different approaches to European integration presented in this volume ('Comparative perspective') and then map core issues and relevant research questions which European integration theories stand to elaborate more extensively in the future ('Outlook: constitutional roots and external politics in the twenty-first century').

Comparative Perspective

In the introduction, we proposed a comparison of the theoretical approaches to the analysis of European integration included in this volume along two dimensions, their purpose or function, and the specific area of integration they study. We also argued that the different approaches together would form a mosaic providing a multifaceted and never complete picture of European integration and governance. To demonstrate this, we asked contributors to present a case that they thought their approach addressed particularly well ('best case'), as well as to apply their approach to the 'test case' of enlargement. Our expectation was that contributors would select different aspects of European integration and governance as their 'best case', which they would analyse for different purposes. Furthermore, we expected that they would approach the analysis of EU enlargement from different angles, depending on the main purpose of their approach, and focusing consequently on different aspects or areas of enlargement. If this was the case, the various approaches would neither be directly comparable or testable against each other, nor would they be incompatible. Instead, they could be seen as each shedding a different light on European integration and governance, and therefore adding another stone to the mosaic of integration theory.

Overall, the chapters in this volume have met our expectations, as the overview provided by Table 13.1 demonstrates. With a few exceptions, the best cases differ widely, and where they overlap, such as in liberal intergovernmentalism's and neofunctionalism's attempt to explain outcomes of integration, they focus on different aspects of the integration process, which are not mutually exclusive, even though their relative importance can be tested empirically. Similarly, the selected 11 approaches have very different things to say about enlargement. They focus, for example, on the explanation of enlargement (Moravcsik and Schimmelfennig; Pollack; Risse), an analysis of the demands of enlargement on EU institutions (Pollack; Peterson; Niemann with Schmitter), a critical assessment of the effects of enlargement on the societies within the new member states, in terms of economic equality or the expected differential treatment of women and men despite the implementation of the conditionality rules that preceded enlargement (Cafruny and Ryner; Locher and Prugl)—or admit that they have little to contribute to

Table 13.1 Comparative perspective

Chapter number	Author	Approach	Best case	Test case (enlargement)
2	Burgess	Federalism	Normative: constitutional evolution	Normative: maintaining *acquis communautaire*
3	Niemann with Schmitter	Neofunctionalism	Explaining integration outcomes (in cycles)	Predicting effects of enlargement on spillover
4	Moravcsik and Schimmelfennig	Liberal intergovernmentalism	Explaining the consolidation of the Single Market	Explaining outcomes of bargaining in membership negotiations
5	Peters and Pierre	Governance approaches	Describing changes to governance and assessing their normative implications	Describing and assessing the effects of enlargement for governance
6	Peterson	Policy networks	Explaining policy outcomes in CAP	Predicting effects of enlargement on policy networks
7	Pollack	New institutionalism	Explaining executive, judicial, and legislative politics	Explaining decision to enlarge, outcome of negotiations, and effect
8	Risse	Social constructivism	Understanding the construction of European/ national identity	Explaining the EU's decision to enlarge
9	Wæver	Discursive approaches	Explaining/critically assessing policies towards integration	Critically assessing enlargement discourse; explaining decision to enlarge
10	Locher and Prügl	Gender approaches	Explaining/understanding and critically assessing policy, politics, and theories of European integration	Critically assessing enlargement discourse; explaining decision to enlarge
11	Bellamy with Attucci	Political theory	Understanding and scrutinizing processes of polity formation according to normative standards of legitimacy	Pointing towards enlargement as a potential test case of the prevalence, legitimacy, and endurance of the norms which had been constituted through European integration
12	Cafruny and Ryner	Political economy	Explaining economic policy (especially Single Market) in order to highlight societal problems	Critically assessing the incorporation of new member states into liberal market model

this discussion (Bellamy and Attucci), thereby making these approaches more appropriate for the analysis of deepening integration than for the purpose of analysing the territorial scope of membership.

Taking the test case as an example, the emerging mosaic of enlargement is one that focuses first on the decision of the European Union to enlarge (Pollack, Risse, Wæver), proposing that norms and previous commitments were decisive in this respect. Generally, the decision to apply for EU membership by the candidate countries is seen as less problematic—the puzzle in the case of the EU is that rationalist explanations are ultimately not convincing. However, this does not mean that the membership candidacies are uncontested, or that there were no important bargaining processes between the EU and its current member states and the candidate countries, explaining the outcome of which is at the core of the liberal intergovernmentalist agenda (Moravcsik and Schimmelfennig). Given the focus on explanation in their best cases, surprisingly many contributors were concerned with the effect of enlargement. They predict, perhaps less surprisingly, that European governance and further integration will become more complicated: spillover may be hindered (Niemann with Schmitter); that the problem of the 'joint decision-making trap' as described by Scharpf (1988) may become even more of a problem (Peters and Pierre); and that inexperienced civil servants may make decision-making more difficult, while reform of governance will be less likely due to the increased number of member states (Peterson); and path-dependency may dictate continued variation and therefore increased administrative complexity, while Europeanization may decrease this problem but only in the long run (Pollack). Given these complications, a federalist is, from a normative point of view, alarmed, and insists that the *acquis* cannot be jeopardized (Burgess). Finally, discursive and gender approaches, respectively, add critical voices as to the terms on which enlargement proceeds (Wæver) and the effect it has on the gendered structures of social relations in the new member states as well as across the EU (Locher and Prügl).

It should be obvious that such an account is incomplete in a double sense. First, it is a reflection of the most pressing questions that have been raised for European integration theory so far, but others will remain, to be sure. After the new member states had joined, for instance, competing explanations of the outcome of the negotiation processes have been put forward and assessed, and more specific questions about both domestic and EU institutional effects of enlargement have been asked. Secondly, both the angle provided on enlargement by each contribution, as well as the selected best case and how to approach it, do not necessarily cover all the work done from within one particular approach. With this caveat in mind, Table 13.2 represents an attempt to approximate what we call a 'mosaic of European integration theory' by filling in the boxes of Table 1.2. Whatever the limitations of such an exercise, we do suggest that a debate about where one would preferably place each approach contributes to a better understanding both from the perspective of the editors and that of the readers.

Three features of the table immediately catch the eye and need to be addressed. The first and probably least problematic one is that a number of approaches appear twice, whereas gender approaches appear four times. In these chapters, there is a differentiation between different strands that result in more radically different variations than in

Table 13.2 The functions and areas of (integration) theory

	Polity	Policy	Politics
Explanatory/understanding	Neofunctionalism; liberal intergovernmentalism	Policy network; discursive approaches; political economy	New institutionalism; social constructivism
Analytical/descriptive	Governance	Governance; gender approaches	Governance
Critical/normative	Federalism; governance; normative political theory; gender approaches	Discursive approaches; gender approaches; political economy	Gender approaches; normative political theory

the case of, for example, neo-institutionalism. Among the discursive approaches, there is a split between those trying to explain member states' policies towards integration and those problematizing the assumptions on which integration policies are based, although in practice both enterprises often go hand in hand. Gender analysis is clearly the most prolific approach, generating multiple perspectives on both theory and practice. The table sustains our argument that it is preferable to see integration theory as a mosaic in which different perspectives come together in their own right. Ultimately, the problem with the grand theory route that tries to combine different approaches into a single framework, is that it has to impose particular ontological and epistemological assumptions on the analytical possibilities included within this framework. Those closer to a narrow scientific understanding of theory may see this as a good thing, but it does not conform with the spirit of theoretical diversity, and doing justice to the different purposes and areas of theory as set out in Chapter 1.

The second and perhaps most obvious characteristic of Table 13.2 is—except for gender approaches and governance—the absence of entries in the 'analytical/descriptive' row. In Chapter 1, we proposed that it was one of the functions of theory to provide new conceptualizations of particular social and political phenomena, and that this was particularly important in relation to the EU as a new kind of polity. We further argued that European integration theory evolved in phases, starting, after a period of normative pre-theorizing, with an explanatory phase, which was then followed by an analytical phase as the EU was taken more seriously as a polity of its own right in the 1980s, and then by a renewed interest in normative questions, and, following the epistemological debates in the wider social sciences, in problematizing European integration and governance and particular policies.

A revised model of the three phases of theorizing would locate the approaches within the historical context of integration. From a hermeneutic standpoint, it is interesting to observe how these phases reflect distinct theoretical foci in relation to the relevance and place of institutions in theory and practice. Thus European integration theory develops gradually including the three phases of integration (explaining integration as supranational institution-building, Part One of this book), Europeanization (analysing governance, Part Two of this book), and politicization (constructing the polity, Part Three of this book). Table 13.3 summarizes the three phases and their respective focus on institution-building.

As this book's contributions demonstrate, the first two phases are well-developed sets of theoretical approaches. The third phase has begun to shed light on substantial constitutional questions such as the legal status of the EU, the constitutional status of the Charter of Rights, the role of the Church, and the application of Qualified Majority Voting in high politics such as Common Foreign and Security Policy.[4] It is strengthened by the increasing appreciation of the EU as a powerful civilian actor in world politics. This is not only due to a stronger role in the foreign policy portfolio (Whitman and Manners 2000). It is also demonstrated by a positive influence on de-escalating border conflicts (Diez *et al.* 2008). In addition, recent studies have suggested that the EU's experience with cross-border justice and home affairs policy has also sustained the EU's perception as a civilian power (Edwards and Meyer 2008). These issues lead beyond the erstwhile considerably radical challenges of political relations beyond nation state boundaries, presented by the practice of pooling sovereignty as well as by the legal principles of supremacy and direct effect— and their potentially unintended consequences that have sunk in with social scientists only gradually (Craig and de Búrca 1998).

Table 13.3 Three phases of theorizing European integration

Phase	Focus	Place	Dynamic
	Normative pretheorizing	World politics	
1960–85	Integration	Supranational level	Bottom-up
1985–	Europeanization	Domestic, regional level in member and candidate countries	Top-down
1993–	Politicization	Europolity	Trickle-across, bottom-up, top-down

A closer look at the governance approach, the policy network approach, and new insti-tutionalism in Part Two demonstrates that they do take integration and the EU as a new kind of polity as a given, and therefore shift the emphasis from explaining or advocating integration to questions about how governance within this new polity works. Yet it also emerges from these chapters that none of these approaches is content with the provision of new conceptualizations of governance alone, although this was an important con-tribution to the debate. Instead, they strive to explain specific phenomena within this system of governance, such as particular policies or particular aspects of its politics. While they are, in this sense, analysing governance rather than explaining integration as such, they are moving beyond the analysis of governance in the sense of a purpose of theory as set out in Chapter 1.

As Table 13.2 highlights, the predominant purpose of theoretical approaches within European integration theory is to explain or understand either the process of integration and its outcomes, or particular aspects of European integration and governance. Even an approach such as discourse analysis, the roots of which can be traced to post-structuralism, is used at least by some in European integration theory to understand member states' poli-cies towards integration, and although its usage of the term 'explanation' is different from its usage, say, in liberal intergovernmentalism, the purpose is sufficiently similar to the latter's—indeed, Wæver (1998b: 103–4) in his own work sets out explicitly to bridge the gap between critique and explanation. This heavy bias towards explanation may be seen as one symptom of the tendency to make claims beyond the scope of one's theory, which we have identified as problematic in our introduction. Be this as it may, the emphasis on the expla-nation of particular integration policies and outcomes in terms of polity has until recently led to a relative neglect of addressing the issue of politicization, both in the form of attempts to analyse the increasing politicization of integration and governance among societies, and in the form of contributing to a critical debate about the desired shape of the EU.

Outlook: Constitutional Roots and External Politics in the Twenty-first Century

How do integration theories fare 50 years on? What is the state of the discipline which has now developed an impressive corpus of texts, produced a stable research context based on international learned associations, and has, last but not least, generated a widely acknowledged teaching profile? The discipline now encompasses a broad spectrum of theoretical approaches ranging from the period of normative pre-integration theorizing that emerged largely from US-American IR theory (see, most prominently, Mitrany's as well as Deutsch's work) via grand theory debates (Hoffmann, Haas, Schmitter, Deutsch, Lindberg, and Scheingold) to a more refined set of approaches in the early twenty-first century. This volume presents a selection of its core approaches. The overview of the past, present, and future of theorizing about European integration suggests that as an increasingly independent subfield in the social sciences, integration theory has come full circle *and* been able to move towards the proverbial higher plane. The following briefly elaborates on this observation.

Given that in the early days of integration theory, normative issues of integration were discussed within the framework of international relations theory, bringing in interest-oriented and institutional approaches to world politics, it appears that in the light of today's clearly discernable and distinguished, albeit interdisciplinary European studies discipline, theoretical approaches to integration have moved on. More specifically, the normative dimension of European integration is back on the table. However, the focus has changed. While in the 1950s the theoretical emphasis on explaining regional integration and supranational institution-building was put on the necessity and probability of endur-ing institutions in the international system of sovereign states with a view to constructing a civilized Kantian world community, today's normative approach is focused on the issue of democratic legitimacy (or the lack of it) under conditions of supranational constitu-tional integration. This shift from the former normative perspective on world politics that built on the idealist Grotian tradition in IR, to conditions of democratic governance in regionally integrated political orders, is embedded in a broad change in IR theories regarding the acceptance of institutions in world politics. Thus, institutional approaches developed both inside and outside European integration theories have contributed to a widely accepted role of 'hard' institutions such as international organizations, treaties, conventions, and written agreements in world politics (March and Olsen 1989, 1998; Hall and Taylor 1996; Ruggie 1998; Onuf 2002). In particular, the various new institutional-isms have been able to sustain the role of institutions in world politics as enhancing coop-eration among states, monitoring policy implementation, facilitating information, and safeguarding norms (Keohane 1988; Garrett 1992; Goldstein and Keohane 1993; Pollack 1996; see also the Pollack and Risse chapters in this volume, respectively).

With its explicit focus on finality, community, and a constitutionalized polity, the dual process of enlargement and constitution-building presents a challenge to the majority of integration theories that study interests and institutions. The limit of such an exclusive focus compared with approaches that allow for a broader perspective on polity formation, governance, and constitutional principles is thus brought to the fore. This challenge is well presented by the choice of best and test cases by the contributors of this volume, and the fact that far more contributors chose to focus on the effects of enlargement than on its explanation, while explanation dominated in the selection of best cases. Surely, interests and institutions play a key role in explaining enlargement. The pressure for institutional change which has been created by the massive enlargement process launched in Copen-hagen 1993, affects member states and candidate countries as well as the Europolity itself.

Problematizing both institutional change and adaptation on the one hand, as well as the interest in enlargement on the other, can therefore be characterized as organic research objectives. Logically, they build on a long-standing tradition of explaining institution-building on the supranational level as well as institutional adaptation, or, Europeanization in the respective domestic member state contexts. Yet, different from previous enlargement rounds, this time constitutional reform has developed a much stronger momentum than previous Treaty revisions at intergovernmental conferences (Christiansen and Jørgensen 1999; Moravcsik and Nicolaïdes 1999; Falkner and Nentwich 2000; Wiener and Neunreither 2000; de Búrca and Scott 2000; Beaumont *et al.* 2002; Bogdandy 2003; Weiler and Wind 2003; Tully 2006; Schimmelfennig and Rittberger 2006; Rosamond and Wincott 2006; Shaw 2007; Walker and Loughlin 2007).

Constitutional politics has turned into a political issue in the EU. More specifically, in distinction from states that cooperate under anarchy in world politics, on the one hand, and EU member states that have been cooperating towards integration, on the other (Wiener 2002), the current EU member states and, albeit to a limited extent, candidate countries have been cooperating towards a shared constitutional agreement. The constitutional turn has generated a new importance of constitutional norms, principles, and routinized practices. These so-called 'soft' institutions have been addressed by a large and growing literature on constructivism in IR, that studied the influence of world views, principled beliefs, routinized practices, and norms to the fore (Kratochwil and Ruggie 1986; Katzenstein 1993, 1996; Sikkink 1993; Koslowski and Kratochwil 1994; Risse-Kappen 1996; Ruggie 1998; Wiener 2002). In European integration studies, the constructivist focus on soft institutions has offered a new interdisciplinary perspective on European integration as a process that involves the constitutionalization of shared European norms, principles, and procedures including both law and the social sciences.

In sum, the constitutional turn in the 1990s and the constitutional 'no' votes raise deeper questions about the constitutive role of *social practices* and (*social*) *legitimacy* in supranational politics more generally. While the constitutional turn pinpointed the debate over the impact of social and material facts, respectively (as the rationalist versus constructivist debates demonstrate quite well), the constitutional votes in the following decade highlighted the impact of invisible yet powerful implications attached to the 'language' of constitutionalism. In fact, it could be argued that, had the constitutional optimists not sped up the constitutional process before its time, many might not have cared to object, i.e. a treaty amendment following routine treaty revisions over the years of European integration might have gone unnoticed to many, while actually implying the same factual change. Consequently, the role of language and, more generally, discourse approaches that are able to reveal distinct patterns of cultural validation became vital for a better understanding of the no-votes in France and the Netherlands (Wiener 2008).

While the EU is a non-state, it does evolve around and works on the basis of core constitutional norms, principles, and procedures akin to the central constitutional reference frame of national states such as the rule of law, fundamental and citizenship rights, and the principle of democracy (Article 6, Treaty on European Union) and some thus endorse the concept of European constitutional law.[5] These fundamental—constitutional—principles have evolved over time in interrelation with the fundamental constitutional principles and practices of the respective EU member states.[6] Their substance carries meaning created through a process from which candidate countries are by definition excluded. The routinized practices, procedures, and norms that have been constitutive for the constitutionalization of these fundamental principles therefore remain a foreign discourse with little meaning for candidate countries that were excluded from their constitution.[7] Politically speaking, different understandings generate issues of conflict. As a research theme, conflictive developments that are brought to the fore by the double process of enlargement and constitutional revision raise different types of research questions, pending on the perspective, goal, and context from which the issue is assessed. Thus, for example, from a prescriptive analytical standpoint certain institutional conditions are necessary (types of constitution; political order; types of democracy; etc.). In turn, a normative analytical standpoint would focus on the question of whether it is possible, and if so, how to establish particular constitutional principles to keep such a diverse polity with its different understandings together.

Conclusion

This volume's contributions have demonstrated that theorizing European integration involves at least three main factors. They include the choice of the *research object* (polity: supranational institution-building; policy: specific EU policies or member states' policies towards integration; politics: quality of integration), the analytical *research purpose* (explanatory/understanding; descriptive/analytical; normative/critical), and the *context* in which the research project has been designed (historical and disciplinary perspectives). The choice of research object and purpose does matter. It generates a distinct theoretical focus and impact which is highlighted by the volume's organization in three parts presenting at least three core theoretical perspectives in three different phases of European integration. These phases are distinguished according to the respective analytical focus on explaining integration (Part One), analysing governance (Part Two), and constructing the Europolity (Part Three). In order to substantiate the main message of each approach, the contributors have been asked to choose a best case scenario (quality of governance; market consolidation; labour market policy; committee governance; agricultural policy; constitutional policy; and so forth) and then, in addition, apply their respective analytical perspective to the test case scenario of enlargement. The combination of best and test case scenarios in all contributions demonstrates nicely how research object and goal are subject to the choice of the individual researcher, yet never under conditions of their own choosing. The clearly opposing views in each part sustain this point.

While theoretical approaches do indeed raise general questions that are shared by a range of different approaches, for example the questions of how to explain institution-building above the state, how to account for governance as a process that develops across national boundaries, and how to assess the emergence of a sociopolitical system critically, their respective ways of addressing these questions are not necessarily *competitive*. They are first and foremost *complementary* in style.

These observations, above all, invite the student of European integration not to think in closed boxes and traditions, but creatively about theorizing European integration and governance, and not to dismiss other approaches all too easily. They also ask those engaged in this process of theorizing to perhaps be more humble than has been the case in the past, and to be aware of the scope of the approach proposed and its place in the overall mosaic of *European Integration Theory*. Finally, they propose to take a closer look at the issues involved in the linked processes of constitutionalization and politicization (see Table 13.3).

The mosaic of integration theory will never be finished. In order to keep providing fresh and relevant perspectives, however, it will have to be pushed forward by creativity, self-reflexivity, and the study of fundamental issues underlying the core debates of past, present, and future.

▦ NOTES

1. See, for example, European Parliament, Committee of Institutional Affairs (2000), Report on the Constitutionalisation of the Treaties, Final A5–0289/2000, PE 286.949.

2. As Dieter Grimm notes:

   > [W]hen a constitution for Europe is talked about today, what is meant is a basic legal order for the polity of the sort that arose at the end of the eighteenth century in the wake of two successful revolutions in America and in France . . .

   > (Grimm 1995: 284)

   For the discussion of the term see an overview with Schepel (2000), and an extensive discussion with Craig (2001).

3. However, the European constitutional debate is characterized by the absence of a shared constitutionalist approach. As Armin von Bogdandy notes '[T]he divergence in approach and even the lack in systematic approaches to European Union law render an assessment of key approaches, main directions, and plausible decisions in the constitutional debate, an enormously complex exercise' (Bogdandy 2000: 209). Indeed, to some it appears 'astonishing that so many scholars and politicians speak about the future constitution of Europe' (Zuleeg 2001: 1).

4. See the draft text of the Treaty that was intended to establish a 'Constitution' of the EU, and which was adopted by members of the *Convention on the Future of Europe*, Brussels, 13 June 2003. For the text see: Draft Convention Volume I including Part I and Part II (CONV 797/1/03) and Volume II including Parts III, IV, and V (CONV 805/03). For the Lisbon Treaty, see *Treaty of Lisbon amending the Treaty on European Union and the Treaty establishing the European Community*, signed at Lisbon, 13 December 2007; Official Journal of the European Union; 2007/C 306/01; 17 December 2007, http://eurlex.europa.eu/JOHtml.do?uri=OJ:C:2007:306:SOM:EN:HTML.

5. The existence of European constitutional law is usually derived from the constitutionalization of the Treaties going back to the process of 'integration through law', see also Chapter 9 in this volume; for a few contributions to the burgeoning literature on the subject, see e.g. Pernice (1999); Bogdandy (1999); Weiler (1999); Walker (2002); Beaumont *et al.* (2002); Bogdandy (2003); Stone Sweet (2002).

6. This interrelation between European and member state constitutional norms, values, and understandings is well encapsulated by the concept of 'multilevel constitutionalism' developed by Ingolf Pernice; see for details Pernice (1999: 707–9).

7. In the legal literature the term 'constitutionalization' is applied with reference to the growing body of legal rules and procedures included in constitutional documents (Craig 2001; Schepel 2000).

■ **STUDY QUESTIONS**

1. Which theoretical approach to the analysis of European integration do you find most convincing and why?

2. What are the differences between the development of a 'grand theory' of European integration and a 'mosaic' of integration theory?

3. In what ways do the constitutional developments within the EU since the late 1990s challenge the state of the art in European integration theory?

4. Are the currently available approaches in European integration theory able to analyse enlargement in any interesting way?

5. Should norms play an important part in our theorizing of European integration? Is this only an empirical question?

■ REFERENCES

ABDELAL, R. (2007) *Capital Rules* (Boston, MA: Harvard University Press).

ABELS, G. (2001) 'Das "Geschlechterdemokratiedefizit" der EU: Politische Repräsentation und Geschlecht im europäischen Mehrebenensystem', in Kreisky, E., Sauer, B. and Lang, S. (eds) *EU. Geschlecht. Staat* (Vienna: WUV-Universitäts-Verlag) 185–202.

—— and BONGERT, E. (eds) (1998) 'Europäische Integration aus feministischer Perspektive', *Femina Politica*, special issue 7(2).

ACHEN, Christopher H. (2006) 'Evaluating Political Decision-Making Models', in Thomson, R., Stokman, F. N., Achen, C. H., and König, T. (eds) *The European Union Decides* (Cambridge: Cambridge University Press) 264–98.

ACHERMANN, A. (1995) 'Asylum and Immigration Policies: From Co-operation to Harmonisation', in Bieber, R. and Monar, J. (eds) *Justice and Home Affairs in the European Union: The Development of the Third Pillar* (Brussels: European Interuniversity Press) 127–40.

ACKERLY, B., STERN, M., and TRUE, J. (eds) (2006) *Feminist Methodologies for International Relations* (Cambridge: Cambridge University Press).

ADLER, E. (1997) 'Seizing the Middle Ground: Constructivism in World Politics', *European Journal of International Relations*, 3(3), 319–63.

—— (2002) 'Constructivism in International Relations', in Carlsnaes, W. *et al.* (eds) *Handbook of International Relations* (London: Sage) 95–118.

—— and BARNETT, M. (eds) (1998) *Security Communities* (Cambridge: Cambridge University Press).

AGLIETTA, M. and ORLÉAN, A., (1982) *La violence de la monnaie* (Paris: PUF).

AGNEW, J. (2001) 'How Many Europes? The European Union, Eastward Enlargement and Uneven Development', *European Urban and Regional Studies*, 8(1), 29–38.

ALBERT, M. (1993) *Capitalism against Capitalism* (London: Whurr).

—— (2003) 'Comment on Qualified Majority Voting: the Effect of the Quota', in Holler, M.J., Kliemt, H., Schmidtchen, D., and Streit, M.E.

(eds) *European Governance*, (Tübingen: Mohr Siebeck) 144–8.

ALBO, G. (1994) 'Competitive Austerity and the Impasse of Capitalist Employment Strategy', *Socialist Register*, 144–70.

ALKER, H. (1996) *Rediscoveries and Reformulations: Humanistic Methodologies for International Relations* (Cambridge: Cambridge University Press).

ALMOND, G.A. and POWELL, G.B. (1966) *Comparative Politics: A Developmental Approach* (Boston, MA: Little, Brown).

ALTER, K.J. (1998) 'Who Are the "Masters of the Treaty"? European Governments and the European Court of Justice', *International Organization*, 52(1), 121–47.

—— (2001) *Establishing the Supremacy of European Law: The Making of an International Rule of Law in Europe* (New York: Oxford University Press).

ANCHIMBE, E.A. (2008) ' "Veto the war but let no French head fall": Linguistic avoidance strategies in Jacques Chirac's pre-Iraq war interview transcripts', *Journal of Language and Politics*, 7(1), 156–70.

ANDERSEN, S.S. and ELIASSEN, K.A. (eds) (2001) *Making Policy in Europe* (London and Thousand Oaks, CA: Sage).

ANDERSON, B. (1991) *Imagined Communities. Reflections on the Origin and Spread of Nationalism*, revised edn (London and New York: Verso).

ANDERSON, L.S. (2006) 'European Union gender regulations in the East: the Czech and Polish accession process', *East European Politics and Society*, 20(1), 101–25.

ANDREWS, D. (1993) 'The Global Origins of the Maastricht Treaty on EMU: Closing the Window of Opportunity', in Cafruny, A. and Rosenthal, G. (eds) *The State of the European Community: The Maastricht Debates and Beyond* (Boulder, CO: Lynne Rienner) 107–24.

ANSELL, C.K. *et al.* (1997) 'Dual Networks in European Regional Development Policy', *Journal of Common Market Studies*, 35(3), 347–75.

APELDOORN, B. VAN (2002) *Transnational Capitalism and the Struggle over European Order* (London: Routledge).

ARMSTRONG, K. and BULMER, S. (1998) *The Governance of the Single European Market* (New York: Manchester University Press).

ASPINWALL, M.D. and SCHNEIDER, G. (eds) (2001) *The Rules of Integration: Institutionalist Approaches to the Study of Europe* (New York: Manchester University Press).

ATKINSON, T. (2002) 'Reassessing the Fundamentals: Social Inclusion and the European Union', *Journal of Common Market Studies*, 40(4), 625–43.

ATTUCCI, C. (2004) 'An Institutional Dialogue on Common Principles : Reflections on the Significance of the EU Charter of Fundamental Rights', in Dobson, L. and Foellesdal, A., *Political Theory and the European Constitution* (London: Routledge) 151–62.

—— (2006) 'European Values and Constitutional Traditions in the EU Charter of Fundamental Rights', in Heit, H. (ed.) *Die Werte Europas. Verfassungspatriotismus und Wertegemeinschaft* (Münster-Hamburg: LIT Verlag) 243–58.

AZOULAY, L. (2002) 'The Judge and the Community's Administrative Governance', in Dehousse, R. (ed.) *Good Governance in Europe's Integrated Market* (Oxford and New York: Oxford University Press) 107–37.

BACHE, I. (1998) *The Politics of European Union Regional Policy* (Sheffield: Sheffield Academic Press).

—— and FLINDERS, M.V. (2004) *Multi-Level Governance* (Oxford: Oxford University Press).

—— and GEORGE, S. (2001) *Politics in the European Union* (Oxford: Oxford University Press).

—— and JONES, R. (2000) 'Has EU regional policy empowered the regions? A study of Spain and the United Kingdom', *Regional and Federal Studies*, 10(3), 1–20.

BAILEY, M. *et al.* (1997) 'The Institutional Roots of American Trade Policy', *World Politics*, 49(3), 309–38.

BAKER, P. *et al.* (2008) 'A useful methodological synergy? Combining critical discourse analysis and corpus linguistics to examine discourses of refugees and asylum seekers in the UK press', *Discourse & Society*, 19(3), 273–306.

BALASSA, B.A. (1962) *The Theory of Economic Integration* (London: Allen and Unwin).

—— (1997) 'Trade Creation and Trade Diversion in the European Common Market: An Appraisal of the Evidence', *Manchester School of Economic and Social Studies*, 42(1), 93–135.

BALDWIN, R. *et al.* (2001) *Nice Try: Should the Treaty of Nice be Ratified?*, Monitoring European Integration 11 (London: Centre for Economic Policy Research). Consulted online 3 October 2002 at www.cepr.org/pubs/books/P140.asp.

BANCHOFF, T. (1999) 'German Identity and European Integration', *European Journal of International Relations*, 5(3), 259–90.

——and SMITH, M. (eds) (1999) *Legitimacy and the European Union: The Contested Polity* (London: Routledge).

BANERJEE, S. (1997) 'The Cultural Logic of National Identity Formation: Contending Discourses in Late Colonial India', in Hudson, V.M. (ed.) *Culture and Foreign Policy* (Boulder, CO: Lynne Rienner) 27–44.

BARBER, T. (2007) 'Brussels' heart ponders Brown absence', *Financial Times*, 13 December, p. 2.

BARNETT, M.A. and FINNEMORE, M. (1999) 'The Politics, Power and Pathologies of International Organizations', *International Organization*, 53(4), 699–732.

BARRY, N. (2004) 'Constitutional deliberations over Europe', *Economic Affairs*, 24(1), 2–4.

BARTELSON, J. (1995) *A Genealogy of Sovereignty* (Cambridge: Cambridge University Press).

BAUER, M.W. (2002) 'Limitations to Agency Control in European Union Policymaking: the Commission and Poverty Programmes', *Journal of Common Market Studies*, 40(3), 381–400.

BEAUMONT, P. *et al.* (2002) *Convergence and Divergence in European Public Law* (Oxford and Portland, OR: Hart Publishing).

BEETHAM, D. and LORD, C. (1998) *Legitimacy and the European Union* (London: Longman).

BEHNKE, A. (2000) 'Inscriptions of Imperial Order: NATO's Mediterranean Initiative', *International Journal of Peace Research*, 5(1), available online at www.gmu.edu/academic/ijps/vo15_1/behnke.htm; accessed 15 October 2003.

BEITZ, C. (1979) *Political Theory and International Relations* (Princeton, NJ: Princeton University Press).

BELLAMY, R. (2003) 'Sovereignty, Post-Sovereignty and Pre-Sovereignty: Reconceptualising the State, Rights and Democracy in the EU', in

N. Walker (ed.) *Sovereignty in Transition* (Oxford: Hart) 167–90.

—— (2006a) 'The Challenge of European Union', in Dryzek, J., Phillips, A., and Honig, B. (eds) *The Oxford Handbook of Political Theory* (Oxford: Oxford University Press) 245–61.

—— (2006b) 'The European Constitution is Dead, Long Live European Constitutionalism', *Constellations: An International Journal of Critical and Democratic Theory,* 13(2), 181–9.

—— (2006c) 'Between Past and Future: the Democratic Limits of EU Citizenship', in Bellamy, R., Castiglione, D., and Shaw, J. (eds) *Making European Citizens. Civic Inclusion in a Transnational Context* (Basingstoke and New York: Palgrave Macmillan) 238–65.

—— (2006d) 'Still in Deficit: Rights, Regulation and Democracy in the EU', *European Law Journal,* 12(6), 725–42.

—— (2007) *Political Constitutionalism: A Republican Defense of the Constitutionality of Democracy* (Cambridge: Cambridge University Press).

—— (2008a) 'Republicanism, Democracy and Constitutionalism', in Laborde, C. and Maynor, J. (eds) *Republicanism and Political Theory* (Oxford: Blackwell) 159–89.

—— (2008b) 'Evaluating Union Citizenship: Belonging, Rights and Participation within the EU', *Citizenship Studies,* 12(6), 597–611.

—— (2009) 'The Republic of Reasons: Public Reasoning, Depoliticisation and Non-Domination', in Besson, S. and Marti, J.-L. (eds) *Legal Republicanism: National and International* (Oxford: Oxford University Press), 103–20.

—— and Castiglione D. (1997) 'Building the Union: The Nature of Sovereignty in the Political Architecture of Europe', *Law and Philosophy,* 16(4), 421–45.

—— and —— (2000) 'Democracy, Sovereignty and the Constitution of the European Union: The Republican Alternative to Liberalism', in Bankowski, Z. and Scott, A. (eds) *The European Union and its Order* (Oxford: Blackwell) 170–90.

—— and —— (2003) 'Legitimising the Euro-polity and its Regime: The Normative Turn in EU Studies', *European Journal of Political Theory,* 2(1), 7–34.

—— and Schönlau, J. (2004a) 'The Normality of Constitutional Politics: An Analysis of the Drafting of the EU Charter of Fundamental Rights', *Constellations: An International Journal of Critical and Democratic Theory,* 11(4), 412–33.

—— and —— (2004b) 'The Good, the Bad and the Ugly: The Need for Constitutional Compromise and the Drafting of the EU Constitution', in Dobson, L. and Andreas F. (eds) *Political Theory and the European Constitution* (London: Routledge) 57–71.

—— and Warleigh, A. (1998) 'From an Ethics of Integration to an Ethics of Participation: Citizenship and the Future of the European Union', *Millennium: Journal of International Studies,* 27(3), 447–70.

Berger, P.L. and Luckmann, T. (1966) *The Social Construction of Reality: A Treatise in the Sociology of Knowledge* (New York: Doubleday).

Berger, T.U. (1996) 'Norms, Identity and National Security in Germany and Japan', in Katzenstein, P.J. (ed.) *The Culture of National Security: Norms and Identity in World Politics* (New York: Colombia) 317–56.

Berghahn, S. (1998) 'Zwischen marktvermittelter Geschlechtergleichheit im europäischen "Herrenclub" und den patriarchalischen Traditionalismen von Mitgliedstaaten: Gibt es einen "Mehrwert" der europäischen Gleichheitsentwicklung für Frauen?', *Femina Politica,* 2(1), 46–55.

—— (2004) 'The Influence of European Union Legislation on Labour Market Equality for Women', in Zollinger Giele, J. and Holst, E. (eds) *Changing Life Patterns in Western Industrial Societies* (Oxford: Elsevier) 211–30.

Beyers, J. (2002) 'Multiple Embeddedness and Socialization in Europe: The Case of Council Officials', *Arena Working Papers,* WP 02/33.

—— and Dierickx, G. (1998) 'The Working Groups of the Council of the European Union: Supranational or Intergovernmental Negotiations?', *Journal of Common Market Studies,* 36(3), 289–317.

Bhagwati, J. and Panagariya, A. (1996) *The Economics of Preferential Trading Agreements* (Washington, DC: American Enterprise Institute).

Bieler, A. (2002) 'The Struggle over EU Enlargement: A Historical Materialist Analysis of European Integration', *Journal of European Public Policy,* 9(4), 575–97.

—— and Morton, A. (2001) *Social Forces in the Making of New Europe* (London: Palgrave).

Bieling, H.J. and Lerch, M. (eds) (2005) *Theorien der europäischen Integration* (Wiesbaden: VS Verlag).

—— and Steinhilber, J. (eds) (2000) *Die Konfiguration Europas: Dimensionen einer kritischen Integrationstheorie* (Münster: Westfälisches Dampfboot).

Biersteker, T.J. (2002) 'Targeting Terrorist Finances: the New Challenges of Financial Market Globalization', in Booth, K. and Dunne, T. (eds) *Worlds in Collision: Terror and the Future of Global Order* (Basingstoke and New York: Palgrave) 74–84.

Blanchflower, D. and Shadforth, C. (2007) *Fear, Unemployment and Migration*, National Bureau of Economic Research Working Paper 13506 (Washington, DC: National Bureau of Economic Research).

Blom-Hansen, J. (1997) 'A "New Institutional" View of Policy Networks', *Public Administration*, 75(4), 669–93.

—— (2008) 'The Origins of the EU Comitology System: a Case of Informal Agenda-setting by the Commission', *Journal of European Public Policy*, 15(2), 208–26.

Bogason, P. and Musso, J.A. (2006) 'The Democratic Prospects of Network Governance', *The American Review of Public Administration*, 36(1), 3–18.

Bogdandy, A. von (1999) 'The Legal Case for Unity: The European Union as a Single Organization with a Single Legal System', *Common Market Law Review*, 36, 887–910.

—— (2000) 'Information und Kommunikation in der Europäischen Union föderale Strukturen in supranationalem Umfeld', in Hoffmann-Riem, W. and Schmidt-Aßmann, E. (eds) *Verwaltungsrecht in der Informationsgesellschaft* (Baden-Baden: Nomos) 133–94.

—— (ed.) (2003) *Europäisches Verfassungsrecht. Theoretische und dogmatische Grundzüge* (Heidelberg: Springer).

Bohle, D. (2006) 'Neoliberal Hegemony, Transnational Capital and the Terms of EU Enlargement', *Capital and Class*, 88, 57–86.

Bomberg, E. (1998) 'Issue Networks and the Environment: Explaining European Union Environmental Policy', in Marsh, D. (ed.) *Comparing Policy Networks* (Buckingham: Open University Press) 167–84.

——and Peterson, J. (1998) 'European Union Decision-Making: the Role of Sub-National Authorities', *Political Studies*, 46(2), 219–35.

—— et al. (2008) *The European Union: How Does it Work?*, 2nd edn (Oxford: Oxford University Press).

Bonham, G.M. *et al.* (1987) 'Cognition and International Negotiation: The Historical Recovery of Discursive Space', *Cooperation and Conflict*, 22(1), 1–19.

Booth, C. and Bennett, C. (2002) 'Gender mainstreaming in the European Union', *The European Journal of Women's Studies*, 9(4), 430–46.

Bornschier, V. (ed.) (2000) *Statebuilding in Europe: The Revitalization of Western European Integration* (Cambridge: Cambridge University Press).

Borras, S. and Jacobssen, K. (2004) 'The Open Method of Coordination and New Governance Patterns in Europe', *Journal of European Public Policy*, 11(2), 185–208.

Börzel, T.A. (1997) 'Zur (Ir-)Relevanz der "postmoderne" für die Integrationsforschung: Eine Replik auf Thomas Diez's Beitrag "Postmoderne und europäische Integration"', *Zeitschrift für internationale Beziehungen*, 4(1), 125–37.

—— (1998) 'Organising Babylon: on the Different Conceptions of Policy Network', *Public Administration*, 76(2), 253–73.

—— (2001) 'Non-compliance in the European Union: Pathology or Statistical Artefact?', *Journal of European Public Policy*, 8(5), 803–24.

—— and Hosli, M. (2003) 'Brussels Between Berne and Berlin: Comparative Federalism Meets the European Union', *Governance*, 16(2), 179–202.

—— and Risse, T. (2000) 'When Europe Hits Home: Europeanization and Domestic Change', *European Integration online Papers*, 4(15), http://eiop.or.at/eiop/texte/2000–015a.htm.

—— and —— (2003) 'Conceptualizing the Domestic Impact of Europe', in Featherstone, K. and Radaelli, C.M. (eds) *The Politics of Europeanization* (Oxford: Oxford University Press) 57–81.

—— and —— (2007) 'Europeanization: The Domestic Impact of EU Politics', in Jørgensen, K.E., Pollack, M.A., and Rosamond, B. (eds) *The Handbook of European Union Politics* (New York: Sage) 483–504.

—— et al. (2007) *Recalcitrance, Inefficiency, and Support for European Integration. Why Member States Do (Not) Comply with European Law* (Cambridge, MA: Center for European Studies, Harvard University).

Boudette, N. (2004) 'As Jobs Head to Eastern Europe Unions in West Start to Bend', *Wall Street Journal*, 11 March.

BOYER, R. (2000) 'The Unanticipated Fallout of the European Monetary Union: The Political and Institutional Deficits of the Euro' in Crouch, C. (ed.) *After the Euro: Shaping Insitutions for Governance in the Wake of the European Monetary Union* (Oxford: Oxford University Press), 24–88.

BOYM, S. (2000) 'Leningrad into St. Petersburg: The Dream of Europe at the Margins', in Stråth, B. (ed.) *Europe and the Other and Europe as the Other* (Brussels: P.I.E.-Peter Lang) 311–24.

BRAITHWAITE, M. (2000) 'Mainstreaming gender in the European structural funds'. Paper prepared for the *Mainstreaming Gender in European Public Policy* Workshop, University of Wisconsin-Madison, 14–15 October.

BRANCH, A.P. and ØHRGAARD, J.C. (1999) 'Trapped in the Supranational–Intergovernmental Dichotomy: A Response to Stone Sweet and Sandholtz', *Journal of European Public Policy*, 6(1), 123–43.

BRÄUNINGER, T. and KÖNIG, T. (2001) 'Voting Power in the Post-Nice European Union, Department of Politics and Management', University of Konstanz, manuscript consulted online 3 October 2002 at www.unikonstanz.de/FuF/Verwiss/koenig/manuskript1.pdf.

BRETHERTON, C. (2002) 'Gender mainstreaming and enlargement: the EU as negligent actor?', National Europe Centre Paper No. 24.

BROWNING, C. and JOENNIEMI, P. (2004) 'Contending Discourses of Marginality: The Case of Kaliningrad', *Geopolitics*, 9(3), 699–730.

BRUTER, M. (2005) *Citizens of Europe? The Emergence of a Mass European Identity* (Basingstoke and New York: Palgrave).

BUENO DE MESQUITA, B. and STOKMAN, F.N. (eds) (1994) *European Community Decision Making: Models, Applications and Comparisons* (New Haven, CT and London: Yale University Press).

BULMER, S. (1994) 'The Governance of the European Union: A New Institutionalist Approach', *Journal of Public Policy*, 13(4), 351–80.

BÚRCA, G. DE and SCOTT, J. (2000) *Constitutional Change in the EU: From Uniformity to Flexibility?* (Oxford: Hart).

BURGESS, J.P. (1997a) 'On the Necessity and the Impossibility of a European Cultural Identity', in Burgess, J.P. (ed.) *Cultural Politics and Political Culture in Postmodern Europe* (Amsterdam and Atlanta, GA: Postmodern Studies) vol. 24, 19–39.

—— (ed.) (1997b) *Cultural Politics and Political Culture in Postmodern Europe* (Amsterdam and Atlanta, GA: Postmodern Studies) vol. 24.

—— (2000) 'The Securitization of Economic Identity: Reason and Culture in the European Monetary Union', in Burgess, J.P. and Tunander, O. (eds) *European Security Identities: Contested Understandings of EU and NATO* (Oslo: PRIO Report 2/2000) 57–80.

—— (2001) 'The Historiography of European Space', in Burgess, J.(ed.) *Culture and Rationality: European Frameworks of Norwegian Identity* (Kristiansund: Norwegian University Press) 125–44.

BURGESS, M. (1989) *Federalism and European Union: Political Ideas, Influences and Strategies in the European Community, 1972–1987* (London: Routledge).

—— (1996) 'Federalism and the European Union', Special Issue of *Publius: The Journal of Federalism*, 26(4), 1–162.

—— (2000) *Federalism and European Union: The Building of Europe, 1950–2000* (London: Routledge).

—— (2006) *Comparative Federalism in Theory and Practice* (London: Routledge).

BURLEY, A. and MATTLI, W. (1993) 'Europe before the Court: A Political Theory of Legal Integration', *International Organization*, 47(2), 41–76.

BUZAN, B. *et al.* (1998) *Security: A New Framework of Analysis* (Boulder, CO: Lynne Rienner).

CAFRUNY, A. and RYNER, M. (eds) (2003) *A Ruined Fortress? Neoliberal Hegemony and Transformation in Europe* (Lanham, MD: Rowman and Littlefield).

—— and —— (2007) *Europe at Bay: In the Shadow of US Hegemony* (Boulder, CO: Lynne Rienner).

CALLEO, D. (1982) *The Imperious Economy* (Cambridge, MA: Harvard University Press).

—— (2003) 'Balancing America: Europe's International Duties', *International Politics and Society*, 1(1), 43–60.

CALLONI, M. (2003) 'From Maternalism to Mainstreaming: Femocrats and the Reframing of Gender Equality Policy in Italy', in Liebert, U. (ed.) *Gendering Europeanisation* (Brussels: P.I.E.-Peter Lang) 117–84.

CAMERON D. (1995) 'Transnational Relations and the Development of European Economic and Monetary Union', in Risse-Kappen, T. (ed.) *Bringing Transnational Relations Back In: Non-State Actors, Domestic Structures and International Institutions* (Cambridge: Cambridge University Press) 37–78.

CAMPBELL, D. (1992) *Writing Security: United States Foreign Policy and Politics of Identity* (Manchester: Manchester University Press).

CAPORASO, J. (1996) 'The European Union and Forms of State: Westphalian, Regulatory or Post-Modern?', *Journal of Common Market Studies*, 34(1), 29–52.

—— (2007) 'The Promises and Pitfalls of an Endogenous Theory of Institutional Change: A Comment', *West European Politics*, 30(2), 392–404.

—— and JUPILLE, J. (2001) 'The Europeanization of Gender Equality Policy and Domestic Structural Change', in Green Cowles, M., Caporaso, J., and Risse, T. (eds) *Transforming Europe: Europeanization and Domestic Change* (Ithaca, NY: Cornell University Press) 21–43.

——and KEELER, J.T.S. (1995) 'The European Union and Regional Integration Theory', in Rhodes, C. (ed.) *The State of the European Union*, vol. 3 (Boulder, CO: Lynne Rienner) 29–62.

CAPPELLETTI M. *et al.* (1985) *Integration Through Law* (Berlin and New York: Walter de Gruyter).

CARCHEDI, G. (2001) *For Another Europe: A Class Analysis of European Economic Integration* (London: Verso).

CARDOZO, R. (1987) 'The Project for a Political Community, 1952–54', in Pryce, R. (ed.) *The Dynamics of European Union* (London: Croom Helm) 49–77.

CARNEY, F.S. (ed.) (1995) *Politica: Johannes Althusius* (Indianapolis, IN: Liberty Fund).

CARPENTER, D.P. *et al.* (1998) 'The Strength of Ties in Lobbying Networks: Evidence from Health-Care Policies in the United States', *Journal of Theoretical Politics*, 10(4), 417–44.

CASTELLS, M. (1998) *End of Millennium* (Oxford and Malden, MA: Blackwell).

CAVIEDES, A. (2004) 'The Open Method of Coordination in Immigration Policy: A Tool for Prying Open Fortress Europe', *Journal European of Public Policy*, 11(3), 289–310.

CEDERMAN, L.-E. (ed.) (2001) *Constructing Europe's Identities: The External Dimension* (Boulder, CO: Lynne Rienner).

CHECKEL, J. (2001a) 'Social Construction and Integration', in Christiansen, T., Jørgensen, K.E., and Wiener, A. (eds) *The Social Construction of Europe* (London: Sage) 50–64.

—— (2001b) 'Why Comply? Constructivism, Social Norms, and the Study of International Institutions', *International Organization*, 55(3), 553–88.

—— (2001c) 'From Meta- to Substantive Theory? Social Constructivism and the Study of Europe', *European Union Politics*, 2(2), 219–26.

—— (2003) '"Going Native" in Europa? Theorizing Social Interaction in European Institutions', *Comparative Political Studies*, 36(1–2), 209–31.

—— (2005) 'International Institutions and Socialization in Europe: Introduction and Framework', *International Organization*, 59(4), 801–26.

—— and KATZENSTEIN, P.J. (eds) (2008) *The Politics of European Identity Construction* (Cambridge: Cambridge University Press).

CHILTON, P. (1996) *Security Metaphors: Cold War Discourse from Containment to Common House* (Berne and New York: Peter Lang Publishing).

——and ILLYIN, M. (1993) 'Metaphor in Political Discourse: the Case of the "Common European House"', *Discourse and Society*, 4(1), 7–31.

CHOULIARAKI, L. and FAIRCLOUGH, N. (1999) *Discourse in Late Modernity: Rethinking Critical Discourse Analysis* (Edinburgh: Edinburgh University Press).

CHRISTIANSEN, T. (2001) 'Introduction', in Christiansen, T. *et al.* (eds) *The Social Construction of Europe* (London: Sage) 1–19.

—— and JØRGENSEN, K.E. (1999) 'The Amsterdam Process: A Structurationist Perspective on EU Treaty Reform', *European Integration Online Papers* 3, 23.

—— and LARSSON, T. (2007) *The Role of Committees in the Policy Process of the EU* (Cheltenham: Edward Elgar).

—— and PIATTONI, S. (eds) (2003) *Informal Governance in the European Union* (Cheltenham: Edward Elgar).

—— *et al.* (eds) (1999) 'The Social Construction of Europe', *Journal of European Public Policy*, 6(4).

—— *et al.* (2001) *The Social Construction of Europe* (London: Sage).

CHRISTENSEN, T. and LAEGREID, P. (2006) *Autonomy and Regulation: Coping with Agencies in the Modern World* (Cheltenham: Edward Elgar).

CHURCH, C. and DARDANELLI, P. (2005) 'The Dynamics of Confederalism and Federalism: Comparing Switzerland and the EU', *Regional and Federal Studies*, 15(2), 163–85.

CICHOWSKI, R.A. (2007) *The European Court and Civil Society: Litigation, Mobilization and Governance* (Cambridge: Cambridge University Press).

CITRIN, J. and SIDES, J. (2004) 'More than Nationals: How Identity Choice Matters in the New Europe', in Herrmann, R.K., Risse, T., and Brewer, M. (eds) *Transnational Identities. Becoming European in the EU* (Lanham, MD: Rowman and Littlefield) 161–85.

COASE, R.H. (1960) 'The Problem of Social Cost', *Journal of Law and Economics*, 3(1), 1–44.

COLEMAN, W.D. (2001) 'Policy Networks, Non-State Actors and Internationalized Policy-Making: A Case Study of Agricultural Trade', in Wallace, W. (ed.) *Non-State Actors in World Politics* (Basingstoke and New York: Palgrave) 93–112.

CONANT, L. (2002) *Justice Contained: Law and Politics in the European Union* (Ithaca, NY: Cornell University Press).

—— (2007) 'Judicial Politics', in Jørgensen, K.E., Pollack, M.A., and Rosamond, B. (eds) *The Handbook of European Union Politics* (New York: Sage) 213–29.

CONNELL, R.W. (1998) 'Masculinities and Globalization', *Men and Masculinities*, 1(1), 3–23.

CONNOLLY, W.E. (1983) *The Terms of Political Discourse* (Princeton, NJ: Princeton University Press).

COOTER, R.D. and GINSBURG, T. (1996) 'Comparative Judicial Discretion', *International Review of Law and Economics*, 16(3), 295–313.

COSS, S. (2002) 'Knight of the Realms: Albert Bore', *European Voice*, www.europeanvoice .com/article/imported/profile-knight-of-the-realms-albert-bore/44910.aspx.

COUDENHOVE-KALERGI, R.G. (1971) *Weltmacht Europa* (Stuttgart: Seewald).

COX, R.W. with SINCLAIR, T.J. (1996) *Approaches to World Order* (Cambridge: Cambridge University Press).

CRAIG, P. (2001) 'Constitutions, Constitutionalism, and the European Union', *European Law Journal*, 7(1), 125–50.

—— and DE BÚRCA, G. (1998) *EU Law: Text, Cases, and Materials*, 2nd edn (Oxford: Oxford University Press).

CRAWFORD, N. (2002) *Argument and Change in World Politics: Ethics, Decolonization, and Humanitarian Intervention* (Cambridge: Cambridge University Press).

CROMBEZ, C. *et al.* (2000) 'Understanding the EU Legislative Process: Political Scientists' and Practitioners' Perspectives', *European Union Politics*, 1(3), 363–81.

CROSBIE, J. (2008) 'EU member states seek more powers for Eurojust', *European Voice*, 17 January 2008, www.europeanvoice. com/archive/article.asp?id=29622.

CZEMPIEL, E.O. and ROSENAU, J.N. (eds) (1992) *Governance without Government: Order and Change in World Politics* (Cambridge: Cambridge University Press).

DALY, M. (2006) 'EU Social Policy After Lisbon', *Journal of Common Market Studies*, 44(3), 461–81.

DAMGAARD, B (2006) 'Do Policy Networks Lead to Network Governing?', *Public Administration*, 84(3), 673–91.

DAUGBJERG, C. (1999) 'Reforming the CAP: Policy Networks and Broader Institutional Structures', *Journal of Common Market Studies*, 37(3), 407–28.

——and MARSH, D. (1998) 'Explaining Policy Outcomes: Integrating the Policy Network Approach with Macro-Level and Micro-Level Analysis', in Marsh, D. (ed.) *Comparing Policy Networks* (Buckingham: Open University Press) 52–71.

DAVIS, S.R. (1978) *The Federal Principle: A Journey Through Time in Quest of a Meaning* (London: University of California Press).

DE GRAUWE, P. (2003) *Economics of Monetary Union*, 5th edn (Oxford: Oxford University Press).

—— (2006) 'Germany's Pay Policy Points to Eurozone Design Flaw', *Financial Times*, 5 May.

—— (2007) 'Some Thoughts on Monetary and Political Union', Paper Presented at the Workshop on the Future of EMU (London School of Economics, 12 October).

DEHOUSSE, R. (1997) 'Regulation by Networks in the European Community: the Role of European Agencies', *Journal of European Public Policy*, 4(2), 246–61.

—— (2002) 'Misfits: EU Law and the Evolution of European Governance', in Dehousse, R. (ed.) *Good Governance in Europe's Integrated Market* (Oxford and New York: Oxford University Press) 207–30.

—— *et al.* (2004) *La Stratégie de Lisbonne et la méthode ouverte de coordination: 12 recommandations pour une stratégie à plusieurs niveaux plus efficace* (Paris: Notre Europe).

—— *et al.* (2007) *Élargissement: Comment l'Europe s'adapte* (Paris: Les Presses Sciences Po).

De Jong, M. and Edelenbos, J. (2007) 'An Insider's look into Policy Transfer in Transnational Expert Networks', *European Planning Studies*, 15(5), 687–706.

Delanty, G. (1995a) *Inventing Europe: Idea, Identity, Reality* (London: Macmillan).

—— (1995b) 'The Limits and Possibility of a European Identity: A Critique of Cultural Essentialism', *Philosophy and Social Criticism*, 21(4), 15–36.

—— (1998) 'Social Theory and European Transformation: Is there a European Society?', *Sociological Research Online*, 3(1), www.socreson-line.org.uk/socreson-line/3/1/1.html.

Delgado Moreira, J.M. (2000) 'Cohesion and Citizenship in EU Cultural Policy', *Journal of Common Market Studies*, 38(3), 449–70.

Den Boer, M. (1994) 'The quest for European Policing: Rhetoric and Justification in a Disorderly Debate', in Anderson, M. and den Boer, M. (eds) *Policing Across National Boundaries* (London: Pinter) 174–96.

Den Boer, P. et al. (1995 [1993]) *The History of the Idea of Europe* (London: Rouledge; originally: Open University Press 1993).

Deppe, F. (ed.) (1976) *Arbeiterbewegung und westeuropäische Integration* (Cologne: Pahl-Rugenstein).

Derrida, J. (1974 [1967]) *Of Grammatology* (Baltimore, MD: Johns Hopkins University Press).

—— (1978 [1967]) 'Structure, Sign and Play in the Discourses of the Human Sciences', in Derrida, J., *Writing and Difference* (London: Routledge and Kegan Paul) 278–93.

—— (1992 [1991]) *The Other Heading: Reflections on Today's Europe* (Bloomington, IN: Indiana University Press).

Deutsch, K.W. et al. (1957) *Political Community and the North Atlantic Area: International Organization in the Light of Historical Experience* (Princeton, NJ: Princeton University Press).

—— (1967) *France, Germany and the Western Alliance: A Study of Elite Attitudes on European Integration and World Politics* (New York: Scribner's Sons).

Dicey, A.V. (1915) *Introduction to the Study of the Law of the Constitution* (London: Macmillan).

Diez, T. (1995) *Neues Europa, altes Modell: Die Konstruktion von Staatlishckeit im politischen Diskurs zur Zukunft der europäischen Gemeinshaft* (Frankfurt/M: Haag+Herchen).

—— (1996) 'Postmoderne und europäische Integration: Die Dominanz des Staatsmodells, die Verantwortung gegenüber dem Anderen und die Konstruktion eines alternativen Horizonts', *Zeitschrift für internationale Beziehungen*, 3(2), 255–81.

—— (1997) 'International Ethics and European Integration: Federal State or Network Horizon', *Alternatives*, 22(3), 287–312.

—— (1998) 'Perspektivenwechsel. Warum ein "postmoderner" Ansatz für die Integrationsforschung doch relevant ist', *Zeitschrift für internationale Beziehungen*, 5(1), 139–48.

—— (1999a) 'Speaking "Europe": the politics of integration discourse', *Journal of European Public Policy*, 6(4) 598–613.

—— (1999b) *Die EU lesen: Diskursive Knotenpunkte in der britischen Europadebatte* (Opladen: Leske und Budrich).

—— (1999c) 'Riding the AM-Track through Europe. Or: The Pitfalls of a Rationalist Journey through European Integration', *Millennium: Journal of International Studies*, 28(2), 355–69.

—— (2001) 'Europe as a Discursive Battleground: Discourse Analysis and European Integration Studies', *Cooperation and Conflict*, 36(1), 5–38.

—— (2004) 'Europe's Others and the Return of Geopolitics', *Cambridge Review of International Affairs*, 17(2), 319–35.

—— (2005) 'Constructing the Self and Changing Others: Reconsidering "Normative Power Europe"', *Millennium: Journal of International Studies*, 33(3), 613–36.

—— (2007) 'Expanding Europe: The Ethics of Turkey-EU Relations', *Ethics and International Affairs*, 21(4), 415–22.

—— and Manners, I. (2008) 'Reflecting on Normative Power Europe', in Berenskoetter, F. and Williams, M.J. (eds) *Power in World Politics* (London: Routledge) 173–88.

—— et al. (eds) (2008) *The European Union and Border Conflicts: The Power of Integration and Association* (Cambridge: Cambridge University Press).

Dinan, D. (2006) *Origins and Evolution of the European Union* (Oxford: Oxford University Press).

DOBSON, L. (2006) 'Normative Theory and Europe', *International Affairs,* 83(2), 511–23.

—— and FØLLESDAL, A. (eds) (2004) *Political Theory and the European Constitution* (London: Routledge).

DOGAN, R. (2000) 'A Cross-sectoral View of Comitology: Incidence, Issues and Implications', in Christiansen, T. and Kirchner, E. (eds) *Committee Governance in the European Union* (New York: St Martin's Press) 45–61.

DOORNBOS, M. (2003) '"Good Governance": The Metamorphosis of a Policy Metaphor', *Journal of International Affairs,* 57(1), 3–17.

DORE, R. (2000) 'Will Global Capitalism Be Anglo-Saxon Capitalism?', *New Left Review,* 6(2), 101–19.

DOWDING, K. (1995) 'Model or metaphor? A Critical Review of the Policy Network Approach', *Political Studies,* 43(1), 136–58.

—— (2000) 'Institutionalist Research on the European Union: A Critical Review', *European Union Politics,* 1(1), 125–44.

—— (2001) 'There must be an End to Confusion: Policy Networks, Intellectual Fatigue, and the Need for Political Science Methods Courses in British Universities', *Political Studies,* 49(1), 89–105.

DREYFUS, H.L. and RABINOW, P. (1982) *Michel Foucault: Beyond Structuralism and Hermeneutics* (New York: Harvester Wheatsheaf).

DROR, Y. (2001) *The Capacity to Govern* (London: Routledge).

DRULAK, P. (2006) 'Motion, Container and Equilibrium: Metaphors in the Discourse about European Integration', *European Journal of International Relations,* 12(4), 499–531.

DUCHESNE, S. and FROGNIER, A.-P. (1995) 'Is There a European Identity?', in Niedermayer, O. and Sinnott, R. (eds) *Public Opinion and Internationalized Governance* (Oxford: Oxford University Press) 194–226.

DUNCAN, S. (2002) 'Policy discourses on "reconciling work and life" in the EU', *Social Policy and Society,* 1(4), 305–14.

DUNFORD, M. (2005) 'Old Europe, New Europe, and the USA: Comparative Economic Performance, Inequality, and Market-Led Models of Development', *European Urban and Regional Studies,* 12(2), 149–76.

—— and SMITH, A. (2000) 'Catching Up or Falling Behind? Economic Performance and the Trajectories of Economic Development in an Enlarged Europe', *Economic Geography,* 76(2), 169–95.

DUNN, J.A. and PERL, A. (1994) 'Policy Networks and Industrial Revitalization: High Speed Rail Initiatives in France and Germany', *Journal of Public Policy,* 14(3), 311–43.

DYSON, K. (2000) *The Politics of the Eurozone* (Oxford: Oxford University Press).

EASTON, D. (1953) *The Political System: An Inquiry into the State of Political Science* (New York: Alfred A. Knopf).

ECONOMIST, THE (2007) 'Swan Songs: The Crises to Watch For in 2008', *The Economist,* 22 December, p. 120.

EDER, K. and GIESEN, B. (eds) (1999) *European Citizenship and the National Legacies* (Oxford: Oxford University Press).

—— and KANTNER, C. (2000) 'Transnationale Resonanzstrukturen in Europa. Eine Kritik der Rede vom Öffentlichkeitsdefizit', in Bach, M. (ed.) *Die Europäisierung nationaler Gesellschaften* (Wiesbaden: Westdeutscher Verlag) 306–31.

EDWARDS, G. and MEYER, C.O. (2008) 'Introduction: Charting a Contested Transformation', *Journal of Common Market Studies,* 46(1), 1–26.

EGAN, M. (1998) 'Gendered integration: social policies and the European market', *Women and Politics,* 19(4), 23–52.

EGEBERG, M. (1999) 'Transcending Intergovernmentalism? Identity and Role Perceptions of National Politicians in EU Decision-Making', *Journal of European Public Policy,* 6(3), 456–74.

EILSTRUP SANGIOVANNI, M. (ed.) (2006) *Debates on European Integration: A Reader* (Basingstoke: Palgrave).

EISENSTADT, S.N. and GIESEN, B. (1995) 'The Construction of Collective Identity', *European Journal of Sociology,* 36, 72–102.

EISING, R. and KOHLER-KOCH, B. (1999) 'Introduction: Network Governance in the European Union', in Kohler-Koch, B. and Eising, R. (eds) *The Transformation of Governance in the European Union* (London: Routledge) 1–29.

EL-AGRAA, A.M. (1982) 'The theory of economic integration', in El-Agraa, A.M. (ed.) *International Economic Integration* (Basingstoke: Macmillan) 10–27.

ELAZAR, D.J. (1987) *Exploring Federalism* (Tuscaloosa, AL: University of Alabama Press).

—— (1995) 'From Statism to Federalism: A Paradigm Shift', *Publius: The Journal of Federalism,* 25(2), 5–18.

—— (2001) 'The United States and the European Union: Models for Their Epochs', in Nicolaïdis, K. and Howse, R. (eds) *The Federal Vision: Legitimacy and Levels of Governance in the United States and the European Union* (Oxford: Oxford University Press) 31–53.

ELLINA, C.A. (2003) *Promoting Women's Rights: the Politics of Gender in the European Union* (New York: Routledge).

ELMAN, R.A. (ed.) (1996) *Sexual Politics and the European Union: The Feminist Challenge* (Oxford: Berghahn).

ELSTER, J. (1989) *Nuts and Bolts for the Social Sciences* (Cambridge: Cambridge University Press).

EPSTEIN, D. and O'HALLORAN, S. (1999) *Delegating Powers: A Transaction Cost Politics Approach to Policy Making under Separate Powers* (New York: Cambridge University Press).

EPSTEIN, R. (2005) 'Diverging Effects of Social Learning and External Incentives in Polish Central Banking and Agriculture', in Schimmelfennig, F. and Sedelmeier, U. (eds) *The Europeanization of Central and Eastern Europe* (Ithaca, NY: Cornell University Press) 178–98.

EUROPEAN BANK FOR RECONSTRUCTION AND DEVELOPMENT (2007) *Life in Transition: A Survey of People's Experiences and Attitudes* (Paris: EBRD).

EUROPEAN COMMISSION (1985) *White Paper on the Internal Market,* COM (85) 331 final (Brussels: Commission of the European Communities).

—— (1988) *Europe 1992: The Overall Challenge,* Brussels, 13 April, SEC (88) 524 final (Brussels: Commission of the European Communities).

—— (1992) 'The Principle of Subsidiarity', SEC (92) 1990 final, 27 October (Brussels: Commission of the European Communities.

—— (1997) *Agenda 2000 for a Stronger and Wider Europe,* COM (97) vol. I (Brussels: Commission of the European Communities).

EUROPEAN PARLIAMENT (2000) Report on the Constitutionalisation of the Treaties, Final A5–0289/2000, PE 286.949 (Brussels: European Parliament).

EUROPEAN ROUNDTABLE (1991) *Reshaping Europe* (Brussels).

EUROPEAN WOMEN'S LOBBY (2002) 'Convention on the Future of Europe: Where are the Women?' Press release, 26 February.

FAIRCLOUGH, N. (1992) *Discourse and Social Change* (Cambridge: Polity Press).

—— (1995) *Critical Discourse Analysis: The Critical Study of Language* (London: Longman).

FALKNER, G. (1999) 'European Social Policy: Towards Multi-Level and Multi-Actor Governance', in Eising, R., *The Transformation of Governance in the European Union* (London and New York: Routledge) 83–97.

—— (2000) 'Policy Networks in a Multi-Level System: Convergence Towards Moderate Diversity?', *West European Politics,* 23(4), 94–120.

——and M. NENTWICH (2000) 'Enlarging the European Union: The Short-Term Success of Incrementalism and De-Politicisation' (Cologne: Max-Planck-Institut für Gesellschaftsforschung, MPIfG Working Paper 00/4, July).

—— et al. (2005) *Complying With Europe: EU Harmonization and Soft Law in Member States* (Cambridge: Cambridge University Press).

FARRELL, H. and HÉRITIER, A. (2005) 'A Rationalist-Institutionalist Explanation of Endogenous Regional Integration', *Journal of European Public Policy,* 12(2), 273–90.

—— and —— (2007) 'Introduction: Contested Competences in the European Union', *West European Politics,* 30(2), 227–43.

FEARON, J.D. (1998) 'Domestic Politics, Foreign Policy and Theories of International Relations', *Annual Review of Political Science,* 1, 259–83.

—— and WENDT, A. (2002) 'Rationalism and Constructivism in International Relations Theory', in Carlinaes, W., Risse, T., and Simmons, B.A. (eds) *Handbook of International Relations* (London: Sage) 52–72.

FEATHERSTONE, K. and RADAELLI, C.M. (eds) (2003) *The Politics of Europeanization* (Oxford: Oxford University Press).

FELSENTHAL, D. and MACHOVER, M. (2001) 'The Treaty of Nice and Qualified Majority Voting', London School of Economics, paper consulted online on 4 October 2002 at www.lse.ac.uk/ Depts/cpnss/projects/VPPpdf/niceqmv .pdf.

FIERKE, K.M. (2002) 'Links Across the Abyss: Language and Logic in International Relations', *International Studies Quarterly,* 46(3), 331–54.

—— and WIENER, A. (1999) 'Constructing Institutional Interests: EU and NATO Enlargement', *Journal of European Public Policy* 6(5), 721–42.

FINANCIAL TIMES (2007) 'It's a Multi-currency World we Live In: The Dollar is Becoming Merely the First among Many', *Financial Times*, 27 December, p. 8.

FLIGSTEIN, N. and STONE SWEET, A. (2001) 'Constructing Polities and Market: An Institutionalist Account of European Integration', *American Journal of Sociology*, 107(5), 1206–43.

FLYNN, L. (1996) 'The Body Politic(s) of EU Law', in Hervey, T. and O'Keeffe, D. (eds) *Sex Equality Law in the European Community* (Chichester: Wiley) 279–97.

FØLLESDAL, A. (1997) 'Democracy and Federalism in the EU: a Liberal Contractualist Perspective', in Føllesdal, A. and Koslowski, P. (eds) *Democracy and the European Union: Studies in Economic Ethics and Philosophy* (Berlin: Springer) 231–53.

—— (2001) 'Federal Inequality among Equals: A Contractualist Defense', in Pogge, T. (ed.) *Global Justice* (Oxford: Blackwell) 242–61.

—— (2006a) 'Justice, stability and toleration in a Federation of Well-ordered Peoples', in Martin, R. and Reidy, D. (eds) *Rawls's Law of Peoples: A realistic Utopia?* (Oxford: Blackwell) 299–317.

—— (2006b) 'Survey Article: The Legitimacy Deficits of the European Union', *Journal of Political Philosophy*, 14(4), 441–68.

—— and HIX, S. (2006) 'Why There is a Democratic Deficit in the EU: A Response to Majone and Moravcsik', *Journal of Common Market Studies*, 44(3), 533–62.

FORSYTH, M. (1981) *Unions of States: The Theory and Practice of Confederation* (Leicester: Leicester University Press).

FORTESCUE, J.A. (1995) 'First Experiences with the Implementation of the Third Pillar Provisions', in Bieber, R. and Monar, J. (eds) *Justice and Home Affairs in the European Union: The Development of the Third Pillar* (Brussels: European Interuniversity Press) 19–28.

FOSSUM, J.E. and SCHLESINGER, P. (eds) (2007) *The European Union and the Public Sphere. A Communicative Space in the Making?* (London: Routledge).

FOUCAULT, M. (1972) *The Archeology of Knowledge* (London: Pantheon).

—— (1991) 'Politics and the Study of Discourse', in Burchell, G. *et al.* (eds) *The Foucault Effect. Studies in Governmentality* (Hemel Hempstead: Harvester Wheatsheaf) 53–72.

FRANCHINO, F. (2000) 'Control of the Commission's Executive Functions: Uncertainty, Conflict and Decision Rules', *European Union Politics*, 1(1), 63–92.

—— (2002) 'Efficiency or Credibility? Testing the Two Logics of Delegation to the European Commission', *Journal of European Public Policy*, 9(5), 677–94.

—— (2004) 'Delegating Powers in the European Community', *British Journal of Political Science*, 34(2), 449–76.

—— (2007) *The Powers of the Union. Delegation in the EU* (Cambridge: Cambridge University Press).

FREDERICKSON, H.G. (2006) 'Whatever Happened to Public Administration? Governance, Governance Everywhere', in Ferlie, E., Lynn, L.E., and Pollitt, C. (eds) *Oxford Handbook of Public Management* (Oxford: Oxford University Press) 247–59.

FRIEDEN, J. (1991) 'Invested Interests: The Politics of National Economic Policies in a World of Global Finance', *International Organization*, 45(4), 425–51.

FRIEDRICHS, J. (2004) *European Approaches to International Relations Theory: A House with Many Mansions* (London: Routledge).

FRIIS, L. and MURPHY, A. (1999) 'The European Union and Central and Eastern Europe, Governance and Boundaries', *Journal of Common Market Studies*, 37(2), 211–32.

—— and —— (2000) '"And Never the Twain Shall Meet": The EU's Quest for Legitimacy and Enlargement', in Kelstrup, M. and Williams, M.C. (eds) *International Relations Theory and the Politics of European Integration. Power, Security and Community* (London: Routledge) 226–49.

FUNK, N. and MÜLLER, M. (1993) *Gender Politics and Post-Communism: Reflections from Eastern Europe and the former Soviet Union* (New York: Routledge).

GALATI, G. and WOOLDRIDGE, P. (2006) 'The Euro as a Reserve Currency: A Challenge to the Pre-Eminence of the US Dollar?' (Basel: Bank of International Settlements Working Papers) No. 218.

GÁNDARA, L. (2004) '"They That Sow the Wind . . . ": Proverbs and Sayings in Argumentation', *Discourse and Society*, 15(2–3), 345–59.

GARCÍA, S. (ed.) (1993) *European Identity and the Search for Legitimacy* (London: Pinter).

GARRETT, G. (1992) 'International Cooperation and Institutional Choice: The European Community's Internal Market', *International Organization*, 46(2), 533–60.

—— (1995) 'The Politics of Legal Integration in the European Union', *International Organization*, 49(1), 171–81.

——and TSEBELIS, G. (1996) 'An Institutional Critique of Intergovernmentalism', *International Organization*, 50(2), 269–99.

——, ——, and CORBETT, R. (2001) 'The EU Legislative Process: Academics vs. Practitioners—Round 2', *European Union Politics*, 2(3), 353–66.

——and WEINGAST, B. (1993) 'Ideas, Interests, and Institutions: Constructing the European Community's Internal Market', in Goldstein, J. and Keohane, R. (eds) *Ideas and Foreign Policy* (Ithaca, NY: Cornell University Press) 173–206.

—— *et al.* (1998) 'The European Court of Justice, National Governments, and Legal Integration in the European Union', *International Organization*, 52(1), 149–76.

GAUTHIER, D. (1986) *Morals by Agreement* (Oxford: Oxford University Press).

GEORGE, S. (1991) *Politics and Policy In the European Community*, 2nd edn (Oxford: Clarendon Press).

—— (1996) *Politics and Policy in the European Community*, 3rd edn (Oxford: Clarendon Press).

—— and BACHE, I. (2006) *Politics in the European Union*, 2nd edn (Oxford: Oxford University Press).

GHECIU, A. (2005) *NATO in the 'New Europe': The Politics of International Socialization after the Cold War* (Stanford, CA: Stanford University Press).

GIDDENS, A. (1982) 'Hermeneutics and Social Theory', in Giddens, A. (ed.) *Profiles and Critiques in Social Theory* (Berkeley, CA: University of California Press) 1–17.

—— (1984) *The Constitution of Society: Outline of a Theory of Structuration* (Cambridge: Polity).

GIESEN, B. (1993) *Die Intellektuellen und die Nation. Eine deutsche Achsenzeit* (Frankfurt/M: Suhrkamp).

—— (1999) *Kollektive Identität. Die Intellektuellen und die Nation 2* (Frankfurt/M: Suhrkamp).

GILL, S. (1998) 'European Governance and New Constitutionalism: EMU and Alternatives to Disciplinary Neoliberalism in Europe', *New Political Economy*, 3(1), 5–26.

GILPIN, R. (1981) *War and Change in World Politics* (Cambridge: Cambridge University Press).

GLARBO, K. (2001) 'Reconstructing a Common European Foreign Policy', in Christiansen, T. *et al.* (eds) *The Social Construction of Europe* (London: Sage) 140–57.

GOLDSTEIN, J. and KEOHANE, R.O. (1993) 'Ideas and Foreign Policy: An Analytical Framework', in Goldstein, J. and Keohane, R.O. (eds) *Ideas and Foreign Policy: Beliefs, Institutions, and Political Change* (Ithaca, NY: Cornell University Press) 3–30.

GÖLER, D. (2006) *Deliberation—Ein Zukunftsmodell europäischer Entscheidungsfindung? Analyse der Beratungen des Verfassungskonvents 2002–2003* (Baden-Baden: Nomos).

GOREN, N. and NACHMANI, A. (eds) (2007) *The Importance of Being European: Turkey, the EU and the Middle East* (Jerusalem: The European Forum at the Hebrew University).

GRABBE, H. and HUGHES, K. (1998) *Enlarging the EU Eastwards* (London: Pinter).

GRAHL, J. (2001) *European Monetary Union: Problems of Legitimacy, Development and Stability* (London: Kogan Page).

——and TEAGUE, P. (1989) 'The Cost of Neo-Liberal Europe', *New Left Review*, 174, 33–50.

——and —— (1990) *The Big Market* (London: Lawrence and Wishart).

GRAMSCI, A. (1971) *Selections from the Prison Notebooks* (New York: International Publishers).

GRANDE, E. and PESCHKE, A. (1999) 'Transnational Cooperation and Policy Networks in European Science Policy-Making', *Research Policy*, 28(1), 43–61.

GRANOVETTER, M.S. (1973) 'The Strength of Weak Ties', *American Journal of Sociology*, 78(5), 1360–80.

GREEN COWLES, M. (1995) 'Setting the Agenda for a New Europe: The ERT and EC 1992', *Journal of Common Market Studies*, 33(4), 501–26.

—— and CURTIS, S. (2004) 'Developments in European Integration Theory: The EU as "Other"', in Cowles, M.G. and Dinan, D. (eds) *Developments in the European Union II* (Basingstoke: Palgrave) 296–309.

—— *et al.* (eds) (2001) *Transforming Europe: Europeanization and Domestic Change* (Ithaca, NY: Cornell University Press).

GREIF, A. and LAITIN, D.D. (2004) 'A Theory of Endogenous Institutional Change', *American Political Science Review*, 98(4), 633–52.

GREILSAMMER, I. (1979) 'Some Observations on European Federalism', in Elazar, D.J. (ed.) *Federalism and Political Integration* (Tel Aviv: Turtledove Publishing) 107–31.

GRIECO, J.M. (1990) *Cooperation among Nations: Europe, America and Non-Tariff Barriers to Trade* (Ithaca, NY: Cornell University Press).

—— (1996) 'State Interests and Institutional Rule Trajectories: A Neorealist Interpretation of the Maastricht Treaty and European Economic and Monetary Union', *Security Studies*, 5(3), 261–305.

GRIGOREVICH MIRKIN, B. (1996) *Mathematical Classification and Clustering* (Boston, MA: Kluwer Academic).

GRIMM, D. (1995) 'Does Europe Need a Constitution?', *European Law Journal*, 1, 282–302.

—— (1997) 'Does Europe Need a Constitution?', in Gowan, P. and Anderson, P. (eds) *The Question of Europe* (London: Verso) 239–58.

GROENENDIJK, N. (2006) 'Lisbon not delivering?', *EUSA Review*, 19(4), 4–7.

GROOM, A.J.R. (1978) 'A Case of Mistaken Identity', *Political Science*, 30(1), 15–28.

GROSSMAN, G.M. and HELPMAN, E. (1994) 'Protection for Sale', *American Economic Review*, 84(4), 833–50.

GSTÖHL, S. (2002) *Reluctant Europeans. Norway, Sweden, and Switzerland in the Process of European Integration* (Boulder, CO: Lynne Rienner).

GUERRINA, R. (2002) 'Mothering in Europe: Feminist Critique of European Policies on Motherhood and Employment', *The European Journal of Women's Studies*, 9(1), 49–68.

HAAHR, J.H. (2003) ' "Our Danish Democracy": Community, People and Democracy in the Danish Debate on the Common Currency', *Cooperation and Conflict*, 38(1), 27–47.

HAAS, E.B. (1958) *The Uniting of Europe: Political, Social, and Economic Forces 1950–57* (Stanford, CA: Stanford University Press).

—— (1960) *Consensus Formation in the Council of Europe* (Berkeley, CA: University of California Press).

—— (1961) 'International Integration: the European and the Universal Process', *International Organization*, 15(3), 366–92.

—— (1964a) 'Technocracy, Pluralism, and the New Europe', in Graubard, S.R. (ed.) *A New Europe?* (Boston, MA: Hougton Mifflin) 62–88.

—— (1964b) *Beyond the Nation State: Functionalism and International Organization* (Stanford, CA: Stanford University Press).

—— (1967) 'The "Uniting of Europe" and the "Uniting of Latin America" ', *Journal of Common Market Studies*, 5(2), 315–43.

—— (1968) *The Uniting of Europe: Political, Social and Economic Forces 1950–1957*, 2nd edn (Stanford, CA: Stanford University Press).

—— (1970) 'The Study of Regional Integration: Reflections on the Joy and Anguish of Pretheorizing', *International Organization*, 24(4), 607–46.

—— (1976) 'Turbulent fields and the theory of regional integration', *International Organization*, 30(2), 173–212.

—— (2001) 'Does Constructivism Subsume Neofunctionalism?', in Christiansen, T. *et al.* (eds) *The Social Construction of Europe* (London: Sage) 22–31.

—— (2004) 'Introduction: Institutionalism or constructivism?', in *The Uniting of Europe: Politics, Social and Economic Forces, 1950–1957*, 3rd edn (Notre Dame, IN: University of Notre Dame Press) xiii–lvi.

—— and HAAS P.M. (2002) 'Pragmatic Constructivism and the Study of International Institutions', *Millennium: Journal of International Studies*, 31(3), 573–601.

——and SCHMITTER, P. (1964) 'Economics and Differential Patterns of Political Integration: Projections About Unity in Latin America', *International Organization*, 18(4), 705–37.

HAAS, P.M. (1992) 'Epistemic Communities and International Policy Coordination', *International Organization*, 46(1), 1–35.

—— (1999) 'Compliance with EU Directives: Insights from International Relations and Comparative Politics', *Journal of European Public Policy*, 5(1), 17–37.

HABERMAS, J. (1981) *Theorie des kommunikativen Handelns*, 2 vols (Frankfurt/M: Suhrkamp).

—— (1992a) *Faktizität und Geltung. Beiträge zur Diskurstheorie des Rechts und des demokratischen Rechtsstaats* (Frankfurt/M: Suhrkamp).

—— (1992b) 'Citizenship and National Identity: Some Reflections on the Future of Europe', *Praxis International*, 12(1), 1–19.

—— (1994) 'Staatsbürgerschaft und nationale Identität', in Dewandre, N. and Lenoble, J. (eds) *Projekt Europa. Postnationale Identität: Grundlage für eine europäische Demokratie* (Berlin: Schelzky und Jeep) 11–29.

—— (1996a) 'Der europäische Nationalstaat—Zu Vergangenheit und Zukunft von Souveränität und Staatsbürgerschaft', in Habermas, J., *Die Einbeziehung des Anderen* (Frankfurt/M: Suhrkamp) 154–84.

—— (1996b) *Between Facts and Norms* (Cambridge: Polity Press/Blackwell).

—— (1997) 'Braucht Europa eine Verfassung? Eine Bemerkung zu Dieter Grimm', in Habermas, J. *Die Einbeziehung Des Anderen. Studien Zur Politischen Theorie* (Frankfurt/M: Campus) 185–91.

—— (1998) *The Inclusion of the Other: Studies in Political Theory* (Cambridge, MA: MIT Press).

—— (2001a) *The Postnational Constellation. Political Essays* (Cambridge: Polity Press/ Blackwell).

—— (2001b) 'Why Europe Needs a Constitution', *New Left Review*, 11, 5–26.

HAGEN, J. VON (1996) 'The Political Economy of Eastern Enlargement of the EU', in Ambrus-Lakatos, L. and Schaffer, M. (eds) *Coming to Terms with Accession* (London: CEPR, Institute for East–West Studies) 1–41.

HAGGARD, S. and MORAVCSIK, A. (1993) 'The Political Economy of Financial Assistance to Eastern Europe, 1989, 1991', in Keohane, R.O., Nye, J.S. Jr, and Hoffmann, S. (eds) *After the Cold War: International Institutions and State Strtegies in Europe, 1989–1991* (Cambridge, MA: Center of International Affairs) 246–85.

HALL, P.A. and SOSKICE, D. (eds) (2001) *Varieties of Capitalism: The Institutional Foundations of Comparative Advantage* (Oxford: Oxford University Press).

——and TAYLOR, R.C.R. (1996) 'Political Science and the Three New Institutionalisms', *Political Studies*, 44(5), 936–57.

—— and THELEN, K. (2006) 'Varieties of Capitalism and Institutional Change', *APSA European Politics & Society: Newsletter of the European Politics and Society Section of the American Political Science Association*, 5(1), 1, 3–4.

HANSEN, L. (1997) 'Nation-Building on the Balkan Border', *Alternatives*, 21, 473–96.

—— (2001) 'Sustaining Sovereignty: the Danish approach to Europe', in Hansen, L. and Wæver, O. (eds) *European Integration and National Identity: The Challenge of the Nordic States* (London: Routledge) 50–87.

—— (2007) *Security as Practice: Discourse Analysis and the Bosnian War* (London: Routledge).

——and WÆVER, O. (eds) (2002) *European Integration and National Identity: The Challenge of the Nordic States* (London: Routledge).

——and WILLIAMS, M.C. (1999) 'The Myths of Europe: Legitimacy, Community and the "Crisis" of the EU', *Journal of Common Market Studies*, 37(2), 233–49.

HANSEN, R. (1973) 'European Integration: Forward March, Parade Rest, or Dismissed?', *International Organization*, 27(2), 225–54.

HANTRAIS, L. (ed.) (2000a) *Gendered Policies in Europe: Reconciling Employment and Family Life* (Basingstoke: Macmillan).

—— (2000b) 'From Equal Pay to Reconciliation of Employment and Family Life', in Hantrais, L. (ed.) *Gendered Policies in Europe: Reconciling Employment and Family Life* (Basingstoke: Macmillan Press) 1–26.

HASSNER, P. (1997) 'The European Nation State versus Transnational Forces', in Tunander, O. *et al.* (eds) *Geopolitics in Post-Wall Europe* (London: Sage) 45–58.

HAY, C. (2000) 'Contemporary Capitalism, Globalization, Regionalization and the Persistence of National Variations', *Review of International Studies*, 26(4), 509–31.

—— (2004) 'Common Trajectories, Variable Paces, Divergent Outcomes? Models of European Capitalism under Conditions of Complex Economic Interdependence', *Review of International Political Economy*, 11(2), 231–62.

—— and ROSAMOND, B. (2002) 'Globalization, European Integration and the Discursive Construction of Economic Imperatives', *Journal of European Public Policy*, 9(2), 147–67.

HAY, D. (1968) *Europe. The Emergence of an Idea*, 2nd edn (Edinburgh: Edinburgh University Press).

HAYES-RENSHAW, F. *et al.* (1992) 'The Permanent Representations of the Member States to the European Communities', *Journal of Common Market Studies*, 28(2), 119–37.

—— and WALLACE, H. (2006) *The Council of Ministers*, 2nd revised and updated edn (London: Palgrave).

HECLO, H. (1978) 'Issue Networks and the Executive Establishment', in King, A., *The New*

American Political System (Washington, DC: American Enterprise Institute) 87–124.

HEIDEBREDER, E. G. (2008) *Expansion of the European Union and Public Policy: The Impact of Policy on Politics*, Unpublished Dissertation, European University Institute, Florence, October.

HELFERICH, B. and KOLB, F. (2001) 'Multilevel Action Coordination in European Contentious Politics: The Case of the European Women's Lobby', in Imig, D. and Tarrow, S. (eds) *Contentious Europeans: Protest and Politics in an Emerging Polity* (Lanham, MD: Rowman and Littlefield) 143–61.

HELMBERG M. (2007) 'Eurojust and Joint Investigation Teams: how Eurojust can Support JITs', *ERA Forum*, 8(2), 245–51.

HÉRITIER, A. (1998) 'The European Polity, Deadlock and Development', paper given in EUI seminar on the Amsterdam Treaty, Florence, March.

—— (1999) *Policy-Making and Diversity in Europe: Escape from Deadlock* (Cambridge and New York: Cambridge University Press).

—— *et al.* (2001) *Differential Europe—New Opportunities and Restrictions for Policy Making in Member States* (Lanham, MD: Rowman and Littlefield).

HERRMANN, R.K. *et al.* (eds) (2004) *Transnational Identities. Becoming European in the EU* (Lanham, MD: Rowman and Littlefield).

HIRST, P. (1994) *Associative Democracy: New Forms of Economic and Social Governance* (London: Polity).

HIX, S. (1994) 'The Study of the European Community: the Challenge to Comparative Politics', *West European Politics*, 17(1), 1–30.

—— (1999) *The Political System of the European Union* (Basingstoke: Macmillan).

—— (2001) 'Legislative Behaviour and Party Competition in EP: An Application of Nominate to the EU', *Journal of Common Market Studies*, 39(4), 663–88.

—— (2002) 'Constitutional Agenda-Setting through Discretion in Rule Interpretation: Why the European Parliament Won at Amsterdam', *British Journal of Political Science*, 32(2), 259–80.

—— (2005) *The Political System of the European Union*, 2nd edn (New York: Palgrave).

—— (2007) 'The European Union as a Polity (1)', in Jørgensen, K.E., Pollack, M.A., and Rosamond, B. (eds) *The Handbook of European Union Politics* (New York: Sage) 141–58.

—— *et al.* (2007) *Democratic Politics in the European Parliament* (Cambridge: Cambridge University Press).

HOBBES, T. (1996 [1651]) *Leviathan* (Cambridge: Cambridge University Press).

HODSON, D. and MAHER, I. (2001) 'The Open Method as a New Mode of Governance', *Journal of Common Market Studies*, 39(4), 719–46.

HOFFMANN, S. (1966) 'Obstinate or Obsolete? The Fate of the Nation-State and the Case of Western Europe', *Daedalus*, 95, 862–915.

—— (1982) 'Reflections on the Nation-State in Western Europe Today', *Journal of Common Market Studies*, 21(1–2), 21–37.

—— (1995) *The European Sisyphus. Essays on Europe, 1964–1994* (Boulder, CO: Westview Press).

HOLLAND, S. (1980) *UnCommon Market: Capital, Class and Power in the European Community* (London: Macmillan).

HOLLIS, M. and SMITH, S. (1990) *Explaining and Understanding International Relations* (Oxford: Clarendon).

HOLM, U. (1992) *Det Franske Europa* (Aarhus: Aarhus Universitetsforlag).

—— (1997) 'The French Garden is Not What it Used To Be', in Jørgensen, K.-E. (ed.) *Reflective Approaches to European Governance* (London: Macmillan) 128–46.

HOLMAN, O. (2001) 'The Enlargement of the EU Towards Central and Eastern Europe: The Role of Supranational and Transnational Actors', in Bieler, A. and Morton, A.D. (eds) *Social Forces in the Making of the New Europe: The Restructuring of European Social Relations in the Global Political Economy* (Basingstoke: Palgrave Macmillan) 161–84.

—— (2006) 'Socialising Structural Policy: Disembedding Neoliberalism and the Transnational Dimension of Core–periphery Relations in the EU', Paper presented at the 4th convention of the Central and East European Studies Association, University of Tartu, Estonia.

HOLZSCHEITER, A. (2005) 'Discourse as Capability: Non-State Actors' Capital in Global Governance', *Millennium: Journal of International Studies*, 33(3), 723–46.

HOOD, C. (1976) *The Tools of Government* (Chatham, NJ: Chatham House).

HOOGHE, L. and MARKS, G. (2001) *Multi-Level Governance and European Integration* (Lanham, MD: Rowman and Littlefield).

—— (2005) 'Calculation, Community, and Cues. Public Opinion on European Integration', *European Union Politics,* 6(4), 419–43.

—— (2007) *Understanding Euroscepticism.* Special Issue of *Acta Politica* (Basingstoke: Palgrave).

HOSKYNS, C. (1996) *Integrating Gender: Women, Law and Politics in the European Union* (London: Verso).

—— (2000) 'A Study of Four Action Programmes on Equal Opportunities', in M. Rossilli (ed.) *Gender policies in the European Union* (New York: Peter Lang) 43–59.

HOWE, P. (1995) 'A Community of Europeans: The Requisite Underpinnings', *Journal of Common Market Studies,* 33(1), 27–46.

HRBEK, R. (1972) *Die SPD–Deutschland und Europa: Die Haltung der Sozialdemokratie zum Verhältnis von Deutschland-Politik und West-Integration* (Bonn: Europa Union).

HUBER, J.D. (2004) *Delegation* (Cambridge: Cambridge University Press).

—— and SHIPAN, C. (2000) 'The Costs of Control: Legislators, Agencies, and Transaction Costs', *Legislative Studies Quarterly,* 25(1), 25–52.

HUEGLIN, T.O. (1999) *Early Modern Concepts for a Late Modern World: Althusius on Community and Federalism* (Waterloo, ON: Wilfrid Laurier University Press).

HUYSMANS, J. (2000) 'The European Union and the Securitization of Migration', *Journal of Common Market Studies,* 38(6), 751–77.

IMMERGUT, E. (2006) 'From Constraints to Change', *APSA European Politics & Society: Newsletter of the European Politics and Society Section of the American Political Science Association,* 5(2), 4–6.

IVANOVA, M. (2007) 'Why There Was No "Marshall Plan" for Eastern Europe and Why This Still Matters', *Journal of Contemporary European Studies,* 15(3), 345–76.

JABKO, N. (1999) 'In the Name of the Market: how the European Commission Paved the Way for Monetary Union', *Journal of European Public Policy,* 6(4), 475–96.

JACHTENFUCHS, M. (1995) 'Theoretical Perspectives on European Governance', *European Law Journal,* 1, 115–33.

—— (1997) 'Die Europäische Union—Ein Gebilde Sui Generis?', in Wolf, K.D. (ed.) *Projekt Europa Im Übergang? Probleme, Modelle Und Strategien Des Regierens in Der Europäischen Union* (Baden-Baden: Nomos) 15–35.

—— (2001) 'The Governance Approach to European Integration', *Journal of Common Market Studies,* 39(2), 245–64.

—— (2002) *Die Konstruktion Europas. Verfassungsideen und institutionelle Entwicklung* (Baden-Baden: Nomos).

——and KOHLER-KOCH, B. (1996) 'Einleitung: Regieren im dynamischen Mehrebenensystem', in Jachtenfuchs, M. and Kohler-Koch, B. (eds) *Europäische Integration* (Opladen: Leske und Budrich) 15–44.

—— *et al.* (1998) 'Which Europe? Conflicting Models of a Legitimate European Political Order', *European Journal of International Relations,* 4(4), 409–46.

JACOBY, W. (2004) *The Enlargement of the European Union and NATO: Ordering from the Menu in Central Europe* (Cambridge: Cambridge University Press).

JEFFERY, C. (2006) 'Social and Regional Interests: the Economic and Social Committee and Committee of the Regions', in Peterson, J. and Shackleton, M. (eds) *The Institutions of the European Union* (Oxford: Oxford University Press) 312–30.

JILEVA, E. (2004) 'Do Norms Matter? The Principle of Solidarity and the EU's Eastern Enlargement', *Journal of International Relations and Development,* 7(1), 3–23.

JOENNIEMI, P. (2003) 'Can Europe be Told from the North? Tapping into the EU's Northern Dimension', in Pehkonen, S. and Möller, F. (eds) *Encountering the North: Cultural Geography, International Relations and Northern Landscapes* (Aldershot: Ashgate) 221–60.

JOERGES, C. and NEYER, J. (1997a) 'Transforming Strategic Interaction into Deliberative Problem-solving: European Comitology in the Foodstuffs Sector', *Journal of European Public Policy,* 4(4), 609–25.

—— and —— (1997b) 'From Intergovernmental Bargaining to Deliberative Political Process: The Constitutionalization of Comitology', *European Law Journal,* 3(3), 273–99.

JOHANSEN, A. (1997) 'Fellowmen, Compatriots, Contemporaries: On the Formation of Identity within the Expanding "Now" of Communication', *Post-modern Studies,* 24(2), 169–209.

JOHNSON, K. (2008) 'We agreed to agree, and forgot to notice', *New York Times Week in Review,* 6 January.

JÖNSSON, C. et al. (2000) *Organizing European Space* (London: Sage).

JORDAN, A. and SCHOUT A. (2006) *The Coordination of the European Union: Exploring the Capacities of Networked Governance* (Oxford: Oxford University Press).

—— et al. (2005) 'The Rise of "New" Policy Instruments in Comparative Perspective: Has Governance Eclipsed Government?', *Political Studies*, 53(3), 477–96.

JORDAN, G. (1981) 'Iron Triangles, Woolly Corporatism and Elastic Nets: Images of the Policy Process', *Journal of Public Policy*, 1(1), 95–123.

—and SCHUBERT, K. (1992) 'A Preliminary Ordering of Policy Network Labelling', *European Journal of Political Research*, 21(special issue), 7–28.

JØRGENSEN, K.E. (1997) 'PoCo: the Diplomatic Republic of Europe', in Jørgensen, K.E. (ed.) *Reflective Approaches to European Governance* (Basingstoke: Macmillan) 167–80.

—— (2000) 'Continental IR Theory: the Best Kept Secret', *European Journal of International Relations*, 6(1), 9–42.

—— and CHRISTIANSEN, T. (1999) 'The Amsterdam Process: A Structurationist Perspective on EU Treaty Reform', European Integration Online Papers 3(1), http://eiop.or.at/eiop/texte/1999-001a.htm.

—— et al. (eds) (2007) *Handbook of European Union Politics* (London: Sage).

JOSSELIN, D. and WALLACE, W. (eds) (2001) *Non-State Actors in World Politics* (Basingstoke and New York: Palgrave).

JUNG, S. (1999) *Europa, made in France. Eine Analyse des politischen Diskurses Frankreichs zur Zukunft der Europäischen Gemeinschaft–von den Anfängen bis heute* (Baden-Baden: Nomos).

JUPILLE, J. and CAPORASO, J.A. (1999) 'Institutionalism and the European Union: Beyond International Relations and Comparative Politics', *Annual Review of Political Science*, 2, 429–44.

—— et al. (2003) 'Integrating Institutions. Rationalism, Constructivism, and the Study of the European Union', *Comparative Political Studies*, 36(1–2), 7–40.

KADAYIFEI, A. (1996) *Discourse Analysis and Conflict: Turkish Identity Creation*, Ph.D. University of Kent at Canterbury.

KADELBACH, S. (2003) 'Unionsbürgerschaft', in Bogdandy, A. von (ed.) *Europaeisches Verfassungsrecht. Theoretische und dogmatische Grundzuege* (Heidelberg: Springer) 539–82.

KAMARCK, E.C. (2007) *The End of Government as We Know It: Making Public Policy Work* (Boulder, CO: Lynne Rienner).

KANTNER, C. (2004) *Kein modernes Babel. Kommunikative Voraussetzungen europäischer Öffentlichkeit* (Wiesbaden: VS Verlag für Sozialwissenschaften).

KASSIM, H. (1993) 'Policy Networks, Networks and European Union Policy-Making: a Sceptical View', *West European Politics*, 17(4), 15–27.

KATZENSTEIN, P. (1978) *Between Power and Plenty: Foreign Economic Policies of Advanced Industrial States* (Madison, WI: University of Wisconsin Press).

—— (1984) *Corporatism and Change: Austria, Switzerland and the Politics of Industry* (Ithaca, NY: Cornell University Press).

—— (1993) 'Coping with Terrorism: Norms and Internal Security in Germany and Japan', in Goldstein, J. and Keohane, R.O. (eds) *Ideas and Foreign Policy. Beliefs, Institutions, and Political Change* (Ithaca, NY: Cornell University Press) 265–95.

—— (ed.) (1996) *The Culture of National Security* (New York: Columbia University Press).

KAZAN, I. (1994) Omvendt Osmannisme og Khanaternes Kemalisme: Tyrkiets udenrigspolitik—en diskurs udfordret af EFs integration og Sovjetunionens opløsning (Copenhagen: Institut for Statskundskab, Københavns Universitet).

KECK, M.E. and SIKKINK, K. (1998) *Activists Beyond Borders: Advocacy Networks in International Politics* (Ithaca, NY and London: Cornell University Press).

KELLEY, J. (2004) 'International Actors on the Domestic Scene: Membership Conditionality and Socialization by International Institutions', *International Organization*, 58(4), 425–57.

KELSTRUP, M. (1998) 'Integration Theories: History, Competing Approaches and New Perspectives', in Wivel, A. (ed.) *Explaining European Integration* (Copenhagen: Copenhagen Political Studies Press) 15–55.

—and WILLIAMS, M.C. (eds) (2000) *International Relations Theory and the Politics of European Integration: Power, Security and Community* (London: Routledge).

KEOHANE, R. (1984) *After Hegemony. Cooperation and Discord in the World Political Economy* (Princeton, NJ: Princeton University Press).

—— (1986) 'Theory of World Politics: Structural Realism and Beyond', in Keohane, R. (ed.) *Neorealism and Its Critics* (New York: Columbia University Press) 158–203.

—— (1988) 'International Institutions: Two Approaches', *International Studies Quarterly*, 32, 379–96.

—— (1989) *International Institutions and State Power* (Boulder, CO: Westview).

—— (2001) 'Governance in a Partly Globalized World', *American Political Science Review*, 95, 1–13.

——and HOFFMANN, S. (eds) (1991) *The New European Community: Decision-making and Institutional Change* (Boulder, CO and Oxford: Westview).

——and NYE, J. (1975) 'International Inter-dependence and Integration', in Greenstein, F. and Polsby, N. (eds) *Handbook of Political Science* (Reading, MA: Addison-Wesley) 363–77.

—— and —— (1977) *Power and Interdependence. World Politics in Transition* (Boston, MA: Little, Brown).

KIELMANSEGG, P.G. (1996) 'Integration und Demokratie', in Jachtenfuchs, M. and Kohler-Koch, B. (eds) *Europäische Integration* (Opladen: Leske und Budrich) 47–71.

KILROY, B. (1999) *Integration Through Law: ECJ and Governments in the EU*, Ph.D. dissertation, UCLA.

KINDERMAN, D. (2005) 'Pressure from Without: Subversion from Within: The Two-Pronged German Employer Offensive', *Comparative European Politics*, 3(4), 432–63.

KING, G. *et al.* (1994) *Designing Social Inquiry: Scientific Inference in Qualitative Research* (Princeton, NJ: Princeton University Press).

KING, P. (1982) *Federalism and Federation* (Baltimore, MD: Johns Hopkins University Press).

—— and BOSCO, A. (eds) (1991) *A Constitution for Europe: A Comparative Study of Federal Constitutions and Plans for the United States of Europe* (London: Lothian Foundation Press).

KINSKY, F. (1979) 'Personalism and Federalism', *Publius: The Journal of Federalism*, 9(4), 131–56.

KISBY, B. (2008) 'Analysing Policy Networks: Towards an Ideational Approach, *Policy Studies*, 28(1), 71–90.

KISSINGER, H.A. (1957) *A World Restored: Castlereagh, Metternich and the Restoration of Peace, 1812–1822* (Boston, MA: Houghton Mifflin).

KLEINE, M. (2008) 'All Roads Lead Away from Rome? A Theory of Institutional Adaptation in the European Union', Paper presented at the International Relations Graduate Research Seminar, 2 October, Princeton University.

—— and RISSE, T. (2007) Constitutional Talk. Exploring Institutional Scope Conditions for Effective Arguing, Paper presented at the Biannual Meeting of the European Union Studies Association, Montreal, Canada.

KLOTZ, A., and LYNCH, C. (2007) *Strategies for Research in Constructivist International Relations* (Armonk, NY: M.E. Sharpe).

KNOKE, D. (1998) 'Who Steals My Purse Steals My Trash: the Structure of Organizational Influence Reputation', *Journal of Theoretical Politics*, 10(4), 507–30.

KODRÉ, P. and MÜLLER, H. (2003) 'Shifting Policy Frames: EU Equal Treament Norms and Domestic Discourses in Germany', in Liebert, U. (ed.) *Gendering Europeanisation* (Brussels: P.I.E.-Peter Lang) 83–116.

KOHLER-KOCH, B. (2000) 'Framing: the Bottleneck of Constructing Legitimate Institutions', *Journal of European Public Policy*, 7(4), 513–31.

—— and EISING, R. (eds) (1999) *The Transformation of Governance in the European Union* (London: Routledge).

KOOIMAN, J. (ed.) (1993) *Modern Governance. New Government–Society Interactions* (London: Sage).

KOOPENJAAN, J. and KLIJN, E.-H. (2006) *Managing Uncertainty in Policy Networks* (London: Routledge).

KOOPMANS, R. (2007) 'Who Inhabits the European Public Sphere? Winners and Losers, Supporters and Opponents in Europeanised Political Debates', *European Journal of Political Research*, 46(2), 183–210.

KOREMENOS, B. *et al.* (2001) 'The Rational Design of International Institutions', *International Organization*, 55(4), 761–99.

KOSLOWSKI, R. (2001) 'Understanding the European Union as a Federal Polity', in Christiansen, T. *et al.* (eds) *The Social Construction of Europe* (London: Sage) 32–49.

——and KRATOCHWIL, F. (1994) 'Understanding Change in International Politics: The Soviet

Empire's Demise and the International System', *International Organization*, 48, 215–47.

KOSTAKOPOULOU, T. (1997) 'Why a "Community of Europeans" Could be a Community of Exclusion: A Reply to Howe', *Journal of Common Market Studies*, 35(2), 301–14.

—— (2001) *Citizenship, Identity, and Immigration in the European Union: Between Past and Future* (Manchester: Manchester University Press).

—— (2006) 'Security Interests: Police and Judicial Cooperation', in Peterson, J. and Shackleton, M. (eds) *The Institutions of the European Union*, 2nd edn (Oxford and New York: Oxford University Press) 231–51.

KRASNER, S.D. (1976) 'State Power and the Structure of International Trade', *World Politics*, 28(3), 317–47.

KRATOCHWIL, F. (1989) *Rules, Norms, and Decisions* (Cambridge: Cambridge University Press).

—— and RUGGIE, J.G. (1986) 'International Organization: A State of the Art on an Art of the State', *International Organization*, 40, 753–75.

KREHBIEL, K. (1991) *Information and Legislative Organization* (Ann Arbor, MI: University of Michigan Press).

KREPPEL, A. (1999) 'The European Parliament's Influence over EU Policy Outcomes', *Journal of Common Market Studies*, 37(3), 521–38.

—— (2001) *The European Parliament and Supranational Party System: A Study in Institutional Development* (Cambridge: Cambridge University Press).

KRIESI, H., ADAM, S., and JOCHUM, M. (2006) 'Comparative Analysis of Policy Networks in Western Europe', *Journal of European Public Policy*, 13(3), 341–61.

KRIZSÁN, A. and ZENTAI, V. (2006) 'Gender Equality Policy or Gender Mainstreaming? The Case of Hungary on the Road to an Enlarged Europe', *Policy Studies*, 27(2), 135–51.

KRONSELL, A. (2005) 'Gender, Power and European Integration Theory', *Journal of European Public Policy*, 12(6), 1022–40.

KUHN, T.S. (1964) *The Structure of Scientific Revolutions* (Chicago, IL: University of Chicago Press).

KUPER, A. (2004) *Democracy Beyond Borders. Justice and Representation in Global Institutions* (Oxford: Oxford University Press).

LACLAU, E. and MOUFFE, C. (1985) *Hegemony and Socialist Strategy: Towards a Radical Democratic Politics* (London: Verso).

LADEUR, K.-H. (1997) 'Towards a Legal Theory of Supranationality—the Viability of the Network Concept', *European Law Journal*, 3(1), 33–54.

LAFFAN, B. (1996) 'The Politics of Identity and Political Order in Europe', *Journal of Common Market Studies*, 34(1), 81–102.

—— (2004) 'The European Union and Its Institutions as "Identity Builders"', in Herrmann, R.K., Risse, T., and Brewer, M. (eds) *Transnational Identities: Becoming European in the EU* (Lanham, MD: Rowman and Littlefield) 75–96.

—— et al. (2000) *Europe's Experimental Union. Rethinking Integration* (London: Routledge).

LAHAV, G. (2004) *Immigration and Politics in the New Europe. Reinventing Borders* (Cambridge: Cambridge University Press).

LAKE, D.A. and POWELL, R. (1999) 'International Relations: A Strategic Choice Approach', in Lake, D.A. and Powell, R. (eds) *Strategic Choice and International Relations* (Princeton, NJ: Princeton University Press) 3–38.

LARSEN, H. (1997a) *Foreign Policy and Discourse Analysis: France, Britain, and Europe* (London: Routledge).

—— (1997b) 'British Discourses on Europe: Sovereignty of Parliament, Instrumentality and the Non-Mythical Europe', in Jørgensen, K.-E. (ed.) *Reflective Approaches to European Governance* (London: Macmillan) 109–27.

—— (1999) 'British and Danish European Policies in the 1990s: A Discourse Approach', *European Journal of International Relations*, 5(4), 451–83.

—— (2000) 'Danish CFSP Policy in the Post-Cold War Period: Continuity or Change', *Cooperation and Conflict*, 35(1), 37–64.

LASCOUMBES, P. and LE GALES, P. (2004) *Les instruments de politique publique* (Paris: Presses de Sciences Po).

LA TORRE, M. (2002) 'The Law beneath Rights' Feet: Preliminary Investigations for the Study of the Charter of Fundamental Rights of the European Union', *European Law Journal*, 8(4), 515–35.

LAVENEX, S. and WALLACE, W. (2005) 'Justice and home affairs: towards a European public order?', in Wallace, H., Wallace, W., and Pollack, M. (eds) *Policy-Making in the European Union* (Oxford: Oxford University Press) 457–80.

LEBORGNE, D. and LIPIETZ, A. (1988) 'New Technologies, New Modes of Regulation: Some

Spatial Implications', *Environment and Planning D: Society and Space*, 6, 263–80.

LE GALÈS, P. and THATCHER, M. (eds) (1995) *Les Reseaux de Politique Publique* (Paris: L'Harmattan).

LEGRO, J.W. (1996) 'Culture and Preferences in the International Cooperation Two-Step', *American Political Science Review*, 90(1), 118–37.

—— (2007) *Rethinking the World: Great Power Strategies and International Order* (New York: Cornell University Press).

—— and MORAVCSIK, A. (1999) 'Is Anybody Still a Realist?', *International Security*, 24(2), 5–55.

LEHMBRUCH, G. and SCHMITTER, P. (eds) (1979) *Trends towards Corporatist Intermediation* (London: Sage).

LEHNING, P.B. and Percy, B. (1997) 'Pluralism, Contractarianism and the European Union', in Lehning, P.B. and Weale, A. (eds) *Citizenship, Democracy and Justice in the New Europe* (London and New York: Routledge) 107–24.

—— and WEALE, A. (eds) (1997) *Citizenship, Democracy and Justice in the New Europe* (London and New York: Routledge).

LEONARD, M. and POPESCU, N. (2007) *A Power Audit of EU–Russia Relations* (Brussels: European Council on Foreign Relations).

LESSER, I.O. (1999) 'Countering the New Terrorism: Implications for Strategy', in Lesser, I.O., Hoffman, B., Arquilla, J. *et al.* (eds) *Countering the New Terrorism* (Santa Monica, CA: Rand Corporation) 85–143.

LIEBERT, U. (1999) 'Gender Politics in the European Union: The Return of the Public', *European Societies*, 1(2), 197–239.

—— (2002) 'Europeanising Gender Mainstreaming: Constraints and Opportunities in the Multilevel Euro-polity', *Feminist Legal Studies*, 10(2), 241–56.

—— (ed.) (2003) *Gendering Europeanisation* (Brussels: P.I.E.-Peter Lang).

LIM, E. (2006) *The Euro's Challenge to the Dollar: Different Views from Economists and Evidence from COFER and Other Data* (Washington, DC: IMF Working Paper) 06/153.

LINDBERG, L.N. (1963) *The Political Dynamics of European Economic Integration* (Stanford, CA: Stanford University Press).

—— and SCHEINGOLD, S.A. (1970) *Europe's Would-Be Polity: Patterns of Change in the European Community* (Englewood Cliffs, NJ: Prentice Hall).

—— and —— (1971) *Regional Integration: Theory and Research* (Cambridge, MA: Harvard University Press).

LIPGENS, W. (1982) *A History of European Integration, 1945–1947: The Formation of the European Unity Movement*, vol. 1 (Oxford: Clarendon Press).

—— (ed.) (1985) *Documents on European Integration*, vols 1 and 2 (Berlin: De Gruyter).

LIPIETZ, A. (1985) *Mirages and Miracles: The Crisis of Global Fordism* (London: Verso).

—— (1987) 'Rebel Sons: The Regulation School', *French Politics and Society*, 5, 3–17.

—— (1989) 'The Debt Problem: European Integration and the New Phase of World Crisis', *New Left Review*, 178 (old series), 37–50.

LISBON COUNCIL (2007) *European Human Capital Index* (Brussels: European Council).

LISTER, F. K., (1996) *The European Union, the United Nations and the Revival of Confederal Governance* (London: Greenwood Press).

LOCHER, B (2002) 'Internationale Normen und regionaler Policy-Wandel: Frauenhandel in der Europaeischen Union', *WeltTrends*, 10, 59–80.

—— (2002) *Trafficking in Women in the European Union. A Norm-based Constructivist Approach*, University of Bremen, unpubl. dissertation.

—— (2007) *Trafficking in Women in the European Union: Norms, Advocacy Networks, and Policy Change* (Wiesbaden: VS Verlag für Sozialwissenschaften).

LOCKE, J. (1988 [1680–90]) *Two Treatises on Govern-ment* (Cambridge: Cambridge University Press).

LOHMANN, K. (2005) 'The impact of EU Enlargement on the Civic Participation of Women in Central and Eastern Europe—The perspective of the Karat Coalition', *Sociologický ústav AVČR*, 1111–17.

LORENTOWICZ, A., MARIN, D., and RAUBOLD, A. (2002) *Ownership, Capital or Outsourcing: What Drives German Investment to Eastern Europe?* (Munich: Center for Economic Policy Research).

LOWI, T. (1979) *The End of Liberalism* (New York: W.W. Norton).

LOWNDES, V. (1996) 'Varieties of New Institutionalism: a Critical Appraisal', *Public Administration*, 74(2), 181–97.

LUDLOW, N.P. (2006) *The European Community and the Crises of the 1960s. Negotiating the Gaullist Challenge* (London: Routledge).

LUDLOW, P. (1991) 'The European Commission', in Keohane, R.O. and Hoffmann, S. (eds) *The New European Community. Decision-making and Institutional Change* (Boulder, CO: Westview) 85–132.

LUNDSTRÖM, K. (1999) *Jämlikhet mellan Kvinnor och män i EG-rätten. En feministisk Analys* (Gothenburg: Iustus).

MACRAE, H. (2006) 'Rescaling Gender Relations: The Influence of European Directives on the German Gender Regime', *Social Politics,* 13(4), 522–50.

MCCUBBINS, M. and SCHWARTZ, T. (1987) 'Congressional Oversight Overlooked: Police Patrols versus Fire Alarms', in McCubbins, M. and Sullivan, T. (eds) *Congress: Structure and Policy* (New York: Cambridge University Press) 426–40.

MCDONALD, M. (2000) 'Identities in the European Commission', in Nugent, N. (ed.) *At the Heart of the Union: Studies of the European Commission* (Basingstoke: Macmillan) 49–70.

MCELROY, G. (2007) 'Legislative Politics', in Jørgensen, K.E., Pollack, M.A., and Rosamond, B. (eds) *The Handbook of European Union Politics* (New York: Sage) 175–94.

MCKAY, D. (2001) *Designing Europe: Comparative Lessons from the Federal Experience* (Oxford: Oxford University Press).

MCLAREN, L. (2006) *Identity, Interests and Attitudes to European Integration* (Basingstoke: Palgrave Macmillan).

—— (2007) 'Explaining Opposition to Turkish Membership in the EU', *European Union Politics,* 8(2), 251–78.

MCNAMARA, K.R. (1993) 'Common Markets, Uncommon Currencies: Systems Effects and European Community', in Snyder, J. and Jervis, R. (eds) *Coping with Complexity, in the International System* (Boulder, CO: Westview Press) 303–27.

—— (1998) *The Currency of Ideas: Monetary Politics in the European Union* (Ithaca, NY: Cornell University Press).

—— (2002) 'Managing the Euro: the European Central Bank', in Shackleton, M. (ed.) *The Institutions of the European Union* (Oxford: Oxford University Press) 164–85.

—— (2006) 'Managing the Euro: the European Central Bank', in Peterson, J. and Shackleton, M. (eds) *The Institutions of the European Union*, 2nd edn (Oxford: Oxford University Press), 169–89.

MADEKER, E. (2008) *Türkei und europäische Identität. Eine wissenssoziologische Analyse der Debatte um den EU-Beitritt* (Wiesbaden: VS Verlag für Sozialwissenschaften).

MAJONE, G. (1994) 'The Rise of the Regulatory State in Europe', *West European Politics,* 17(3), 77–101.

—— (1996) *Regulating Europe* (London: Routledge).

—— (1998) 'Europe's "Democracy Deficit": the Question of Standards', *European Law Journal,* 4(1), 5–28.

—— (2001) 'Two Logics of Delegation: Agency and Fiduciary Relations in EU Governance', *European Union Politics,* 2(1), 103–21.

—— (2005) *Dilemmas of European Integration: the Ambiguities and Pitfalls of Integration by Stealth* (Oxford and New York: Oxford University Press).

—— (2006a) 'The common sense of European integration', *Journal of European Public Policy,* 13(5), 607–26.

—— (2006b) 'Managing Europeanization: the European Agencies', in Peterson, J. and Shackleton, M. (eds) *The Institutions of the European Union*, 2nd edn (Oxford and New York: Oxford University Press) 190–209.

MALMBERG, M. and STRÅTH, B. (eds) (2002) *The Meaning of Europe* (Oxford: Berg).

MALMVIG, H. (2002) *Sovereignty Intervened: Constitutions of State Sovereignty during Interventionary and Non-Interventionary Practices in Kosovo and Algeria*, University of Copenhagen: unpubl. Ph.D. dissertation.

MANDEL, E. (1968) *Die EWG und die Konkurrenz Europa-Amerika* (Frankfurt/M: Europäische Verlagsanstalt).

MANNERS, I. (2002) 'Normative Power Europe: A Contradiction in Terms', *Journal of Common Market Studies,* 40, 235–58.

—— (2006) 'Normative Power Europe Reconsidered: Beyond the Crossroads', *Journal of European Public Policy,* 13, 182–99.

—— (2007) 'Another Europe is Possible: A Critical Perspective on European Union Politics', in Jorgensen, K.E., Pollack, M., and Rosamond, B. (eds) *Handbook of European Union Politics* (London: Sage) 77–95.

MARCH, J.G. and OLSEN, J.P. (1989) *Rediscovering Institutions: The Organizational Basis of Politics* (New York: Free Press).

—— (1995) *Democratic Governance* (New York: The Free Press).

—— (1998) 'The Institutional Dynamics of International Political Orders', *International Organization,* 52, 943–69.

MARCUSSEN, M. (1998) 'Central Bankers, the Ideational Life-Cycle and the Social Construction of EMU', Working Paper RSC 98/33 (Florence: European University Institute).

—— (1999) 'The Dynamics of EMU Ideas', *Cooperation and Conflict,* 34(4), 383–413.

—— (2000) *Ideas and Elites. Danish Marco-Economic Policy Discourse in the EMU Process* (Aalborg: Aalborg University Press).

—— and RISSE, T. (1997) 'A Europeanisation of Nation-state Identities? Conceptual Considerations and Research Design', paper presented at the workshop on National Identities. Florence: Robert Schuman Centre, European University Institute, 21–22 November.

—— and TORFING, J. (2007) *Democratic Network Governance in Europe* (Basingstoke: Palgrave).

—— et al. (1999) 'Constructing Europe. The Evolution of French, British, and German Nation-State Identities', *Journal of European Public Policy,* 6(4), 614–33.

—— et al. (2001) 'Constructing Europe? The Evolution of French, British and German Nation-State Identities', in Christiansen, T., Jørgensen, K.E., and A. Wiener (eds) *The Social Construction of Europe* (London: Sage) 101–20.

MARINETTO, M. (2003) 'Governing Beyond the Centre: A Critique of the Anglo-Governance School', *Political Studies,* 51(4), 592–608.

MARKS, G. (1992) 'Structural Policy and Multi-level Governance in the EC', in Rosenthal, G.G. (ed.) *The State of the European Community II* (Boulder, CO and Ilford: Lynne Rienner and Longman) 390–410.

—— HOOGHE, L., and BLANK, K. (1996) 'European Integration from the 1980s: State-Centric v. Multi-level Governance', *Journal of Common Market Studies,* 34(3), 341–78.

—— and McADAM, D. (1996) 'Social Movements and the Changing Structure of Political Opportunities in the EU', in Marks, G., Scharpf, F.W., Schmitter, P. *et al.* (eds) *Governance in the EU* (London: Sage) 95–120.

—— et al. (1996) *Governance in the European Union* (London: Sage).

MARSH, D. (ed.) (1998) *Comparing Policy Networks* (Buckingham: Open University Press).

—— and RHODES, R.A.W. (eds) (1992) *Policy Networks in British Government* (Oxford: Clarendon Press).

—— and SMITH, M. (2000) 'Understanding Policy Networks: Towards a Dialectical Approach', *Political Studies,* 48(1), 4–21.

—— and —— (2001) 'There is More than One Way to do Political Science: on Different Ways to Study Policy Networks', *Political Studies,* 49(3), 528–41.

MARTINOTTI, G. and STEFFANIZZI, S. (1995) 'Europeans and the Nation-State', in Niedermayer, O. and Sinnott, R. (eds) *Public Opinion and Internationalized Governance* (Oxford: Oxford University Press) 163–89.

MARX FERREE, M. (ed.) (2004) 'Gender Politics in the EU: Feminist Discourses and Policy Debates', Special Issue of *Social Politics,* 11(1), 1–145.

MASTENBROEK, E. (2005) 'EU Compliance: Still a "Black Hole"?', *Journal of European Public Policy,* 12(6), 1103–20.

MATLARY, J.H. (1997) *Energy Policy in the European Union* (London: Macmillan Press).

MATTILA, M. (2004) 'Contested Decisions–Empirical Analysis of Voting in the EU Council of Ministers', *European Journal of Political Research,* 43(1), 29–50.

MATTLI, W. (1999) *The Logic of Regional Integration. Europe and Beyond* (Cambridge: Cambridge University Press).

—— and SLAUGHTER, A.-M. (1995) 'Law and Politics in the European Union: A Reply to Garrett', *International Organization,* 49(1), 183–90.

—— and —— (1998) 'Revisiting the European Court of Justice', *International Organization,* 52(1), 177–209.

MAYNTZ, R. (2003) 'New challenges to Governance Theory', in Bang, H.P. (ed.) *Governance as Social and Political Communication* (Manchester and New York: Manchester University Press) 27–40.

MAZEY, S. (1998) 'The European Union and Women's Rights: from the Europeanization of National Agendas to the Nationalization of European Agendas?', *Journal of European Public Policy,* 5(1), 131–52.

—— (2001) *Gender Mainstreaming in the EU: Principles and Practice* (London: Kogan Page).

—— (2002) 'The development of EU gender policies: toward the recognition of difference', *EUSA Review,* 15(3), 1–2.

—— and RICHARDSON, J. (eds) (1993) *Lobbying in the European Community* (Oxford and New York: Oxford University Press).

—— and —— (1997) 'The Commission and the lobby', in Edwards, G. and Spence, D. (eds) *The European Commission*, 2nd edn (London: Cathermill) 178–98.

MEARSHEIMER, J.J. (1990) 'Back to the Future: Instability in Europe after the Cold War', *International Security,* 15(1), 5–56.

MEEHAN, E. (1993) *Citizenship and the European Community* (London: Sage).

MENON, A. (2008) *Europe: The State of the Union* (London: Atlantic).

—— and SCHAIN, M. (eds) (2006) *Comparative Federalism: The European Union and the United States in Comparative Perspective* (Oxford: Oxford University Press).

MERLINGEN, M. (2001) 'Identity, Politics and Germany's Post-TEU Policy on EMU', *Journal of Common Market Studies*, 39(3), 463–83.

METCALFE, L. (2000) 'Reforming the Commission: Will Organizational Efficiency Produce Effective Governance?', *Journal of Common Market Studies*, 38(5), 817–41.

MEYER, C. (2007) 'The Constitutional Treaty Debates as Revelatory Mechanisms. Insights for Public Sphere Research and Re-Launch Attempts' (Oslo: ARENA), University of Oslo, July.

MILLER, D. (1998) 'The Left, the Nation-State, and European Citizenship', *Dissent*, 45(3), 47–51.

—— (2000) *Citizenship and National Identity* (Cambridge: Polity Press).

MILLIKEN, J. (1999) 'The Study of Discourse in International Relations: A Critique of Research and Methods', *European Journal of International Relations*, 5(2), 225–54.

MILNER, H.V. (1998) 'Rationalizing Politics: The Emerging Synthesis of International, American, and Comparative Politics', *International Organization,* 52(4), 759–86.

MILWARD, A.S. (1992) *The European Rescue of the Nation State* (London: Routledge).

—— et al. (1993) *The Frontier of National Sovereignty: History and Theory 1945–1992* (London: Routledge).

—— (2000) *The European Rescue of the Nation State,* 2nd edn (London: Routledge).

MITRANY, D. (1943) *A Working Peace System: An Argument for the Functional Development of International Organization* (London: Royal Institute of International Affairs).

—— (1966) 'The Prospect of Integration: Federal or Functional', *Journal of Common Market Studies*, 4(2), 119–49.

—— (1975) *The Functional Theory of Politics* (London: Macmillan).

MOE, T. (1984) 'The New Economics of Organization', *American Journal of Political Science,* 28(4), 739–77.

MONNET, J. (1978) *Memoirs* (New York: Doubleday).

MONTPETIT, E. (2003) *Misplaced Trust: Policy Networks and the Environment in France* (Vancouver: University of British Columbia Press).

MORAVCSIK, A. (1989) 'Disciplining Trade Finance: The OECD Export Credit Arrangement', *International Organization,* 43(1), 173–205

—— (1991) 'Negotiating the Single European Act: National Interests and Conventional Statecraft in the European Community', *International Organization,* 45, 19–56.

—— (1993) 'Preferences and Power in the European Community: A Liberal Intergovernmentalist Approach', *Journal of Common Market Studies,* 31, 473–524.

—— (1994) 'Why the European Community Strengthens the State: Domestic Politics and International Cooperation', Center for European Studies, Working Paper Series No. 52 (Harvard University).

—— (1995) 'Liberal Intergovernmentalism and Integration: A Rejoinder', *Journal of Common Market Studies,* 33(4), 611–28.

—— (1997) 'Taking Preferences Seriously: A Liberal Theory of International Politics', *International Organization,* 51(4), 513–53.

—— (1998) *The Choice for Europe. Social Purpose and State Power From Messina to Maastricht* (Ithaca, NY: Cornell University Press).

—— (1999a) 'The Choice for Europe: Current Commentary and Future Research: A Response to James Caporaso, Fritz Scharpf, and Helen Wallace', *Journal of European Public Policy,* 6(1), 168–79.

—— (1999b) 'A New Statecraft? Supranational Entrepreneurs and International Cooperation', *International Organization,* 53(2), 267–306.

—— (1999c) 'The Future of European Integration Studies: Social Science or Social Theory',

Millennium: Journal of International Studies, 28(2), 371–91.

—— (1999d) 'Theory and Method in the Study of International Negotiation: A Rejoinder to Oran Young', *International Organization,* 53(4), 811–14.

—— (2001a) 'Federalism in the European Union: Rhetoric and Reality', in Nicolaïdis, K. and Howse, R. (eds) *The Federal Vision: Legitimacy and Levels of Governance in the United States and the European Union* (Oxford: Oxford University Press) 161–87.

—— (2001b) 'Bringing Constructivist Integration Theory Out of the Clouds: Has it Landed Yet?', *European Union Politics,* 2(2), 226–40.

—— (2001c) 'Constructivism and European Integration: A Critique', in Christiansen, T. et al. (eds) *The Social Construction of Europe* (London: Sage) 176–88.

—— (2001d) 'De Gaulle between Grain and Grandeur: The Political Economy of French Economic Policy, 1958–1970 (Part I)', *Journal of Cold War Studies,* 2(2), 3–43.

—— (2001e) 'De Gaulle between Grain and Grandeur: The Political Economy of French Economic Policy, 1958–1970 (Part II)', *Journal of Cold War Studies,* 2(3), 4–68.

—— (2002) 'In Defence of the Democratic Deficit: Reassessing Legitimacy in the European Union', *Journal of Common Market Studies,* 40(4), 603–24.

—— (2005) 'The European Constitutional Compromise and the Neofunctionalist Legacy', *Journal of European Public Policy,* 12(2), 349–86.

—— (2006) 'What Can We Learn from the Collapse of the European Constitutional Project?', *Politische Vierteljahresschrift,* 47(2), 219–41.

—— (2007) 'The European Constitutional Settlement', in McNamara, K. and Meunier, S. (eds) *Making History: European Integration and Institutional Change at 50* (Oxford: Oxford University Press) 158–83.

—— (2008) 'The New Liberalism', in Reus-Smit, C. and Snidal, D. (eds) *The Oxford Handbook of International Relations* (Oxford: Oxford University Press) 234–54.

——and Nicolaïdis, K. (1998) 'Keynote Article: Federal Ideals and Constitutional Realities in the Treaty of Amsterdam', *Journal of Common Market Studies,* 36, 13–38.

—— and —— (1999) 'Explaining the Treaty of Amsterdam: Interests, Influence, Institutions', *Journal of Common Market Studies,* 37(1), 59–85.

——and Vachudova, M.A. (2002) 'Bargaining Among Unequals: Enlargement and the Future of European Integration', *EUSA Review,* 15(4), 1, 3–5.

—— and —— (2003) 'National Interests, State Power, EU Enlargement', *East European Politics and Societies,* 17(1), 42–57.

Morgan, G. (2004) *The Idea of a European Superstate: Public Justification and European Integration* (Princeton, NJ: Princeton University Press).

Morth, U. (ed.) (2004) *Soft Law in Governance and Regulation: An Interdisciplinary Analysis* (Cheltenham: Edward Elgar).

Müller, H. (1994) 'Internationale Beziehungen als kommunikatives Handeln. Zur Kritik der utilitaristischen Handlungstheorien', *Zeitschrift für Internationale Beziehungen,* 1(1), 15–44.

Mutimer, D. (1989) '1992 and the Political Integration of Europe: Neofunctionalism Reconsidered', *Journal of European Integration,* 13, 75–101.

Naurin, D. and Wallace, H. (2008) 'Introduction: From Rags to Riches', in Naurin, D. and Wallace, H. (eds) *Unveiling the Council: Games Governments Play in Brussels* (London: Palgrave).

Nelsen, B.F. and Stubb, A.C.-G. (1994) *The European Union: Readings on the Theory and Practice of European Integration* (Boulder, CO: Lynne Rienner).

Neumann, I.B. (1996a) *Russia and the Idea of Europe: A Study in Identity and International Relations* (London: Routledge).

—— (1996b) 'Self and Other in International Relations', *European Journal of International Relations,* 2(2), 139–74.

—— (1998) 'European Identity, EU Expansion, and the Integration/Exclusion Nexus', *Alternatives,* 23, 397–416.

——(1999) *Uses of the Other: the 'East' in European Identity Formation* (Manchester: Manchester University Press).

—— (2001) 'This Little Piggy Stayed at Home: Why Norway is Not a Member of the EU', in Hansen, L. and Wæver, O. (eds) *European Integration and National Identity: The Challenge of the Nordic States* (London: Routledge) 88–129.

—— (2002) 'Returning Practice to the Linguistic Turn: The Case of Diplomacy', *Millennium,* 31, 627–51.

NEYER, J. (2002) 'Politische Herrschaft in nicht-hierarchischen Mehrebenensystemen', *Zeitschrift für Internationale Beziehungen,* 9(1), 9–38.

NICOLAÏDIS, K. and HOWSE, R. (eds) (2001) *The Federal Vision: Legitimacy and Levels of Governance in the United States and the European Union* (Oxford: Oxford University Press).

—— and —— (2002) '"This is my EUtopia": the EU, the WTO, global governance and global justice', *Journal of Common Market Studies,* 40(4), 767–89.

NIEMANN, A. (1998) 'The PHARE programme and the concept of spillover: neofunctionalism in the making', *Journal of European Public Policy,* 5, 428–46.

—— (2000) *The Internal and External Dimensions of European Union Decision-Making: Developing and Testing a Revised Neofunctionalist Framework,* Ph.D. Thesis, University of Cambridge.

—— (2004) 'From pre-theory to theory? Developing a revised neofunctionalist framework for explaining EU decision-making outcomes', *Dresdner Arbeitspapiere Internationale Beziehungen,* 11.

—— (2006) *Explaining Decisions in the European Union* (Cambridge: Cambridge University Press).

—— (2008) 'Dynamics and countervailing pressures of visa, asylum and immigration policy Treaty revision: explaining change and stagnancy from the Amsterdam IGC to the IGC 2003/2004', *Journal of Common Market Studies,* 46(3), 559–91.

NORMAN, P. (2003) *The Accidental Constitution. The Story of the European Convention* (Brussels: EuroComment).

NORTH, D.C. (1990) *Institutions, Institutional Change and Economic Performance* (Cambridge: Cambridge University Press).

NOZICK, R. (1974) *Anarchy, State and Utopia* (New York: Basic Books).

NUGENT, N. (1995) 'The Leadership Capacity of the European Commission', *Journal of European Public Policy,* 2(4), 603–23.

NUNAN, F. (1999) 'Policy Network Transformation: the Implementation of the EC Directive on Packaging and Packaging Waste', *Public Administration,* 77(3), 621–38.

NYE, J. (1971) *Peace in Parts: Integration and Conflict in Regional Organization* (Boston, MA: Little, Brown).

OBERHUBER, F. *et al.* (2005) 'Debating the European Constitution: On Representations of Europe/the EU in the Press', *Journal of Language and Politics,* 4(2), 227–71.

OECD (ed.) (2001) *Governance in the 21st Century* (Paris: OECD).

OFFE, C. (2000) 'The Democratic Welfare State in an Integrating Europe', in Green, M. and Pauly, L. (eds) *Democracy beyond the State? The European Dilemma and the Emerging Global Order* (Lanham, MD: Rowman and Littlefield) 63–89.

—— (2003) 'The European Model of "Social" Capitalism: Can it Survive European Integration?', *Journal of Political Philosophy,* 11(4), 437–69.

ØHRGAARD, J.C. (1997) 'Less than Supranational, More than Intergovernmental: European Political Cooperation and the Dynamics of Intergovernmental Integration', *Millennium: Journal of International Studies,* 26(1) 1–29.

O'LEARY, S. (1996) *The Evolving Concept of Community Citizenship: From the Free Movement of Persons to Union Citizenship* (The Hague: Kluwer).

OLSEN, J.P. (2001) 'Four Faces of Europeanization' (Oslo: ARENA paper).

—— (2002a) 'The Many Faces of Europeanization', *Journal of Common Market Studies,* 40(5), 921–52.

—— (2002b) 'Reforming European Institutions of Governance', *Journal of Common Market Studies,* 40(4), 581–602.

ONUF, N. (1989) *World of Our Making: Rules and Rule in Social Theory and International Relations* (Colombia, SC: University of South Carolina Press).

—— (2002) 'Institutions, Intentions and International Relations', *Review of International Studies,* 28, 211–28.

ORDESHOOK, P.C. and SCHWARTZ, T. (1987) 'Agenda and the Control of Political Outcomes', *American Political Science Review,* 81(1), 179–200.

O'REILLY, D. and STONE SWEET, A. (1998) 'The Liberalisation and Reregulation of Air Transport', *Journal of European Public Policy,* 5(3), 447–66.

Ostner, I. (2000) 'From equal pay to equal employability: four decades of European gender policies', in Rossilli, M. (ed.) *Gender policies in the European Union* (New York: Peter Lang) 25–42.

—— and Lewis, J. (1995) 'Gender and the evolution of European social policies', in Leibfried, S. and Pierson, P. (eds) *European Social Policy: Between Fragmentation and Integration* (Washington, DC: Brookings Institution) 159–93.

Padoa-Schioppa, T. (1988) 'The EMS: A Long Term View', in Giavazzi, F. and Micossi, S., and Miller, M. (eds) *The European Monetary System* (Cambridge: Cambridge University Press) 369–84.

Page, E.C. (1997) *People Who Run Europe* (Oxford: Oxford University Press).

Pagden, A. (ed.) (2002) *The Idea of Europe: From Antiquity to the European Union* (Cambridge: Cambridge University Press).

Painter, M. and Pierre, J. (eds) (2005) *Challenges to State Policy Capacity* (Basingstoke: Palgrave).

Panitch, L. (1981) 'Trade Unions and the Capitalist State', *New Left Review,* 125 (old series), 21–43.

Pantel, M. (1999) 'Unity-Diversity: Cultural Policy and EU Legitimacy', in Banchoff, T. and Smith, M. (eds) *Legitimacy and the European Union* (London: Routledge) 46–65.

Parker, N. (2002) 'Differentiating, Collaborating, Outdoing: Nordic Identity and Marginality in the Contemporary World', *Identities: Global Studies in Culture and Power,* 9(3), 355–81.

Parsons, C. (2000) 'Domestic Interests, Ideas and Integration: Lessons from the French Case', *Journal of Common Market Studies,* 38(1), 45–70.

Parsons, T. (1951) *The Social System* (London: Routledge and Kegan Paul).

Parsons, C (2003) *A Certain Idea of Europe* (Ithaca, NY: Cornell University Press).

Parsons, W. (2004) 'Not Just Steering but Weaving: Relevant Knowledge and Craft of Building Policy Capacity', *Australian Journal of Public Administration,* 63(1), 43–57.

Pedersen, T. (1998) *Germany, France and the Integration of Europe: A Realist Interpretation* (London: Pinter).

Pentland, C. (1973) *International Theory and European Integration* (London: Faber and Faber).

Pernice, I. (1999) 'Multilevel Constitutionalism and the Treaty of Amsterdam: European Constitution-Making Revisited?', *Common Market Law Review,* 36, 703–50.

—— (2001) 'The European Constitution', 16th Sinclair-House Talks in Bad Homburg, 11–12 May.

Peters, B.G. (1998) 'Policy Networks: Myth, Metaphor and Reality', in Marsh, D. (ed.) *Comparing Policy Networks* (Buckingham: Open University Press) 21–32.

—— (1999) *Institutional Theory in Political Science* (London and New York: Continuum).

—— (2001) 'Agenda-Setting in the European Union', in Richardson, J.J. (ed.) *European Union: Power and Policy-Making,* 2nd edn (London: Routledge) 66–91.

—— (2007) 'Forms of Informality: Identifying Informal Governance in the European Union', *Perspectives on European Politics and Society,* 7(1), 25–40.

—— and Pierre, J. (2004) 'Multi-Level Governance: A Faustian Bargain?', in Bache, I. and Flinders, M. (eds) *Multi-Level Governance* (Oxford: Oxford University Press) 75–91.

Peterson, J. (1992) 'The European Technology Community: Policy Networks in a Supranational Setting', in Marsh, D. and Rhodes, R.A.W. (eds) *Policy Networks in British Government* (Oxford: Clarendon Press) 226–48.

—— (1995a) 'Decision-making in the European Union: Towards a Framework for Analysis', *Journal of European Public Policy,* 2(1), 69–93.

—— (1995b) 'EU Research Policy: the Politics of Expertise', in Mazey, S. (ed) *The State of the European Union vol. 3: Building a European Polity?* (Boulder, CO and Ilford: Lynne Rienner and Longman) 391–412.

—— (2001) 'The Choice for EU Theorists: Establishing a Common Framework for Analysis', *European Journal of Political Research,* 39(3), 289–318.

—— (2008) 'Enlargement, Reform and the Commission: Weathering a Perfect Storm?', *Journal of European Public Policy,* 15(5), 761–80.

—— and Bomberg, E. (1999) *Decision-making in the European Union* (Basingstoke and New York: Palgrave).

—— and —— (2000) 'The European Union After the 1990s: Explaining Continuity and Change', in Cowles, M.G. and Smith, M. (eds) *The State of the European Union, vol. 5: Risks, Reform, Resistance and Revival* (Oxford and New York: Oxford University Press) 19–41.

——and JONES, E. (1999) 'Decision Making in an Enlarging European Union', in Sperling, J., *Two Tiers or Two Speeds? The European Security Order and the Enlargement of the European Union and NATO* (Manchester and New York: Manchester University Press) 25–45.

—— and O'TOOLE JR, L.J. (2001) 'Federal Governance in the United States and the European Union: a Policy Network Perspective', in Howse, R., *The Federal Vision: Legitimacy and Levels of Governance in the United States and the European Union* (Oxford and New York: Oxford University Press) 300–34.

——and SHACKLETON, M. (eds) (2006) *The Institutions of the European Union*, 2nd edn (Oxford and New York: Oxford University Press).

——and SHARP, M. (1998) *Technology Policy in the European Union* (Basingstoke: Macmillan).

PETERSON, V. S. (ed.) (1992) *Gendered States: Feminist (Re)Visions of International Relations Theory* (Boulder, CO: Lynne Rienner).

PETTIT, P. (1997) *Republicanism: A Theory of Freedom and Government* (Oxford: Oxford University Press).

—— (2004) 'Depoliticising Democracy', *Ratio Juris*, 17(1), 52–65.

PFETSCH, B. (2004) 'The Voice of the Media in European Public Sphere: Comparative Analysis of Newspaper Editorials', Integrated Report WP3: Europub.com.

PFISTER, T. (2007) The Changing Nature of Citizenship in the European Union: The European Employment Strategy and its Gender Equality Dimension, Unpubl Ph.D. Dissertation, Queen's University of Belfast.

PIERRE, J. (ed.) (2000) *Debating Governance: Authority, Steering and Democracy* (Oxford and New York: Oxford University Press).

—— and PETERS, B.G. (2005) *Governing Complex Societies: Trajectories and Scenarios* (Basingstoke: Palgrave).

PIERSON, P. (1996) 'The Path to European Integration: a Historical Institutionalist Analysis', *Comparative Political Studies*, 29(2), 123–63.

—— (1998) 'The Path to European Integration: A Historical-Institutionalist Analysis', in Sandholtz, W. and Stone Sweet, A., *European Integration and Supra-national Governance* (Oxford: Oxford University Press) 27–58.

—— (2000) 'Increasing Returns, Path Dependence, and the Study of Politics', *American Political Science Review*, 94(2), 251–67.

—— (2004) *Politics in Time: History, Institutions, and Social Analysis* (Princeton, NJ: Princeton University Press).

—— and LEIBFRIED, S. (1995) 'Multi-Tiered Institutions and the Making of Social Policy', in Leibfried, S. and Pierson, P. (eds) *European Social Policy: Between Fragmentation and Integration* (Washington, DC: Brookings Institution) 1–40.

PINDER, J. (1986) 'European community and nation-state: a case for a neofederalism?', *International Affairs*, 62(I), 41–54.

—— (1991) *European Community: The Building of a Union* (Oxford: Oxford University Press).

—— (1993) 'The New European Federalism: The Idea and the Achievements', in Burgess, M. and Gagnon, A-G. (eds) *Comparative Federalism and Federation: Competing Traditions and Future Directions* (Hemel Hempstead: Harvester Wheatsheaf) 45–66.

—— (ed.) (1998) *Altiero Spinelli and the British Federalists* (London: Federal Trust).

POCOCK, J.G.A. (1991) 'Deconstructing Europe', *London Review of Books*, 19 December, 6–10.

POGGE, T.W. (1989) *Realizing Rawls* (Ithaca, NY: Cornell University Press).

—— (1994) 'An Egalitarian Law of Peoples', *Philosophy and Public Affairs*, 23(3), 195–224.

—— (1997) 'Creating Supra-national Institutions Democratically: Reflections on the European Union's "Democratic Deficit"', *Journal of Political Philosophy*, 5(2), 163–82.

—— (2002) *World Poverty and Human Rights. Cosmopolitan Responsibilities and Reforms* (Cambridge: Polity Press).

POLLACK, M.A. (1996) 'The New Institutionalism and EU Governance: The Promise and Limits of Institutionalist Analysis', *Governance*, 9(4), 429–58.

—— (1997) 'Delegation, Agency and Agenda Setting in the European Community', *International Organization*, 51(1), 99–135.

—— (2001) 'International Relations Theory and European Integration', *Journal of Common Market Studies*, 39(2), 221–44.

—— (2003) *The Engines of European Integration: Delegation, Agency and Agenda-Setting in the EU* (New York: Oxford University Press).

—— (2005) 'Theorizing the European Union: International Organization, Domestic Polity, or Experiment in New Governance', *Annual Review of Political Science*, 8, 357–98.

—— (2007) 'Rational Choice and EU Politics', in Jørgensen, K.E., Pollack, M.A., and Rosamond, B. (eds) *The Handbook of European Union Politics* (New York: Sage) 31–55.

——and HAFNER-BURTON, E. (2000) 'Mainstreaming Gender in the European Union', *Journal of European Public Policy*, 7(4), 432–56.

POLLITT, C. and TALBOT, C. (2004) *Unbundled Government: A Critical Analysis of the Global Trend to Agencies, Quangos and Contractualisation* (London: Routledge).

POULANTZAS, N. (1974) 'Internationalisation of Capitalist Relations and the Nation State', *Economy and Society*, 2(1), 145–79.

—— (1975) *Political Power and Social Classes* (London: New Left Books).

PRÜGL, E. (2004) 'Gender Orders in German Agriculture: From the Patriarchal Welfare State to Liberal Environmentalism', *Sociologia Ruralis*, 44(4), 349–72.

—— (2009) 'Does Gender Mainstreaming Work? Feminist Engagements with the German Agricultural State', *International Feminist Journal of Politics*, 11(2).

PRZEWORSKI, A. and TEUNE, H. (1982) *The Logic of Comparative Social Inquiry* (Malabar, FL: Krieger).

PUCHALA, D.J. (1972) 'Of Blind Men, Elephants and International Integration', *Journal of Common Market Studies*, 10(3), 267–84.

QUAGLIA, L. *et al.* (2008) 'Committee Governance and Socialization in the European Union', *Journal of European Public Policy*, 15(1), 155–66.

RADAELLI, C.M. (1999) *Technocracy in the European Union* (Harlow and New York: Addison-Wesley Longman).

—— (2007) 'Whither Better Regulation for the Lisbon Agenda?', *Journal of European Public Policy*, 14(2), 190–207.

RAWLS, J. (1971) *A Theory of Justice* (Cambridge, MA: Belknap Press).

—— (1993) *Political Liberalism* (New York: Columbia University Press).

—— (1999) *The Law of Peoples* (Cambridge, MA and London: Harvard).

—— and VAN PARIJS, P. (2003) *Autour de Rawls*, special issue of *Revue de philosophie économique*, 8, 7–20.

RAY F.U. and HENNING, H.C.A. (1999) 'The Organization of Influence on the EC's Common Agricultural Policy: A Network Approach', *European Journal of Political Research*, 36(2), 257–81.

REES, T. (1998). *Mainstreaming Equality in the European Union: Education, Training and Labour Market Policies* (New York: Routledge).

RETHEMEYER, R.K. (2007) 'Policymaking in the Age of the Internet: Is the Internet Tending to Make Policy Networks More or Less Inclusive?', *Journal of Public Administration—Research and Theory*, 17(2), 259–84.

RHODES, M. (2002) 'Why the EMU Is—or May Be—Good for the European Welfare States,' in Dyson, K. (ed.) *European States and the Euro: Europeanization, Variation and Convergence* (Oxford: Oxford University Press) 305–34.

RHODES, R.A.W. (1990) 'Policy Networks: a British Perspective', *Journal of Theoretical Politics*, 2(2), 293–317.

—— (1996) 'The New Governance: Governance Without Government', *Political Studies*, 44(4), 652–67.

—— (1997) *Understanding Governance. Policy Networks, Governance, Reflexivity and Accountability* (Buckingham: Open University Press).

RICHARDSON, J. (ed.) (1982) *Policy Styles in Western Europe* (London: Allen and Unwin).

—— (2000) 'Government, Interest Groups and Policy Change', *Political Studies*, 48(5), 1006–25.

—— (2004) *European Union: Power and Policy-Making* (London: Routledge).

RIKER, W. (1980) 'Implications from the Disequilibrium of Majority Rule for the Study of Institutions', *American Political Science Review*, 74(3), 432–47.

RILEY, P. (1973) 'The Origins of Federal Theory in International Relations Ideas', *Polity*, 6(1), 87–121.

RISSE, T. (2000) ' "Let's Argue!" Communicative Action in International Relations', *International Organization*, 54(1), 1–39.

—— (2001) 'A European Identity? Europeanization and the Evolution of Nation-State Identities', in Cowles, M.G. *et al.* (eds) *Transforming Europe. Europeanization and Domestic Change* (Ithaca, NY: Cornell University Press) 198–216.

—— (2005) 'Neo-Functionalism, European Identity, and the Puzzles of European Integration', *Journal of European Public Policy*, 12(2), 291–309.

—— (2004) 'European Institutions and Identity Change: What Have We Learned?', in Herrmann, R.K. *et al.* (eds) *Europeanization: Institutions and the Evolution of Social Identities* (Lanham, MD: Rowman and Littlefield).

—— (2009) *We the European Peoples? Identity, Public Sphere, and European Democracy* (Ithaca, NY: Cornell University Press).

—— and KLEINE, M. (2007) 'Assessing the Legitimacy of the EU's Treaty Revision Methods', *Journal of Common Market Studies*, 45(1), 69–80.

—— and VAN DE STEEG, M. (forthcoming) 'The Emergence of a European Community of Communication: Insights from Empirical Research on the Europeanization of Public Spheres', *Journal of European Public Policy*.

—— and WIENER, A. (1999) ' "Something Rotten" and the Social Construction of Social Constructivism: A Comment on Comments,' *Journal of European Public Policy*, 6, 775–82.

—— and —— (2001) 'The Social Construction of Social Constructivism', in Christiansen, T. *et al.* (eds) *The Social Construction of Europe* (London: Sage) 199–205.

—— *et al.* (1999) 'To Euro or Not to Euro. The EMU and Identity Politics in the European Union', *European Journal of International Relations*, 5(2), 147–87.

RISSE-KAPPEN, T. (1996) 'Exploring the Nature of the Beast: International Relations Theory and Comparative Policy Analysis Meet the European Union', *Journal of Common Market Studies*, 34(1), 53–80.

RITTBERGER, B. and SCHIMMELFENNIG, F. (2006) *Die Europäische Union auf dem Weg in den Verfassungsstaat* (Frankfurt/M: Campus).

ROEMHELD, L. (1990) *Integral Federalism: Model for Europe—a Way towards a Personal Group Society* (Frankfurt/M: Peter Lang).

ROSAMOND, B. (1995) 'Mapping the European Condition: the Theory of Integration and the Integration of Theory', *European Journal of International Relations*, 1(3), 391–408.

—— (1999) 'Discourses of Globalization and the Social Construction of European Identities', *Journal of European Public Policy*, 6(4), 652–68.

—— (2000) *Theories of European Integration* (Basingstoke: Macmillan).

—— (2001) 'Discourses of Globalisation and European Identities', in Christiansen, T. *et al.* (eds) *The Social Construction of Europe* (London: Sage) 158–73.

—— (2005) 'The Uniting of Europe And the Foundation of EU Studies: Revisiting the Neofunctionalism of Ernst B. Haas', *Journal of European Public Policy*, 12, 237–54.

—— and WINCOTT, D. (2006) 'Constitutionalism, European Integration and British Political Economy,' *British Journal of Politics and International Relations*, 8, 1–14.

ROSS, G. (1995) *Jacques Delors and European Integration* (Cambridge: Polity).

ROSSITER, C. (ed.) (1961) *The Federalist Papers* (New York: The New York American Library).

ROTHSTEIN, B. and TOERELL, J. (2008) 'What is Quality of Governance? A Theory of Impartial Government Institutions', *Governance*, 21(1), 165–90.

ROUSSEAU, J.J. (1968 [1792]) *The Social Contract and Other Later Political Writings* (Cambridge: Cambridge University Press).

RUGGIE, J.G. (1993) 'Territoriality and Beyond: Problematizing Modernity in International Relations', *International Organization*, 47(1), 139–74.

—— (1997) 'The Past as Prologue? Interest, Identity, and American Foreign Policy', *International Security*, 21(4), 89–125.

—— (1998) 'What Makes the World Hang Together? Neo-Utilitarianism and the Social Constructivist Challenge', *International Organization*, 52(4), 855–85.

RUMINSKA-ZIMNY, E. (2002) *Gender Aspects of Changes in the Labour Markets in Transition Economies* (Geneva:UNECE Issue Paper).

RUSSELL, R. (1975) 'L'Engrenage, Collegial Style, and the Crisis Syndrome: Lessons from Monetary Policy in the European Community', *Journal of Common Market Studies*, 13, 61–86.

RYNER, M. (2007) 'US Power and the Crisis of European Social Democracy in Europe's Second Project of Integration', *Capital and Class*, 93, 101–20.

RYTKØNEN, H.L. (2002) 'Europe and its "Almost-European" Other: A Textual Analysis of Legal and Cultural Practices of Othering in Contemporary Europe', Stanford University: unpubl. Ph.D. dissertation.

SABATIER, P.A. (1993) 'Policy Change Over a Decade or More', in Sabatier, P.A. and Jenkins-Smith, H.C. (eds) *Policy Change and Learning: An Advocacy Coalition Approach* (Boulder, CO and Oxford: Westview) 1–19.

—— and JENKINS-SMITH, H.C. (eds) (1993) *Policy Change and Learning: an Advocacy Coalition Approach* (Boulder, CO and Oxford: Westview).

—— and —— (1998) *Policy Change and Learning: an Advocacy Coalition Approach*, 2nd edn (Boulder, CO and Oxford: Westview).

SAGEMAN, M. (2004) *Understanding Terrorist Networks* (Philadelphia, PA: University of Pennsylvania Press).

—— (2007) *Leaderless Jihad: Terror Networks in the Twenty-First Century* (Philadelphia, PA: University of Pennsylvania Press).

SALAMON, L.M. (2001) Introduction, in Salamon, L.M. (ed.) *The Handbook of Policy Instruments* (New York: Oxford University Press) 1–47.

SANDHOLTZ, W. (1992) *High-Tech Europe: The Politics of International Co-operation* (Berkeley, CA: University of California Press).

—— (1993) 'Institutions and Collective Action: The New Telecommunications in Western Europe', *World Politics*, 45, 242–70.

—— (1996) 'Membership Matters: Limits of the Functional Approach to European Institutions', *Journal of Common Market Studies*, 34(3), 403–29.

——and STONE SWEET, A. (eds) (1998) *European Integration and Supranational Governance* (Oxford: Oxford University Press).

——and ZYSMAN, J. (1989) '1992: Recasting the European Bargain', *World Politics*, 42(1), 99–128.

SAUER, B. (2001a) 'Das "bewundernswert Männliche" des Staates: Überlegungen zum Geschlechterverhältnis in der Politik', *Femina Politica*, 2, 50–62.

—— (2001b) 'Vom Nationalstaat zum Europäischen Reich? Staat und Geschlecht in der Europäischen Union', *Feministische Studien*, 1, 8–20.

—— (2001c) *Die Asche des Souveräns: Staat und Demokratie in der Geschlechterdebatte* (Frankfurt/M, New York: Campus).

SBRAGIA, A. (1992) 'Thinking about the European Future: the Uses of Comparison', in Sbragia, A. (ed.) *Euro-Politics: Institutions and Policy-Making in the New European Community* (Washington, DC: The Brookings Institution) 257–91.

—— (1993) 'EC Environmental Policy: Atypical Ambitions and Typical Problems?', in Cafruny, A. and Rosenthal, G. (eds) *The Maastricht Treaty and Beyond* (Boulder, CO: Lynne Rienner) 337–52.

—— (2001) 'Italy Pays for Europe: Political Leadership, Political Choice, and Institutional Adaptation', in Cowles, M.G. *et al.* (eds) *Transforming Europe. Europeanization and Domestic Change* (Ithaca, NY: Cornell University Press) 79–98.

SCANLON, T. (1998) *What We Owe to Each Other* (Cambridge, MA: Belknap Press).

SCHARPF, F.W. (1988) 'The Joint-Decision Trap: Lessons from German Federalism and European Integration', *Public Administration*, 66(3), 239–78.

—— (1994) 'Community and Autonomy. Multi-Level Policy-Making in the European Union', *Journal of European Public Policy*, (1), 219–42.

—— (1996) 'Negative and Positive Integration in the Political Economy of European Welfare States' in Marks, G., Scharpf, F.W., Schmitter, P., and Streeck, W., *Governance in the European Union* (London: Sage), 15–39.

—— (1997) *Games Real Actors Play. Actor-Centered Institutionalism in Policy Research* (Boulder, CO: Westview).

—— (1999) *Governing in Europe: Effective and Democratic?* (Oxford and New York: Oxford University Press).

—— (2002) 'The European Social Model: Coping with the Challenges of Diversity', *Journal of Common Market Studies*, 40(4), 645–69.

SCHEPEL, H. (2000) 'Reconstructing Constitutionalization: Law and Politics in the European Court of Justice', *Oxford Journal of Legal Studies*, 20, 457–68.

SCHIMMELFENNIG, F. (1997) 'Rhetorisches Handeln in der internationalen Politik', *Zeitschrift für Internationale Beziehungen*, 4(2), 219–54.

—— (2001) 'The Community Trap: Liberal Norms, Rhetorical Action, and the Eastern Enlargement of the European Union', *International Organization,* 55(1), 47–80.

—— (2003a) 'Strategic Action in a Community Environment: The Decision to Enlarge the European Union to the East', *Comparative Political Studies,* 36(1–2), 156–83.

—— (2003b) *The EU, NATO and the Integration of Europe: Rules and Rhetoric* (Cambridge: Cambridge University Press).

—— (2005) 'Strategic Calculation and International Socialization: Membership Incentives, Party Constellations, and Sustained Compliance in Central and Eastern Europe', *International Organization,* 59(4), 827–60.

—— and RITTBERGER, B. (2006) 'Explaining the Constitutionalization of the European Union', *Journal of European Public Policy,* 13, 1148–67.

—— and SEDELMEIER, U. (2002) 'Theorizing EU Enlargement: Research Focus, Hypotheses, and the State of Research', *Journal of European Public Policy,* 9(4), 500–28.

—— and —— (eds) (2005a) *The Europeanization of Central and Eastern Europe* (Ithaca, NY: Cornell University Press).

—— and —— (2005b) 'Introduction: Conceptualizing the Europeanization of Central and Eastern Europe', in Schimmelfennig, F. and Sedelmeier, U. (eds) *The Europeanization of Central and Eastern Europe* (Ithaca, NY: Cornell University Press) 1–28.

SCHLESINGER, P. (1991) *Media, State and Nation: Political Violence and Collective Identities* (London: Sage).

SCHMIDT, S.K. (1997) 'Sterile Debates and Dubious Generalisations: European Integration Theory Tested by Telecommunications and Electricity', *Journal of Public Policy,* 16(3), 233–71.

SCHMITTER, P. (1969) 'Three Neo-Functional Hypotheses about International Integration', *International Organization,* 23(0), 562–64.

—— (1970) 'A Revised Theory of Regional Integration', *International Organization* (Autumn), 836–68. Also published in Lindberg, L. and Scheingold, S. (eds) *Regional Integration: Theory and Research* (Cambridge, MA: Harvard University Press, 1971) 232–65.

—— (1996) 'Imagining the Future of the Euro-Polity with the Help of New Concepts', in Marks, G., Scharpf, F.W., Schmitter, P. *et al.*

(eds) *Governance in the European Union* (London: Sage) 121–50.

—— (1997) 'The Emerging Europolity and Its Impact on National Systems of Production', in Rogers Hollingsworth, J. and Boyer, R. (eds) *Contemporary Capitalism: The Embeddedness of Institutions* (Cambridge: Cambridge University Press) 395–430.

—— (2004) 'Neo-Neofunctionalism', in Wiener, A. and Diez, T. (eds) *European Integration Theory,* 1st edn (Oxford: Oxford University Press) 46–74.

SCHNEIDER, H. (1977) *Leitbilder der Europapolitik I: Der Weg zur Integration* (Bonn: Europa Union).

SCHONLAU, J. (2005) *Drafting the EU Charter: Rights, Legitimacy and Process* (Basingstoke: Palgrave Macmillan).

SCHOUT, A. and JORDAN, A. (2005) 'Coordinated European governance: self-organizing or centrally steered?', *Public Administration,* 83(1), 201–20.

SEDELMEIER, U. (2000) 'Eastern Enlargement: Risk, Rationality, and Role-Compliance', in Green Cowles, M. and Smith, M. (eds) *State of the European Union Volume 5: Risk, Reforms, Resistance, and Revival* (Oxford: Oxford University Press) 164–85.

—— (2002) 'Sectoral Dynamics of EU Enlargement: Advocacy, Access, and Alliances in a Composite Policy', *Journal of European Public Policy,* 9(4), 627–49.

—— (2005) *Constructing the Path to Eastern Enlargement: The Uneven Policy Impact of EU Identity* (Manchester: Manchester University Press).

SELCK, T. J. and STEUNENBERG, B. (2004) 'Between Power and Luck: The European Parliament in the EU Legislative Process', *European Union Politics,* 5(1), 25–46.

SERVAN-SCHREIBER, J.-J. (1969) *The American Challenge* (New York: Athenaeum).

SHAW, J. (2000) 'Importing Gender: the Challenge of Feminism and the Analysis of the EU Legal Order', *Journal of European Public Policy,* 7(3), 406–31.

—— (2001a) 'European Union Governance and the Question of Gender: A Critical Comment', in Meny Joerges, M. and Weiler, J., *Mountain or Molehill?*, www.jeanmonnetprogramme.org. papers/01/010601.

—— (2001b) 'Postnational Constitutionalism in the European Union', in Christiansen, T., Jørgensen, K.E., and Wiener, A. (eds) *The Social Construction of Europe* (London: Sage) 66–84.

—— (2007) *The Transformation of Citizenship in the European Union: Electoral Rights and the Restructuring of Political Space* (Cambridge: Cambridge University Press).

Shepsle, K.A. (1979) 'Institutional Arrangements and Equilibrium in Multi-dimensional Voting Models', *American Journal of Political Science*, 23(1), 27–60.

—— (1986) 'Institutional Equilibrium and Equilibrium Institutions', in Weisberg, H. (ed.) *Political Science; The Science of Politics* (New York: Agathon) 51–81.

——and Weingast, B.R. (1984) 'Uncovered Sets and Sophisticated Voting Outcomes with Implications for Agenda Control', *American Journal of Political Science*, 28(1), 49–74.

Sifft, S. (2003) 'Pushing for Europeanisation: how British Feminists Link with the EU to Promote Parental Rights', in Liebert, U. (ed.) *Gendering Europeanisation* (Brussels: P.I.E.-Peter Lang) 149–86.

—— et al. (2007) 'Segmented Europeanization: Exploring the Legitimacy of the European Union from a Public Discourse Perspective', *Journal of Common Market Studies*, 45 (1), 127–55.

Sikkink, K. (1993) 'The Power of Principled Ideas: Human Rights Policies in the United States and Western Europe', in Goldstein, J. and Keohane, R. (eds) *Ideas & Foreign Policy. Beliefs, Institutions, and Political Change* (Ithaca, NY: Cornell University Press) 139–70.

Sjursen, H. (2006a) 'The EU as a "Normative" Power: How Can This Be?', *Journal of European Public Policy*, 13(2), 235–251.

—— (2006b) *Questioning EU Enlargement. Europe in Search of Identity* (London and New York: Routledge).

Skelcher, C. (2005) 'Jurisdictional Integrity, Polycentrism and the Design of Democratic Governance', *Governance*, 18(1), 89–110.

Smith, A.D. (1992) 'National Identity and the Idea of European Unity', *International Affairs*, 68(1), 55–76.

Smith, D.L. and Ray, J.L. (1993) 'European Integration: Gloomy Theory Versus Rosy Reality', in Smith, D.L. and Ray, J.L. (eds) *The 1992 Project and the Future of Integration in Europe* (Armonk, NY: Sharpe) 19–44.

Smith, M.E. (2000) 'Conforming to Europe: The Domestic Impact of EU Foreign Policy Coordination', *Journal of European Public Policy*, 7(4), 613–31.

Smith, S. (2000) 'Wendt's World', *Review of International Studies*, 26(1), 151–63.

Sørenson, E. and Torfing, J. (2007) *Theories of Democratic Network Governance* (Basingstoke: Macmillan).

Spinelli, A. (1966) *The Eurocrats—Conflict and Crisis in the European Community* (Baltimore, MD: The Johns Hopkins Press).

—— and Rossi, E. (2006 [1944]) *Il Manifesto di Ventotene* (Milan: Mondadori).

Stacey, J. and Rittberger, B. (2003) 'Dynamics of Formal and Informal Change in the EU', *Journal of European Public Policy*, 10(6), 858–83.

Stark, D. (1992) 'Path Dependence and Privatization Strategies in East Central Europe', *East European Politics and Society*, 6(1), 17–54.

Stavrakakis, Y. (2005) 'Passions of Identification: Discourse, Enjoyment and European Identity', in Howarth, D. and Torfing, J. (eds) *Discourse Theory and European Politics* (Basingstoke: Palgrave) 68–92.

Steinhilber, S. (2002) 'Women's Rights and Gender Equality in the EU Enlargement. An Opportunity for Progress', WIDE Briefing Paper.

Steunenberg, B., Koboldt, C., and Schmidtchen, D. (1996) 'Policymaking, Comitology, and the Balance of Power in the European Union', *International Review of Law and Economics*, 16(2), 329–44.

Stone Sweet, A. (2002) 'Constitutional Courts and Parliamentary Democracy', *West European Politics*, 25(1), 77–100.

—— and Brunell, T.L. (1998) 'Constructing a Supranational Constitution: Dispute Resolution and Governance in the European Community', *American Political Science Review*, 92(1), 63–81.

——and Caporaso, J.A. (1998) 'From Free Trade to Supranational Polity: The European Court and Integration', in Sandholtz, W. and Stone Sweet, A. (eds) *European Integration and Supranational Governance* (New York: Oxford University Press) 92–133.

—— and Sandholtz, W. (1997) 'European Integration and Supranational Governance', *Journal of European Public Policy,* 4(3), 297–317.

Story, J. and Walter, I. (1997) *Political Economy of Financial Integration in Europe: The Battle of the Systems* (Cambridge, MA: MIT Press).

Straehle, C. *et al.* (1999) 'Struggle as Metaphor in European Union Discourses on Unemployment', *Discourse and Society,* 10(1), 67–100.

Stråth, B. (2000a) 'Introduction: Europe as a Discourse', in Stråth, B. (ed.) *Europe and the Other and Europe as the Other* (Brussels: P.I.E.-Peter Lang) 13–44.

—— (2000b) 'Multiple Europes: Integration, Identity and Demarcation to the Other', in Stråth, B. (ed.) *Europe and the Other and Europe as the Other* (Brussels: P.I.E.-Peter Lang) 385–420.

Stratigaki, M. (2004) 'The cooptation of gender concepts in EU policies: the case of "reconciliation of work and family"', *Social Politics,* 11(1), 30–56.

Streeck, W. (1992) *Social Institutions and Economic Performance: Studies on Industrial Relations in Advanced European Capitalist Countries* (London: Sage).

—— and Schmitter, P. (1991) 'From National Corporatism to Transnational Pluralism: Organized Interests in the Single European Market', *Politics and Society,* 19(2), 133–64.

—— and Thelen, K. (2005) 'Introduction: Institutional Change in Advanced Political Economies', in Streeck, W. and Thelen, K. (eds) *Beyond Continuity: Institutional Change in Advanced Political Economies* (Oxford: Oxford University Press) 1–39.

Sunnus, M. (2003) 'EU challenges to the pioneer in gender equality: the case of Sweden', in Liebert, U. (ed.) *Gendering Europeanisation* (Brussels: P.I.E.-Peter Lang) 223–54.

Talani, L. S. (2000) *Betting For and Against EMU: Who Wins and Who Loses in Italy and the UK from the Process of European Monetary Integration* (London: Ashgate).

—— (2003) 'Interests and Expectations: A Critical Political Economy Approach to the Credibility of Exchange Rates: The Cases of Italy and the UK in the EMS and EMU', in Cafruny, A. and Ryner, M. (eds) *A Ruined Fortress: Neoliberal Hegemony and Transformation in Europe* (Lanham, MD: Rowman and Littlefield) 123–46.

Tallberg, J. (1999) *Making States Comply: The European Commission, the European Court of Justice and the Enforcement of the Internal Market* (Lund, Sweden: Lund Political Studies 09, Department of Political Science, Lund University).

—— (2000) 'The Anatomy of Autonomy: An Institutional Account of Variation in Supranational Influence', *Journal of Common Market Studies,* 38(5), 843–64.

—— (2007) 'Executive Politics', in Jørgensen, K.E., Pollack, M.A., and Rosamond, B. (eds) *The Handbook of European Union Politics* (New York: Sage) 195–212.

Taylor, C. (1995) *Philosophical Arguments* (Cambridge, MA: Harvard University Press).

Taylor, P. (1983) *The Limits of European Integration* (London: Croom Helm).

——(1989) 'The New Dynamics of EC in the 1980s', in Lodge, J. (ed.) *The European Community and the Challenge of the Future* (New York: St Martin's Press) 3–25.

Thatcher, M. (1998) 'The Development of Policy Network Analyses: From Modest Origins to Overarching Frameworks', *Journal of Theoretical Politics,* 10(4), 389–416.

—— and Coen, D. (2008). 'Reshaping European Regulatory Space: An Evolutionary Analysis', *West European Politics,* 31(4), 806–36.

Thelen, K. (1999) 'Historical Institutionalism in Comparative Politics', *Annual Review of Political Science,* 2, 369–404.

Thomson, R. (2007) 'The Impact of Enlargement on Legislative Decision Making in the European Union', paper presented at the General Conference of the European Consortium for Political Research, Pisa, Italy, 6–8 September.

—— *et al.* (2006) *The European Union Decides* (Cambridge: Cambridge University Press).

Thompson, G. (2003) *Between Hiearchies and Markets: the Logic and Limits of Network Forms* (Oxford and New York: Oxford University Press).

Threlfall, M. (2005) *The European Employment Strategy and Women's Work,* manuscript, Loughborough University.

THWAITES, N. (2006) 'Eurojust: Beacon in EU Judicial Co-operation', *Revue Internationale de Droit Penal,* 77(1–2), 293–8.

TIIHONEN, S. (2005) *From Governing to Governance: The Process of Change* (Tampere, FL: Tampere University Press).

TITKOW, A. (1998) 'Polish Women in Politics: An Introduction', in Rueschemeyer, M. (ed.) *Women in the Politics of Postcommunist Eastern Europe* (New York: M.E. Sharpe) 24–32.

TITSCHER, S. *et al.* (2000) *Methods of Text and Discourse Analysis* (London: Sage).

TOOLEY, M.J. (ed.) (1955) *Six Books of the Commonwealth* (Oxford: Basil Blackwell).

TORFING, J., (1999) *New Theories of Discourse: Laclau, Mouffe and Žižek* (Oxford: Blackwell).

TRANHOLM-MIKKELSEN, J. (1991) 'Neofunctionalism: Obstinate or Obsolete? A Reappraisal in the Light of the New Dynamism of the European Community', *Millennium: Journal of International Studies,* 20(1), 1–22.

Treaties Establishing The European Communities (ECSC, EEC, EAEC) (abridged edn) (1987) (Luxembourg: Office for Official Publications of the EC).

Treaty of Lisbon amending the Treaty on European Union and the Treaty establishing the European Community (2007), signed at Lisbon, 13 December; Official Journal of the European Union; 2007/C 306/01, 17 December.

TRENZ, H.J. (2006) *Europa in den Medien. Die europäische Integration im Spiegel nationaler Öffentlichkeit* (Frankfurt/M and New York: Campus).

TRIANTAFILLOU, P. (2007) 'Governing the Formation and Mobilization of Governance Networks', in Sørenson, E. and Torfing, J. (eds) *Theories of Democratic Network Governance* (Basingstoke: Macmillan) 183–198.

TRONDAL, J. (2002) 'Beyond the EU membership-nonmembership dichotomy? Supranational identities among national EU decision-makers', *Journal of European Public Policy,* 9, 468–87.

TSEBELIS, G. (1994) 'The Power of the European Parliament as a Conditional Agenda Setter', *American Political Science Review,* 88(1), 129–42.

—— (1997) 'Maastricht and the Democratic Deficit', *Aussenwirtschaft,* 52(1), 29–56.

——and GARRETT, G. (2001a) 'Legislative Politics in the European Union', *European Union Politics,* 1(1), 9–36.

—— and —— (2001b) 'The Institutional Foundations of Intergovernmentalism and Supranationalism in the European Union', *International Organization,* 55(2), 357–90.

TULLY, J. (2002) 'The Unfreedom of the Moderns in Comparison to their Ideals of Constitutionalism and Democracy', *Modern Law Review,* 65, 204–28.

—— (2006) 'A New Kind of Europe? Democratic Integration in the European Union'. ConWEB Papers on Constitutionalism and Governance Beyond the State 4/2006.

—— (2008) *Public Philosophy in a New Key, vol. 2.* (Cambridge: Cambridge University Press).

ULLRICH, H. (2002) 'The Impact of Policy Networks in the GATT Uruguay Round: the Case of US-EC Agricultural Negotiations', *Government and International Relations* (London: London School of Economics).

UNICEF (1999) *Women in Transition.* The MONNEE Project Cee/CIS/Baltics.

UNITED NATIONS DEVELOPMENT PROGRAM (2008) *Human Development Indices: A Statistical Update 2008,* www.hdr.undp.org/statistics/data.

VACHUDOVA, M.A. (2005) *Europe Undivided: Democracy, Leverage, and Integration after Communism* (Oxford: Oxford University Press).

—— (2007) 'Historical Institutionalism and the EU's Eastward Enlargement', in Meunier, S. and McNamara, K. (eds) *The State of the European Union,* vol. 8 (Oxford: Oxford University Press) 105–22.

VALIENTE, C. (2003) 'Pushing for Equality Reforms: the European Union and Gender Discourse in Post-authoritarian Spain', in Liebert, U. (ed.) *Gendering Europeanisation* (Brussels: P.I.E.-Peter Lang) 187–222.

VAN APELDOORN, B. (2002) *Transnational Capitalism and the Struggle over European Integration* (London: Routledge).

—— et al. (eds) (2008) *Contradictions and Limits of Neoliberal European Governance: From Lisbon to Lisbon* (London: Palgrave).

—— OVERBEEK, H., and RYNER, M. (2003) 'Theories of European Integration: A Critique', in Cafruny, A. and Ryner, M. (eds) *A Ruined Fortress? Neoliberal Hegemony and Transformation in Europe* (Lanham, MD: Rowman and Littlefield) 17–44.

VAN DE STEEG, M. (2006) 'Does a Public Sphere Exist in the European Union? An Analysis of the Content of the Debate on the Haider Case', *European Journal of Political Research*, 45, 609–34.

VAN DER MOLEN, I. and NOVIKOVA, I. (2005) 'Mainstreaming Gender in the EU-accession Process: the Case of the Baltic Republics', *Journal of European Social Policy*, 15(2), 139–56.

VAN DER PIJL, K. (1984) *The Making of an Atlantic Ruling Class* (London: Verso).

—— (1996) *Vordenker der Weltpolitik* (Opladen: Leske and Budrich).

—— (2001) 'From Gorbachev to Kosovo: Atlantic Rivalries and the Reincorporation of Eastern Europe', *Review of International Political Economy*, 8(2), 275–310.

—— and HOLMAN, O. (2003) 'Structure and Process in Transnational European Business', in Cafruny, A. and Ryner, M. (eds) *A Ruined Fortress? Neoliberal Hegemony and Transformation in Europe* (Lanham, MD: Rowman and Littlefield) 71–94.

VAN DER VLEUTEN, A. (2004) 'Snail or snake? Shifts in the domain of EU gender equality policies', Paper presented at the Second Pan-European Conference on EU Politics of the ECPR Standing Group on the European Union, 24–26 June, Bologna.

—— (2007) *The Price of Gender Equality: Member States and Governance in the European Union* (Aldershot: Ashgate).

VAN PARIJS, P. (1995) *Real Freedom for All: What (If Anything) Can Justify Capitalism?* (Oxford: Clarendon Press).

—— (1997a) 'Basic Income and the Political Economy of the New Europe', in Lehning, P.B. and Weale, B. (eds) *Citizenship, Democracy and Justice in the New Europe* (London and New York: Routledge), 161–74.

—— (1997b) 'Should the European Union Become More Democratic?', in Føllesdal, A. and Koslowski, P. (eds) *Democracy and the European Union* (Berlin and New York: Springer) 287–301.

VERNON, R. (ed.) (1979) *The Principle of Federation by P.-J. Proudhon* (Toronto: University of Toronto Press).

VIBERT, F. (1995) *A Constitution for the Millennium* (Aldershot: Dartmouth).

—— (2002) *Europe Simple. Europe Strong: The Future of European Governance* (Cambridge: Polity Press).

—— (2007) *The Rise of the Unelected* (Cambridge: Cambridge University Press).

VINER, J. (1950) *The Customs Union Issue* (New York: Carnegie Endowment for International Peace).

WÆVER, O. (1989) 'Ideologies of Stabilization— Stabilization of Ideologies: Reading German Social Democrats', in Harle, V. and Sivonen, P. (eds) *Europe in Transition: Politics and Nuclear Strategy* (London: Frances Pinter) 110–39.

—— (1990) 'Three Competing Europes: German, French, Russian', *International Affairs*, 66(3), 477–93.

—— (1991) 'Det tyske problem i 1990erne' (The German Problem in the 1990s), *Internasjonal Politikk*, (4), 401–19.

—— (1994) 'Resisting the Temptation of Post Foreign Policy Analysis', in Carlsnaes, W. and Smith, S. (eds) *European Foreign Policy: The EC and Changing Perspectives in Europe* (London: ECPR/Sage) 238–73.

—— (1995) 'Power, Principles and Perspectivism: Understanding Peaceful Change in Post-Cold War Europe', in Patomäki, H. (ed.) *Peaceful Changes in World Politics* (Tampere, FL: TAPRI) 208–82.

—— (1996a) ' "The Struggle for Europe": A Discourse Analysis of France, Germany and European Union', Center for International Studies, School of International Relations, University of Southern California, 'Re-thinking Security' Seminar Paper No. 11, 23 October (62 pages).

—— (1996b) 'The Rise and Fall of the Inter-paradigm Debate', in Smith, S., Booth, K., and Zalewski, M. (eds) *International Theory: Positivism and Beyond* (Cambridge: Cambridge University Press) 149–85.

—— (1996c) 'European Security Identities', *Journal of Common Market Studies*, 34(1), 103–32.

—— (1998a) 'The Sociology of a Not so International Discipline: American and European Developments in International Relations', *International Organization*, 52(4), 687–727.

—— (1998b) 'Explaining Europe by Decoding Discourses', in Wivel, A. (ed.) *Explaining European Integration* (Copenhagen: Political Studies Press) 100–46.

—— (2000) 'The EU as a Security Actor: Reflections from a Pessimistic Constructivist on Post-sovereign Security Orders', in Kelstrup, M. and Williams, M.C. (eds) *International Relations Theory and the Politics of European Integration. Power, Security and Community* (London: Routledge) 250–94.

—— (2005) 'European Integration and Security: Analysing French and German Discourses on State, Nation, and Europe', in Howarth, D.R. and Torfing, J. (eds) *Discourse Theory in European Politics: Identity, Policy and Governance* (Basingstoke: Macmillan) 33–67.

—— and KELSTRUP, M. (1993) 'Europe and its Nations', in Wæver, O. *et al.* (eds) *Identity, Migration and the New Security Agenda in Europe* (London: Pinter) 62–92.

—— *et al.* (1991) *The Struggle for Europe: French and German Concepts of State, Nation and European Union* (unpublished book ms).

WAGSTYL, S. (2008) 'Dark Clouds Approaching From the West', *Financial Times*, 2 April.

WALBY, S. (2004) 'The European Union and gender equality: emergent varieties of gender regime', *Social Politics*, 11(1), 4–29.

WALKER, N. (2002) 'The Idea of Constitutional Pluralism', *The Modern Law Review*, (65), 317–59.

—— and M. LOUGHLIN (2007) *The Paradox of Constitutionalism: Constituent Power and Constitutional Form* (Oxford: Oxford University Press).

WALL, S. (2008) *A Stranger in Europe: Britain and the EU from Thatcher to Blair* (Oxford: Oxford University Press).

WALLACE, H. (2000) 'Analysing and Explaining Policies', in Wallace, W., *Policy-Making in the European Union* (Oxford: Oxford University Press) 65–81.

—— (2000a) 'EU Enlargement: A Neglected Subject', in Green Cowles, M. and Smith, M. (eds) *State of the European Union volume 5: Risk, Reforms, Resistance, and Revival* (Oxford: Oxford University Press) 149–63.

—— (2007) 'Adapting to Enlargement of the European Union: Institutional Practice since May 2004', TEPSA Working Paper (Brussels: TEPSA).

—— *et al.* (eds) (2005) *Policy-making in the European Union* (Oxford: Oxford University Press).

WALLACE, W. (1990) 'Introduction: The Dynamics of European Integration', in Wallace, W. (ed.) *The Dynamics of European Integration* (London: Pinter) 1–24.

—— (1996) 'Truth and Power, Monks and Technocrats: Theory and Practice in International Relations', *Review of International Studies*, 22(3), 301–21.

WALTERS, W. (2002) 'The Power of Inscription: Beyond Social Construction and Deconstruction in European Integration Studies', *Millennium*, 31(1), 83–108.

WALTZ, K.N. (1979) *Theory of International Politics* (New York: McGraw-Hill).

WARD, S. and WILLIAMS, R. (1997) 'From Hierarchy to Networks? Subcentral Government and EU Urban Environment Policy', *Journal of Common Market Studies*, 35(3), 439–64.

WEALE, A. (2006) *Democratic Citizenship and the European Union* (Manchester: Manchester University Press).

WEBB, C. (1983) 'Theoretical Perspectives and Problems', in Wallace, H. *et al.* (eds) *Policy-making in the European Community* (Chichester: Wiley) 1–41.

WEBER, C. (2001) *International Relations Theory: A Critical Introduction* (London: Routledge).

WEBER E.P. and KHADEMIAN, A.M. (2008) 'Wicked problems, knowledge challenges, and collaborative capacity builders in network settings', *Public Administration Review*, 68(2), 334–49.

WEILER, J. (1994) 'A Quiet Revolution: The European Court of Justice and Its Interlocutors', *Comparative Political Studies*, 26(4), 510–34.

—— (1995) 'The State "über alles": Demos, Telos, and the German Maastricht Decision', in Due, O. *et al.* (eds) *Festschrift für Ulrich Everling* (Baden-Baden: Nomos) 1651–88.

—— (1999) *The Constitution of Europe. 'Do the New Clothes Have an Emperor?' and Other Essays on European Integration* (Cambridge: Cambridge University Press).

—— (2002) 'A Constitution for Europe? Some Hard Choices', *Journal of Common Market Studies*, 40, 563–80.

—— (2003) *Un'Europa Cristiana* (Milan: BUR Saggi).

—— and Wind, M. (eds) (2003) *European Constitutionalism Beyond the State* (Cambridge: Cambridge University Press).

Wendt, A. (1992) 'Anarchy is what states make of it: the social construction of power politics', *International Organization,* 88(2), 384–96.

—— (1999) *Social Theory of International Politics* (Cambridge: Cambridge University Press).

Whitman, R.G. and Manners, I. (2000) *The Foreign Policies of European Union Member States* (Manchester: Manchester University Press).

Wiener, A. (1998) *'European' Citizenship Practice: Building Institutions of a Non-State* (Boulder, CO: Westview).

—— (2002) 'Finality vs. Enlargement. Opposing Rationales and Constitutive Practices towards a New Transnational Order', Jean Monnet Working Paper 8/02, NYU School of Law.

—— (2003) 'Institutionen', in Bogdandy, A. von (ed.) *Europäisches Verfassungsrecht. Theoretische und dogmatische Grundzüge* (Heidelberg: Springer) 121– 47.

—— (2006) 'Soft Institutions', in Bogdandy, A. von and Bast, J. (eds) *Principles of European Constitutional Law* (Oxford: Hart Publishing) 419–49.

—— (2007) 'The Dual Quality of Norms and Governance Beyond the State: Sociological and Normative Approaches to Interaction', *Critical Review of International Social and Political Philosophy,* 10(1), 47–69.

—— (2008) *The Invisible Constitution of Politics. Contested Norms and International Encounters* (Cambridge: Cambridge University Press).

—— (2009) 'Enacting Meaning-in-Use. Qualitative Research on Norms and International Relations', *Review of International Studies* (in press).

——and Neunreither, K. (2000) 'Introduction: Amsterdam and Beyond', in Neunreither, K. and Wiener, A. (eds) *European Integration After Amsterdam* (Oxford: Oxford University Press) 1–11.

Wight, C. (2002) 'Philosophy of Science and International Relations', in Carlsnaes, W. *et al.* (eds) *Handbook of International Relations* (London: Sage) 23–51.

Wilkinson, J.D. (1981) *The Intellectual Resistance in Europe* (Cambridge, MA: Harvard University Press).

Williams, M.C. and Neumann, I.B. (2000) 'From Alliance to Security Community: NATO, Russia, and the Power of Identity', *Millennium: Journal of International Studies,* 29(2), 357–87.

Wimmel, A. (2006) *Transnationale Diskurse in Europa. Der Streit um den Türkei-Beitritt in Deutschland, Frankreich und Großbritannien* (Frankfurt/M and New York: Campus).

Wincott, D. (1995) 'Institutional Interaction and European Integration: Towards an Everyday Critique of Liberal Intergovernmentalism', *Journal of Common Market Studies,* 33(4), 597–609.

—— (2003) 'Beyond Social Regulation? New Instruments and/or a New Agenda for Social Policy at Lisbon?', *Public Administration,* 81(3), 533–53.

Wind, M. (2001) *Sovereignty and European Integration. Towards a Post-Hobbesian Order* (London and New York: Palgrave Macmillan).

Wobbe, Th. (2003) 'From Protecting to Promoting: Evolving EU Sex Equality Norms in an Organisational Field', *European Law Journal,* 9, 88–108.

Wodak, R. and Krzyzanowski, M. (eds) (2008) *Qualitative Discourse Analysis for the Social Sciences* (Basingstoke: Palgrave).

Wodak, R. and Weiss, G. (2000) 'The Globalization Rhetoric in Discourses of the European Union', in Suess, A. (ed.) *Globalisierung: Ein wissenschaftlicher Diskurs?* (Vienna: Passagen) 209–39.

Wolf, E. (1997) *Europe and the People without History* (Berkeley, CA: University of California Press).

Wolff, R.P. (1970) *In Defense of Anarchism* (New York: Harper and Row).

Woods, N. (1996) 'The Uses of Theory in the Study of International Relations', in Woods, N. (ed.) *Explaining International Relations since 1945* (Oxford: Oxford University Press) 9–31.

Woodward, A.E. (2001) 'Gender Mainstreaming in European Policy: Innovation or Deception?', WZB Discussion Paper FS I 01–103 (Berlin: Wissenschaftszentrum Berlin).

—— (2003) 'European Gender Mainstreaming: Promises and Pitfalls of Transformative Policy', *Review of Policy Research,* 20(1), 65–88.

Wright, M. (1988) 'Policy Community, Policy Network and Comparative Industrial Policies', *Political Studies,* 36(2), 593–612.

YAVUZ, M.H. (2006) 'Islam and Europeanization in Turkish-Muslim socio-political movements', in Byrnes, T.A. and Katzenstein, P.J. (eds) *Religion in an Expanding Europe* (Cambridge: Cambridge University Press) 225–55.

YESILKAGIT, K. and BLOM-HANSEN, J. (2007) 'Supranational governance or national business-as-usual? The national administration of EU structural funds in the Netherland and Denmark', *Public Administration,* 85(2), 503–24.

YOUNG, B. (2000) 'Disciplinary Neoliberalism in the European Union and Gender Politics', *Political Economy,* 5(1), 77–98.

ZEITLIN, J. and POCHET, P. (2005) T*he Open Method of Co-Ordination in Action: The European Employment and Social Inclusion Strategies* (Brussels: Peter Lang).

ZIELONKA, J. (2007) 'Plurilateral Governance in the Enlarged European Union', *Journal of Common Market Studies,* 45(1), 187–209.

ZIPPEL, K. (2004) 'Transnational advocacy networks and policy cycles in the European Union: the case of sexual harassment', *Social Politics,* 11(1), 57–85.

ZULEEG, M. (2001) 'Comment', *German Law Journal,* 2(14), 2.

ZÜRN, M. and CHECKEL, J.T. (2005) 'Getting Socialized to Build Bridges: Constructivism and Rationalism, Europe and the Nation-State', *International Organization,* 59(4), 1045–79.

ZYSMAN, J. (1983) *Governments, Markets and Growth: Financial Systems and the Politics of Industrial Change* (Ithaca, NY: Cornell University Press).

■ INDEX